W9-AQO-661

RELIGION IN AMERICA SINCE 1945: A HISTORY

Columbia Histories of Modern American Life

Columbia Histories of Modern American Life

The books in this new series are concise interpretive histories focusing on major aspects of the American experience since World War II. Written by leading historians, the books draw on recent scholarship to create a lively and interesting account of the subject at hand. The books are written accessibly with a general reader/student audience in mind. Each volume includes an excellent bibliography and a detailed index.

RELIGION IN AMERICA SINCE 1945: A HISTORY

Patrick Allitt

COLUMBIA UNIVERSITY PRESS   NEW YORK

Columbia University Press
Publishers Since 1893
New York   Chichester, West Sussex

© 2003 Columbia University Press
All rights reserved

Library of Congress Cataloging-in-Publication Data
Allitt, Patrick.
    Religion in America since 1945 : a history / Patrick Allitt.
       p. cm. — (Columbia histories of modern American life)
    Includes bibliographical references and index.
    ISBN 0–231–12154–7 (alk paper)
    1. United States—Religion—1945– I. Title. II. Series.
  BL2525.A44 2003
  200'.973'09045—dc21   2003055288

∞

Columbia University Press books are printed on permanent and durable
acid-free paper.

Printed in the United States of America
c 10 9 8 7 6 5 4 3 2 1

For Thomson Smillie

Contents

Preface

Hundreds of people have written about American religious history since the Second World War, but few have taken on the whole subject. In 1999 James Warren of Columbia University Press asked me to try it, and this book is the result. It is a narrative of the main religious events, trends, and movements of the fifty-six years between two explosive events—the American use of atomic weapons against Japan in August 1945 and Al Qaeda's attack on the World Trade Center and the Pentagon in September 2001. It concentrates partly on changes within religious groups and partly on the connection between religion and major issues in national life.

Recent American religious history is paradoxical. America is, in one respect, the great exception to the rule of secularization in the Western industrialized nations. As rates of church attendance and faith in a transcendent God declined steadily throughout twentieth-century Europe, in America they remained high and sometimes climbed higher. While religion was declining into a vestige of its former self in England, France, Spain, the Netherlands, and Scandinavia, it was becoming more vigorous than ever in America. Spectacular new churches enhanced the landscape; well-funded and religiously motivated groups like Moral Majority intensified the religiosity of American political life; and spiritual seekers found an ever-growing range of religious groups from which to choose.

At the same time, however, America was in other ways profoundly secular. A strong tradition of church-state separation kept religious considerations out of legislation, to the disappointment of evangelical lobbyists. American commerce, science, and technology operated entirely without reference to the divine, and the nation's approach to problem solving was rigorously rational and this-worldly. Citizens who wanted to spend their private lives deep in the embrace of religious communities could do so, but all except the most dedicated separatists had to move out into the secular world for their working lives. Citizens who wanted nothing to do with religion of any kind rarely found it impinging on them. Postwar America, in other words, was simultaneously a highly religious and a highly secular place. This is the paradox around which the book is organized.

Other paradoxes confront us as well. A second is the fact that America in the latter half of the twentieth century was the world's richest nation, with a population much better provided for materially than at any other time in its history and wealthier than almost all other contemporary nations. The workings of the massive market economy and its success as a wealth generator profoundly affected religion, enabling Americans to build imposing churches and to fund them to the tune of billions of dollars. Such wealth and ostentatiousness might have sat awkwardly with a majority-Christian population whose inspirational figure, Jesus, spoke vigorously against wealth and against having a care for the future. In fact the Christianity and the money rubbed along together easily enough, partly because Americans contributed very generously to religious charities and partly because they, like earlier Christian generations, had worked out an array of rationalizations.

A third paradox is that many American religious groups were, at least in their rhetoric and their social ideas, nostalgic and traditionalist, but in their methods innovative and technologically sophisticated. Preachers had been among the first Americans, back in the 1920s, to exploit radio. By 1950 they were also coming to terms with the new medium of television, and by the 1970s they had complemented televangelism with satellite feeds, direct-mail fund-raising, and computers. Evangelists unself-consciously used the best technologies of their day to produce shows with names like Charles Fuller's *Old-Fashioned Revival Hour* on radio or Jerry Falwell's *Old-Time Gospel Hour* on television. Anti-technology religious groups like the Amish (who drove around their Pennsylvania lands by horse and buggy and farmed without tractors or combines) were the exception, a colorful anomaly to the general rule of adapting eagerly to each new technology.

A fourth paradox is that America, the most technologically advanced nation, with near-universal literacy, an immense educational infrastructure, and instantaneous coast-to-coast communications, included populations that disagreed with one another on the most basic questions about the nature of life itself. The members of some religious groups believed they were witnessing the advance of society to steadily greater achievements of human creativity. The members of others believed they were witnessing the deterioration of society to a condition of such chaos that only the miraculous return of Jesus—or the arrival of benign extraterrestrials—could save it. Immense diversity existed, not only between religious groups but within them, with clashing ideas about the nature of God, the nature of the world, and the prospects for its inhabitants.

A book of this kind draws heavily on other historians' work. My preparation for writing it has consisted largely of reading their books, along with works of theology, religious sociology, and religious journalism. I have supplemented this reading with an oral history project, asking a wide variety of people to talk about their religious lives as children. For the most recent years, about which there is little historical literature so far, I have relied heavily on journalists' accounts. Despite many years of involvement in the study of American religious history, I can make no claim to comprehensiveness. Readers will note vast areas of American religious history, including entire religions and denominations, that are merely mentioned in passing or even omitted completely. To prevent the book from taking the form of a mere list or set of encyclopedia entries, as it could easily have done, I decided to develop some themes at the cost of ignoring others. The book provides a general introduction to the American religious landscape since World War II, but readers must turn to detailed works, of which there are thousands, for further information about particular groups, incidents, and problems.

Certain sociologists and historians, notably Robert Wuthnow, Peter Berger, and R. Laurence Moore, have influenced my way of thinking about this entire subject. Wuthnow's *The Restructuring of American Religion* (1988) is the classic statement of an argument that seems to me profoundly right. He points out that American religion, having been divided along *denominational* lines in the early postwar period, had come by the 1980s to be divided along *political* lines instead. Protestants' sharp antagonism toward Catholics in the 1950s was a distant memory by the 1980s. By then an alliance of conservative Protestants and conservative Catholics was working together on "family," educational, and foreign policy issues against a coalition of liberal Protestants and liberal Catholics, with each faction enjoying support from a sharply divided Jewish community. The shift that Wuthnow describes, from denominational division to political division, can be witnessed in many of the issues described here.

Peter Berger's *A Rumor of Angels* (1969) and *The Heretical Imperative* (1979) have also had a lasting influence on me. Both books deal with the difficulties that religious bodies face in the modern world, with its characteristics of skepticism and relativism. The first, written in response to the theological "death of God" affair that made headlines in the 1960s, shows how difficult it had become by the mid-twentieth century to enjoy religious certainty. Anyone who thought about or studied his or her religion at once became aware that its truths were not the truths of the religions surrounding it. Berger's insight was that the academic posture of relativism with which one studied these competing truth claims did not necessarily annihilate the possibility of religious truth; in the book's catch-phrase he "relativized the relativizers." He then sought out auguries of tran-scendence in the midst of America's modern rational society in a way that seemed to me highly plausible. *The Heretical Imperative*, written ten years later, noted that the word "heresy" originally meant "choice." American religious peo-ple were, in effect, forced to be "heretics," he said, because they had to choose their own religious way of life. There was no national religious orthodoxy against which deviations could be measured. Even those who chose something they thought of as rigorously orthodox could not fail to be aware that they were making the choice in a world full of people who had *not* made that choice.

Berger's idea that the American situation of religious choice makes everyone a heretic meshes with R. Laurence Moore's idea, in *Selling God* (1994), of America as a religious marketplace. Strict separation of church and state, said Moore, meant that throughout most of American history no one got social or political advantages from being religious. Ministers, priests, and rabbis depended on having an audience (one satisfied enough to give money) if they wanted a livelihood. Therefore they had to give the public what it wanted. Comparing religious life to consumer life (without ever being dismissive about it), Moore showed that numerous episodes throughout American history could be understood as efforts to manipulate the religious "market" in pursuit of the maximum number of "customers." This insight, which many other writers on American religious history have shared to some degree, helps explain, for exam-ple, the growth of "megachurches" in the 1980s and 1990s, which modeled themselves on commercial malls, concentrating worship, education, entertain-ment, retail, and amenities all in the same massive structures.

Informed by these three interpreters (but often taking advantage of other scholars' insights), I begin with a survey of the American religious landscape at the end of World War II. It featured a strong Roman Catholic Church, an array of Protestant churches divided between theologically liberal "mainline" denominations and theologically conservative evangelical ones, an ethnically distinct Greek and Russian Orthodox Christian Church, a largely Western Mormon Church, and a Jewish community split three ways, into Orthodox, Conservative, and Reform branches. Immigration law reform in the 1960s enabled large numbers of Muslims, Hindus, Buddhists, Sikhs, Confucians, and others to migrate to America, further diversifying America's religious profile. America showed an astonishing capacity to absorb new immigrant generations, often from culturally remote origins, and was even more pluralistic by 2001 than it had been in 1945.

While describing elements of life within each of America's main religious communities and the way they adapted to new circumstances, I have also tried to show how religious beliefs contributed to public and political conflicts. The book considers, among many other themes, the civil rights movement as a religious event that was led by ministers, fortified by Scripture, exhorted in massive church meetings, and buoyed by gospel music (chapter 3). It considers the public controversy over the election of a Catholic as president in 1960, the outcry over the Supreme Court's decisions, in the early 1960s, to prohibit the use of prayers and Bible reading in public schools, and the public scandal over some theologians' claims, later in that decade, that "God is dead" (chapter 4). It shows how religious beliefs influenced Americans' views of Communism and of the ethics of becoming involved in the Vietnam War (chapters 2, 4, and 5), and how religious ideas led some Americans to welcome the feminist and gay liberation movements while others condemned them (chapters 6 and 11).

Later chapters trace religious reactions to the political and social issues of the 1980s and 1990s, such as the attempt of evangelical conservatives to re-Christianize a society that its members thought of as too secular and too humanistic. Other issues include religion and environmentalism, the rise of American Islam from indigenous and immigrant sources, the mushroom growth of "megachurches," and the strange life of revival groups like Promise Keepers. The book closes with the millennium and the religious impact of the traumatic attacks on New York and Washington of September 11, 2001.

In addition to paying tribute to the many writers on whose work I have drawn, I would like to give special thanks to James Warren for the invitation to write this book and to Jim Fisher, who originated the project. Thanks also to my colleagues in the Emory University Department of History, especially Jamie Melton, our heroic chair, and Jeff Lesser, whose arrival made the place better than ever. Frank Lechner, also at Emory, gave me a crucial insight, while Ernie Freeberg at Colby-Sawyer College and John McGreevy at Notre Dame gave the whole manuscript helpful and sympathetic readings. The dedication is to a wonderful new friend, Thomson Smillie of Louisville, the wittiest Scotsman in Kentucky.

RELIGION IN AMERICA SINCE 1945: A HISTORY

Chapter 1

ANXIOUS VICTORY: 1945–1952

The War's End

The Second World War ended in August 1945 after two nuclear explosions destroyed the Japanese cities of Hiroshima and Nagasaki. Even nonreligious people groped for religious language to describe the power and destructiveness of the bombs. J. Philip Oppenheimer, one of the scientific leaders of the bomb project, witnessing the dazzling light of the first test explosion in New Mexico, thought of a passage from the Bhagavad Gita, the Hindu scripture: "If the radiance of a thousand suns were to burst into the sky, that would be like the splendour of the Mighty One." A moment later, seeing the immense mushroom cloud that followed the detonation, he found that another passage from the Gita came to mind: "I am become Death, the shatterer of worlds."[1] The tail gunner of the *Enola Gay*, the plane that dropped the bomb on Hiroshima, watched the terrifying fireball and mushroom cloud beneath him and said: "It's like a peep into Hell."[2] Throughout that year, on Germany until May and on Japan until August, bombs had rained down from the sky to tear cities apart and incinerate the rubble, killing tens of thousands of men, women, and children. Air war planners called it "the Jupiter Complex," invoking the old God of Thunder flinging fire bolts down from Olympus to satisfy his righteous anger.

How should religious people think about the firestorms that consumed Hamburg, Dresden, and Tokyo and then the two nuclear blasts? Had an inhumane enemy brought a justified destruction on itself? Many Americans believed that it had. The editors of the *Christian Herald* compared the atom bomb to an unrepentant Austrian Nazi who had worked as an executioner at Auschwitz. "Fearful as the bomb is," they wrote, "it isn't as bad as this 40-year-old barbarian. We can choose between the bomb controlled by decent men or this [Nazi] philosophy running riot during and after battle."[3]

Others were not so sure, and feared that America had descended to the savage level of its foes by making indiscriminate war on civilians. Twenty-two theologians from the Federal Council of Churches, an ecumenical Protestant group, wrote that "the surprise bombings of Hiroshima and Nagasaki are morally indefensible" and that America, by using nuclear weapons, "has sinned grievously against the law of God."[4] The editor of the *Catholic World* agreed, declaring: "We the people of the United States . . . have struck the most powerful blow ever delivered against Christian civilization and the moral law."[5]

Religious opponents of war were even more dismayed by this new level of destructiveness. Dorothy Day, leader of the Catholic Worker movement and an outspoken pacifist, had declared after Pearl Harbor, "We are still pacifists. Our manifesto is the Sermon on the Mount, which means that we will try to be peacemakers." When atomic bombs were dropped on Hiroshima and Nagasaki, she wrote: "Our Lord Himself has already pronounced judgment on the atomic bomb. When James and John (John the beloved) wished to call down fire from heaven on their enemies, Jesus said: 'You know not of what Spirit you are. The Son of Man came not to destroy souls but to save.'"[6] Mennonite and Quaker leaders, from churches that had always opposed war in all its forms, condemned these new weapons of mass destruction in the same uncompromising terms.

The war had been raging since the German attack on Poland in September 1939, and America had been directly involved since the Japanese attack on Pearl Harbor in December 1941. Several million Americans had been drafted into military service, while millions more on the "home front" had moved to take up war-related work. Even for a country like the United States, with a high level of mobility, this uprooting of millions was extraordinary. Families everywhere were broken, sometimes briefly, others for years, and, when men died in battle, forever. No wonder that military men, living away from the people they loved and enduring months of harsh discipline and monotony punctuated by moments of terror, craved spiritual aid and comfort. Their chaplains watched previously indifferent men suddenly begin to pray when they went into combat or when enemy shells fell around them. In a book based on interviews with army chaplains and published at war's end, Christopher Cross and William Arnold included this exchange:

These men of his congregation—have they changed at all in their attitude toward religion? "Yes," says Chaplain [Joseph H.] Hogan. "It is fear that has been an important contributing factor. Flattened in a foxhole under a heavy enemy barrage with death buzzing in every flying fragment, men are afraid. One becomes conscious of a helplessness and dependency and turns to the only one who can help—God."

Fear and death, observes Chaplain Hogan, make the average soldier think more deeply than at any time in his life. Sudden violent death flings the challenging questions: "Why are you on earth? What is the purpose of life? What comes after death? What if that shell had sought me out?"

More easily the non-essentials are sifted away and the great truths stand out. As one soldier put it to Chaplain Hogan: "I was afraid. I just prayed. Nothing fancy, mind you—just a direct wire: 'Help me, God!'"[7]

Chaplains also had to counsel men and help them through personal crises. Paratrooper chaplain James Mormon described how often men under his care received news of sexual betrayal from home. "One reads over and over the same sordid, shameful story of infidelity and adultery, many times told the soldier by the woman herself." The distressed man, to console himself, "goes into sin and on and on the vicious circle goes." Mormon saw this state of affairs as evidence that "too many Americans have forgotten that 'the wages of sin is death.'"[8]

The chaplains themselves, slightly more than 8,000 in all, came from Protestant, Catholic, and Jewish backgrounds. Seventy-six were killed in battle, 67 others died of illness and disease, 233 were wounded, and 1,213 were decorated for bravery. Soldiers could not always depend on finding a chaplain of their own particular church when they needed help. "Captain Rothschild is there [in a military hospital] with the wounded and dying. This time the Chaplain happens to be Jewish. But one's faith is only of academic interest here. 'They're all children of God,' as every Chaplain says."[9] This experience of wartime interfaith and interdenominational cooperation contributed to the ecumenical spirit that marked postwar religious life, and to the gradual decline of religious prejudice.

The soldiers' and sailors' families back home prayed for their men's safety with the same fervor as the combatants. Many clergy reported rising attendance in their churches, and attendance levels stayed high when the war ended. Chaplains believed that the reason was the gratitude men felt for surviving when they too could so easily have been killed.

Despite the separation, fear, and loneliness that the war caused, it was certainly possible to see the war itself as a spiritual contest, one with religious consequences, and not just as a brutal struggle between the world's great powers. Many American Christians saw it that way and eagerly supported the government's call for enlistment and personal sacrifices.

If Christians could see the war in this positive light, Jews were even more likely to do so. Hitler's persecution of German Jews had been well reported before the war began, and a trickle of Jewish refugees from Nazism had entered America in the 1930s, bringing news of persecution by the Third Reich. Once the war had begun, and especially when Germany and America were openly at war, it became more difficult to get reliable news. Jewish relief agencies heard rumors of an extermination policy in the concentration camps and then more definite news from agents in Nazi-occupied Europe and from neutral countries. That the Nazis were trying systematically to annihilate the whole Jewish population seemed almost too incredible to believe. Ironically, many Americans, recalling that they had believed anti-German atrocity stories during the First World War that had then proved false, conscientiously refused to believe that what we now know as the Holocaust was taking place. Even so, America's Jewish population was virtually unanimous in supporting the Allied war effort against Germany and giving it their blessing.

America's experience of the Second World War was different from that of most combatant countries. There was no fighting on American soil and no bombing of its cities. The onset of the war swept away the lingering Great Depression and created in its place an economic boom. As working men enlisted in the armed forces, employers scrambled to find new sources of labor. Thousands of women entered the industrial workforce as shipbuilders, manufacturers of tanks, aircraft, and munitions, and steam train drivers, earning more money than ever before and enjoying a new sense of economic independence. The war, then, seemed to many Americans to be a time of achievement; the cause was a good one, citizens' sense of patriotism was high, and the conflict ended with two evil enemies forced into unconditional surrender. The end of the war brought forth prayers of thanks to God for the men whose lives he had saved, and expressions of hope for a better postwar world. Compared to the millions of casualties suffered by many European nations (Russia alone probably lost more than twenty million people), American casualties (around three hundred thousand) seemed relatively small.

But if some Americans thought the world was decidedly better at the end of this conflict, others believed that it had never been worse. Victory, after all, had been won only in alliance with the Soviet Union, which was under the brutal dictatorship of Joseph Stalin, an atheist and Communist. How could Christians and Jews take pride in a victory of this kind—defeating one totalitarian monster by joining up with another? Besides, had American military men acted like soldiers in a righteous cause? Not always; reports of brutality against prisoners in the Pacific War, desecration of the bodies of the dead, epidemic rates of venereal disease among troops, widespread prostitution and alcohol abuse in port cities—all bespoke a different kind of spiritual crisis. Perhaps America had defeated the Nazis and Japanese only by descending to their level of immorality.

Americans, depending on their experiences in the war, their temperament, and their religious background, varied widely in their interpretation of the situation by 1945. But nearly all agreed that they were standing at one of the cross-roads of history, faced with choices that would have consequences not only in the everyday world but for the future of their entire civilization.

The American Religious Landscape

The overwhelming majority of Americans in 1945 were Protestants, Catholics, or Jews. The Protestant denominations included the Methodists, Baptists, Lutherans, Congregationalists, Presbyterians, Quakers, Episcopalians, Disci-ples of Christ, Assemblies of God, various Pentecostalist sects, and Unitarians, along with members of several denominations founded in America, including the Mormons, the Jehovah's Witnesses, and the Christian Scientists. Protes-tants traced their origins to the Reformation in sixteenth-century Europe, when most of northern Europe had split off from the Roman Catholic Church, under the inspiration of Martin Luther in Germany and Scandinavia, John Calvin in France, Switzerland, and the Netherlands, and as a result of King Henry VIII's divorce from Catherine of Aragon in Britain. Americans with north German ancestors were likely to be Protestants, as were those with ethnic origins in Nor-way, Sweden, the Netherlands, England, Scotland, and Wales.

Luther, himself a Catholic friar, had at first criticized specific corrupt prac-tices in the Catholic Church, but prolonged controversy soon enlarged the scope of his criticisms. Christians, he had come to believe, should depend on the Bible alone as their sole source of religious guidance, rejecting the Catholics' equal reliance on Scripture and tradition. *Sola Scriptura* or "the Bible alone" was therefore the foundation of the Protestant churches, which translated the Scriptures from Latin into the common languages of Europe. Protestantism spread through much of northern Europe in the sixteenth century and was car-ried to America by the first generations of British settlers after 1607.

It remained overwhelmingly the dominant religious identity of most settlers in the British colonies up to the Revolution but took many different forms. Mass-achusetts was a Congregationalist colony, holding to a severe Puritan theology teaching that God predestined every soul to heaven or hell and that people were powerless to change their fate. Virginia was an Anglican colony, following the milder teaching of the Church of England, in which religious observance, good moral conduct, and love of neighbor held out the promise of a heavenly reward. Swedish and German Lutherans, Dutch Calvinists, and Scottish Presbyterians in the middle colonies complicated this picture, as did the development of a Quaker colony in Pennsylvania, but all these groups traced their origins to the Reformation. Lacking a strong central authority (such as the Papacy that they had discarded), Protestant churches were prone to split, along doctrinal lines, because of disagreements over biblical interpretation, because of settlers' differ-ent ethnic and national traditions, and because of social class tensions.

From the colonial period to the late nineteenth century most Americans regarded the English-speaking part of the New World to be an essentially Protestant place. Protestants were numerically dominant and made an indelible mark on America's institutions, its moral and civil traditions, and (after the Revolution) its principle of church-state separation. Few Protestant churches actually favored religious pluralism or even toleration from the outset (colonial Massachusetts persecuted a wide variety of dissenters). However, the reality of denominational fragmentation gradually persuaded most of them to accept the idea, embodied in the First Amendment, that they should accept one another's ways of worshiping God and should avoid consecrating any one denomination as the national church. The First Amendment prohibited only the *federal* government from creating an established church, but by 1833 the last of the established *state* churches had also been disbanded.

Many Americans understood themselves as having created a republic that corresponded to the theological insights of the Reformation. The theoretical equality of America's citizens was a secular counterpart of the equality of every man in the eyes of God, what Luther had called "the priesthood of all believers." They believed, further, that the republic would prosper only if it was inhabited by virtuous Christian citizens. Legislators began their daily deliberations with prayers from a Protestant chaplain, and judges (including those on the Supreme Court) did not hesitate to assert that America was a Protestant Christian nation. Regular Protestant prayer and Bible reading were central to Horace Mann's plans for a universal public school system.

Moreover, a secular transfiguration of Protestantism was already apparent by the early nineteenth century. The rhetoric of "Manifest Destiny," for example, expressed the idea that God had singled out the United States to dominate the North American continent. It inspired successive American wars against the Indians and then against Mexico in the 1840s. Manifest Destiny could be traced back to the idea of being a chosen people that enjoys God's special favor while being held to his high standards. American Protestants in the Puritan tradition believed that this favor, granted first to Abraham and the ancient Jews, had been inherited by the early Christian church after the Jews failed to recognize Jesus as the promised Messiah, had next been inherited by the sixteenth-century reformers of a corrupt Christendom, and had finally descended to themselves as the people who had fully "purified" English Protestantism of its Catholic vestiges. They understood America as the fulfillment of a Protestant ideal and its uninterrupted continental expansion between 1780 and the 1860s as a sign of God's special favor.

America's nineteenth-century Protestant leaders were theoretically committed to reuniting their many squabbling denominations—whose existence seemed like a scandalous betrayal of the gospel—but could never manage it. To the contrary, denominations continued to subdivide over moral, doctrinal, and political disputes. The Methodists, Presbyterians, and Baptists, for example, all split into proslavery Southern branches and antislavery Northern ones before the Civil War. "The Bible alone" and the "priesthood of all believers" authorized everyone to interpret Scripture in his or her own way. Not surprisingly, the existence of many interpreters continued to lead to many interpretations, around which new groups formed. European governments had presided over state churches and enforced a degree of uniformity, but conditions in America—its size, Constitution, and ethnic diversity—facilitated the proliferation of new denominations. Many were American inventions, including the Shakers, the Assemblies of God, the Disciples of Christ, the Mormons, the Christian Scientists, and the Jehovah's Witnesses.

In the late nineteenth century, intellectual disputes contributed to more Protestant fragmentation. Religious scholars, as they began the historical-critical study of the ancient world, came to regard the Hebrew Bible (the Old Testament) as one of many collections of religious writings from the ancient Near East. They discovered that in these different texts could be found similar myths about creation, floods, the origin of languages, and God's intervention on earth. Such insights made it difficult to believe that the Bible alone was true and divinely inspired, and all the others (despite striking parallels) false. Moreover, the ethics of some characters in the Hebrew Bible seemed impossible to justify: the dirty tricks by which Jacob stole his brother Esau's birthright and his father's blessing, and the apocalyptic anger of God himself in flooding the world and killing everyone except Noah's family. Some Protestants concluded that they could still place their faith in Jesus and the teachings of the New Testament but not in the whole of the Old Testament. Charles Lyell's discoveries in geology and Charles Darwin's theory of evolution also transformed scholars' understanding of the nature of the earth and of life itself, casting doubt on whether the beginning of the Book of Genesis described actual historical events.

Men and women following these lines of thought, whom we remember as liberal Protestants, were not able to persuade all their contemporaries. Conservative Protestants, their opponents, were convinced that the Bible was completely unlike all other historic literature. It was, they said, the revealed word of God, all of which was absolutely true. God himself would not lie. They pointed out that liberal Protestants, in picking and choosing which parts of the Bible to accept, were really making themselves, not God, supreme judges of what was true and right. How, they asked, can you *worship* a God whom you have judged? They were willing to admit that Charles Darwin was a fine empirical biologist, but they considered his evolutionary theory mere speculation. Therefore they felt justified in rejecting evolution and affirming that the biblical account of the Creation was true. Some even argued that fossilized shells, dinosaur bones, the Grand Canyon, and other evidences of an ancient Earth were tests sent by God to challenge the strength of humans' faith.

These disagreements led to more divisions among Protestants. Those who insisted on biblical infallibility got the name "fundamentalists" after the publication, early in the twentieth century, of a series of booklets (*The Fundamentals*) summarizing their views. Fundamentalists were strongest in rural areas and the South, and their adherents were on the whole less highly educated and poorer than liberal Protestants. By 1945 most Protestant leaders with national reputations were theological liberals. The Episcopal, Methodist, Northern Baptist, Congregational, and Presbyterian churches to which they belonged made up, collectively, what was called the "Protestant mainstream." By then, a famous court case to decide whether Tennessee schoolchildren could study evolution, the Scopes "Monkey Trial" of 1925, had intellectually discredited fundamentalists among educated Americans.

This split between intellectually advanced liberal Protestants and biblical fundamentalist Protestants developed gradually between 1860 and 1925. Meanwhile, the continuation of a long tradition of evangelical revivals preserved a large middle ground between the two extremes. The whole history of American Protestantism was one of recurrent revivals in which charismatic preachers aroused spiritual enthusiasm in entire communities, temporarily eclipsing denominational differences. George Whitefield in the colonial period, Charles Grandison Finney and Dwight Moody in the nineteenth century, and Billy Sunday in the early twentieth century were shining stars in this evangelical revival tradition, which, after World War II, Billy Graham would continue. Until the mid-nineteenth century a personal crisis of faith and a conversion experience, the dawning assurance that you were saved by God, had been required for membership in many churches. The twentieth-century equivalent, being "born again," remained a central feature of Protestant life across a broad spectrum of the denominations. Some liberal Protestants, especially those who were more educated and those of higher social status, had become uncomfortable with the emotionalism of revivals, but such meetings were nevertheless still a central feature of American Protestant life.

—

Alongside the Protestant majority by 1945 lived a large Catholic minority. Maryland had been the first Catholic settlement among the English colonies in North America, but most American Catholics traced their ancestry to Ireland, Italy, Poland, southern Germany, and the Slavic countries of southeastern Europe. The Reformation split of the sixteenth century had led to mistrust and hatred between Catholics and Protestants, which migrants from both sides of the divide had carried with them to America. The Catholic Church taught that it alone was true Christianity and that all Protestants, as heretics, were damned. Protestants replied that Catholics, having failed to reform themselves, were parts of a corrupt and decadent organization, remote from real Christianity, and that their leader, the pope, was a tyrannical foreign monarch. American circumstances had begun to temper these opinions by the 1940s; it is hard to live next door to a family whose everyday life is similar to your own and yet believe that they are all damned to hell while you are not, because you attend different churches every Sunday morning. Harder still is it to share a foxhole under enemy bombardment and believe that, in the event of a direct hit, half of your comrades will go to eternal bliss, the other half to eternal suffering, depending on their particular religious upbringing. Even so, anti-Catholicism remained intellectually respectable among both Fundamentalist and liberal Protestants. It had played a role in foiling the candidacy of the only Catholic to run for president on a major party ticket (Al Smith, Democrat, in 1928) and would still plague John F. Kennedy's candidacy in 1960.

The Catholic population had been small until the early nineteenth century (just one signer of the Declaration of Independence was a Catholic) but had grown rapidly with migrations from Ireland and Germany in the 1830s, 1840s, and 1850s and from southern Europe later in that century. Most Catholics had become working-class city dwellers at first and had come to dominate political life in New York, Chicago, Boston, and several other big cities by the early twentieth century. Their priests' and bishops' fear that Catholic immigrants would be tempted to join Protestant churches had led them to set up their own educational system, the parochial schools, so that each new generation of Catholics could learn their religious tradition from the inside. Most urban Catholics between 1850 and 1920 lived in ethnic enclaves, to which newcomers arrived from Europe. The end of open immigration in the 1920s began to weaken these communities, and by the 1940s the Catholic population was spreading out into America's rapidly growing suburbs. Catholic neighborhoods, first in town, later in the suburbs, devoted themselves to raising funds for their schools and churches, and maintaining a high degree of religious distinctiveness.

The Catholic Church, unlike the Protestant denominations, had a strong principle of centralized leadership. Catholic bishops ruled like princes in their dioceses. Although they were uncompromising in defending their faith, they were eager to reassure their American neighbors that it was possible to be both fully Catholic and a fully loyal American citizen. They had long discouraged (or, in World War I, forbidden) the use of immigrant languages in church. At their behest priests urged their parishioners, during both world wars, to contribute to bond drives (in effect lending money to the government to help finance the war effort) and, if they were men, to enlist and fight. At the same time they worked to ensure that Rome, the international center of their church, would have no need to fear for their orthodoxy.

In addition to these ethnic, organizational, and social contrasts, Catholicism had a different style of religious activity than Protestantism. Mass, the principal

Catholic service, was recited by the priest in Latin, with his back to the congregation. Preaching and Bible study, central to the Protestant tradition, played a far smaller role for Catholics, who placed more weight on church tradition in shaping their beliefs. The pope's teachings commanded widespread assent from American Catholics. Among them was a ban on contraception, which deliberately separates sex from procreation and, it was argued, violates the natural law. By the 1940s, accordingly, Catholic families tended to have more children than Protestants, among whom there was no comparable ban. The Catholic ideal family consisted of a working father and six or more children, each named after one of the saints, under the protection of a self-sacrificing stay-at-home mother.

—

American Jews, like American Catholics, were mainly the descendants of immigrants who had arrived since 1850. There was a tiny Jewish population from the colonial era, but the first large-scale Jewish immigration came from Germany in the 1840s and 1850s. They were members of the Reform tradition, urban, and already highly assimilated to the way of life of a mainly Christian nation. What Jews called the Bible, Christians called the Old Testament. Christians believed that the Messiah foretold in the Hebrew Scriptures was Jesus. Jews did not; they still awaited his coming, meanwhile living according to the laws that God gave to Moses. In order to facilitate everyday life in Germany and America, Reform Jews had abandoned many of the complicated regulations laid down in the books of Deuteronomy and Leviticus. They emphasized the ethical rather than the legalistic side of Judaism.

A second wave of Jewish immigration arrived in America at the end of the nineteenth and early in the twentieth centuries, this time from Poland, Russia, and the Austro-Hungarian Empire (southeastern Europe). These newcomers were Orthodox Jews, who had been forced to live in segregated ghettos and had made fewer compromises with the modern world than their Reform cousins. They kept the kosher food laws and preserved taboos against touching or eating with non-Jews, grew their hair and beards long, segregated men and women in the synagogue, and accorded high status to talmudic scholars. Subject to persecution in Russia and sometimes forced to flee from pogroms (government-backed popular attacks on Jews), they found adaptation to America a challenge. Living at first in high-density ethnic enclaves, notably on the Lower East Side of New York City, most adjusted to American conditions in a generation. American public schools taught their children English, and, through a combination of hard work and high academic achievement, the second generation began a spectacular ascent to prosperity and professional success that was well advanced by 1945.

Anti-Semitism was a source of permanent anxiety for American Jews, who, by the time of World War II, numbered about 4 million in an American population of about 135 million. For two thousand years Jews had suffered from Christian accusations that they were the killers of Christ. Expelled periodically from European kingdoms, often cheated of their property and denied access to law, Jews had learned to be sensitive to the mood and prejudices of those around them. America was certainly not free of anti-Semitism, but most Jews discovered that conditions in the New World were generally much better than they had been in the Old. The principle of church-state separation enabled them to worship without hindrance. They were no longer segregated, unless by choice. They were free to carry on their businesses, their work, and their faith without political or legal harassment, and some among them rose to distinguished positions in American public life. Louis Brandeis, scion of a German Reform family, became America's first Jewish Supreme Court justice in 1916. The most prominent newspaper columnist in America by 1945 was Walter Lippmann. Lionel Trilling became the first Jew to teach English literature at an Ivy League university when he was appointed to the faculty of Columbia University.

Since the late nineteenth century many Jews in Europe had devoted themselves to the Zionist movement. Zionism, the ideal of Theodore Herzl (1860–1904), aimed to gather Jews from all over the world and return them to their historic homeland, Israel, from which they had dispersed after two failed rebellions against the Roman Empire in the years 70 and 135 C.E. Only by having their own promised land, said Herzl and his followers, would the Jews be safe from recurrent bouts of persecution. But where was the promised land? To growing numbers of immigrants America itself seemed ideal. After all, America already existed, already gave Jews civil protection and religious freedom, and enabled many of them to live unexpectedly well. Israel, in 1945, was still just an idea. The land in question was called Palestine, had a large Arab population, and was controlled politically by the British Empire, which had acquired it from the defeated Turkish Empire at the end of the First World War. Jews had been moving there, buying land, and setting up utopian communities, called kibbutzim, since the early 1920s, but only the most optimistic or ideologically committed Zionist would have thought of leaving America to settle there in 1945. Palestine was on the brink of civil war as rival Jewish, Palestinian, and British groups vied for control.

Hanging over Jews everywhere by then was news of the Holocaust, whose scale and horrors began to be laid bare in 1945 when Allied troops liberated Dachau, Bergen-Belsen, Auschwitz, and the other Nazi death camps. Coming to terms with the fact that the Nazi regime had killed literally millions of Jews would take decades—the process is still going on today. It is not surprising that the first reaction of many American Jews was to cling to the security and pros-

perity that America offered rather than to jump into another conflict whose outcome then seemed so uncertain.

Cold War of the Spirit

The end of the war affected almost everybody in America. Millions of men
returned from the armed forces, while millions of women left their temporary
industrial jobs. The marriage rate and the birth rate soared, accelerating a baby
boom that had begun while the war was still being fought. Churches and synagogues found their membership increasing and, as we shall see, undertook
ambitious building programs to keep pace with the era's surprising turn to traditional religion. As young American families crowded into new churches, their
ministers, priests, and rabbis led them in prayers for a world in upheaval. On
the one hand the Nazis and the Japanese had been defeated and history's most
destructive war brought to a victorious end. Most American men had jobs and
more money than ever before. But was this good life secure? Some feared that,
without the stimulus of war, Depression conditions would recur, with widespread unemployment and poverty. That fear eventually proved groundless, but
the vitality of the postwar economy was itself based partly on preparations for
new and more devastating wars.

Although many churches placed their hopes in the United Nations (a senior
Presbyterian layman, John Foster Dulles, was one of the American architects of
the UN) it was clear by 1946 that America's wartime alliance with the Soviet
Union was breaking down. The hot war against Hitler's Germany was being
replaced by the Cold War against Stalin's Soviet Union. Nuclear weapons had
not disappeared; attempts to arrange an international pool of nuclear knowledge and resources failed because of mistrust among the victors, and now the
Russians were developing their own nuclear bombs as fast as possible. Worse,
Klaus Fuchs and Julius and Ethel Rosenberg, Soviet spies in the American
nuclear program, had passed information to the Russians, helping them complete their own bomb by 1949.

No one voiced the fear that the world was coming to a crisis more convinc-
ingly than evangelical and fundamentalist preachers. A staple of their preaching had always been that the Second Coming of Christ, foretold in the New
Testament Book of Revelation, was imminent and that everyone should prepare
for the end of the world. Revelation is an extremely cryptic book of visions.
More than a century of intense efforts by American fundamentalists to unravel
its exact meaning had brought plenty of ingenious theories and obscurantist
wrangling but little agreement. Most of these interpreters believed that the Second Coming would be preceded by certain "signs of the times," including the
appearance of an Antichrist who carried "the Mark of the Beast" and would be
a powerful worldly tyrant. The world would degenerate until Jesus intervened,

carried off those who were already saved in an event called the Rapture, and left everyone else to fight out the terrible last Battle of Armageddon. Then Christ would return in glory to preside over a thousand-year reign of peace on earth. Fundamentalists looked on the world as a great battleground for the conflict between God and the Devil, good and evil. Mankind alone, they believed, could never build the Kingdom of God (the great hope of liberal Protestants) and must concentrate on saving souls rather than reforming society. Therefore, a ministry to the poor and on behalf of social reform, while not irrelevant, was strictly secondary business. The great thing was to convert individuals.

Fundamentalists were an argumentative lot and feuded, sometimes roughly, with each other, with nonfundamentalist Protestants, and with the rest of the world. For example, in the 1930s Frank Norris (1877–1952), a spellbinding preacher from Fort Worth, Texas, had criticized the town's Catholic mayor so harshly that one of the mayor's friends got drunk and went to call on Norris to demand an apology. Norris killed him with four gunshots. On another occasion he set fire to his own church and burned it to the ground, alleging that his enemies had done it. He denounced all Baptists who doubted the exact word-for-word accuracy of the Bible. After the war he called President Truman a Communist and condemned academic freedom in American schools and colleges as an entering wedge for Communist subversion.

Norris and other abrasive ministers hampered rather than helped the spread of the fundamentalist message. In 1942 two evangelical ministers, J. Elwin Wright and Harold Ockenga, trying to create a more upbeat and harmonious image for their brand of Protestantism, founded the National Association of Evangelicals. It was a pointedly nondenominational organization, drawing members from many different churches and trying to restore the old revival tradition, emphasizing Jesus' love and personal salvation, while avoiding Norris-style polemics and doctrinal hairsplitting. It also aimed to modernize the image of evangelicalism. Whereas old evangelists had traveled what was known as the "sawdust trail," preaching in tents to small-town audiences, the new evangelicalism looked for ways to come into the big cities that increasingly dominated American life.

A radio show, Charles Fuller's *Old-Fashioned Revival Hour*, was an early sign of changing evangelical methods. Begun in 1937, by 1940 it was broadcasting on 450 stations every week. Fuller, originally from California, was a well-spoken middle-American personality, with none of the dangerous sharp edges that made figures like Norris such a public relations problem. His wife read listeners' letters over the air, with news of their conversions or requests for prayers, and a tuneful quartet played and sang gospel hymns. As the historian Joel Carpenter has written, the Fullers "did not sound like high-voltage haranguers but rather like trusted friends."[10] By 1943 theirs was the single most popular broadcast in the nation, with twenty million weekly listeners.

Having adapted to radio, one of the great twentieth-century technologies, evangelical religion began picking up other innovations. The Youth for Christ movement, which developed in the last years of the war, was a self-conscious effort to make the evangelical message attractive to urban teenagers and to get crowds of unattached soldiers and sailors out of city bars and brothels and into church. Its ministers wore the youth fashions of the day, and its musicians, far from playing the homely hymns of the revival tradition, imitated Harry James and Glenn Miller, the popular jazz and swing musicians of the time. Preachers tried to imitate the cadence of radio announcers rather than the florid sermon rhetoric of their elders, to underline the point that their message was as up-to-date and relevant now as it had been in the era of the Bible.

Youth for Christ's greatest triumph was its Chicago rally on Memorial Day, 1945, when an audience of seventy thousand filled Soldier Field, the Chicago Bears' football stadium. Soldiers and nurses marched, missionary representatives paraded the costumes of all the nations still awaiting the gospel, a band of three hundred played upbeat music and a choir of five thousand sang, while a giant neon sign over the stadium declared JESUS SAVES. The main preacher was Percy Crawford, one of YFC's founders and chief strategists, but also on the platform that night was Billy Graham.

Graham, born in 1918, a North Carolina farm boy, converted by traveling evangelist Mordecai Fowler Ham as a sixteen-year-old in 1934, and educated at Bob Jones College, Florida Bible Institute, and then Wheaton College, Illinois, was about to transform evangelical Christianity. He was already its brightest new star. After a string of brilliant preaching successes for Youth for Christ, he became America's youngest college president in 1947 when he was appointed to head a trio of Minnesota evangelical colleges. A handsome and intelligent man with a spellbinding preacher's manner and a piercing gaze, Graham had the knack of filling his listeners first with dread that they were sinners, fragments of a world rushing headlong to catastrophe, and then with the desire to turn their lives around, put their trust in Jesus, and be saved. Listeners would troop forward at the end of his revival sermons to repent of their sins, turn to Jesus, and dedicate their lives to God.

The turning point of Graham's career, which converted him from an evangelical circuit star to a national celebrity, came in 1949 when he preached a revival in Los Angeles. Immediately before the meetings he was feeling depressed, plagued by intellectual doubts. His friend Chuck Templeton had shown him how strong the scholarly evidence was against fundamentalist claims, and argued that it was no longer possible for an intelligent man to believe that the whole of the Bible was literally true. Graham acknowledged the power of Templeton's arguments, and at various times in the following days his friends found him weeping, groaning, and lying prostrate on the grass, begging for God's guidance. Recalling the crisis years later, Graham wrote:

> Dropping to my knees there in the woods, I opened the Bible at random on a tree stump in front of me. . . . "Oh God! There are many things in this book I do not understand. There are many problems with it for which I have no solution. There are many seeming contradictions. There are some areas in it that do not seem to correlate with modern science. I can't answer some of the philosophical and psychological questions Chuck and the others are raising." I was trying to be on the level with God, but something remained unspoken. At last the Holy Spirit freed me to say it. "Father, I am going to accept this as Thy Word—by *faith*! I'm going to allow faith to go beyond my intellectual questions and doubts, and I will believe this to be Your inspired Word."[11]

He came out of this crisis determined to uphold the full evangelical message and preached in Los Angeles with unprecedented verve. When a group of minor celebrities, including Olympic athlete Louis Zamperini and a popular disc jockey, Stuart Hamblen, converted, the word of Graham's mission began to spread in the mainstream media, and the crowds at his revival tent swelled accordingly.

Stories in the Hearst newspapers and picture spreads of Graham's revival in *Life* magazine primed him for an equally spectacular success in Boston that winter, and evangelicals everywhere began to hope that a new Great Awakening would sweep through America, as it had in the 1740s and again in the 1820s, turning the nation away from sin and preparing the people for Christ's return. Graham himself dared to wonder whether he was the reincarnation of the great revivalists Whitefield and Finney, or even of such biblical prophets as Elisha or Amos. Harold Ockenga, pastor of Boston's Park Street Church, helped host Graham's Boston revival. Delighted by its success, he thought he was witnessing the onset of Christ's Second Coming. "It may be that God is now taking out his elect . . . before the awful wrath of God will be loosed in the atomic warfare of this day."[12]

Graham's success quieted evangelicals' fears that their brand of Christianity (in their view the only true version) no longer spoke to Americans. At Wheaton College, Illinois, in February 1950, a start-of-semester prayer meeting turned suddenly into a general confession of sins. One by one students stood to declare their transgressions against God, to beg his forgiveness, and to join hands in Christian fellowship. The meeting lasted for two complete days and was followed by a wave of campus revivals there and across the American evangelical college landscape. Despite Graham's and Ockenga's hopes, this chain of events did not inaugurate the end times, but they did shift the balance of power among American religious groups. They showed mainstream Protestants that evangelicalism and fundamentalism, far from being dead and forgotten, were more powerful, more up-to-date, and more influential than at any time in the twentieth century and that they would continue to play an important role in national life.

Spiritual Peace in the 1940s

What was religion *for*? Was it a way of forcing you to reckon with your sins, to feel the full weight of your unworthiness before God, to admit that without him you were hopeless, and then to get ready for the Apocalypse? Or was it a kind of therapy, something to make you feel good about yourself and help you to get along more easily in everyday life? Billy Graham gave the first answer, but a string of religious best-sellers in the late 1940s gave the second, and they came from many parts of the religious spectrum. Among them were Rabbi Joshua Loth Liebman's *Peace of Mind* (1946) and Norman Vincent Peale's *Guide to Confident Living* (1948). Each in his own way was concerned with the problem of anxiety. If wartime terror was the dominant emotion of the early 1940s, a more diffuse anxiety seemed to be the dominant emotion of the decade's later years. Secular and religious writers alike argued that Americans, while victorious and materially well endowed, remained anxious, adrift, unsure of their identity and purpose. David Riesman's *The Lonely Crowd* (1950) was a brilliant and influential sociological study of anxious middle-class Americans, but it offered no easy solutions. Liebman and Peale provided techniques for overcoming anxiety.

Liebman, of Temple Israel in Boston, and Peale, of the Marble Collegiate Church on New York's Fifth Avenue, were among the first American clergy to blend Christianity and psychoanalysis. The Viennese founder of psychoanalysis, Sigmund Freud (1856–1939), had first become a household name in America during the 1920s, when inaccurate popular summaries of his work implied that the source of many human problems was sexual repression. Ministers had been horrified, especially when it became clear that Freud was an atheist. His 1927 book *The Future of an Illusion* argued that God was merely an infantile projection of the father figure, a towering male presence both loved and feared by the powerless child in its cradle. Freud expected that as civilization and science advanced, humanity would outgrow such childish delusions. Coming as he did from a secularized Jewish family, he had no patience with Christianity. But by the late 1940s, Rabbi Liebman—and Peale (with his assistant, Smiley Blanton, who had known and been psychoanalyzed by Freud)—were arguing that religion and psychiatry both had the same mission: to promote health and human well-being.

"The express purpose of religion is the achievement of the good life," wrote Liebman, and peace of mind, not material riches, is the highest attainment of the good life.[13] Psychoanalysis, he argued, was a useful addition to the techniques of religion but not a replacement for them. By religion Liebman meant "the accumulated spiritual wisdom and ethical precepts dating from the time of the earliest Prophets and gradually formulated into a body of tested truths for man's moral guidance and spiritual at-homeness in the universe" (12). He was careful to make no particular claims for Judaism or any other single religion, and he quoted freely from Buddha, Lao-tzu, and Marcus Aurelius as well as from the Psalms and the Prophets.

For orthodox Christianity and Judaism he had harsh words. Their concept of sin, he believed, had encouraged a repression that was all too likely to become neurotic. Much better to bring your dark rages and antisocial impulses into the light of day by talking frankly about them than to bottle them up and try to pretend they did not exist. Did not Catholics do exactly that in the confessional? Not really, because the confessional priest urged people to repent of their sinful acts and thoughts, whereas psychoanalysis, recognizing that they were perfectly natural, asked people instead to *outgrow* them. Religion should learn from psychiatry that peace of mind came from self-knowledge, not self-condemnation. Liebman ended with his own ten commandments, not the harsh "thou shalt nots" of the Hebrew God but a series of "shalts" for a therapeutic generation:

"Thou shalt learn to respect thyself and then thou wilt love thy neighbor as thyself.

"Thou shalt transcend inner anxiety . . .

"Thou shalt search thy heart for the traces of immaturity and the temptations of childishness . . . " and so on (202–3). It is difficult to believe that Freud would have endorsed Liebman's book, which made peace of mind sound like an end in itself rather than inquiring into what the possessor of a peaceful mind would do next. Neither did it make any of the more imperious demands that were the staples of traditional religion.

Norman Vincent Peale also offered a *technique* for feeling better, an antidote to the anxiety, tension, guilt, and fear he found among the people who came to his church and his counseling service. He described church services as a form of group therapy, whose goodwill atmosphere would overcome common mental problems:

> One technique used in the service of public worship that has produced amazing results is the period of directed quietness. Attendance at Quaker meetings taught me the value of creative silence. In meeting with the Friends, I derived great personal strength over fear and mental clarification which helped me in one or two instances to the most astounding solution of problems.[14]

Where Liebman sought to give his readers peace, Peale offered energy or power, but it had the same life-affirming character. "Christianity . . . is a throbbing, pulsating, vibrant, creative energy, even in such manner as the sunlight is energy. . . . It is a deep therapy which can drive to the heart of a personality or of society . . . in breaking down infection centers, building up life centers, transforming, endowing with new energy" (9). Peale's *Guide to Confident Living* then told readers how to apply this energy-Christianity to overcoming their problems. He even suggested to those with disabilities, inferiority complexes, and anxieties that they should stare boldly at themselves in the mirror and declare: "With men things are impossible but with God all things are possible" (58). About Jesus and about the Apocalypse he had nothing to say. Even more than Liebman, Peale was offering a technique for getting on well in this world rather than dwelling on Jesus' words "My Kingdom is not of this world." Peale's next and even greater best-seller, *The Power of Positive Thinking* (1952), which sold more than two million copies, took this trend further, draining away its religious content almost completely.

Monsignor Fulton Sheen, a talented speaker and writer for the Catholic Church, protested against works like Liebman's and Peale's in *Peace of Soul* (1949). In his view they were both evidence of a drastically truncated vision of life itself. Where once men had lived poised between heaven above and hell beneath and had striven to overcome the animal side of their nature by fulfilling their divine potentialities, now they were reduced to "a single dimension . . . the surface of the earth."

> Jailed by self, he [modern man] attempts to compensate for the loss of the three-dimensional universe of faith by finding three new dimensions within his own mind. Above his *ego*, his conscious level, he discovers, in place of heaven, an inexorable tyrant whom he calls the *superego*. Below his consciousness, in place of hell, he substitutes a hidden world of instincts and urges, primitive longings and biological needs, which he calls the *id*.[15]

In the rest of the book Sheen debunked the Freudian system as one of many secular substitutes for Christianity thrown up in the last few centuries by secularized men with delusions of omniscience. Marxism and Enlightenment rationalism were others. All were pernicious because they willfully turned away from the God who alone can fulfill human aspirations. Sheen's book was far richer than Liebman's or Peale's (citing Augustine, Kierkegaard, Jung, and Heidegger), much more conscious of a valuable intellectual tradition than theirs, and much more outspoken in refusing to come to terms with the modern world. Liebman and Peale were looking for ways to get along and adapt to new conditions and feel good, but Sheen was standing in judgment over sinners. Peace of mind, he warned, is not at all the same thing as peace of soul. Liebman and Peale urged anxious Americans not to blame themselves but to understand the subconscious forces that had created their anxieties. Sheen insisted that anxiety springs from our separation from God, from our uncontrolled desires, and from our eagerness to avoid taking responsibility for our actions.

Sheen's objective was to reconcile people with God—that was the only way in which they would be reconciled to themselves and to each other, he believed—"there can be no world peace unless there is soul peace" (1). Another religious best-seller of the early postwar years, Thomas Merton's *The Seven Storey Mountain* (1948), also shows a greater Catholic resistance to the modern world than that of liberal Protestants and Reform Jews. Merton (1915–1968), the religiously indifferent son of an artist, was a handsome young man who had spent many of the interwar years in England and France. He had had a series of love affairs, aspired to write novels, was a talented cartoonist, and a dabbler in social radicalism during the Depression years, even joining the Communist Party for a while. Merton detested the modern commercial world but eventually found Catholic philosophers, not Communists, to be its most persuasive critics. He converted to Catholicism as a Columbia University graduate student in 1938. Eager to live out his new faith to the full, he entered the Trappist monastery at Gethsemani, Kentucky, in 1941. Trappists take vows of perpetual silence, converse in a simple sign language, and use their voices only to sing Gregorian chant in seven daily chapel services. They work hard on their subsistence farm between services, however, growing their own food. Merton took to the life, survived the arduous Trappist novitiate (apprenticeship), and was ordained a priest in 1947. His abbot, learning of his former literary ambitions, and seeing that he was a talented writer of devotional pamphlets, encouraged him to write his spiritual autobiography. It appeared the next year, and, to their amazement, it became a best-seller.

Have you ever read a book in total rapture, convinced that every word is true and that the author is showing you how to live your own life from now on? That's what *The Seven Storey Mountain* is like. Merton gets under your skin and convinces you, at least while you are actually in the midst of it, that the modern materialistic world is futile and evil and that a life of monastic contemplation is the antidote. He delights in hardship and mortification and makes you see all the attractions of asceticism. He loves to flay himself for recurrent lapses into sin.

> It cannot have been much more than two weeks after that that I was in the infirmary myself . . . with influenza. It was the Feast of St. Gregory the Great. I remember entering the cell assigned to me with a sense of secret joy and triumph, in spite of the fact that it had just been vacated two days before by Brother Hugh, whom we had carried out to the cemetery, lying in his open bier with that grim smile of satisfaction that Trappist corpses have.
>
> My secret joy at entering the infirmary came from the thought: "Now at last I will have some solitude and I will have plenty of time to pray." . . . I was fully convinced that I was going to indulge all the selfish appetites that I did not yet know how to recognize as selfish because they appeared so spiritual in their new dis-

guise. All my bad habits, disinfected, it is true, of formal sin, had sneaked into the monastery with me and had received the religious vesture along with me: spiritual gluttony, spiritual sensuality, spiritual pride.[16]

Merton's autobiography led to an unprecedented rush by young men to join the Trappists, and the order was forced to open new monasteries to deal with the crowd. Still, far more people read the book as a kind of religious entertainment than as a gateway to actual self-renewal or repudiation of society. The historian Mark Massa shrewdly points out that *The Seven Storey Mountain* was not as different from religious therapeutic literature as its admirers liked to think. Instead, "Merton legitimized the possibility of a sophisticated, accessible Catholic spirituality for a middle-class suburban constituency without really 'converting' them to the radical implications of Cistercian or Benedictine Spirituality."[17]

As for Merton himself, he was still not sure that he was living a sufficiently isolated life, and he often wished he had joined the even more penitential and contemplative Carthusians instead. "Here at Gethsemani," he wrote, "we are at the same time Cistercians and Americans. It is in some respects a dangerous combination. Our energy runs away with us."[18]

The literary success of Liebman, Peale, Sheen, and Merton, and the electric response of Billy Graham's audiences, all bear witness to a religious longing in postwar America, mixed with feelings of anxiety and insecurity that victory and prosperity had not been able to dispel. Although Billy Graham made several successful visits to England and although postwar Europe, shattered by years of war, had an equal or greater need of spiritual renewal, the American postwar religious revival had no European counterpart. America became, increasingly, the one special case of modernization and religion going forward hand in hand rather than one at the expense of the other.

Chapter 2

RELIGION AND MATERIALISM: 1950–1970

Fighting Godless Communism

In the 1930s the apparent breakdown of the American capitalist system prompted some Americans to look for radical alternatives. Was it not intolerable to have productive factories standing unused and fields lying fallow at a time when millions of people were short of food, clothes, and housing? The alternative to this weird situation, a few Americans believed, was Communism. The Russian Revolution of 1917 had collectivized all production and distribution of goods. Now, at least in theory, the society made what it needed and distributed it justly and equitably, having abolished profits and class differences. Backward Russia was hurrying forward into the twentieth century; could not an already advanced America leap further into the future under Communism?

The American Communist Party was never large, but in the mid-1930s it was vigorous and outspoken, organizing labor unions, strikes, and demonstrations for social justice. Religious onlookers didn't like its philosophical atheism, but a radical minority, including Catholic Worker founder Dorothy Day, admired its active spirit and its theoretical commitment to social and economic equality. Day reminded audiences that "it is atheistic Communism which we oppose, but as for economic Communism—it is a system which has worked admirably in religious orders for two thousand years."[1] Conversely, Communists them-

selves sometimes admitted that the movement had become for them a substitute religion, calling forth a spirit of self-denial, a golden vision of the future,
and even occasionally demanding heroic suffering on behalf of the cause.
Whittaker Chambers, for example, became a Communist in 1925 and
described Communism as "a great faith," whose vision of "Man without God"
rivaled Christianity's vision "of God and man's relationship to God."[2]

America's alliance with the Soviet Union during the Second World War
gave Communism, briefly, good press in the United States. The end of the war
soon changed that. Wartime warmth became Cold War chill when the Soviet
Union refused to permit open elections in Eastern Europe, set up Communist
dictatorships there instead, and began to persecute Christians and Jews. America and the Soviet Union almost went to war in 1948 over access to Berlin and
Soviet intervention in Czechoslovakia. In 1949 the completion of the first Russian atom bomb and then the Chinese Communist revolution under Mao
Zedong exacerbated the Cold War confrontation. In 1950 American soldiers
poured into South Korea to repel a North Korean Communist invasion that was
backed by Communist China, and they fought there until the truce of 1953.

Inside America, first the government and then numerous private agencies
began searching for evidence of internal espionage and Communist subversion. They discovered that Soviet spies had infiltrated the Manhattan Project
(creator of the atom bomb) and that Communist sympathizers and Party members had worked in many federal agencies during their era of rapid expansion
in the 1930s. The Korean War heightened anti-Communist fears and gave Senator Joseph McCarthy (Republican, Wisconsin) his chance to exploit them
with claims of an immense conspiracy to subvert America and the Christian
civilization it led. McCarthy was a rough-and-ready opportunist who never
lacked for critics, but even liberal Democrats, who saw him as a mere Republican scoundrel, agreed that Communism was a severe threat.

American religious groups, terrified of Russian aggression and horrified by
the Communists' militant atheism, were among the most enthusiastic anti-
Communists. Several historians have shown in recent years that the issue was
particularly welcome to American Catholics. The Vatican had condemned
socialism for nearly a century by 1950, and America's Catholics had opposed
Communism right from the beginning. Their leaders had warned during the
Second World War that America's Soviet ally was potentially as big a threat as
the Nazi enemy, that its ideology was based on falsehoods, and that it was the
implacable foe of religion. The archbishop of Dubuque, Iowa, for example,
during the wartime alliance, had served notice on the Soviet Union that "the
Christ-haters of Moscow and their international brethren . . . may well take note
of the church militant when she becomes aroused."[3] As the Cold War intensified, New York's Catholic policemen turned out en masse for prayer breakfasts
with Senator McCarthy and Cardinal Spellman (the archbishop of New York).

Brent Bozell, an ardent Catholic convert, pointed out that Americans held a stronger hand when it came to nuclear "brinksmanship" than the Communists did. After all, Americans, being Christians, believed in life after death and felt confident that if even the world itself were destroyed in a righteous cause, they would go to their heavenly reward. Communists, by contrast, were atheists, held out no hope of life after death, and would be correspondingly less willing to escalate a confrontation all the way to nuclear exchange.[4]

Anti-Communism suited Catholic philosophical and theological principles; it also gave Catholics what might be thought of as a sociological opportunity. For a hundred years they had endured accusations that they could not be wholehearted Americans because they were loyal to the pope, a despotic foreign monarch, and because Catholic authoritarianism violated the republican ideal of liberty. An anti-Catholic tract, Paul Blanshard's *American Freedom and Catholic Power*, had restated the case as recently as 1949 and enjoyed royal treatment from Protestant and secular reviewers. Imagine Catholics' relief and righteous indignation, then, on noting that many of the Communists and spies turned up by the era's loyalty investigations—men like Alger Hiss—had come from privileged Protestant families. It enabled Catholics to depict themselves as the real champions of freedom, the surest defenders of Christendom against its anti-Christian enemies. As the historian Charles Morris has noted:

> By the 1950s . . . American mass opinion . . . became strongly anti-Communist— arguably the first time that a national political consensus had come to track so closely a long-held and identifiably Catholic view. It was a watershed in Catholic history: the nagging Catholic grievance that their patriotism and Americanism had never been fully appreciated was, in Catholic eyes, finally and gloriously put to rest.[5]

This alignment came from the heart—not merely from the public relations department—of the Catholic Church; it had supernatural backing as well as papal writ in its favor. In 1917, the year of the Russian Revolution, the Blessed Virgin Mary had appeared to three Portuguese children in the village of Fatima, amazed them by causing the sun to spin visibly in the sky, and told them a series of secrets. One was that two of them would die young. They did. Another was that World War I would end the following year (it did), but that an even more catastrophic war would break out under Pope Pius XI (it did). The Virgin also told the children that people everywhere should pray the rosary for the conversion of the Russian people to Christianity because the future of the world was in jeopardy. Last, she confided to Lucia, the child who survived into adulthood (and became a nun), a third secret, along with the instruction to whisper it to the pope in 1960.

Catholics from Europe and America went on pilgrimage to Fatima almost as enthusiastically as they went to Lourdes, where the Virgin had appeared to another poor rural girl, Bernadette, half a century before. A Hollywood film about Lourdes, *Song of Bernadette* (1943), won four Oscars and may have contributed to the inspiration of a nine-year-old Catholic boy, Joseph Vitelo, from the Bronx, who said that *he* had seen the Virgin, blond-haired and wearing a blue dress, in his backyard in November 1945. She promised him that water would burst from the ground there on November 14, just as it had at Lourdes. Thousands of hopeful New Yorkers gathered beside his house that rainy night expecting a miracle, only to suffer a drenching disappointment. The Catholic authorities, aware that popular devotions often go haywire, had given Vitelo no encouragement, but they had given their blessing to Lourdes and Fatima, which formed part of the spiritual backdrop to Cold War Catholicism. Parishioners took seriously the injunction to pray for the conversion of the Russians. In the late 1940s, "block rosaries" brought together groups of Catholic neighbors for collective prayer sessions, often groups of women who had prayed for their menfolks' safety during World War II and now switched to the Russian issue.

In 1950 a Wisconsin farmer's wife, Mrs. Mary-Ann van Hoof, also saw an apparition of the Virgin and received from her urgent instructions to pray for Russia and against Communism. Crowds gathered around her too. Church authorities again gave them no encouragement and were wary of Mrs. van Hoof because earlier in her life she had frequented spiritualists and clairvoyants. Still, that such apparitions should be happening at all, and gathering big audiences, showed how religiously significant American Catholics felt the issue of anti-Communism to be. At the other end of the Catholic spectrum, one of their most learned theologians, John Courtney Murray, S.J., also wrote that "it would be almost impossible to set limits to the danger of Communism as a spiritual menace." Christianity and Communism could not coexist, and America, the Christian leader, must prepare itself for war to the uttermost against this evil, implacable foe.[6]

Former Communists played a leading role in the era's Christian anti-Communism. Louis Budenz, born and raised a Catholic, had worked his way into the upper reaches of the American Communist Party during the 1930s, and by 1945 he was editor of the Communists' *Daily Worker*. That year, however, he abandoned Communism, reverted to the faith of his youth, and became a professor of economics at one of the great bastions of American Catholicism, the University of Notre Dame. Still a journalist too, he began a regular column, syndicated to Catholic newspapers nationwide, on the dangers of Communism and appeared frequently as a witness in court cases and congressional hearings against alleged Communists. Catholics regarded him as a prodigal son, returned to the fold after a misspent youth. Leftists regarded him as the worst kind of traitor to their cause.

Catholics were by no means alone in their anti-Communism. A wide array of Protestants was equally assertive on the topic. The most indefatigable was Fred Schwarz, a doctor and evangelical preacher (originally an immigrant from

Australia), who made opposition to Communism his life's work. In 1952 he met Billy Graham, who encouraged him to create an organization explicitly linking evangelism and anti-Communism. The Christian Anti-Communist Crusade, founded in 1953, was the result. Schwarz regarded Communism as a vicious parody of Christianity.

> My opposition to Communism was not based upon economics or politics but upon its false doctrines about God and man. . . . Communism had a doctrine of God—that God did not exist but that the idea of God had been projected into human consciousness by the universal existence of the Class Struggle; that it had a doctrine of Man—that man was a collection of atoms and molecules without soul or spirit and that all human ideas and emotions were derived from experiences provided by the economic environment; that it had a doctrine of Sin—that sin resulted from the experience provided by Capitalism; that it had a doctrine of Redemption—a Communist revolution; and that it had a doctrine of the future— that the Communist victory was inevitable due to the progressive nature of being. I also pointed out that it had a Creator—Karl Marx; a Messiah—Vladimir Lenin; a Pope—Joseph Stalin; and a devil—Leon Trotsky.[7]

In speeches, a newsletter, and the best-selling book *You Can Trust the Communists (to Be Communists)* (1960), Schwarz spent four decades warning Americans of the intellectual treachery, the danger of educational subversion, and the remorseless threat to Christianity that Communism posed.

It is not surprising that in this atmosphere many of the churches should have undertaken "Red hunts" of their own, or that some of their more unconventional and radical members should have come under suspicion of pro-Communist sympathies. In February 1950, for example, journalist Stanley High described the Methodist Federation for Social Action, which worked for economic justice and racial integration, as "Methodism's pink fringe" ("pink" implying partial allegiance to "red" Communism). The horrified Methodist bishops reacted first with denial but then issued a statement to dissociate their church from the federation, asking it to drop the word "Methodist" from its name. They went on to declare: "We reject its [Communism's] materialism, its methods of class war, its use of dictatorship, its fallacious economics, and its false theory of social development." Having made the point clear beyond any doubt, they recovered a little self-confidence and added: "We know that the only way to defeat it [Communism] permanently is to use the freedom of our own democracy to establish economic justice and racial brotherhood."[8] Accusations of Communism were thick in the air of the 1950s, and often hit the wrong target. The Reverend Martin Luther King Jr., for example, who never showed any interest in Communism, was plagued by allegations that he was a "Red" during the early days of the civil rights movement, and his alleged Communism was standard fare among the defenders of racial segregation.

Religious Intellectuals in the 1950s

The 1950s were the last decade in which theologians played a major role in American public life. Reinhold Niebuhr (1892–1971) and Paul Tillich (1886–1965), both Protestant writers, Jacques Maritain (1882–1973), a Catholic, and Will Herberg (1909–1977), a Jew, gave intellectual substance to the religious revival of the postwar era. They were often featured in the press as spokesmen not only on religious issues but also on political and cultural affairs. Like the popular religious writers of the late 1940s whom we met in the previous chapter, they were all interested in the relationship between religion and psychology. In addition they reacted to America's new role as leader of the non-Communist world and speculated on whether the country possessed the political, social, and spiritual qualities to prevail. Their answer was in each case a guarded yes. Audiences were particularly receptive because Tillich and Maritain were both European exiles (German and French, respectively) who had carved out prominent places for themselves in their adopted America, and now acted as interpreters between the Old World and the New.

Reinhold Niebuhr, a professor at Union Theological Seminary in New York, had been born and raised in rural Missouri and small-town Illinois, the son of German evangelicals (and brother of another talented theologian, H. Richard Niebuhr of Yale Divinity School). He had been a socialist and pacifist in the 1920s but changed his mind in the early 1930s as he became convinced that socialism and pacifism were based on the fallacy of human perfectibility, and that they could not come to terms with the ineradicable reality of sin. In an immensely influential book of Christian ethics, *Moral Man and Immoral Society* (1932), Niebuhr argued that while individuals might aspire to, and even occasionally achieve, moral purity, *groups* of people can never do so. A society, acting collectively, cannot duplicate the moral exaltation of an individual and should not attempt it. Instead it must strive for responsibility and maturity, avoiding messianic plans. Societies that strive for perfection, Niebuhr argued, are intolerant of human frailties and eventually perpetrate great evils.

The events of the 1930s and 1940s had borne out his words in unexpectedly vivid ways. He had watched the growth of Nazism with dismay—it seemed to him a terrifying form of parody religion. In January 1941 he had broken with his liberal Protestant brethren, nearly all of them isolationists, by advocating American intervention in World War II, and had founded a new journal to lobby for war, *Christianity and Crisis*. When the war ended he was equally ready to believe that America's Cold War posture against the Soviet Union was defensible on Christian grounds and that Communism represented an evil of the same magnitude as Nazism.

Niebuhr, at the height of his fame in the early Cold War years, published one of the most influential religious books of the era, *The Irony of American His-*

tory (1952). Despite his own belief that Communism was a terrible, evil system, Niebuhr now warned Americans against self-righteousness, against assuming that their nation represented the antithesis of Communism or that it could play the role of God's earthly surrogate in overcoming Communism. Far from being polar opposites, he pointed out, the two antagonists were similar in many ways: "Our orators profess abhorrence of the communist creed of 'materialism' but we are rather more successful practitioners of materialism as a working creed than the communists, who have failed so dismally in raising the general standards of well-being."[9] Americans must now recognize that "the evils against which we contend are frequently the fruit of illusions which are similar to our own" (16).

Niebuhr emphasized more forcefully than any contemporary that America's global responsibilities entailed a heavy moral burden; its only effective way of opposing the great foe was with nuclear weapons so fearsome in their destructive power that to use them would be to annihilate all claims to moral superiority. America must learn humility from its situation rather than indulge in a mood of moral self-righteousness; it could no longer claim to be an "innocent" nation exempt from the ugly realities of power politics. It must chart a course into the future cautiously, realistically, and with a full awareness of its imperfections.

Paul Tillich, Niebuhr's faculty colleague at Union Theological Seminary, was another star of American Protestant theology. A veteran of the German armies of World War I and an ardent anti-Nazi in the late 1920s and early 1930s, he wrote later that his whole life had been lived "on the boundary," between faith and doubt, between the collapsing old order into which he had been born and the new one that rose out of a war-torn world, between Germany and America, and between conventional and revolutionary moral principles. He had been expelled from his German professorship by Hitler in 1933 and had come to America at Niebuhr's behest, becoming a citizen in 1940.

Niebuhr's strong suit was politics and ethics; Tillich's was philosophical theology, and in works of great intellectual daring he showed a willingness to slough off much of the traditional heritage of Christianity. His postwar books, notably *The Courage to Be* (1952), outlined a new way of thinking about God and a new vocabulary. God, he argued, should no longer be thought of as a *being*. Instead, God should be reconceptualized as "Being itself." The fact that there is anything at all in the universe, when there could be nothing, is what we mean by "God." Faith, he added, is not intellectual assent to a set of doctrinal propositions about God. Instead, it is the willingness to carry on living in the face of the existential anxieties we all feel: the dread of death, meaninglessness, and personal guilt. Faith is, as his title put it, "the courage to be." Anything about which we feel "ultimately concerned," moreover, *is* God, and we need not worry ourselves about finding particular Christian doctrines implausible in light of our scientific knowledge. As he wrote elsewhere, but in the same vein, "Religion is not a sphere alongside others, but the dimension of depth in all spheres of human life. As God cannot be enclosed in a temple or a church, so theology cannot be restricted to Biblical and ecclesiastical tradition."[10]

How were these formulas connected to Americans and their midcentury situation? Tillich answered that the courage to be, in the face of the threat of non-being, consisted of two elements: the courage to be as oneself, an individual, and the courage to be as part of a collectivity. America might pride itself on being a nation of individualists, but what struck him (as it struck the sociologist David Riesman and other social critics of the 1950s) was the high degree of voluntary conformity shown by citizens. Was "democratic conformism" stifling Americans? No, because they saw their conformity as a way of joining in "the creative development of mankind." In a characteristic paragraph linking his highly abstract definitions to the immediate situation of Americans in the 1950s, Tillich wrote:

> There is something astonishing in the American courage for an observer who comes from Europe: although mostly symbolized in the early pioneers it is present today in the large majority of people. A person may have experienced a tragedy, a destructive fate, the breakdown of convictions, even guilt and momentary despair: he feels neither destroyed nor meaningless nor condemned nor without hope. . . . The typical American, after he has lost the foundations of his existence, works for new foundations. This is true of the individual and it is true of the nation as a whole. One can make experiments because an experimental failure does not mean discouragement. The productive process in which one is a participant naturally includes risks, failures, catastrophes. But they do not undermine courage. This means that it is the productive act itself in which the power and the significance of being is present.[11]

In other words, the American manifestation of the courage to be was a faith in progress deep enough to withstand shocks and reversals. And, Tillich added, Americans' cooperativeness in a complex industrial world and in the great fight against totalitarianism kept at bay the existential feeling of isolation. In an idiom remote from Niebuhr's he also was becoming aware of the irony of American history: The struggle against Soviet collectivism was forcing a collectivist mentality on the Americans too. Luckily "the courage to be as oneself" provided a counterweight to "the courage to be as a part" and prevented the destruction of individualism.

Jacques Maritain, like Paul Tillich, ended up in America because of the Nazis. The central figure in the early-twentieth-century Catholic revival of Thomism (philosophy in the tradition of Saint Thomas Aquinas), he had made frequent visits to Canada in the 1930s and was there, lecturing in Toronto, when the German army overran France in 1940. Maritain was a convert to

Catholicism; so was his wife, Raissa, but she was racially Jewish, so a return to France would have been suicidal. Instead he spent the war years teaching at Toronto, Chicago, and Notre Dame, revisited Europe for three years at war's end as French ambassador to the Vatican, but then returned to America, accepting a professorship at Princeton, where he worked from 1948 to 1961. He became, like Niebuhr and Tillich, a highbrow religious figurehead during the 1950s. His work also helped to augment Protestant intellectuals' respect for their still-often-despised Catholic neighbors.

Maritain's *Reflections on America* (1958), based on a series of Chicago speeches from 1956, was an enthusiastic defense of America against its European detractors. The United States, he declared, was not in its essence either greedy or materialistic. Although its citizens were certainly capable of money-making, they did it with a high sense of moral responsibility, spent it generously, philanthropically, and in accordance with elevated idealistic schemes. Nowhere else in the world was there so much enthusiasm for education in the humanities or such an abundance of spiritual vitality. He even argued that the United States was the closest approximation in practice to the ideal form of society he had outlined in his book *Integral Humanism* (1936) twenty years earlier. America certainly had its problems—Maritain mentioned racial segregation and an unhealthy preoccupation with sex—but it also possessed "a certain hidden disposition that is Christian in origin, and appears to me as a kind of humble and remote reminiscence of the Gospel in the inner attitude of the people. Behind the facade of violence and callousness of modern life, this something of old, subtle Christian flavor lies, I think, deep in the soul of this country."[12]

The nation's first settlers, he added, had migrated to avoid religious persecution, and many later immigrants had fled from "moral persecution, moral distress," and poverty. In the profoundly optimistic American environment, however, "the tears and sufferings of the persecuted and unfortunate are transmuted into a perpetual effort to improve human destiny and to make life bearable; they are transfigured into optimism and creativity." This transformation struck Maritain as a secular embodiment of Christian hope. "Except under the shade of the Gospel such a phenomenon could neither take place nor make sense in human history" (85). Maritain, like Niebuhr and Tillich, was aware of the dangers of America's situation and expressed some annoyance at educated Americans' reluctance to develop a more systematic philosophical justification of their society. Nevertheless, he believed that America was the best possible leader for the free world: "What the world expects from America is that she keep alive, in human history, a fraternal recognition of the dignity of man, in other words, the terrestrial hope of men in the Gospel" (199).

Among the distinguished Jewish intellectuals of the 1950s was Will Herberg. Born in New York in 1909, the son of Russian Jewish immigrants, he had joined the Communist Party as a teenager and become a leading Marxist theoretician in the debates of the 1930s. He left the Party after the Soviet show trials and the Hitler-Stalin pact, bitterly disillusioned, recalling:

> Marxism was to me, and to others like me, a religion, an ethic, and a theology; a vast all-embracing doctrine of man and the universe, a passionate faith endowing life with meaning, vindicating the aims of the movement, idealizing its activities and guaranteeing its ultimate triumph.[13]

By the late 1940s he had become attracted to the political aspects of Reinhold Niebuhr's theology, its use of such concepts as irony and paradox, and its hardheaded recognition of human sinfulness. He approached Niebuhr about the possibility of becoming a Christian. Niebuhr, in what has now become a famous conversation in the history of American religious pluralism, told him that he ought to rediscover the riches of his own Jewish heritage first and see whether he might not find a home there. Herberg took Niebuhr's advice to heart and became a practicing Jew, though of an eclectic and unconventional kind.

Accepting an appointment at Drew University (a Methodist foundation), Herberg published *Protestant, Catholic, Jew* (1955), one of the twentieth century's best books about religion, which explored the complicated relationship between religious and ethnic identity. He began by noting the apparent half-heartedness of many Americans' religious faith. He cited a survey in which 80 percent of Americans said they believed the Bible to be the revealed word of God and yet 53 percent, when asked to name one of the first four books of the New Testament, could not do so. How was this paradox to be explained? On the one hand, he said, Americans' membership in religious groups was widespread and apparently sincere. And yet

> there cannot be much doubt that, by and large, the religion which actually prevails among Americans today has lost much of its authentic Christian (or Jewish) content. Even when they are thinking, feeling, or acting religiously, their thinking, feeling, and acting do not bear an unequivocal relation to the faiths they profess. Americans think, feel, and act in terms quite obviously secularist at the very time that they exhibit every sign of a widespread religious revival. It is this secularism of a religious people, this religiousness in a secularist framework, that constitutes the problem posed by the contemporary religious situation in America.[14]

The solution lay, he argued, in the fact that religion was as much a matter of identity as a matter of faith.

The idea of America as a "melting pot," said Herberg, had always been more a matter of pious hope than a reality. What had actually happened to America's successive waves of immigrants was rather different. In the first generation, Irish boys had married Irish girls, Polish Jewish boys had married Polish Jewish girls, and so on. In the second generation, however, Irish Catholic boys sometimes married Italian Catholic girls. They had been to Catholic school together, grown up speaking English, and were not separated by the kind of gulf that had separated their parents. In the same way, second-generation Polish Jewish boys sometimes married German or Russian Jewish girls. Marriage across ethnic lines became common, but marriage across religious lines remained rare. According to Herberg, to be a "hyphenated" American was impermissible but to be a Protestant American, a Catholic American, or a Jewish American was fine. America, in other words, had developed a "triple melting pot." This theory of the triple melting pot solved the paradox of religionless religiosity by showing that religion was as much a matter of identity as of faith, an attenuated remnant of the strong ethnicity that had had to be left behind.

Herberg himself was an advocate of the idea of the "Judeo-Christian tradition." As the historian Mark Silk has shown, the idea was an American twentieth-century invention, designed to emphasize the shared aspects of these two religions in an era when fascism and Communism seemed to threaten both. Orthodox Christians and Jews both rejected the idea—to them Judaism and Christianity were almost polar opposites—but it proved to be an influential way of thinking about religion in general, especially in the context of World War II and the Cold War. Herberg's experiences, and his books *Judaism and Modern Man* (1951) and *Four Existentialist Theologians* (1958) also bore witness to the fact that "Judeo-Christian" was not necessarily a watery or halfhearted faith position; rather, it had a distinguished intellectual pedigree of its own.

Eisenhower Spirituality

Churchgoing among Americans continued to increase in the 1950s amid plentiful signs of everyday religiosity, of which the intellectuals' version was merely the most articulate. Dwight Eisenhower, elected president in 1952 and inaugurated early in 1953, is alleged to have declared in one early speech that America's institutions made no sense without "a deeply held religious faith—and I don't care what it is!"[15] He read a prayer of his own composition at his inauguration, referred frequently to "the Supreme Being," and went to church most Sundays. After hearing a Washington preacher, the Reverend George Docherty, advocate the idea in a February 1954 sermon, he endorsed the inclusion of the words "under God" in the pledge of allegiance and later directed that the words "In God We Trust" should be stamped on the currency.

Many commentators at the time and many historians since have scoffed at this kind of daily, almost casual, religiosity. William Lee Miller remarked that "President Eisenhower, like many Americans, is a very fervent believer in a very vague religion."[16] Eisenhower-era spirituality did indeed have a frivolous side. In 1950, for example, there was a craze among church groups to sponsor public Bible-reading marathons. A Springfield, Missouri, Bible marathon, organized by the Assemblies of God, put its readers on display in department store windows, with a public address system to amplify their words for shoppers and passersby. The Syracuse, New York, Salvation Army ran its own marathon and, beginning at six in the morning, kept at it for nineteen hours, until one o'clock the following morning, even being helped along at one point by a blind reader of the Braille New Testament.

But along with the frivolity was much earnestness and idealism. These qualities were personified in Dr. Tom Dooley, whose experiences remind us that Christian anti-Communism could inspire passionate dedication and selflessness. Dooley, a young St. Louis Catholic and graduate of Notre Dame, became a U.S. Navy doctor and was present in 1955 when Navy ships evacuated North Vietnamese Christians from Haiphong, after the Geneva Accords had ended the French phase of the Vietnam War. Vietnam, a country whose whereabouts and significance few Americans then knew, had been temporarily partitioned into a Communist north under Ho Chi Minh and a non-Communist south under Ngo Dinh Diem. Elections were scheduled to take place after a period of pacification and settlement. Dooley, however, after witnessing the sufferings of North Vietnamese Christians, many of whom had been persecuted and tortured for their faith by the Communists, supported the American decision to boycott the elections (which Ho Chi Minh was almost certain to win) and underwrite the continued existence of South Vietnam.

Such views were common enough at the time. What added force to them was that Dooley, a gifted and emotional writer, penned a best-seller on the subject, *Deliver Us from Evil* (1956). Its wrought-up emotional and religious tone won it half a million sales and serialization in *Reader's Digest*, where it was read by millions more. Sample the rhetoric:

> At Notre Dame the priests had tried to teach me philosophy. But out here in this Communist hellhole I had learned many more profound and practical facts about the true nature of man. I had watched tough US sailors become tender nurses for sick babies and dying old men. I had seen inhuman torture and suffering elevate weak men to lofty heights of spiritual nobility. I knew now why organized godlessness can never kill the divine spark that burns within even the humblest human.[17]

Leaving the Navy soon after the book appeared, Dooley devoted the rest of his life to establishing simple, low-tech medical centers in Vietnam, Cambodia, and Laos, bringing what he thought of as the best of American medical know-how to people who previously had had no medical care of any kind. He financed the centers from the proceeds of his books, from lecture tours of the United States, and from successful lobbying of American pharmaceutical corporations for big contributions and free medicines. He staffed them by appealing to the religious service idealism of other young doctors and nurses, whom he persuaded to volunteer for jungle duty.

The proximity of one of his hospitals to the Lao-Chinese border led to Chinese accusations that he was really a CIA agent, merely posing as a doctor while gathering intelligence information. The Chinese were not entirely wrong, but they were no more likely to have guessed the whole story than Dooley's admiring Catholic fans. Not until the historian James Fisher investigated previously classified sources in the 1990s for his book *Dr. America: The Lives of Thomas A. Dooley, 1927–1961* (1997) did hidden elements of the case emerge. Fisher found that Dooley *was* reporting regularly to the CIA. He also found that the reason for Dooley's premature resignation from the Navy was that it had discovered him to be a promiscuous homosexual. No sooner had it built him up as one of its first Cold War heroes than it found out about his predilection for gay sailors. Rather than tarnish an idol, the Navy released him to begin his civilian work, while holding over him the threat of exposure. After months of back-breaking work in southeast Asia and in high-spirited fund-raising tours of America, he would disappear into the gay underworld of Bangkok for days at a time, then emerge, his conscience wracked by guilt. His premature death from melanoma, coming in 1961 when he was just thirty-four, made him a martyr figure to many Cold War Christians (and, of course, made subsequent revelations about his paradoxical personality all the more shocking).

Church Buildings

The majority of Americans were anti-Communist in a general way, and knew of Dr. Dooley through their newspapers or *Reader's Digest*. More directly relevant to their religious lives were the churches and synagogues in which they worshiped and socialized during the postwar decades. Thousands of new churches and synagogues were built throughout America in the years 1946–1966; many of them still stand today as brick-and-mortar (wood, glass, and concrete) testimony to the postwar revival.

Various factors contributed to the building boom. First, the hard years of the Great Depression had deprived most congregations of sufficient funds for building projects. World War II had drawn away manpower and created a building-material shortage. By the mid- and late 1940s, therefore, a backlog amounting almost to twenty years had to be overcome. Second, these postwar decades witnessed the mass suburbanization of America. Low-interest veterans' loans to returning service personnel enabled hundreds of thousands to buy modest suburban homes for the first time. The new standardized, low-cost suburbs, of which Levittown, New York, has come to stand as a symbol for all the others, grew up on land that had until recently been farmed. Churches, as social and worship centers for the new communities, had to be built quickly and economically, along with highways, schools, and shops. Affluent suburbs, growing rapidly in the same years, also founded new churches and synagogues or relocated previously urban congregations in their new neighborhoods. Between 1945 and 1959, for example, in the suburbs of New York City alone fifty-seven Reform, sixty-eight Conservative, and thirty-five Orthodox synagogues were built as the rapidly assimilating Jewish population moved to the suburbs. Third, huge numbers of the young families living in the new suburbs decided to join their local churches. Their plentiful children, the baby boom, needed not only sanctuaries but also playgrounds, youth groups, and Sunday schools.

What should a church look like and of what materials should it be built? If the congregation chose, it usually decided on something profoundly traditional. If architects were consulted, by contrast, they advanced daring plans, to make the best use of new styles and new materials, of which earlier generations had known nothing. Modernist architects, especially exponents of the international style, rarely enjoyed public support, however. After a survey of churches built in the late 1940s and 1950s, one modernist wrote irritably: "Unfortunately, timidity, conservatism, and ignorance have prevented most congregations from experimentation."[18] Another added: "One must traverse miles of suffocating mediocrity before finding one instance of strikingly fresh church design."[19] Architectural writers less dogmatic about the modern style were more optimistic. "Not since the close of the Middle Ages," wrote one, "has there been promise of such able advance in the building arts of the church. The universal longing of our people can be supported by a universal will to build and to give in order to carry out in new church buildings our cultural and spiritual ideals."[20]

A variety of designs appeared, reflecting the variety of decision-making bodies and the variety of available budgets. Nevertheless, certain trends soon became clear. Suburbs were heavily dependent on cars, and some communities actually required by law that churches provide parking lots commensurate with their size (for example, one parking space for every six seats in the church). As a result, they tended to sprawl over large "campuses" rather than being hemmed in by other buildings, as their urban predecessors had been. Second, many were consciously designed as social and educational centers as well as places for worship, in which parlors, kitchens, meeting spaces, and classrooms for Sunday school and adult education classes were given high priority. Similarly, ministers' offices and pastoral counseling rooms were integral to the designs from the start, rather than being squeezed later into available spaces around the sanctuary.

The demand for new churches was so great that church-planning consultancy firms and a genre of advice books on building churches developed in the 1940s and 1950s. William Harrell, Martin Anderson, William Watkin, and Katharine Morrison McClinton, for example, all wrote books packed with highly practical advice about how to create building and finance committees, how to allocate space, how to choose architects, buy land, meet local building codes, and persuade parishioners to contribute generously. Anderson even worried that his fund-raising advice might—in a Christian context—sound a bit *too* hardheaded, and concluded his financial-planning chapter with the remark, "In special cases, where there is a crying need, where one can be absolutely sure that God wills it, where there is no other way, we may confidently go forth, even though from a strictly business point of view we may seem to have no solid ground under our feet." Yes, he concluded, God will provide in emergencies, but on the whole, "we believe God expects us to use the good business sense which He has given us."[21]

These how-to authors did not reject modernistic designs out of hand, but in a characteristic statement Anderson, a Lutheran, cautioned readers that "the House of God must be distinctive; it must be at once recognizable as a church. The exterior design must indicate, even to the most casual observer, that this is not an auditorium, a theater, a post office or a library, but a church" (21). After all, modernistic designs "do not yet have the hallowed associations of the older types" (26), and communities, as they planned their churches, should "not despise or ignore values that have been discovered and developed through many generations of consecrated study and toil" (24).

The design options offered in such literature were generally of four types: Gothic, Romanesque, colonial, and modern. Ideally, wrote Watkin, healthy competition between the styles would benefit them all. "A widening of our vista in church building, accepting the capable artistry of modern forms, is appropriate. It becomes a challenge to the traditionalists to do good, clean, beautiful work, of fresh and vital form. . . . The modernist in turn will do better work when he is challenged by able work on the part of the traditionalist."[22] Comparatively few Gothic designs appeared in practice. The neo-Gothic style had been popular among Catholics and Protestants alike in the late nineteenth and early twentieth centuries, and had inspired some American ecclesiastical masterpieces (such as the National Cathedral in Washington, D.C., and Princeton University's Memorial Chapel). However, the price of such buildings, with their soaring arches, high towers and spires, and elaborate stained glass, usually put them out of reach of suburban communities.

Some groups avoided Gothic for theological as well as financial reasons. The long, thin shape of a Gothic church tends to create a hierarchical separation between the priest in the chancel and the laity down in the nave. Changing ideas about human equality and democracy made this arrangement less satisfactory than in earlier times. Catholic designs, for example, were already being influenced by the liturgical movement, which downplayed hierarchy and conceptualized the priest and people as, jointly, members of the Mystical Body of Christ.

In place of Gothic, a minority of communities did experiment with modernist designs (about one in every four by the late 1950s), then looked for ways,
inside their defiantly untraditional new buildings, to bring clergy and people
into intimate and democratic proximity. One method, adopted by scattered
communities throughout the nation, was to create churches "in the round,"
bringing the clergy into the middle of the congregation. Some designs were literally circular, others hexagonal, T-shaped, elliptical, or even Y-shaped, all of
which could certainly achieve intimacy and bring more worshipers close to the
minister. In solving one set of problems, however, they created another. Where
would the choir go? How should the pulpit and the altar table be oriented? A
congregant close to the minister's *back* during the sermon could hardly expect
him to rotate as he preached, and might doubt whether anything had been
gained by comparison with the old system.

The members of churches in the round also had to face, in a more acute
form than their conventionally housed coreligionists, difficulties related to the
clock, the appointment book, and the calendar. Could a church in the round
with a central altar be converted at short notice into a meeting room or a study
hall? And what about the cycles of the liturgical year? Far more Christians came
to church at Christmas and Easter than in June; far more Jews came to the synagogue for Yom Kippur and Passover than in July. How could the intimate
space enjoyed throughout the year by loyal congregation members be
expanded to accommodate seasonal crowds?

Architectural writers admitted that such troubles had to be overcome but
nevertheless greeted modernist designs with delight, while heaping scorn on
traditional ones. Among those most often lauded was Christ Church Lutheran
in Minneapolis, completed in 1950 by Eliel and Eero Saarinen and composed
of austerely plain brick rectangles, and St. Francis de Sales Catholic Church,
Muskegon, Michigan, built in the early sixties by Marcel Breuer and Herbert
Beckhard out of vast, sloping concrete slabs. It is difficult today to wax enthusiastic over their bare walls and stark interiors, or to find them liberating. Still, it
is true that reinforced concrete was one of the keys to modernist church building. Strong both in tension and in compression, it permitted an array of new
structural forms—shallow-angled domes and parabolic walls—and far less massive masonry forms than were needed with brick and stone. Admirers insisted
that churches built of concrete were "honest" and that their form boldly
declared their function. Claiming modernism as a genuine style appropriate to
the age, they also noted with pleasure that some of the most theologically conservative churches, Catholics and Missouri Synod Lutherans, were accepting
the challenge of building them.

Reinforced concrete was useful not only because it looked so different from
masonry but also because it was relatively cheap. So was glass, which played a
major role in the new designs. Modernists used recessed or overhead windows

to create a mystical atmosphere inside their slab-concrete churches. Many of their best opportunities came in the building of college chapels, where the patron was more likely to be impressed by the latest architectural theories. For example, the chapel at the Illinois Institute of Technology (1952) was designed by Ludwig Mies van der Rohe, one of the superstars of architectural modernism. He wanted buildings to be simple, mechanical, and stripped down to the essentials. His chapel was a dull brick box, which you would pass without a second glance unless you were well versed in all the relevant theories. At its dedication, an unabashed Mies van der Rohe declared that "in its smallness it is great, in fact monumental."[23]

Slightly better was Eero Saarinen's chapel at MIT (1955), a murky brick cylinder. Its white marble altar was decorated by a "Jacob's Ladder" mobile of wire rods and aluminum rectangles that picked up light from a recessed window overhead. Much better was the Benedictine monks' chapel at St. Louis Priory in Creve Coeur, Missouri, an imaginative church in the round built of thin white sheet concrete that looked, from a distance, like ingeniously curved and folded paper. Modernist hard cases like Mies van der Rohe liked to leave their concrete untreated so that, after a few years' exposure, it would be as streaked with rust and grime as a Russian trawler just back from the Arctic. Gyo Obata, by contrast, the architect of St. Louis's, coated the concrete with a protective epoxy to preserve its playful good looks for the future.

In addition to concrete and glass, a third inexpensive material, soon standardized in dozens of new churches, was laminated wood. Developed by aviation researchers during the Second World War for its strength and lightness, and secured by powerful new chemical adhesives, it was more supple than conventional wood and could be molded into arches, vaults, and curved walls. Laminated wooden arches for church building first became popular in the Pacific Northwest, where population (and the need for churches) was growing rapidly, where wood was plentiful, and where exchequers could not be overtaxed. To the same region could be traced the A-frame design, which by 1970 had become the hallmark silhouette for hundreds of American churches. A-frame churches were suitable for shedding the heavy rains of the Northwest, but by 1960 they were turning up even in the nation's arid zone.

Pietro Belluschi was one of the two or three most celebrated church architects of the postwar era. He declared that a church "should be a segment of space which reminds the worshipper of the infinity from which it was wrested."[24] Born in Rome, Italy, in 1899, he had emigrated to America in 1924 and gradually built his reputation as a leading architectural modernist from his headquarters in Portland, Oregon. His work on the Equitable Building in Portland, one of the first postwar corporate skyscrapers and the first American building to be fully sealed, air-conditioned, and aluminum-sheathed, made him a national figure. He enjoyed working with church design committees as a contrast to his work for high-powered businessmen, but he found that they could be awkward clients. The pastor of Zion Lutheran Church in Portland (built 1947–1950), for example, flatly rejected Belluschi's first design for a new church on the grounds that it looked "too much like a factory"; pastor and design committee together insisted on a pitched roof and a spire (147). The architect, albeit a little grudgingly, gave them what they wanted, adding laminated wooden arches throughout and a glass-brick pattern in the walls for illumination.

Other church communities, aware of architects' imperious ways and impressed by Belluschi's greater responsiveness to the congregation's wishes, also selected him as their architect. He was a good listener but also a good educator in the modernist aesthetic. In explaining to one congregation why he refused to build in the Gothic style, he said: "If there is a conscious striving for beauty it must come not from cut-rate imitations of the fruits of past civilizations developed in alien lands, but from our own methods, with our own materials, and from a judicious and sensitive use of space, color, and texture."[25] Meanwhile, he continued to enhance his reputation by designing the Presbyterian Church of Cottage Grove, Oregon, which became a widely studied and much-praised modernist classic.

Protestant, Catholic, and Jewish congregations enjoyed, in many ways, the same opportunities while facing the same challenges. All of them, for example, gradually realized that they had more money to spend than ever before. The Great Depression had gone once and for all—in its place came what the economist John Kenneth Galbraith called "the affluent society," in which a large percentage of the population had discretionary income to devote to whatever projects they chose. With each passing year, church and synagogue funds increased, while building committees approved bolder, more costly, and more elaborate designs.

Despite a largely shared situation, points of emphasis kept different religious groups' architectural ideas distinct. Catholics, Episcopalians, and Lutherans, after all, still regarded the church as a sacred place, especially sacred at the altar. The Jesuit writer John LaFarge expressed this view in the comment that

> in a Catholic church, its *sacral* character is strongly emphasized by a style and furnishing tending to produce a sense of reverence, culminating in the reverential elements of the altar, with its tabernacle and reserved Sacrament. . . . [The church] is oriented in both directions; to the mysteries of the unseen world beyond, and to the spiritual needs of struggling humanity.[26]

Jews, and Protestants in the radical Reformation tradition, by contrast, tended to look at their synagogues and churches as gathering places in which the presence of the congregation was more important than the space itself. For them, the delivery of the word was all-important, such that the focal point would be the *bimah*, or lectern, rather than the altar. Jewish contributors to the design debate observed that until now their synagogues had usually just borrowed from the community in which they were placed the dominant form of public building (classical, Romanesque, Moorish, or Gothic), but that finally a moment had arrived for synagogues to take on an architectural distinctiveness of their own. Reform rabbi Maurice Eisendrath wrote in 1953, along these lines, that "Jews can most suitably be inspired to worship God in daily services, on Sabbaths, festivals, and holy days in temple sanctuaries that incorporate the clean lines and untrammelled spaces of contemporary architecture."[27] He was an enthusiastic supporter of modernist synagogues.

Among Protestant contributors to the architecture debate, Reinhold Niebuhr took a relatively conservative position, arguing in the early 1950s that Gothic was, despite everything, still the best expression up to that time of the Christian spirit. "Gothic vaulting and the church spire are fitting symbolic expressions of the yearning of the religious spirit for the ultimate beyond the immediate concerns of life," he wrote. "The broken lines of Gothic are moreover perfect expressions of the Christian concept of the discontinuities of life; of the contrast between man and God, between sin and grace." This did not mean, however, that he was yearning for Gothic medievalism. After all, America's distinctive contribution to religious architecture was its antithesis, the plain, whitewashed colonial Puritan meetinghouse. Now, Niebuhr claimed, the best elements of the two traditions were being united by an innovative generation of American modernists like Pietro Belluschi:

> This represents the union of two great architectural traditions and in Western civilization it represents a vital adaptation of a great architectural tradition to the ethos of a technical age. At its best the new style seeks to preserve the suggestions of aspiration and of concern for the ultimate with chastity of form, and may suggest the ascetic tendencies in the Christian life.[28]

Paul Tillich was less kindly disposed to the Gothic heritage and more iconoclastic than Niebuhr. He pointed out that the only reason Protestants had ever worshiped in Gothic buildings was because they had seized them from the Catholics at the time of the Reformation, cleared out their icons and statues, and continued to use them for lack of more suitable alternatives. To him it seemed grotesque that American Protestant congregations in the nineteenth and early twentieth centuries should have been so misguided as to *choose* a Gothic style for their own buildings, since the style embodied exactly what they did *not* stand for. Protestantism was a religion more of the ear than the eye, he declared, and it should shun elaborate works of art in church and bring the minister into the midst of his congregation.

> Churches that retain a central aisle leading to a removed altar as the holiest place separated from other parts of the building are essentially un-Protestant. With the

abolition of any kind of hierarchical dualism between laymen and clergy, between a secular and holy role—in short, because of the fundamental Protestant concept of the priesthood of all believers—these remnants of the Catholic tradition are religiously inadequate for a Protestant architecture.[29]

Tillich admitted, nevertheless, that Protestant architects still had to find ways of giving their structures a sense of the presence of God. After all, as Christians they had to come to terms with the fact that the remote, omnipotent God of the Old Testament was also the incarnate human God of the New.

> Under the criterion of the manifestation of the transcendent God in Jesus as the Christ, the churches can be filled with symbolic objects of all kinds. All Catholic churches emphasize this side. . . . Protestantism need not reject these elements of Catholic substance but it should subject them to some definite criteria. (124)

After laying down the law about what these criteria should be (a highly eccentric list, which, for instance, said yes to murals but no to individual paintings on canvas), he concluded that "today, genuine Protestant church architecture is possible, perhaps for the first time in our history." Congregations must rise to the challenge and avoid all backsliding into traditionalism. "*Only* by the creation of new forms can Protestant churches achieve an honest expression of their faith" (125). He too gave Belluschi high praise and described his Cottage Grove Presbyterian Church as "truly numinous."[30]

Despite such attempts to demarcate a distinctively Protestant approach to church building, America's religious groups in fact borrowed extensively from one another. This overlap dovetailed nicely with the idea of a united godly America facing down the godless Soviet Union. Interfaith anti-Communist cooperation was actually embodied in one of the most memorable churches built in the whole era: the Cadet Chapel of the Air Force Academy in Colorado Springs (1957–1963), designed by Walter Netsch Jr. and built by Skidmore, Owings, and Merrill (one of the nation's most prestigious architectural firms). Containing Protestant, Catholic, and Jewish worship centers and presenting a magnificent silhouette against the Front Range of the Rocky Mountains, it suggested simultaneously the glorious verticals of Gothic architecture and a bristling row of intercontinental nuclear missiles; its seventeen spiky spires also brought to mind a pair of hands pressed together for prayer.

The great church-building boom began to flag in the mid-1960s, just as the confident Christian anti-Communism of the 1950s, so well expressed by Dr. Tom Dooley and the Air Force Academy chapel, began to drown in the swamps of Vietnam. By then the whole idea of heaping up great monuments in stone, concrete, and glass was under challenge. The civil rights movement, and renewed political attention to the fact that poverty was still widespread in affluent America, prompted critics to assert that the billions of dollars going to church building every year could be better spent on the kind of work the Jew-ish Prophets and Jesus would have approved: feeding the hungry and housing the homeless. Michael Novak, a Young Turk among the Catholics, wrote in 1964 that the Catholic Church should abandon its mammoth building pro-gram altogether. Addressing a conference of the liturgical movement, he deplored the fact that "so many of its [the Catholic Church's] energies are drained off into materialistic interests; into money-raising campaigns, into put-ting up buildings. . . . The Church seems so much engaged in externals, so ter-ribly interested in institutional forms, that the life of the Gospels appears to be by comparison neglected." The time had come, he argued, "to move out of our church buildings" and "to recapture the ideals of those small groups of Chris-tians who met together informally in living rooms, who celebrated the sacra-ments in small groups." The brick-and-mortar structure of Catholicism, achieved at immense cost over the preceding century, now seemed to him no better than a burden "which weighs us down on our pilgrimage."[31]

That was an extreme view, but one shared to some extent more and more widely during the 1960s. When St. Mary's, the Catholic cathedral of San Fran-cisco, burned down in 1962, Archbishop Joseph T. McGucken (fresh to the job six months previously) announced a fund drive so that a new structure could rise in its place. Donations poured in from Catholics and non-Catholics alike, but so did rebukes, in voices like Novak's; one came from a delegation of twenty-seven priests, another from a confrontational committee of laity. This time the architect-hero Pietro Belluschi had to undertake his work against the background rumblings of angry dissenters, who dismissed the immense new modernist concrete structure as an appalling waste of money; money that could, and should, have been spent on the poor. A local columnist described the planned cathedral as "a multi-million dollar Pandora's box of episcopal fan-tasy, civic holiness and financial intrigue."[32]

Another sign of the changing times was that Belluschi himself was no longer the golden boy of American architecture. His collaboration with Walter Gropius on the gargantuan and widely disliked Pan-Am Building in New York had set off a storm of controversy and the beginnings of an antimodernist reac-tion within the architectural profession. The archbishop, loyal to Belluschi and to the creation of another big building, tried to fend off the critics by pointing out that it would be dishonest to raise funds for one project, then spend them on another. Ironically, he was in the unusual position of having raised *too much* money (fifteen million dollars, of which only six million were earmarked for the cathedral), so he hoped to be able to please both constituencies by devoting much of the surplus (with the donors' consent) to good works. But when the Episcopal archbishop of San Francisco offered, in ecumenical spirit, to share his building with the Catholic neighbors, demands to divert *all* the money to public housing projects intensified. The cathedral opened quietly in October

1970, its first services attended by police officers to discourage possible demonstrations or bomb scares. Nevertheless, the official dedication ceremonies were marred by heckling pickets from various Catholic organizations, including a Hispanic priests' group whose leaflets quoted the farmworkers' union leader, Cesar Chavez: "We don't ask for more Cathedrals, we don't ask for bigger churches or fine gifts. We ask for the Church's presence among us" (72).

American churches continued to rise throughout the later twentieth century, though never again at the rate of 1945–1965. Among them were some ingenious and inventive designs, such as the Crystal Cathedral, in Garden Grove, California. Others, as we shall see later, were remarkable more for their size than for their architectural qualities, and soon gained the name "megachurches." The rapid improvement of communications media and the rise of "televangelism" after 1970 and the Internet after 1990 also created the possibility of "virtual" churches, though not in a way the radical critics of St. Mary's would have approved.

Chapter 3

RELIGION, RESPECT, AND
SOCIAL CHANGE: 1955–1968

Martin Luther King Jr., writing his account of the Montgomery bus boycott after its successful conclusion, asked: Why did it happen there, of all places? Was it because there was a large desegregated Air Force base just outside of town where many of the townspeople worked? Was it because there was a vigorous chapter of the National Association for the Advancement of Colored People (NAACP) in the town, providing leadership to black citizens? Was it because of Rosa Parks's willingness to test the bus company's segregation policy, or because he [King] was there to help the movement? It was all these things, he concluded, but above all it was because God chose Montgomery. Similarly his right-hand man, the Reverend Ralph Abernathy, wrote later that "the Good Lord . . . wanted me to be in Montgomery during those years and He provided me with the opportunity to stay there . . . as pastor of the First Baptist Church."[1] Declarations like these make religious historians uneasy. They know that all kinds of things have been done in the world, many of them horrible, with the claim of God's intervention or blessing. Historians can check documentary evidence and interview participants in recent historical events, but they cannot check up on God or get him to confirm or deny his actions. Prescinding, therefore, from the question of whether God was the decisive participant, let us consider the civil rights movement as a religious event, but from a more earthly perspective.

African American Religion

The majority of black Americans in the 1940s and 1950s belonged to evangelical Protestant churches, nearly two-thirds being Baptists and nearly one-third Methodists. In southern Louisiana, most African Americans were Catholics, and throughout the nation others were scattered among Pentecostal and spiritualist churches or the Jehovah's Witnesses. Before the Civil War, slaves had sometimes been obliged to attend white churches but also held their own religious meetings in "brush arbors." As freedmen eager to escape white surveillance, they had created their own denominations. Religion was one aspect of Southern life in which blacks rather than whites pioneered segregation. From Reconstruction right into the mid-twentieth century the black churches were, in the words of E. Franklin Frazier, "a refuge in a hostile white world," which offered fellowship and consolation but at the same time "aided the Negro to become accommodated to an inferior status."[2]

The favored style of preaching in many black churches was a form of chanting, which, as the historian Albert Raboteau shows, had a long history in black (and occasionally white evangelical) communities. "The preacher begins calmly, speaking in conversational, if oratorical and occasionally grandiloquent, prose; he then gradually begins to speak more rapidly, excitedly, and to chant his words in time to a regular beat; finally, he reaches an emotional peak in which his chanted speech becomes tonal and merges with the singing, clapping, and shouting of the congregation."[3] Sermons of this kind, still common throughout the late twentieth century, required a fine balance between preparation and extemporization. They had to seem like spontaneous gifts of the Holy Spirit to draw in and excite their audiences, but they also had to cohere around a central theme.

Congregational response to the sermon could be dramatic. The poet and novelist Maya Angelou recalled a certain Sister Monroe in Stamps, Arkansas, where she was a child, who "made up for her absences by shouting so hard when she did make it that she shook the whole church. As soon as she took her seat, all the ushers would move to her side of the church because it took three women and sometimes a man or two to hold her." When the minister began to preach, "she got the spirit and started shouting, throwing her arms around and jerking her body, so that the ushers went over to hold her down, but she tore herself away from them and ran up to the pulpit. She stood in front of the altar, shaking like a freshly caught trout. She screamed at Reverend Taylor. 'Preach it. I say, preach it.'"[4]

Dramatic conversion experiences and religious ecstasies were central to the religious life of many black as well as white Christians. Members of the Church of God in Christ near Angelou's home "could be heard on Sunday a half mile away, singing and dancing until they sometimes fell down in a dead faint"

(104). The same emotional intensity was carried to Northern cities in the Great Migration of the early and mid-twentieth century. As a Harlem teenager, James Baldwin (later a distinguished novelist) was suddenly converted in a Pentecostalist storefront church after a summer of spiritual anguish.

> I became more guilty and more frightened and kept all this bottled up inside me, and naturally, inescapably, one night, when this woman had finished preaching, everything came roaring, screaming, crying out, and I fell to the ground before the altar. It was the strangest sensation I have ever had in my life. . . . One moment I was on my feet, singing and clapping . . . the next moment, with no transition, no sensation of falling, I was on my back, with the lights beating down into my face and all the vertical saints above me. I did not know what I was doing down so low or how I had got there. And the anguish that filled me cannot be described. . . . All I really remember is the pain, the unspeakable pain; it was as though I were yelling up to Heaven and Heaven would not hear me. And if Heaven would not hear me, if love could not descend from Heaven—to wash me, to make me clean—then utter disaster was my portion. . . . I was on the floor all night. Over me, to bring me "through," the saints sang and rejoiced and prayed. And in the morning, when they raised me, they told me that I was "saved." . . . Well, indeed I was, in a way, for I was utterly drained and exhausted, and released, for the first time, from all my guilty torment.[5]

Middle-class African Americans, by contrast, tended to emulate the decorum of white mainstream Protestant congregations and were less expressive. Ralph Abernathy commented, "You can tell the class of people who go to a black church by how much noise they make during the sermon. The less noise, the higher the class." He went on to say that Dexter Avenue Baptist Church in Montgomery, Alabama, where Martin Luther King Jr. succeeded Vernon Johns in 1954, was a congregation made up largely of Alabama State College professors who were "habitually silent during the sermon."[6]

Black church music as well as preaching had its own traditions, growing partly out of slave music with African roots, partly out of blues and jazz, and partly out of Euro-American hymnody. Many of the great black singers of the postwar era, including Mahalia Jackson and Aretha Franklin, learned their craft as church choir members. Jackson (1911–1972), for example, was the daughter of a Baptist minister in New Orleans. She migrated to Chicago during the 1920s and was part of the movement to bring gospel music into the churches there, but had to work against the wishes of what she called "high-up society Negroes," who considered it undignified. "Some colored ministers objected to it. . . . They didn't like the hand-clapping and the stomping and they said we were bringing jazz into the church and it wasn't dignified. Once at church one of the preachers got up in the pulpit and spoke out against me." Jackson, familiar with the evangelical idiom, rose to reply, justifying herself from Scripture: "I told him I had been reading the Bible every day most of my life and there was

a Psalm that said: 'Oh clap your hands, all ye people! Shout unto the Lord with
the voice of a trumpet!'"[7] Jackson carried her point and gradually established
her reputation as a gospel singer with a national audience that crossed the color
line.

The music remained a point of controversy, however. Leroy Davis (b. 1947)
grew up attending a Louisville Baptist church whose minister, E. M. Elmore, a
local leader and staunch Republican, refused to admit jazz or gospel music in
his services:

> He would talk about it in the pulpit. He knew people wanted to move to the other
> kind of music but he thought it was "Devil-music." We lost a lot of membership
> because of that. . . . Every once in a while the young people's choir would try to
> infuse a bit of gospel music into our singing. We got away with a little bit but I can
> remember that a couple of times, when he thought it was getting too much swing,
> he would stop us. He would actually get up, come to the pulpit, and just say,
> "Hold it! You know I don't like that kind of singing in my church." . . . He even
> chastised me one time when I was playing the trumpet—I think it was Amazing
> Grace. I'd got into jazz music and I improvised a couple of notes. He stopped me
> and told me, "That is not tolerated in my church."[8]

Clergy like Elmore could be autocratic because they were men of high status in the black community, especially in Southern towns. They were often
among the few black professionals not dependent on the goodwill and patron-
age of the white elite. They were, in addition, usually more highly educated
than most of their flock, and more highly paid. They often mediated conflicts
among their parishioners, supervised mutual assistance programs, insurance,
and burial programs, and acted as go-betweens in solving interracial problems.
If they preached well they could gather large, loyal congregations. When a
child was born to the spellbinding preacher Ralph Abernathy and his wife,
Juanita, in 1950, for example, "the people from the church drove across town
to St. Jude Hospital just to file past the glass window and stare in at the tiny
brown ball in the bassinet, and the hospital nurses shook their heads at the
seemingly endless parade of people."[9] Their leadership position sometimes led
ministers into temptation, and did not always deliver them from evil. Fred Shuttlesworth, for example, a Birmingham pastor, was convinced that God spoke to
him directly and had appointed him to lead the civil rights movement there. He
was so autocratic that many black citizens refused to join the movement so long
as he was leading it.

In the black churches on Sunday mornings and Wednesday evenings, everyday roles and marks of status were suspended. Poor churchgoers who dressed
for their weekday jobs in utilitarian clothes came to church in all their finery.
Status inside the church often differed from status outside. As Jesse Jackson
(later a presidential candidate) recalled of his childhood church in Greenville,

South Carolina, "Here, Deacon Foster, who might be only a janitor at the school, he can be chairman of the deacon board and sit on the front row, while the principal of the school, who might be an ole drinkin' sinner, *he* gonna have to sit ten rows back and keep quiet. It's Deacon Foster, guy who can say the most fervent prayers, who got the status *here*. Different kind of reality."[10]

The Civil Rights Movement Begins

In the 1950s and 1960s, activist clergy in the civil rights movement tried to redirect black religious energy away from its otherworldly traditions and toward worldly reforms. It is no coincidence that King and most of the movement's other black leaders, including Ralph Abernathy, Andrew Young, Jesse Jackson, Fred Shuttlesworth, and Joseph Lowery, were young clergymen. Although the civil rights movement is usually dated to the Supreme Court's *Brown* decision of 1954 or the Montgomery bus boycott, its foundations had been laid earlier in the century, also largely by ministers. Martin Luther King Sr., for example, the minister of Ebenezer Baptist Church in Atlanta, had led a black protest march to the Atlanta city hall in 1935, demanding the vote for blacks. King's maternal grandfather, Adam Daniel Williams, also a minister, had led a black protest against a municipal bond issue for education that lacked any provision for black high schools. King's leadership, in other words, could draw from a deep well of ministerial tradition in his own family.

The civil rights movement aimed to desegregate Southern life, but, paradoxically, it drew much of its strength and inspiration from the segregated black churches. A group of Montgomery women and members of the NAACP organized the initial bus boycott to protest the arrest of Rosa Parks on December 1, 1955, when she refused to surrender her bus seat to a white passenger. In black churches, as in white, women constituted a majority of the members even though they were a minority of the leaders. Jo-Ann Robinson, a local black college professor, in her memoir of the boycott, recalls that she and some of her students distributed boycott leaflets throughout the town. They gave copies to Montgomery's black clergy, who were meeting that day in the African Methodist Episcopal Zion Church on Highland Avenue.

It was then that the ministers decided that it was time for them, the leaders, to catch up with the masses. If the people were really determined to stage this one-day protest, then they would need moral support and Christian leadership. The churches could serve as channels of communication as well as altars where people could come for prayer and spiritual guidance. . . . There was no thought of denomination. Baptists, Presbyterians, Episcopalians, Lutherans, Congregationalists, and others joined together and became one band of ministerial brothers, offering their leadership to the masses. . . . The black ministers and their churches made the Montgomery Bus Boycott the success that it was. . . . The ministers gave themselves, their time, their contributions, their minds, their prayers, and their leadership, all of which set examples for the laymen to follow.[11]

After the successful first day of the boycott, a Monday, an estimated six thousand people showed up for a mass meeting at the Holt Street Baptist Church, with one thousand crowding in and the rest thronging the surrounding streets. The assembled black civic leaders created the Montgomery Improvement Association, elected twenty-six-year-old Martin Luther King Jr. as its president after he delivered an electrifying speech, and resolved to continue the boycott until the bus company changed its rules. King told them: "We must keep God in the forefront. Let us be Christian in all of our action."[12] Throughout 1956, Monday evenings witnessed church services for prayer, singing, preaching, and "free-will offerings" of money to sustain the boycott.

The religious fervor of the meetings and the feeling of divine blessing on the boycott were important to offset blacks' fears about becoming involved in the movement and their initial terror of arrest. Virginia Durr, a sympathetic white citizen of Montgomery, recalled that when Rosa Parks first got out of jail and discussed with friends whether to get involved in a boycott movement, her husband urged her against it and kept repeating, over and over: "Rosa, the white folks will kill you."[13] Parks overcame her fears, appealed her conviction, and joined the boycott movement. The religious excitement generated by the boycott throughout 1956, Durr added, assured its success and had some unexpected side effects.

> I had a washwoman who came once a week. . . . She admired Dr. King greatly. She said she had seen the angels come down and stand on his shoulders every Monday night. In everything he said he was speaking with the voice of God. Now everything *she* did was also dictated by the voice of God. She got so she talked to God so much that she didn't do much ironing. She was really a sweet old lady but she was a religious fanatic. (282)

The King family was relatively affluent, and Martin, as the son of an Atlanta community leader, had enjoyed high status as a young man. He had attended nearby Morehouse College, then gone north for ministerial training at Crozer Seminary in Chester, Pennsyslvania. Graduating in 1951 as student body president and valedictorian, he had then studied for a Ph.D. at Boston University, where he read the theology of Reinhold Niebuhr and Paul Tillich, whose ideas would appear in many of his sermons and articles. In his later essay "Pilgrimage to Nonviolence" he paid tribute to their influence. "My reading of the works of Reinhold Niebuhr made me aware of the complexity of human motives and the reality of sin on every level of man's existence. . . . I also came to see that the superficial optimism of liberalism concerning human nature overlooked the fact that reason is darkened by sin."[14] At Boston University he also learned about the work of Gandhi in the Indian independence movement of the immediately preceding years. He had not finished writing his doctoral dissertation, on Tillich and personalist theology, when he accepted a call to minister at Dexter Avenue Baptist Church in Montgomery, in 1954. Accepting the call brought him back into the segregated South. (We now know that parts of his dissertation, hastily finished in Montgomery and turned in during 1955, were plagiarized.)

When the one-day bus boycott proved to be effective and persisted into 1956, white resistance escalated into attacks on King. Segregationists fired bullets into his house, causing him intense anxiety for his own and his family's safety. He regained his resolve after a profound religious experience one night at home.

> I discovered then that religion had become real to me and I had to know God for myself. And I bowed down over that cup of coffee. . . . I prayed a prayer and I prayed out loud that night. I said: "Lord, I'm down here trying to do what's right. . . . But Lord I must confess that I'm weak now. I'm faltering. I'm losing my courage. I can't let the people see me like this because if they see me weak and losing my courage they will begin to get weak. . . . And it seemed at that moment that I could hear an inner voice saying to me, "Martin Luther, stand up for righteousness. Stand up for justice. Stand up for truth. And lo I will be with you, even unto the end of the world." . . . I heard the voice of Jesus saying still to fight on. He promised never to leave me, never to leave me alone.[15]

The reference to Martin Luther suggests close identification with the Reformation leader, and a sense of historic mission. The experience solidified King's determination to accept the risks that went with leadership.

Press publicity around the nation contributed to the success of the Montgomery bus boycott, and it was partly the press that singled out the eloquent and well-educated King as its spokesman. He recognized that his position as a clergyman gave him a crucial advantage. He was able to appeal to white Americans in Bible language, a language that the majority of them understood, respected, and took seriously. He took Bible passages they knew well but applied them in jarringly immediate and contemporary ways, to underscore his belief that segregation was not simply unjust, not simply tactless in view of the Cold War propaganda competition then being waged over the loyalties of postcolonial Africans, but *sinful*.

Segregationists accused King of being a Communist, but this was the 1950s and the best way to deny it was to quote chapter and verse from the Scriptures. King often compared himself in sermons and speeches to Jesus carrying a heavy cross, or to Moses leading his people out of slavery in Egypt and toward the Promised Land. For example, the day after a dynamite bomb had fizzled out on his front porch in 1957 he preached to his congregation: "Tell Montgomery they can keep bombing and I'm going to stand up to them. If I had to die tomorrow morning I would die happy because I've been to the mountain top and I've seen the promised land and it's going to be here in Montgomery."[16] The "mountain top" is a direct reference to Moses, whom God permitted to look down on the Promised Land of Canaan from Mount Pisgah, though he would never enter it (Deuteronomy 34). Similarly, when Ralph Abernathy describes a leaders' strategy meeting, held behind closed doors to exclude possible police informers, he compares it implicitly to Jesus' Last Supper and the danger posed by a Judas Iscariot: "We had come upstairs confused and shaken by the idea that there was a traitor in our midst. We came down with a sense of dedication and unity. We had been together in the Upper Room and we were going into the world to do the Lord's work."[17] The night before the famous Good Friday 1963 march in Birmingham, Abernathy told the marchers: "Almost 2000 years ago Christ died on the cross for us. Tomorrow we will take it up for our people and die if necessary" (246).

King, always a brilliant publicist, preached nonviolent resistance to unjust authority and gave impromptu lessons on the history of nonviolence to his Montgomery followers. Like Henry David Thoreau, the transcendentalist philosopher, and like the Indian independence leader Mohandas "Mahatma" Gandhi, he knew how to exploit his oppressors' bad consciences while preserving the moral high ground. "Gandhism," as the sociologist E. Franklin Frazier noted at the time, "is completely alien to the Negro," but "as Negro students go forth singing the Spirituals or the Gospel hymns when they engage in sit-down strikes or sing their Gospel songs in response to violence, they are behaving in accordance with [their] religious heritage."[18]

The Southern Christian Leadership Conference (SCLC) was founded in 1957 at an Atlanta meeting of sixty black clergy. It maintained the principle of organizing through churches but turned the Christian message outward into the world. Its founders asked black Americans "to accept Christian love in full knowledge of its power to defy evil. We call upon them to understand that non-violence is not a symbol of weakness or cowardice, but, as Jesus demonstrated, non-violent resistance transforms weakness into strength and breeds courage in the face of danger."[19] Civil rights demonstrations were not entirely free of violence, but for the most part the black marchers were able to take the moral high ground, and to be seen on nationwide television as having it. Occasional electrifying moments suggested the power of this self-abnegating approach. Firefighters armed with high-powered hoses confronted about two thousand marchers in Birmingham in 1963. When Bull Connor, the Birmingham public safety officer, ordered his men to "turn the hoses on them," the firefighters refused. "The sight of people kneeling in prayer spoke more eloquently than did Connor's authority. Suddenly, in the face of genuine Christian witness he was powerless to make his own men obey him."[20]

It would be wrong to imagine, however, that the black community united behind the civil rights movement. As participants' memoirs show, King and Abernathy struggled to overcome citizens' fears and were never able to unify an often divided black community. They could not even depend on the other clergy, some of whom thought civil rights work inappropriate. "Some of the older clergy tended to be cautious," wrote Abernathy later, "and many of them were unconcerned with social issues. They preached the Gospel of 'other-worldliness,' of a better time in the sweet by and by. Their ultimate solution to Jim Crow was death—when you died you were equal in the eyes of God."[21] Others felt that their relatively privileged position within the segregated system would be jeopardized by desegregation.

The SCLC's work led to a crisis in the seven-million-member National Baptist Convention, to which King and Abernathy belonged. The convention's autocratic leader, Joseph Jackson of Chicago, had spoken in support of the Montgomery bus boycott in 1956 but by 1960 had decided that the black churches should not be involved in civil rights work. As a friend of Chicago's Mayor Richard Daley and the South Side's black congressman William Dawson, he stood to lose influence and status as King's fame grew and as the segregated system began to crumble. King and other activists supported another candidate for president of the convention in 1960 but were outmaneuvered by Jackson loyalists. Squabbles between the rival factions deteriorated into fistfights at the next year's conference, in Kansas City. One elderly minister fell off the platform and died of head injuries. These events exhausted even King's ability to mediate, and he led an activist minority out of the denomination. They convened in Cincinnati later that year and constituted themselves as the Progressive National Baptist Convention.

News about desegregation of schools, sit-ins, protest marches, and freedom rides spread. Clergy around the country began to see that they were witnessing religiously significant events. While Southern black clergy worked against legal segregation, their Northern brethren were working against racial restrictions in housing and employment. Leon Sullivan, a Philadelphia minister, for example, led a group of four hundred fellow ministers in organizing boycotts of businesses that would not hire or promote black employees. White liberal clergy also came to identify with the aims of the movement and indulged in a good deal of breast beating for not having gotten involved sooner. Several churches published mea culpas for having acquiesced so long in what they now admitted to be glaring injustice. Individuals, too. The Jesuit priest Louis Twomey, for example, admitted that throughout the first part of his life he had been "part of a vast conspiracy, coldly calculated to deprive our Negro fellowmen of the spiritual and material goods to which under God they have an inalienable right."[22]

White Christians and Civil Rights

Southern white clergy sympathetic to the movement had to risk antagonizing their parishioners (and therefore their income) if they were too outspoken on the race question. Pete Daniel (b. 1938) recalled that in his childhood Baptist church in Spring Hope, North Carolina, a minority of rabid segregationists had pressured the pastor not to mention the issue. Not until Daniel became a freshman at Wake Forest College in 1957 did he hear serious discussions about a Christian's duty to help the civil rights movement. It was easier for faculty and seminarians at religious colleges to take a pro–civil rights stand because they were not directly answerable to (and financially dependent on) parishioners' goodwill. Before long, however, some white clergy were willing to take the risk of speaking out for civil rights. A group of fifty-nine North Carolina preachers, black and white, responded favorably to the sit-in movement of 1960 with a statement that read, in part: "We feel that Christ would refuse no man food if he was hungry, no child education if he wanted to learn, and no person fellowship if he sought worship."[23] They urged all North Carolinians to support the movement, but as organizer Frederick West wrote later, many clergy sympathizers could not bring themselves to sign, telling the organizers: "It would split my congregation down the middle," "It would kill my building program at this time," or "It would limit the Christian witness I am now free to make behind the scenes" (18). White clergy ambitious for advancement shied away lest they damage their career prospects, justifying their decisions with the claim that they must minister to all their flock, not just the ones who shared this controversial opinion.

White Christians who broke the color line were indeed exposing themselves to danger. Clarence Jordan, for example, who ran a Christian farm-training program, Koinonia, in Southwest Georgia, encouraged black and white families to attend and learn improved farming techniques. In February 1957 he was visited by one hundred Ku Klux Klan members, who warned him to leave the area. When he refused, three hundred of his orchard trees were hacked down and the roadside stand at which he sold his farm's produce was destroyed by dynamite. Jordan himself was attacked and beaten on the streets of Americus and, to add insult to injury, was then arrested for breach of the peace. A Macon businessman, Herbert Birdsey, who refused to join a white business boycott of Koinonia, also suffered the loss of his warehouse in an immense explosion. Among the few white businessmen who stayed loyal to Jordan was the future U.S. president Jimmy Carter, himself a devout Southern Baptist.

Some Southern white preachers remained convinced that segregation was religiously defensible and the civil rights movement wrong. Humphrey Ezell, a Southern Baptist minister, for example, argued in a 1959 book that segregation according to the "separate but equal" formula was the best way of assuring "the prosperity, the happiness and the divine blessings, of both races." To support this view he repeated the age-old argument that God himself created racial segregation when, after the great flood, he separated Shem, Japheth, and Ham, the sons of Noah, making Ham black and cursing him and his descendants. Ezell's reading of later passages in the Old Testament convinced him that whenever disaster befell the children of Israel, it was because they had failed in their segregationist duty. Jesus, too, he added, had been steadfast in preserving Jewish distinctiveness. Even the new nation of Israel, founded in 1948, had been possible only because the Jews had so scrupulously maintained "their racial identity and purity," and he argued that we should guide ourselves along the same segregationist path.[24]

Lawrence Neff, an Atlanta Methodist, agreed with Ezell and contributed a pamphlet, *Jesus: Master-Segregationist*, to the debate. He noted that Jesus, in sending out his disciples on their first mission (Matthew 10:5), had cautioned them to avoid the Gentiles and Samaritans and to preach only to Jews. And at other turning points in his ministry, he had also declined to involve non-Jews. "Let the fact be calmly and deliberately stated and stressed," Neff concluded. "Jesus was the most consistent and inflexible segregationist the world has ever known. . . . His gospel is equally valid for every nation, tribe and tongue. But it could flow only through specific human channels." The attempt to mingle these "channels" by desegregation, he believed, endangered Christianity itself.[25]

Some defenders of the old status quo got quite rhapsodic about the beauties of race separation. Look at H. C. McGowan's little book *God's Garden of Segregation* (1961), with its line diagrams illustrating God's segregationist intent. It moves through the Old Testament, showing how every act of integration brought down God's wrath, while every act of segregation brought a shower of blessings. McGowan reminded readers that the stakes were high: "The devil established the devil's integration with and among men with Adam and Eve in the garden of Eden when he caused them to integrate themselves with the one and only thing that God, at that time, had withheld from them by commandment. God is a God of separation and not a God of integration. The devil is a devil of integration and not a devil of segregation."[26]

Not all white churchmen were so intractable. Eight Alabama clergy, for example, said in 1963 that they sympathized with King's message but that they considered his march for civil rights in Birmingham "unwise and untimely," tainted by the presence of outside agitators. They urged him to wait for a more suitable moment. Their letter, printed in the *Birmingham News*, stimulated in reply one of King's best-remembered statements, the "Letter from Birmingham Jail." King could match all comers when it came to biblical self-justification. He deflected the "outside agitator" remark with an analogy: "Just as the Apostle Paul left his village of Tarsus and carried the gospel of Jesus Christ to the far corners of the Greco-Roman world, so am I compelled to carry the gospel of freedom beyond my own home town. Like Paul, I must constantly respond to the Macedonian call for aid."[27] In the rest of the letter King made an ostentatious display of learning to place himself squarely in the great tradition of Western philosophy and theology. He moved back and forth between references to current conditions in Birmingham and references to the work of the great ones: Socrates, Amos, Jesus, Augustine, Aquinas, Luther, Bunyan (the author of *Pilgrim's Progress*), Jefferson, Lincoln, Reinhold Niebuhr, Martin Buber (a leading Jewish theologian), and Paul Tillich. Its climax was a scorching indictment of religious leaders in the white South.

> I have been so greatly disappointed with the white church and its leadership. . . .
> When I was catapulted into the leadership of the bus protest in Montgomery,
> Alabama a few years ago, I felt we would be supported by the white church. I felt
> that the white ministers, priests and rabbis of the south would be among our
> strongest allies. Instead some have been outright opponents, refusing to under-
> stand the freedom movement and misrepresenting its leaders; all too many oth-
> ers have been more cautious than courageous and have remained silent behind
> the anesthetizing security of stained-glass windows. . . . In deep disappointment I
> have wept over the laxity of the church. But be assured that my tears have been
> tears of love. There can be no deep disappointment where there is not deep love.
> Yes, I love the church. How could I do otherwise. I am in the rather unique posi-
> tion of being the son, the grandson, and the great-grandson of preachers. Yes, I see
> the church as the body of Christ. But, oh! How we have blemished and scarred
> that body through social neglect and through fear of being nonconformists.[28]

It was time, he told the "moderate" clergy, for them to abandon timid conformity and to revive the heroic, self-sacrificing spirit of the early church. But he was careful to pay tribute to the handful of brave whites whose actions for the movement had "carved a tunnel of hope through the dark mountain of disappointment" (443).

King probably reached the height of his influence on August 26, 1963, with his "I Have a Dream" speech at the March on Washington. Mahalia Jackson, who sang to the two hundred thousand participants crowding the Mall, said that the event "was like marching with a mighty host that had come for deliverance. I kept thinking of the words of the Bible — 'And nations shall rise up. . . .' It seemed to me that here was a nation of people marching together. It was like the vision of Moses that the children of Israel would march over into Canaan."[29] In this deservedly most famous of his speeches, King juxtaposed passages from the Book of Isaiah with pictures of segregated life in the American South and the ideals of the Declaration of Independence. First the appeal to America's own "creed" or civil religion. "I have a dream that one day this nation will rise up and live out the true meaning of its creed — we hold these truths to be self-evident, that all men are created equal." Then a vision of the South transformed. "I have a dream that one day on the red hills of Georgia, the sons of former slaves and the sons of former slave-owners will be able to sit down together at the table of brotherhood." Next, bracketed by the same "dream" formula, a passage straight from the prophet Isaiah. "I have a dream that one day every valley shall be exalted, every hill and mountain shall be made low, the rough places will be made plain and the crooked places will be made straight and the glory of the Lord shall be revealed and all flesh shall see it together." And finally the peroration, quoting the patriotic song "My Country 'Tis of Thee" and enumerating all American people and all their religions: "When we allow freedom to ring . . . we will be able to speed up that day when all of God's children—black men and white men, Jews and Gentiles, Protestants and Catholics—will be able to join hands and sing in the words of the old Negro spiritual, 'Free at last, free at last; thank God Almighty, we are free at last.'"[30]

Nonviolence in Decline

The euphoria generated by the march was abruptly destroyed by a bomb attack on Birmingham, Alabama, churches on September 15, 1963, less than a month later. It killed four girls during their Sunday school classes and did more than anything else to condemn segregation nationwide. President John F. Kennedy and his brother Robert, the attorney general, had moved cautiously on the civil rights front until then because they knew that reelection in 1964 depended on the support of white Southern voters, most of them still prosegregation. From then on, in the two remaining months of his life, the president put his weight behind civil rights and voters' rights legislation.

After Kennedy's assassination in November 1963, President Lyndon Baines Johnson remained committed to the civil rights agenda while further acts of segregationist terrorism intensified the racial crisis. In May 1964, for example, white and black organizers of the "freedom summer" campaign were working to register black voters in rural Mississippi. In the town of Meridian a white mob attacked blacks who had attended a "freedom meeting" in the local Methodist church, beat up four of them, and then burned the church to the ground. They also singled out by name one of the white activists, Michael Schwerner, a Northern Jewish volunteer: "Keep that Red Jew nigger-lover out of here or you'll all wind up in the river."[31] A month later Schwerner, along with another Jewish friend and one black comrade, was murdered by segregationists.

By then, however, many civil rights activists had become dissatisfied with freedom rhetoric, King's policy of Christian nonviolence, and the slow pace of reform. They began to criticize him for persisting with the technique of nonviolent activism. Anne Moody was one. She had grown up in a small, segregated Mississippi town, playing piano for church services as a teenager, had taken part in the lunch counter sit-ins and attempts to desegregate white Southern churches. Now she was involved in the Mississippi voter registration drive. She had been on the Washington Mall during the 1963 march but found it disillusioning. "I sat on the grass and listened to the speakers, to discover we had 'dreamers' instead of leaders leading us. . . . Martin Luther King went on and on talking about his dream. I sat there thinking that in Canton [Mississippi] we never had time to sleep, much less dream."[32] She found her faith in crisis after the 1963 Birmingham church bombings and in one dramatic passage from her superb memoir *Coming of Age in Mississippi*, recalls delivering an ultimatum to God himself.

> As long as I live I'll never be beaten by a white man again. Not like in Woolworth's. Not any more. That's out. You know something else, God? Nonviolence is out. I have a good idea Martin Luther King is talking to you too. If he is, tell him that nonviolence has served its purpose. Tell him that for me, God, and for a lot of other Negroes who must be thinking it today. If you don't believe that, then I know you must be white too. And if I ever find out you are white, then I'm through with you. And if I find out you are black, I'll try my best to kill you when I get to heaven." (318)

The alternative to nonviolence, Black Power, began to upstage King's message and methods in the mid-1960s.

Another religious group, the Black Muslims, also favored a more militant approach than King's. Their movement, the Nation of Islam, had been founded in the 1930s by Elijah Poole, a migrant to Detroit from rural Georgia who had renamed himself Elijah Muhammad. The Nation of Islam worked to take poor black urbanites and prisoners away from a world of alcohol, drugs, and crime. Becoming a Black Muslim meant committing yourself completely to the movement. It meant accepting a puritanical way of life: no tea, coffee, alcohol, or tobacco, and no eating of pork. It meant regular prayer at the mosque, regular work, formal dress, absolute personal rectitude, and an attitude of defiant pride—a life as far removed as possible from the appearance and way of life of the surrounding ghetto. The Black Muslims ran their own schools, businesses, and mosques, each cared for by its own minister and a captain of the "Fruit of Islam," uniformed guards of the movement. Whereas Martin Luther King aimed for an integrated society in which color did not matter, the Nation of Islam was racially separatist and proud of its members' blackness.

Black Muslim theology upended the clichés of white racism and was quite distinct from the Islam practiced in the Middle East and by Arab immigrants to the USA. According to Elijah Muhammad, who said he had received word from a mysterious prophet, Wali Fard Muhammad, "God in person," everyone in the world had once been black. Then an evil genius, Dr. Yacub, a malcontent from Mecca with a deep knowledge of what we would call recessive gene traits, had bred a race of white devils on the island of Patmos, and their descendants still lived as a plague on the earth. They had "set the black men fighting among each other, this devil race had turned what had been a peaceful heaven on earth into a hell torn by quarreling and fighting."[33] Elijah Muhammad had learned racial pride and the importance of self-help from Wali Fard—that he and his people were the descendants of a great civilization, a race of African kings. He talked unselfconsciously about "white devils" in his public statements and foretold that when all American blacks had converted to Islam, Allah would exterminate the whites. The writer James Baldwin was impressed by the charismatic Muhammad despite an early skepticism. They met in about 1960, and Baldwin described the leader as "small and slender, really very delicately put together, with a thin face, large, warm eyes and a most winning smile."[34] Baldwin added that he was "drawn toward his peculiar authority" by a "smile that promised to take the burden of my life off my shoulders" (88).

Despite Elijah Muhammad's charisma, the Black Muslims would have remained a largely unknown sectarian minority had it not been for the electrifying oratory of their most famous member, Malcolm X (1925–1965). Born Malcolm Little in Omaha, he had grown up in Michigan, dropped out of school at the age of fifteen, and moved to Harlem, where he became a pimp, burglar, and drug user. He was jailed in 1946 for burglary and spent his years in prison reading voraciously and trying to finish his education. He was converted by Black Muslim visitors and, emerging from jail in 1952, became a zealous activist. He recalled later his lessons in Islam at Detroit's Black Muslim Temple Number 1.

> The blackboard had fixed upon it in permanent paint, on one side, the United States flag and under it the words "Slavery, suffering, death," then the word "Christianity" alongside the sign of the cross. Beneath the Cross was a painting of a black man hanged from a tree. On the other side was painted what we were taught was the Muslim flag, the crescent and the star on a red background, with the words "Islam, Freedom, Justice, Equality."[35]

The "X" in his name, a common naming technique among Black Muslims, was his way of showing that his real name had been stolen in the era of slavery. He became Elijah Muhammad's most effective missionary, touring black urban districts in the 1950s, making converts and preaching Islam, racial pride, separatism, and the coming catastrophe for whites.

Malcolm X, like the white segregationists, believed "that the only solution to America's serious race problem is complete separation of the two races," and noted that Elijah Muhammad was simply "reiterating what was already predicted for this time by all the Biblical prophets."[36] In a speech to Harvard Law School students in 1961 he compared Elijah Muhammad to Moses and Jesus, religious leaders who had been despised by the higher classes of their times. Denouncing desegregation, he declared that only by giving blacks their own country, carved out of several of the fifty states, could whites avert catastrophe.

Just give us a portion of this country that we can call our own. Put us in it. Then give us everything we need to start our own civilization—that is, support us for twenty to twenty-five years, until we are able to go for ourselves. This is God's plan. This is God's solution. . . . Otherwise America will reap the full fury of God's wrath for her crimes against our people. As your Bible says, "He that leads into captivity shall go into captivity; he that kills with the sword shall be killed by the sword." (126)

He had no patience with King's message of Christian love and turning the other cheek. King's approach to civil rights, he commented, was like coffee. Black coffee is strong and wakes you up, but the 1963 March on Washington, with its large contingent of white marchers, was like coffee with too much milk—it puts you to sleep.

Dressed in a sober suit and tie, with his scholarly spectacles and a muscular bodyguard of Fruit of Islam soldiers, Malcolm X made an imposing appearance and used a menacing rhetoric that terrified white onlookers. He said that Black Muslims, though they must not initiate violence, should never back away if attacked.

There is nothing in our book, the Koran, that teaches us to suffer peacefully. Our religion teaches us to be intelligent. Be peaceful, be courteous, obey the law, respect everyone; but if someone puts his hand on you, send him to the cemetery. That's a good religion. In fact that's the old-time religion. That's the one that Ma and Pa used to talk about: an eye for an eye, and a tooth for a tooth. . . . And nobody resents that kind of religion being taught but a wolf, who intends to make you his meal. This is the way it is with the white man in America. He's a wolf—and you're sheep. Any time a shepherd, a pastor, teaches you and me not to run from the white man and, at the same time, teaches us not to fight the white man, he's a traitor to you and me.[37]

"Yes I'm an extremist," he declared in 1964. "The black race in the United States is in extremely bad shape. You show me a black man who isn't an extremist and I'll show you one who needs psychiatric attention."[38]

King, who met Malcolm X only once, briefly and by chance, was dismayed at the Black Muslims' growing influence after 1960 and was infuriated when a group of them pelted him with eggs when he appeared at a Harlem church to give a speech in June 1963. But even then, Malcolm X was changing. After taking the Muslim's traditional hajj pilgrimage to Mecca in 1964, he left Elijah Muhammad's organization and founded his own, Moslem Mosque Inc. He began to practice a more orthodox version of Islam and to moderate his rhetoric of racial separation. Historians of his life and work believe that, had he lived, he would have been able to join the efforts of the civil rights movement. Early in 1965, however, he was assassinated, shot down while giving a speech, probably by agents of Elijah Muhammad. The leader denied all knowledge of the incident and remained, unindicted, in command of the Nation of Islam until his death in 1975. It continued to attract members but could never compete with the black Christian churches in popularity.

By 1965 racial segregation was illegal throughout the United States, though racial prejudice and economic disparities between the races remained enormous. Black churches and the judiciary had led the way in breaking down the segregation system, joined belatedly by the federal government. Ironically, integration weakened the black churches' influence over their members. E. Franklin Frazier noted in the late 1950s that "the Negro church has lost much of its influence as an agency of social control." One effect of desegregation was that "Negroes have been forced into competition with whites in most areas of social life and their church can no longer serve as a refuge within the American community."[39] King himself remained one of the most important people in America through most of the 1960s, a Nobel Peace Prize winner in 1964 and, by 1967, a vocal opponent of the American role in the Vietnam War. Remaining committed to nonviolence and to racial integration, he witnessed, in the last years of his life, a succession of destructive ghetto riots in black urban areas and an increase in black advocacy of violent resistance to racism. His leadership, already under challenge from Black Power advocates, was cut short by his assassination in 1968.

Mormon America

African American activists in the 1950s and early 1960s used their religion to support their claim to first-class citizenship. American Mormons, by contrast, had endured a long struggle to establish the principle that they were entitled to first-class citizenship *despite* their religion. Their religion was exactly what most other Americans hated, especially in the nineteenth century. Nevertheless, by the mid-twentieth century, the Mormons had found a way to reconcile their faith with wholehearted participation in American life.

The Church of Jesus Christ of Latter-day Saints, founded in the late 1820s and early 1830s by Joseph Smith, an upstate New York farm boy, acknowledged not only the Bible but also the Book of Mormon as sacred literature. Smith said that an angel, Moroni, had brought him a set of golden tablets engraved in an unfamiliar language ("Reformed Egyptian"), along with a pair of stones that, when he held them, enabled him to translate the script. His translation told of the struggles of a lost tribe of Israel on American soil centuries before, whose degenerate descendants were the American Indians. Among its many surprising claims was that Jesus, after his death and resurrection in Roman Palestine, had lived again among these people in America. Smith had returned the tablets to Moroni, so they were not available for skeptics to examine or other linguists to decipher. Nevertheless, he persuaded many of his neighbors of the reality of this divine visitation, and his America-centered brand of Christianity began to grow quickly.

The early history of Smith's movement, which moved successively to Ohio, Missouri, and Illinois, is a story of sustained persecution by suspicious outsiders who hated the Mormons' close-knit community, their business enterprise, and rumors (later confirmed) that they were polygamists. Persecution reached its climax with the lynching of Smith in 1844, after which his successor, Brigham Young, led almost the entire Mormon community on an immense and daring trek across the Great Plains and the Rocky Mountains to Utah. They compared this venture to the exodus of the children of Israel from slavery in Egypt to the land of Zion. Early Mormon maps even emphasized the similarity of Utah's desert terrain, featuring the Great Salt Lake, to the terrain of the Holy Land and its Dead Sea.

Brigham Young founded Salt Lake City in land that was then part of Mexico (though it was ceded to the United States two years later by the treaty that ended the Mexican War). He expected to live there, unmolested, for the indefinite future. In fact, the completion of transcontinental railroads greatly accelerated the rate of nationwide settlement, and by the 1880s even Utah was only a couple of days' travel from the Atlantic and Pacific coasts. Under Young's strong, centralized leadership the community, which was in effect a theocracy, created a network of dams and canals, enabling the arid land to be irrigated and to yield enough food for a population that was growing through natural increase and through vigorous missionary recruitment at home and overseas.

The Mormons came under intense political and legal pressure to abandon polygamy. They did so in 1890 after one of Young's successors, Wilford Woodruff, received divine prompting to suspend it. As a quid pro quo, Utah was granted statehood. Having seemed dangerously radical in its early days (in addition to outraging Victorian principles of propriety and monogamy), the Mormon community became, in the twentieth century, sober, conservative, and ardently patriotic—sharing the rest of America's "God and country" rhetoric. It continued to grow in and beyond Utah by evangelizing in the neighboring states and abroad, and provided its members with a dense network of community welfare institutions. It had worked out a modus vivendi with the rest of America, remaining different from the nation's other religious groups, but not too different. As the religious historian R. Laurence Moore argues in *Religious Outsiders and the Making of Americans* (1986), depicting oneself as an embattled outsider could, paradoxically, be an effective way of asserting a genuine American identity. "One way of becoming American," writes Moore, "was to invent oneself out of a sense of opposition. . . . In defining themselves as being apart from the mainstream, Mormons were in fact laying their claim to it."[40]

The crucial issue in the Mormons' survival and growth, as for every other new religious group, was to define their social and theological boundaries sharply and then to captivate their children with the message, to prevent the group from dying out after one generation. Several other new American religions, also founded in the nineteenth century, succeeding in converting the first generation's inspirations into more durable, organized forms that persisted through the twentieth. Among them were Mary Baker Eddy's Christian Scientists, whose theology subordinated the material world to the spiritual, and Charles Taze Russell's Jehovah's Witnesses, who were even able to withstand the shock of their founders' prediction (that the world would come to its millennial end in 1914) proving to be false. Both of these groups, like the Mormons, made very clear distinctions between insiders and outsiders. Both, moreover, required their members' continuous involvement and gave members, at each stage of the life cycle, plenty to do and a definite theory to explain everything that happened around them. Again like other successful new religions, the Latter-day Saints combined an authoritarian internal structure with a commitment to the American values of freedom and equality in external affairs.

To be a Mormon, even after World War II, was to have all aspects of one's life guided by the church. Church members tithed, giving one-tenth of their pretax income to the church. Membership required attendance at lengthy Sunday church services and dedication of every Monday evening to family activities. This practice, "Family Home Evening," reinforced by periodic edicts from the leadership, was aimed at ensuring that Mormon families would not suffer the social fragmentation that was becoming common in postwar society. For them the family, rather than the individual, was the basic unit of society, and it had a significance that transcended life and death, since Mormons remained "sealed" in marriage even after death.

Teenagers—the group most likely to fall away from religious activity in most denominations—had a special role to play in the practice of proxy baptism. Mormons believed that it was possible to give a Latter-day Saints baptism not only to living members but to everyone else, including the dead. Such baptisms were necessary, they believed, for souls to reach the higher circles of heaven, which they understood to be organized on a series of levels. Mormon teenagers, accordingly, were provisionally given the identity of people from other places or other times and could be baptized on those individuals' behalf, by full immersion.

The Latter-day Saints' belief in this practice of proxy and retrospective baptism also led them to undertake the world's most ambitious genealogical project, with the aim of gathering the names of everybody who had ever lived. An impossible goal, since written records for the majority of people in world history had never existed, it nevertheless enabled them to build up, at the Family History Library in Salt Lake City, an immense international archive that became useful to genealogists with quite different aims. Mormons traveling throughout the world, if they encountered lists of names, were encouraged to submit them to the archive so that the people they represented could enjoy proxy baptism and temple endowments. The practice annoyed Catholics when they discovered that their saints had undergone proxy baptism into Mormonism, and it annoyed Jewish groups even more when they discovered that Holocaust victims had received the same treatment.

Older teenagers graduated from their baptism work to the all-important two-year mission. All Christian churches were theoretically committed to spreading the word, and nearly all of them honored members who decided to undertake missionary work, but none could match the Mormons in their systematic organization of missions as an integral part of a member's progress through life. Working in pairs, in other parts of America or in foreign countries, their job was to visit individuals and try to persuade them to become Mormons, and then to guide them through the early stages of their new faith to ensure that the conversion "stuck."

Conservatively dressed, well mannered, polite yet persistent, these young Mormons, often graduates of the Provo, Utah, Missionary Training Center, visited homes, distributed free copies of the Book of Mormon, and tried to persuade people to attend their meetings. Unpaid and expected to cover all their own expenses, teens on mission were rarely alone, rarely able to relax, and forbidden to date. The partners kept a close watch on one another's behavior to prevent backsliding or the breaking of the spartan regulations. Older mission leaders who knew how to motivate them taught them to endure hundreds of rejections for every success they scored, how to keep meticulous records about their proselytizing along with daily spiritual journals, and how to look on the arduous work as exhilarating rather than grueling.

Missionaries were expected to wear a special undergarment, modeled on one shown by the angel Moroni to Joseph Smith. Ungainly and noticeable (even after modifications to accommodate changing fashions) it signaled wearers' distinction from the non-Mormon population in a tangible way. Boys usually adopted the garments at age nineteen before setting out on their missions; girls (for whom missions were much less common until the 1980s and 1990s) usually adopted them at the time of marriage. Garments were given during an "Endowment" ceremony at the Mormon temple and symbolized adulthood and full membership in the church. A rich folklore about the supernatural protection bestowed by the garments circulated among Mormons—that they could protect wearers against fire and accident, and that they protected wearers against giving way to sexual temptation. When the garments were old and worn they could be thrown out or used for rags, but only after four sacred markings on them were carefully removed first and ritually burned or shredded.

A dedicated Mormon, returning from mission, would be encouraged to attend college, and then to marry and to raise a family, while continuing to devote his or her leisure time to church activities, education, welfare, and missions. The community idealized education, hard work, the dignity of labor, vigorous exercise, and the principle of honoring the pioneer generations by building further on their accomplishments. Because Mormons were also strongly discouraged from the use of tobacco, alcohol, coffee, and all other stimulants, and were expected to live according to what, by the 1950s, were puritanical rules, they had every prospect of enjoying good health and prosperity. By the mid-twentieth century successful Mormons, such as hotel magnate J. Willard Marriott and American Motors chairman George Romney, were nationally significant businessmen. Growing numbers moved from the realm of Utah politics, which Mormons had dominated from the start, to the realm of national politics.

Among Mormon leaders who followed this trajectory to high national office was Ezra Taft Benson (1899–1994), a conservative Republican whom President Eisenhower nominated as his secretary of agriculture in 1953. Benson, a devout Mormon born to hardscrabble Idaho homesteaders, had in 1943 become one of the Quorum of the Twelve Apostles, the Latter-day Saints' leadership, a position that would normally have disqualified him from accepting a major political office. Mormon president David McKay recognized the symbolic significance of the appointment, however, and encouraged Benson to accept, which he did, retaining the job throughout both Eisenhower administrations (1953–1961). Benson was an ardent opponent of New Deal agricultural policies (too centralized and bureaucratic, in his view) and a fanatical anti-Communist whose avowals of red-blooded Americanism rivaled even those of Senator Joseph McCarthy. He was the living embodiment of the Mormon adaptation to American values and, in the last years of his life (1985–1994), would in turn become the church's president. Not that Mormons in American politics were solely Republicans; the Udall family, also devout Latter-day Saints, created a multigenerational Democratic dynasty in Arizona politics and on the national scene. Stewart Udall was secretary of the interior under President Kennedy and President Johnson (1961–1969).

The Mormons' commitment to education had contradictory effects. On the one hand, it enabled generations of young Latter-day Saints to succeed in middle-class careers, for which by the late twentieth century high levels of academic training were essential. On the other hand, it led a few of them, in each generation, to scrutinize Mormon historical and religious claims according to the same skeptical and critical principles they had learned in college research seminars. Historical research on Joseph Smith and the first generation of Mormons could raise unsettling questions, and documentation was much fuller for the 1830s than for research into—for example—ancient Christianity.

Fawn Brodie, niece of future Mormon president David McKay, scandalized the community in 1945 when she published *Nobody Knows My Name*, a critical biography of Smith that claimed he was a "conscious fraud" and that the Book of Mormon was a forgery. Brodie's book was acclaimed by non-Mormon academics as a first-rate work of research and writing, especially for its non-supernatural explanation of Mormon origins, but it was condemned by Mormon officials for contradicting the official version of events. Her father, an LDS elder, refused to read the book or even discuss it with her, and Brodie herself was excommunicated in 1946.

The church set its own scholars to work to refute her, and Smith's early life remained a source of intense scholarly controversy in the ensuing decades. Perhaps the most startling addition to the controversy came in 1984 with Richard Bushman's *Joseph Smith and the Beginnings of Mormonism*. The author was a lifelong Mormon but also a highly regarded academic historian, a professor of history at the University of Delaware. Agreeing with the skeptics that Smith had been a product of his immediate cultural environment in upstate New York, Bushman denied that he had been no more than that. He demolished numerous falsification theories about Book of Mormon and drew the paradoxical conclusion that the miraculous explanation (Smith's own account) was actually more reasonable than all the alternatives. The Quorum of Twelve could relish findings like that, but they remained anxious about other historians' work, even when it was done by their handpicked men. The first head of their Professional History Division, Leonard Arrington (appointed 1972), found his work constantly interrupted and censored by apostolic overseers.

Whatever the rights and wrongs of these historical controversies, the fact remained that Mormonism was among America's most active and dynamic religious groups in the postwar era. Just as it had adapted to American norms in 1890 by bringing an end to polygamy, so it made another crucial reform in 1978 by abandoning a long tradition of racial discrimination. Until then black people—regarded by Joseph Smith and Brigham Young as suffering under God's curse—had been excluded from all degrees of the Mormon priesthood, with the result that they were distinctly second-class citizens, on Earth and in the Kingdom of Heaven. Discrimination of this kind had been rendered socially disgraceful in the United States by the civil rights movement and had led to intense criticism of the Mormons and to boycotts of Brigham Young University's sports teams. Besides, it was an overwhelming obstacle to successful proselytizing in Brazil and Africa.

In the face of growing pressure on this race policy, relief came just in time, taking the form of a divine message to President Spencer W. Kimball and the Quorum of Twelve. One of the Twelve, Gordon Hinckley, recalled of the 1978 meeting at which the change was announced: "No voice audible to our physical ears was heard. But the voice of the Spirit whispered into our minds and our very souls."[41] From that moment, even Mormon leaders previously enthusiastic about the old policy became ardent exponents of the new (though the leadership continued to frown on interreligious dating or marriage). Recruitment of black Americans and black Africans advanced quickly from then on. In the decades after 1945 the Mormon Church enjoyed a period of uninterrupted growth, both in America and worldwide, rising from a membership of roughly one million at the war's end, to about ten million at the end of the century.

Figure 1. Dorothy Day, Catholic editor and pacifist, in about 1960. (AP)

Figure 2. Billy Graham, evangelist, and his wife, Ruth, 1954. (AP)

Figure 3. Norman Vincent Peale, author of *A Guide to Confident Living* (1948) and *How to Win Friends and Influence People* (1952), in 1968. He was pastor of Marble Collegiate Church in New York City from 1932 to 1984. (AP)

Figure 4.   Thomas Merton, Trappist monk and author of *The Seven Storey Montain* (1948), in 1951. (AP)

Figure 5.   Reinhold Niebuhr, America's leading midcentury Protestant theologian, in 1963. (AP)

Figure 6. Christ Church Lutheran, Minneapolis, 1950, designed by Eliel and Eero Saarinen. (AP)

Figure 7. St. Francis de Sales Catholic Church, Muskegon, Michigan, designed by Marcel Breuer and Herbert Beckhard, 1964–1966. (Jim Keating)

Figure 8. St. Louis Priory, designed by Gyo Obata and made of parabolic shells of reinforced concrete and fiberglass walls, 1962. (St. Louis Priory)

Figure 9. Air Force Academy Chapel, 1957–1963, designed by Walter Netsch Jr. (Air Force Academy)

Figure 10. Martin Luther King and Malcolm X in March 1964, at the U.S. Capitol in Washington, D.C. (AP)

Figure 11. The end of the Selma–Montgomery March for civil rights, 1965. On the right is the Dexter Road Baptist Church, where King was minister during the Montgomery Bus Boycott. At left is the Alabama State Capitol. (AP)

Figure 12. Jewish boys from the ultra-Orthodox Hasidic community in Borough Park, New York, with their distinctive earlocks and black hats. (AP)

Figure 13. The Children of God, part of the Jesus movement, sing before lunch at their headquarters in the skid row section of Los Angeles on February 2, 1971. (AP)

Chapter 4

NEW FRONTIERS AND OLD BOUNDARIES: 1960–1969

The Catholic President

Americans like the idea that everyone has an equal chance of growing up to be president. The reality is different. Until now you have had to be a man, and before 1960 you had to be a Protestant man. John F. Kennedy cracked the religious barrier against Roman Catholics in the election of that year. No one ever accused Kennedy of being a *good* Catholic; stories about his ruthless political cynicism and his sexual promiscuity have cast a shadow over the myth of the Kennedy "Camelot" in the decades since his death. Even so, his election marked an important moment in the history of American religious tolerance.

Anti-Catholicism was widespread in America during the 1940s and 1950s, and socially respectable too. For evangelical Protestants, even those like Billy Graham who tried to downplay old animosities, denouncing the Catholic Church was almost as routine as denouncing the Devil himself. Liberal Protestants, some Jews, agnostics, and liberal intellectuals all looked on the Catholic Church as a sinister concentration of alien power, with headquarters in Rome and an authoritarian system of control, the antithesis of American democracy. Paul Blanshard, the most articulate of these critics, compared Catholic power to Communist power—in those days the most damning comparison you could possibly make. Norman Vincent Peale warned that Catholics were a threat to the First Amendment because they did not really believe in religious freedom. The American Civil Liberties Union joined in the chorus.

Catholics had held local and statewide elective office since the mid-nineteenth century, had sat on the Supreme Court, and had dominated the government of many large cities (where ethnic Catholic "machines" had gained a bad reputation for graft and corruption). They had occupied seats in the House of Representatives and the U.S. Senate and held senior Cabinet appointments. But only once before had a major party run a Catholic candidate for president; Al Smith, the governor of New York, had been the Democrats' candidate in 1928. Smith had lost badly, partly because many Democratic voters, especially white Southerners, would not vote for a Catholic.

Was it true that elected Catholic officials took their orders from the pope and violated the principles of democracy? No, but Catholic and Protestant voters did routinely disagree on some matters. One was the question of education. American Catholics had, since the 1880s, built up an independent educational system. By the 1950s it covered the spectrum, from kindergarten to graduate school. Catholics believed that these schools should receive state funding. After all, they taught math, English, social studies, and the other parts of a basic curriculum, just like public schools. Every child that went to Catholic school meant one less child for the public schools to worry about and fund. In cities like Boston, Chicago, Philadelphia, and Milwaukee, a large percentage of all children were attending Catholic schools. Was it right that hard-pressed working-class Catholic parents should have to pay taxes for the public schools, which they did not use, and then pay again for their Catholic schools? They said no. Non-Catholics said yes. In their view, the nonsectarian public school was available to everybody and should be paid for by everybody. If Catholics wanted to patronize an alternative school they were free to do so, but non-Catholics' taxes should not indirectly subsidize it.

Another bone of contention was whether the United States should have an ambassador at the Vatican, a tiny independent state in the middle of Italy. During the Second World War President Roosevelt had had a representative there—a Protestant—but Protestant opinion strongly discouraged leaving him there after the war, lest he too become a malign source of Catholic influence over American life.

Was anti-Catholicism just a matter of blind prejudice or was it rational? On the side of prejudice, Protestants for centuries had regarded themselves as the antithesis of Catholics, inheriting and nurturing the bitter hatreds of the Reformation era. Catholicism and Protestantism by the mid-twentieth century were both utterly different from what they had been in the sixteenth, but old memories and myths lived on, usually intensified in America by ethnic differences. On the side of rationality, it is true that Catholic spokesmen sometimes condemned the ideal of religious freedom. In the official Catholic view, religious freedom when Catholics were in the minority was an acceptable temporary arrangement. But the ideal to strive for was Catholic universalism—after all, Catholicism alone was true Christianity, and error has no rights! Some Catholics still held this abrasive ideal in the 1950s, but by then many others downplayed it as much as possible. When Leonard Feeney, a popular Catholic priest, preached the old doctrine of *extra ecclesiam nulla salus* ("no salvation outside the Catholic Church") at the gates of Harvard University in the late 1940s and early 1950s, his own bishop, Cardinal Richard Cushing of Boston, forced him to stop.

In deciding to run for the Democratic presidential nomination in 1960, Kennedy, already a U.S. senator from Cushing's state, Massachusetts, knew that his Catholic background would be a problem. His campaign speeches included passages in which he emphasized that his religion, a personal matter, would never get in the way of his political decision making. Catholics listening to him had mixed feelings. On the one hand, they could understand and support his claim that a Catholic was fully entitled to be president. On the other hand, many of them *did* think that one's religious convictions sometimes make a political difference. The school funding issue was a case in point, and so was the question of contraception. The Catholic Church opposed all forms of artificial contraception, but by 1960 most other American groups favored family planning within marriage. As president, Kennedy might have to decide whether to permit America to participate in United Nations schemes to distribute contraceptives in overpopulated Third World countries. Surely here was an issue where his religion, if he was serious about it, should contribute to his views. Kennedy denied it. In a 1960 address to a group of Protestant ministers in Houston, vetted for him by the Jesuit intellectual John Courtney Murray, he declared that the Catholic Church had no authority over his political actions. If he ever encountered a situation when he felt unable in conscience to carry out his political duty, he said, he would resign the presidency. He added, pointedly, that the same should be true for candidates from every other church.

Kennedy won his party's nomination and then the election itself in November 1960, in the closest race of the century. If he wasn't a very good Catholic, he could console himself with the thought that neither was his opponent, Richard Nixon, a very good representative of his church, the Society of Friends. Despite the Quakers' venerable pacifist tradition, Nixon had fought in World War II and was a saber-rattling anti-Communist! Whenever Kennedy confronted an issue that touched religious sensibilities, he resolved it in a way least likely to offend non-Catholics. He made no effort to revise educational funding arrangements—Catholic parents therefore still had to pay twice over—and he supported the Supreme Court's decisions in three controversial First Amendment cases that were adjudicated during his administration.

The Supreme Court and Religion in Schools

The section of the First Amendment dealing with religion states: "Congress shall make no law respecting an establishment of religion, or prohibiting the free exercise thereof." By the 1960s, legal scholars and judges usually broke this fragment of the amendment down into two smaller units, which they called the Establishment Clause ("Congress shall make no law respecting an establishment of religion") and the Free Exercise Clause ("Congress shall make no law . . . prohibiting the free exercise thereof"). Legislation, to be acceptable, must not give religion any special advantages, but neither must it prevent anyone from holding, and acting freely on, their religious beliefs. A series of Supreme Court cases in the late 1940s and early 1950s had attempted to define where the line between church and state should be drawn, and where ensuring free exercise crossed over into creating an establishment. In *West Virginia State Board of Education v. Barnette* (1943), a group of Jehovah's Witnesses had protested being forced to salute the American flag; in their view it was an act of idolatry. The Supreme Court agreed with them. In *McCollum v. Board of Education* (1948), the Court had ended an Illinois scheme that permitted religious teaching (voluntary to the students) to take place on public school grounds. In 1952, however, *Zorach v. Clausen* had affirmed that schools were allowed to release students from public school early to attend off-campus religious instruction classes. The First Amendment's Establishment Clause was not breached in these cases, Justice William O. Douglas had written, because government property was not being used. He added that the amendment should not be interpreted to mean that there could be no cooperation between religion and government. After all, "we are a religious people whose institutions presuppose a Supreme Being."[1]

In the first of the controversial cases of the early 1960s, *Engel v. Vitale* (1962), the Supreme Court declared that the New York State Board of Regents had violated the Establishment Clause when it wrote a prayer to be recited in the state's public school classrooms. The regents had written the prayer in the early 1950s to be equally acceptable to Protestants, Catholics, and Jews: ministers, priests, and rabbis had all approved it. It said: "Almighty God, we acknowledge our dependence upon Thee, and we beg thy blessings upon us, our parents, our teachers and our country."[2] Children who did not want to recite it did not have to; they could either stand silent or leave the room. The Supreme Court said that these safeguards made no difference—the prayer still represented an effort by the state to "establish" religion in the classroom. It added: "It is no part of the business of government to compose official prayers for any group of the American people to recite as a part of a religious program carried on by government."[3]

In the second case, decided in the following year, *School District of Abing-*

ton Township v. Schempp (1963), the Court found that a Pennsylvania law requiring the reading of Bible verses and the saying of the Lord's Prayer in public schoolrooms was unconstitutional. The plaintiffs were Unitarians. At the initial trial, a Jewish expert witness, Dr. Solomon Grayzel, had declared that parts of the New Testament were offensive to Jews, adding that to describe Jesus as the Son of God was, to Jews, "practically blasphemous."[4] The Court agreed that the state law's intention had been to give public recognition to Christianity and that, accordingly, it had violated the Establishment Clause.

In an associated case, *Murray v. Curlett* (1963), Madalyn Murray, an outspoken and combative atheist from Baltimore, protested against a similar Maryland law. She resented the fact that her son had to leave the room during the daily prayer and Bible reading. Murray, who later declared herself America's foremost atheist and tried to make sure that American astronauts would not mention God or pray on the Moon, wrote in a letter to *Life* magazine: "We find the Bible to be nauseating, historically inaccurate, replete with the ravings of madmen. We find God to be sadistic, brutal, and a representation of hatred and vengeance. We find the Lord's Prayer to be that muttered by worms, groveling for meager existence in a traumatic, paranoid world."[5] The Court found for Schempp and Murray, with the result that the prayer and Bible laws in both states (and, implicitly, in most others around the nation) were overturned.

Chief Justice Earl Warren, formerly a Republican attorney general and governor of California, had been appointed to the Court by President Eisenhower in 1953 and had become one of the most controversial figures in American public life. In the first year of his tenure, a unanimous Court, with his enthusiastic leadership, had prohibited the racial segregation of public schools in the case of *Brown v. Board of Education of Topeka, Kansas* (1954). It had gone on to relax censorship regulations and now had violated a time-honored tradition of school prayer and Bible reading.

The religion cases caused an immense public outcry, equal in intensity to that over *Brown* in 1954. The public school system, from its early days in the nineteenth century right up to the 1960s, had nearly always and nearly everywhere included time for prayers and readings from the King James (Protestant) Bible. Critics did not see the decisions as preserving the constitutional separation of church and state. Instead they saw them as "taking God out of the classroom," a forcible kind of secularization. "If the extreme position advocated by Justice Douglas [in *Engel*] is adopted," wrote one churchman in a characteristic response, "the logical outcome will be the removal of 'In God We Trust' from our coins, the cessation of prayers at sessions of Congress, the withdrawal of chaplains from the Armed Forces and the deletion of all references to America as a nation 'under God' from our official documents."[6] In the following years a succession of draft constitutional amendments to reverse the decisions appeared before Congress (the Bricker and Dirksen Amendments). They regularly won majorities in both houses but were unable to get the necessary two-thirds majorities that would have sent them out to the states for ratification. A conservative coalition started a movement to impeach Chief Justice Earl Warren, raising the cry, all but inevitable in those years, that he was either an actual Communist himself or at least a dupe of the "international Communist conspiracy."

Vietnam, Part I

America's role in Vietnam escalated in the late 1950s and early 1960s. A former French colony, Vietnam had been occupied by the Japanese during World War II. The French recovered it in 1945, but anti-Japanese resistance fighters, led by Ho Chi Minh and determined to eject all colonial powers, continued to fight against the French. By the time of the Geneva Accords of 1954 they had beaten the French into submission. Ho Chi Minh, however, was not only a Vietnamese nationalist but also a Communist. America therefore refused to ratify the Geneva treaty—in President Eisenhower's view it would deliver another nation into the hands of Communist tyranny. Instead, Eisenhower encouraged the temporary government of South Vietnam, which was designed to be a resettlement zone prior to reunification, to become a permanent, independent, non-Communist country. It did so under the leadership of a corrupt, French-educated oligarchy, which survived only on an increasingly rich diet of American aid.

Its head, General Ngo Dinh Diem, was a Catholic, presiding over a nation whose majority population was Confucian and Buddhist. His sister-in-law, Madame Ngo Dinh Nhu, was a zealous advocate of Catholicism. She hoped to outlaw divorce, contraception, and dancing, and to make the laws of South Vietnam follow Catholic Church teachings. Outspoken, tactless, and fearless, she saw all opposition to the Diem regime as inspired by Communism. When a group of Buddhist monks burned themselves alive in the streets of Saigon to protest the regime's corruption in the early 1960s, threatening its stability, she scornfully dismissed them as "barbecues."[7]

Henry Cabot Lodge, America's ambassador to Saigon, the South Vietnamese capital, learned in the fall of 1963 that a group of South Vietnamese army officers planned to assassinate President Diem, and cabled the news to President Kennedy. Kennedy's advisers told him that Diem was so widely disliked, so corrupt, and so incapable of conducting the war effectively, that America should do nothing to prevent the plot. It went forward, and Diem died in early November 1963. His successors, however, proved to be as bad or worse, and the effort to preserve them in office dragged America ever more deeply into the war in the ensuing years. Only three weeks after Diem's death, President Kennedy too was assassinated.

Orthodox foreign policy opinion in America, under Kennedy and his successor, Lyndon Johnson, favored intervention in Vietnam to prevent its fall to Communism. A vocal minority of religious Americans opposed intervention, however—some because they were pacifists, others because this particular war seemed to them mistaken. Among the absolute pacifists was Dorothy Day, one of the most luminous and charismatic figures in American religious history. Born in Illinois in 1897, she had been a radical journalist in Greenwich Village, New York, during the teens of the twentieth century, and had numbered anarchists and Communists among her lovers. But in the mid-1920s, much to the horror of her radical and bohemian friends, Day had converted to Catholicism and adopted an ascetic way of life among the poor derelicts of New York City. In the early 1930s she had founded a radical newspaper, the *Catholic Worker*, and a House of Hospitality to shelter and feed the homeless. Even when the adversary was Hitler, she was, as we have seen, opposed to American participation in war. She and her followers endured contempt and near starvation on a rural communal farm in the early 1940s rather than aid the war effort. No less zealous in her opposition to the Korean War and to nuclear war preparations, in the 1950s she was arrested and served a short prison term for refusing to participate in civil defense drills. Day's position was that of only a tiny minority among American Catholics; most others shared the hard anti-Communist views of New York's Cardinal Spellman. Nevertheless, her example had inspired a generation of younger Catholic activists.

She and the Trappist monk Thomas Merton (whose autobiography, *The Seven Storey Mountain*, I quoted in chapter 1) were among the distinguished Catholics to lend name and fame to PAX (later Pax Christi), a Catholic peace organization that held workshops and petitioned their bishops and Congress about the war. In November 1965, as Day was returning from a visit to the final session of the Second Vatican Council in Rome, a young man associated with the Catholic Worker movement, Roger LaPorte, emulated the action of the Vietnamese monks by dousing himself with gasoline and setting himself on fire. He did it on the steps of the United Nations in New York and died of burns in the hospital a few days later. Day herself was horrified by the incident, and indignant when she was blamed in parts of the Catholic media for inciting him (in fact, she did not know him). Another of her outspoken pacifist friends, the Jesuit priest Daniel Berrigan, declined to think of LaPorte's death as a suicide (which, because it implies despair and a loss of faith in God, represents the worst possible sin for a Catholic to commit). Berrigan argued: "What if the death reflected not despair, but a self-offering attuned (however naively or mistakenly) to the sacrifice of Christ? Would not such a presumption show mercy toward the dead, as well as honoring the living?"[8] LaPorte's dramatic death, and the intra-Catholic debate over how to interpret it, served notice of the profound religious passions already being stirred by the Vietnam War. They were destined to intensify.

Radical Theology

By the end of the twentieth century, some American Catholics were thinking about making Dorothy Day a saint. Sainthood of the informal Protestant variety was conferred in the early 1960s on Dietrich Bonhoeffer. Bonhoeffer (1906–1945) had been a member of the German Confessing Church in the 1930s, the Protestant minority that refused to submit to Nazi domination. Admired by Reinhold Niebuhr and other American theologians for his intellectual brilliance, he had spent a year at Union Theological Seminary, New York, in 1930, before returning to Germany. When Nazi persecution of Jews had escalated into a policy of extermination, Bonhoeffer had joined Klaus von Stauffenberg's conspiracy to assassinate Hitler in April 1944. The plot failed, Bonhoeffer was arrested, and after a year in Buchenwald and Schoenberg prison, he was executed just before the war's end.

Bonhoeffer's theological writings, mostly unsystematic and unpublished in his lifetime, outlined in the form of letters to a friend, appeared in English in 1953 and soon won American admirers. Among his insights was the idea that as Christian civilization had matured since the Middle Ages it had learned to live without invoking God at every turn. Science and rational thought had replaced God in more and more of the places where he had once reigned supreme, and Christians ought to be content with this development rather than struggling vainly against it. Bonhoeffer showed that Christian attempts to find a place for God in this increasingly secularized world had nearly always failed. He wrote:

> The attack by Christian apologetic upon the adulthood of the world I consider to be in the first place pointless, in the second ignoble, and in the third un-Christian. Pointless, because it looks to me like an attempt to put a grown-up man back into adolescence, i.e., to make him dependent on things on which he is not in fact dependent any more, thrusting him back into the midst of problems which are in fact not problems for him any more. Ignoble, because this amounts to an effort to exploit the weakness of man for purposes alien to him and not freely subscribed to by him. Un-Christian, because for Christ himself is being substituted one particular stage in the religiousness of man.[9]

Christians must forget about trying to turn back the clock. Instead they must now set themselves the task of creating a "religionless Christianity," in which they accept the tasks thrust on them by history without looking for supernatural help. Bonhoeffer's most famous aphorism, quoted widely in the sixties, was, "God would have us know that we must live as men who manage our lives without him" (360).

A second piercing insight from Bonhoeffer was that the Christian God, far from being omnipotent, was conspicuous for his *weakness*.

Man's religiosity makes him look in distress to the power of God in the world; he uses God as a *Deus ex machina*. The Bible however directs him to the powerlessness and suffering of God; only a suffering God can help. To this extent we may say that the process we have described by which the world came of age was an abandonment of a false conception of God, and a clearing of the decks for the God of the Bible, who conquers power and space in the world by his weakness. (361)

The Christian task, then, was to emulate Jesus in living for others *in the world*, without any resort to myths of ultimate salvation, and to acknowledge the same kind of human weakness and frailty that Jesus felt when he cried from the cross: "My God, my God, why hast thou forsaken me?"

A group of American Protestant theologians, more impressed by the cogency of Bonhoeffer's ideas than baffled by his paradoxes, experimented with "secular theology" in the early 1960s. Gabriel Vahanian, for example, a professor of theology at Syracuse University, wrote in *The Death of God* (1961) that "the essentially mythological world-view of Christianity has been succeeded by a thoroughgoing scientific view of reality, in terms of which either God is no longer necessary, or he is neither necessary nor unnecessary: he is irrelevant—he is dead."[10] America believed it had been witnessing a religious revival since World War II, added Vahanian, but it had really been witnessing the substitution of a thin and superstitious *religiosity* for genuine religion. Similarly, Paul Van Buren, a professor at the University of Texas, argued in *The Secular Meaning of the Gospel* (1963) that the concept of "God" and such phrases as "Jesus is Lord," when illuminated by the harsh light of modern philosophical language analysis, lost their ancient meaning. In the foregoing centuries, rigorous thought and careful observation had transformed human realms of inquiry, turning alchemy into chemistry and astrology into astronomy. "In almost every field of human learning, the metaphysical and cosmological aspect has disappeared and the subject matter has been 'limited' to the human, the historical, the empirical. Theology," Van Buren concluded, "cannot escape this tendency if it is to be a serious mode of contemporary thought."[11]

Vahanian and Van Buren were among the leading figures in the mid-sixties' "death of God" theology, along with Thomas Altizer and William Hamilton. This latter pair published *Radical Theology and the Death of God* in 1966, a collection of essays in which they too argued that the traditional idea of God no longer makes sense to modern intellectuals. Jesus of Nazareth as a dynamic figure still "speaks" to us and can give us guidance in the world as we march for civil rights and poverty-reform legislation, they wrote, but we can no longer fall back, superstitiously, on faith in an all-powerful God. Instead of relying on the old "God talk," men must take their cues from the world around them.

Central to the work of these radical theologians was the idea that as the world changed, Christian theology must either change with it or become sterile and irrelevant. Like many intellectuals of their era, they were convinced that electricity, machinery, telephones, and the general advance of high technology were speeding up the rate of history itself and that these changes were benign. We can no longer expect theological statements to suffice once and for all, they argued; theological *systems,* from Thomas Aquinas to Karl Barth and Paul Tillich, are all delusory because they try to resist the corrosions of time. The best we can hope for is provisional statements adequate to the circumstances of the moment. Social, cultural, and technological changes take place faster among Americans than among any other people of the world, they added, making this "death of God" situation a distinctly American phenomenon.

Hamilton in particular did not regard the "death of God" as horrible. Instead he found cause for hope and optimism everywhere, displacing the gloomy mid-century mood of neo-orthodox theology. Consider, he wrote, one symbolically important day, January 4, 1965. On that day died T. S. Eliot, the poet of gloom, alienation, and existential dismay. On the same day President Lyndon Johnson gave a memorable State of the Union address. Hamilton juxtaposed the two events: "President Johnson invited his fellow countrymen not only to enter the world of the twentieth century but to accept the possibility of revolutionary changes in that world. . . . It was somehow unlike political rhetoric of other eras—it was believable."[12] In the social sciences, in art, even in the music of the Beatles, everywhere Hamilton found men sloughing off the old tragic mood and choosing optimism. "Those who were lucky enough to be pulled or pushed . . . to see the Beatles' first movie, *A Hard Day's Night,* will recall the enchanting scene in which the four of them escape from the prison-like television studio . . . and flee to an open field for a few surrealistic moments of jumping, dancing, abandon. This movie, and perhaps even the famous Beatles' sound, is part of this mood of celebration and rejoicing" (163).

Books on "radical" theology sold briskly. The best of the genre, and the best-selling, was Harvey Cox's *The Secular City* (1965). Like Thomas Merton's *Seven Storey Mountain* in the 1940s, it is marvelously representative of its age, and so long as you're actually in the midst of reading it, it seems unquestionably right. Cox himself, a Northern Baptist from small-town Pennsylvania, had become a professor of theology at Harvard Divinity School. A gregarious, likable man, full of enthusiasm for whatever happened to be going on at the moment, with an immense sympathy and tolerance for youth and novelties, and a lover of the urban landscape, he poured so much of himself into this popular, bright-red paperback that what could have been dry and didactic became instead a real page-turner. (In the mid-sixties every intellectual who didn't have a handy copy of Marshall McLuhan's *Understanding Media* in his or her back pocket had *The Secular City* there instead; it sold almost a million copies.) Cox became his generation's Protestant theological superstar, eclipsing the elderly spokesmen of neo-orthodoxy, Niebuhr and Tillich.

Cox's central insight, again taking a lead from Bonhoeffer, was that Christianity had itself been a powerful force for secularization. Ancient religions had had a great pantheon of gods—one for the rivers, another for the trees, one for wine, one for marriage, one for war, and so on. The entire ancient world had been cluttered with supernatural beings, and every step you took was dogged by one deity or another. Judaism and Christianity, however, had swept away the whole lot and left just one remote, omnipotent God presiding over the world. People were then free to manipulate and organize the world without fear that they were stepping on the gods' toes. And having learned that the world was *not* crammed with divinities, they had learned to take the logical next step of pushing back further and further their need for *any* god at all. Secularization and urbanization are not the enemies of Christianity, Cox declared, giving a surprising twist to the usual story, but its logical end product! Robert Ellwood, later a professor of religion, recalls that, as a graduate student, he read *The Secular City* in Chicago, which "was then, as now, a good way this side of paradise." But "I can recall walking the icy streets of that metropolis in this magical book's glow, thinking that, despite all appearances, this place was real, was holy, was the future, was where real life had now to be lived . . . this hard brick and asphalt city was where we were going to build Jerusalem."[13]

The trendy, outlandish, and paradoxical claims of the radical theologians caught the eye of journalists and turned what would have been an esoteric trend in academic theology into a national sensation. John Cogley in the *New York Times* was quite right to note that behind the "catchy, provocative title" "death of God," the movement was "all subtlety, the specialized technical language of the academy, professional abstruseness and lay bafflement."[14] Press oversimplification was bound to lead to controversy and to accusations that men who claimed God was dead had no business teaching theology to aspiring clergy or drawing paychecks from divinity schools. The front cover of *Time* magazine's Easter edition, dated April 8, 1966, all black and red, asked in giant capital letters: "IS GOD DEAD?" A long article inside covered the work of the radical theologians in a gee-whiz style and contributed to their sudden and unexpected publicity boom. The famous *Time* magazine was later used as a prop in the sinister movie *Rosemary's Baby*—one of the film's devil figures browses it!

Letters to the editor of every religious and secular journal jockeyed for the available column inches. A few correspondents, like the secretary of the American Association for the Advancement of Atheism, were delighted: "God is a myth, like Santa Claus. The God-myth is dying. It was born in the minds of ignorant, superstitious Stone Age men and has been exploited by ancient and modern witch doctors to the immense profit of the priest clan."[15] Far more correspondents were outraged. *Time* itself got an earful. One reader spluttered: "Your ugly cover is a blasphemous outrage and, appearing as it does during Passover and Easter week, an affront to every believing Jew and Christian."[16] A retired Army colonel made the almost obligatory allegation: "*Time's* story is biased, pro-atheist, and pro-Communist, shocking, and entirely un-American."[17]

The publicity took the professors by surprise. Hamilton relished the attention, accepted and began to use the label "Christian atheist," and appeared in a long interview with *Playboy* later that year. By contrast, the publicity glare caused at least one of them some anxious moments. Thomas Altizer, a thirty-eight-year-old associate professor of religion at Emory University when the story broke, found himself under attack from this Methodist university's alumni. The university had just launched an appeal to raise $25 million, but now a group of former students, led by a Dr. Robert Shumate, placed a full-page advertisement in the *Atlanta Journal-Constitution* urging other alumni to withhold their contributions until Altizer had been fired. Henry Bowden, chair of the university's board of trustees, told the *New York Times*: "When a man comes here and expounds a principle that is not Christian he is fouling his own nest." Despite these pressures, the university's president gritted his teeth and defended Altizer's academic freedom. The young professor expressed his gratitude for this support, adding, "The traditional Christian faith has become totally meaningless and unreal" so that "a wholly new form of faith is called for as a result."[18]

Evangelicals and fundamentalists, as we have seen already, had been dismayed by liberal Protestant theology's humanistic starting point throughout the twentieth century, even when it took the comparatively sober and rigorous form of Niebuhr's neo-orthodoxy. Bristling with indignation against radical theology, they were in no mood to accept religious instruction from popular culture idols who appeared in *Playboy*. Billy Graham told *Time* that he knew for a fact that God was *not* dead. "I know that God exists because of my personal experience. I know that I know him. I've talked with him and walked with him. He cares about me and acts in my everyday life."[19]

The insights of the radical theologians continued to inform academic theology in the ensuing decades, especially its emphasis on the need for care with "God talk," the need to appreciate the human vantage point from which the theologian's work begins, and the need to connect work in the world with ideas about the divine. Among the most challenging reactions to their work was Peter Berger's *A Rumor of Angels* (1969), which argued that their diagnosis of the theologian's dilemma need not lead to a position of "Christian atheism." The reality in which we live, said Berger, is *socially constructed*—we know what is real and what is right largely because there is a widespread social agreement about the nature of the world around us. Historical study shows us that other societies have had *different* ideas about what is right and true—in other words, different ideas about what "reality" is—and our knowledge of this contrast tends to make us relativists. Members of a society hold religious beliefs only if they can fit them into a "structure of plausibility" that jibes with their idea of reality. The radical theologians' description of modern pluralistic, scientific, ultra-analytical America (or at least its intellectuals, who were their chief concern) had led them to claim that traditional Christian ideas now lacked a structure of plausibility and that Christianity must come to mean something completely new, stripped of its old supernaturalism.

Berger admitted the cogency of their observations and agreed that they were right to begin their work by considering the condition of man in society, rather than trying to make an arbitrary jump to God's point of view (the method of the neo-orthodox theological giant Karl Barth). However, Berger chided the radical theologians for not guarding themselves against the assumption that they stood at the top of an escalator of "progress" and had a better understanding of the world than all their predecessors, and that their particular version of reality was somehow "truer" or more complete than anyone else's. It may be that *their* structure of plausibility left no room for the old Christian verities, but the relativism on which they laid such stress worked both ways. They too could be "relativized," and, Berger added, they should be. Human experience, even the unmystical stuff of ordinary, everyday life, is not really so devoid of religious phenomena as the radicals had implied. Berger offered from everyday life five examples of what he called "signals of transcendence"—signs of a reality beyond the mundane world: order, hope, play, humor, and the human propensity to condemn with the force of damnation.

Each of these five signals of transcendence has a role to play in the human attempt to stave off the terror of death and chaos. All societies create order, though their particular ordering schemes differ. All people express and live by hope, which seems to defy the reality of the death that awaits every individual. All find forms of play—first and most fully in childhood but in later life too—and derive from play's different sense of time a kind of temporary immortality. All use humor to deal with the incongruous fact of "the imprisonment of the human spirit in the world. . . . Humor not only recognizes the comic discrepancy in the human condition, it also relativizes it, and thereby suggests that the tragic perspective on the discrepancies of the human condition can also be relativized."[20] Finally, Berger argued, we cannot simply describe an act of great evil, such as the Holocaust, as the methodical work of a society with different values than our own.

The transcendent element manifests itself in two steps. First our condemnation is absolute and certain . . . we give the condemnation the status of a necessary and universal truth. . . . Second, the condemnation does not seem to exhaust its intrinsic intention in terms of this world alone. Deeds that cry out to heaven also cry out for hell. . . . No human punishment is "enough" in the case of deeds as monstrous as these. These are deeds that demand not only condemnation but *damnation* in the full religious meaning of the word; that is, the doer not only puts himself outside the community of men; he also separates himself in a final way from a moral order that transcends the human community, and thus invokes a retribution that is more than human. (75)

This list of five signals of transcendence was not meant to be exhaustive. Berger believed others could be found in the architecture of the Gothic cathedrals, the music of Mozart, the art of Chagall, the poetry of William Blake, and elsewhere in the modern world, none of them dependent on esoteric or mystical initiation on the part of the observer.

Berger certainly was not claiming that these signals of transcendence vindicated traditional Christianity. Neither was he arguing for a retreat from the world into old dogmatic certainties. In the current highly pluralistic world, where even the most orthodox Christian was constantly encountering different degrees and kinds of Christians, Jews, Muslims, Hindus, skeptics, and atheists, maintaining any one group's "structure of plausibility" was, after all, no easy matter. Everyone was forced to *choose* his or her religion, even if that choice was simply to stay with the one in which he or she had been raised, and to be regularly involved in dealing with anxieties generated by contrasting value structures. He was, however, insisting that the mood represented by the radical theologians was just one more of the many forms of consciousness about which history teaches us, that it enjoyed no special privileges, and that it would be the worst kind of arrogance (and ignorance of history) to assert that it alone now dictated the direction Christianity must take.

In his closing pages Berger sketched out some of his own ideas for a "rediscovery of the supernatural," declaring that—despite all his relativizing sociological work—he was still a Christian, albeit one of a very unorthodox kind. Accepting the full force of pluralism and all the findings of critical-historical and sociological scholarship, he still wanted to "reaffirm the conception of God that emerged in the religious experience of ancient Israel and that is available to us in the literature of the Old Testament" (101). Christ provided a solution to the great theodicy puzzle, the explanation of why an all-powerful God can permit suffering.

> The discovery of Christ implies the discovery of the redeeming presence of God within the anguish of human experience. Now God is perceived not only in terrible confrontation with the world of man, but present within it as suffering love. This presence makes possible the ultimate vindication of the creation, and thus the reconciliation between the power and the goodness of the creator. By the same token it vindicates the hope that human suffering has redeeming significance. (104)

A *Rumor of Angels* was an unusual and fascinating book, especially for the America of 1969, bringing together in barely a hundred pages Berger's clear-eyed, pretense-stripping sociological style and his intensely emotional sense that "rumors" of God's presence were still everywhere among us. Acclaimed at once for its insight and its capacity to expand readers' horizons, it made the radical theologians, scarcely half a decade after their moment of glory, seem slightly pallid and provincial by comparison.

Radical theology provoked not only highly cerebral and serious responses, like Berger's, but also a rash of jokes and cartoons, many of them variations on Mark Twain's old remark: "Reports of my death have been greatly exaggerated." The most accomplished spoof on the whole "death of God" affair was Anthony Towne's little book *Excerpts from the Diaries of the Late God* (1968). Towne, an urbane Episcopalian, used entries from the recently dead God's diary, which he claimed to have discovered, to poke fun at the radical theologians themselves (God feels sick and visits his doctors: "The doctors concluded that my *omnipotens* would respond to treatment but they found further signs of [my] pesky diminishing influence. . . . They were even muttering about some surgeon in Atlanta who might be consulted. Altizer, I think the name was"), at evangelicals ("Billy Graham has halitosis of the soul"), and at Catholics ("It was about their so-called doctrine of original sin that I meant to complain. What twaddle! Can't they find enough sin all around them without trying to discover an *original* sin?").[21] Along with the knowing jokes, ironically, Towne himself seemed almost to make a theological point in line with Bonhoeffer's insight about identifying with God not in his strength but in his *weakness*. In the "editor's preface," he wrote:

> God clearly found it almost as difficult to comprehend the human condition as we humans find it to comprehend the divine condition. . . . As I see it, the diaries engage the following issues:
>
> a) God's perplexity about time
> b) God's perplexity about death
> c) God's perplexity about women
> d) God's perplexity about prayer
> e) God's perplexity about money
> f) God's perplexity about church
> g) God's perplexity about theology
> h) God's perplexity about morals. (7)

In his lighthearted way, Towne was echoing Bonhoeffer's idea that we need to think not of the omnipotent God but of a God in doubt and trouble. The "death of God" affair quickly passed into history, but beneath the froth of publicity it had raised important questions, while its capacity to infuriate evangelicals had further distanced the two halves of American Protestantism.

Catholic Reform

Leaving aside the radicals' question of whether supernatural religion was even possible by the 1960s, consider once again the more pragmatic question of what a religion is supposed to do. Should it preach the same message and stay outwardly the same, yielding to changing times as little as possible? Or should it, as the radical theologians proposed, be the harbinger of social transformation, eagerly picking up new cultural possibilities and giving them a new religious form? Does the truth remain true through the ages or must it be constantly adapted and reformulated? The 1960s was a decade of great social upheaval, in race relations, in politics, in styles of dress, in patterns of youth culture, in music, and in changing ideas about sexuality. Churches certainly were changing as their congregations became more affluent, as they moved from city to suburb, and as the laity's level of education caught up with and surpassed that of their clergy. There was one among them that had always seemed — and had always said that it was — timeless and unchanging: the Catholic Church. But in the early 1960s it too launched an immense program of internal renewal.

Between 1939 and 1958 Eugenio Pacelli had sat on the papal throne with the title Pope Pius XII, and had worn proudly his symbol of royalty, the triple tiara. A brilliant man, formerly the Vatican's nuncio to Nazi Germany, Pius had a reputation for lofty isolation and conservatism, though in some ways he had kept up with the times. He drove by motorcar from Rome to his country estate. He had telephones installed in the Vatican (though priests answering their phones and discovering the pope himself on the other end were expected to fall to their knees before discussing business). Vatican gardeners had instructions to hide behind the trees when Pius took a stroll in his extensive grounds. Lofty, lonely, constantly afflicted with hiccups in the last two years of his life and trusting for his personal comfort to a loyal German nun, Pius was the last of the great Vatican monarchs. The degree to which he had colluded with the fascists and Nazis during the 1930s and World War II, and the ambiguities of his role in protesting and trying to prevent the Holocaust, have remained controversial topics up to the present. Some historians have been sharply critical of his nonconfrontational approach to Hitler, which he took for the sake of preserving religious liberty for German Catholics. Others have argued that he was personally responsible for saving the lives of thousands of German and Italian Jews and that he did as much as was possible under threatening wartime circumstances.

He was replaced by a very different kind of man, Angelo Roncalli, who took the papal name of John XXIII and declined the accoutrements of royalty. John was already over seventy, and the Vatican cardinals did not expect him to live much longer or do anything dramatic. But just as the once unremarkable Earl Warren had amazed everyone by initiating an era of American Supreme Court activism, so John XXIII amazed everyone by declaring that the time had come for a grand Vatican Council, to bring the church up-to-date and to "open a window" into the modern world.

Vatican conservatives dragged their feet but could not prevent the assembling of the council (usually remembered as Vatican II), which met in the fall of 1962 and in each successive autumn until 1965. Every Catholic bishop in the world was invited to discuss the vital issues affecting their Church. Cardinal Cushing of Boston volunteered to install a simultaneous translation system in the Sistine Chapel, modeled on the one at the United Nations. That way each participant in the discussion could use his native language. The Vatican secretaries refused, restricting debate to ecclesiastical Latin, even though more than half of the bishops could speak Latin only haltingly or not at all. Despite this restriction the world's bishops began clamoring for reforms, and got them.

The reform most noticeable to every ordinary Catholic was the switch to vernacular and participatory liturgy. In other words, services that had always been held in Latin, with the priest facing the altar and his back to the congregation, were now held in English with the priest facing the people, involving them more directly. Equally important was the council's decree "The Church in the Modern World," which encouraged Catholics to involve themselves in the daily social and political struggles around them. No longer should they think of Catholicism as the one true religion and all other branches of Christianity as heresies. Instead, they should now think of Protestants as "separated brethren" within the Christian family. The Church itself should no longer be thought of as a hierarchical pyramid, with all power descending from the pope at the top. It redefined itself, democratically, as "the People of God," moving together through history. The hierarchy remained, but no longer as a form of spiritual dictatorship.

Some Catholics loved the reforms and, invoking "the spirit of the Council," tried further experiments of their own. Before long, the twanging of folk guitars and the twirling of liturgical dancers throughout America emphasized the sweeping effects of a new broom in the old Church. Priests and nuns who had grown up with the old system were often impatient of the old ways and pleased by the reforms. Many of them had felt stifled by an educational system that claimed to have a right answer to every question, always grounded in the philosophical system of Saint Thomas Aquinas and always susceptible to phrasing in tidy Latin syllogisms. They were delighted to have the chance to adapt the Church to the modern world, to engage realistically with existential philosophy, new trends in Protestantism, the "death of God" movement, and the social reforms taking place around them.

Other Catholics hated the reforms. Particularly dismaying was the fact that customs they had learned and practiced strictly throughout their lives, such as Friday abstinence from meat, fasting before mass, and regular confession, were no longer required. They could now violate long-honored taboos. Changes like these can be very upsetting—you begin to doubt the sincerity of an organization if it suddenly abandons its previously sacrosanct rules. Just as Protestants were bickering over radical theology, so now Catholics began to fall out over how to apply the teachings of the council and how appropriately to be witnesses to their faith in the modern world.

Catholic children felt the effects of the reforms directly, especially children who spent a large part of every day in Catholic schools. In the pre-council years they had learned an elaborate pattern of conduct, experiences, and sensations. The writer Garry Wills (b. 1934) recalled:

> The habits of our childhood are tenacious, and Catholicism was first experienced by us as a vast set of intermeshed childhood habits—prayers offered, heads ducked in unison, crossings, chants, christenings, grace at meals; beads, altar incense, candles, nuns in the classroom, alternately too sweet and too severe, priests garbed black on the street and brilliant at the altar; churches lit and darkened, clothed and stripped, to the rhythm of liturgical recurrences . . . all things going to a rhythm, memorized, old things always returning, eternal in that sense, no matter how transitory.[22]

Essential to such childhoods was learning rules and rubrics. While fundamentalist kids were busy learning large chunks of the Bible, Catholic kids were learning the catechism, a series of questions and answers that summarized their church's doctrines. They also learned that they must never cross the threshold of a Protestant church, that they must eat no meat on Fridays or during the forty days of Lent, that they must fast between midnight and the taking of the communion wafer on Sunday morning, and that to prepare for communion they must first go to confession to gain absolution from their sins. They knew, too, that unexpected death could overtake them at any time and that, as one put it, "you must be able to recite an Act of Contrition between being hit by the bus and falling lifeless to the ground."[23]

The Catholic child's imaginative world was lurid and violent, partly because the threat of hellfire hung over children who broke the rules and partly because their teachers were willing to use literal physical force. Richard Roesel (b. 1944) recalled a fight at his parochial school in Savannah, Georgia: "I assaulted a bathroom monitor and bloodied his mouth. He bled profusely. When I got back upstairs the nun took me by the ears and slammed my head repeatedly against the blackboard."[24] It was violent also because of the honor given to saints and martyrs who had died hideous deaths, and whose stories were recounted in detail. The novelist Robert Stone recalled tales of gibbets, grills, knives, and crosses, and the importance of dying a noble death: "Dying was an approved Catholic thing to do. You could exist totally within the Catholic culture as a dead person. It was a kind of total resolution of Catholicism. Death was better than fucking, certainly. . . . I think there's a level on which dying was really approved of, practically as a virtuous act in and of itself."[25] Enrique Fernandez, studying with the Christian Brothers in Florida, had a similar memory:

> I grew up with my head filled with stories of two kinds of violence. One kind was the stories of martyrs, which were simply stories of very interesting forms of torture. And the other was stories of eternal damnation, which were *also* stories of very lurid forms of torture. God knows I internalized those. . . . It fills you with a strange drive toward self-immolation, a sense of a need to be hurt in order for some kind of transcendence or something higher to happen.[26]

The Catholic historian Robert Orsi recalled the same pattern in his Italian American family, of attributing a special sanctity to the suffering—a phenomenon brilliantly recalled in his article "Mildred, Is It Fun to Be a Cripple?"

The quality of the education in Catholic schools varied widely but always made a big impression, and former students' memories (pro and con) tended to be strong. Michael Harrington, later a leader of America's democratic socialists, recalled a superbly rigorous education at his St. Louis Jesuit high school. The novelist Mary Gordon, by contrast, recalled that the Josephite nuns who taught her were "very strict but also very dumb. They managed to combine being very ill educated with being very strict about all the wrong things. . . . I had teachers with terrible Brooklyn accents who were illiterate and spoke ungrammatically and a lot of very old nuns who had no business being in classrooms. . . . By the time I was ten years old I was smarter than my teachers."[27] By contrast, Peggy Steinfels, who grew up to become editor of the Catholic journal *Commonweal*, had fond memories of ceremonies that punctuated the year at her Chicago Catholic school, such as crowning a statue of the Blessed Virgin Mary as Queen of May and strewing rose petals before the eucharistic procession. "I wasn't critical of the system which, despite all the recent talk of patriarchy, I think favored girls. The nuns obviously loved the girls and thought the boys were just nuisances."[28]

This entire Catholic way of life, built up over the early twentieth century, began to change after Vatican II. Nuns, who until then had seemed unearthly figures of no gender, heavily draped in black cloth, faces peeking out from elaborate head-coverings with no hair visible, now began to wear much simpler habits or to abandon them altogether and to become recognizable to their students as young women. Catholic school classes studied comparative religion and actually went on expeditions to visit nearby Protestant churches and synagogues rather than shunning them. Confession, now reconceptualized as "reconciliation," lost some of the anxious thrill of the dark confessional box, while the rote learning of the catechism was, in many parishes, discontinued.

Some Catholic children were delighted by the changes in their church, the switch to English liturgy, and the greater sense of involvement in the modern world. Karen Stolley (b. 1955) recalled that in her Erie, Pennsylvania, home, "in the mid-sixties a new church was built, a big brick modern church . . . with a very progressive priest. All the people who had been disaffected with St. Julia's showed up; young families just came out of the woodwork. It was a great church, politically relevant, with sermons on what was happening in the world. As a kid I loved it."[29] Others were dismayed by the changes. Thomas Lanigan Schmidt felt that the move away from elaborate decoration and beautiful robes was a form of "uglification. I didn't mind the liturgy being in English. I just didn't like it being so stupid and ugly and without any sense of reverence."[30] Christopher Buckley (b. 1956), son of the conservative commentator, writes:

> I became immensely resentful of Pope John XXIII. . . . I was enrolled in altar-boy training, the major part of which in those days was having 138 lines of Latin drummed into you. One week after I had it all down pat, Vatican II changed everything, and I felt as though the whole thing had been done to annoy me. So I continued for a while to mumble under my breath: "Ad deum qui laetificat juventutem meum."[31]

Eve Davis, who had grown up in a segregated black parish in New Orleans, recalled that an attempt to make worship more "relevant" actually had the opposite effect: "Two or three women named the Worth Sisters came in with guitars and sang folk hymns. An odd mix for us—folk music is not an indigenous black form at all."[32]

Experimentation with new styles of liturgy proved especially controversial. The movement for charismatic renewal among Catholics introduced behavior in church that until then had been the preserve of Protestant Pentecostalists, including faith healing, speaking in tongues, and being "slain in the spirit" (rendered unconscious by spiritual power). To people finding a new idiom of religious self-expression it could be liberating, but to others it was sometimes profoundly disturbing. In his brilliant memoir *Turbulent Souls*, for example, Stephen Dubner recalls his parents' (both of them Jewish converts to Catholicism) becoming involved in a weekly charismatic prayer meeting:

> The meeting was held in the church hall but Father DiPace didn't come; the songs they sang were different from the regular church songs, and so were the people. . . . They clapped as they sang, in that circular, folksinger way, like mashing hamburger patties. When the song was over they'd close their eyes tight and pray, quietly at first, not together like in church but each of them on his own, voices swarming up like bees. . . . Louder and louder, and soon it would begin; one voice, then a second, jagged outbursts of the strangest syllables, their faces twisted into what looked like pain, their strange syllables then blossoming into shouts, some of them standing as they shouted, a dozen grown-ups, my mother and father among them, crying into the air—and me, petrified, peeking through half-shut eyelids. . . . In church my parents were composed and attentive. But in these prayer meetings my parents went wild. They were the chief clappers and shriek-

ers and then, riding home through the dark, they were totally calm. I would stew in the back seat, angry at the inexplicable madness that had transpired.[33]

These changes in the Catholic Church provoked an extensive literature in the 1960s, 1970s, and 1980s, a subgenre that might be referred to collectively as "my wacky Catholic childhood." It had begun with Mary McCarthy's *Memories of a Catholic Girlhood* (1957), which reminisces about her experiences as a child back in the 1920s. Unlike earlier writings by ex-Catholics, McCarthy's account was not angry and denunciatory. Instead, she wrote in a tone of indulgent amusement, alternating irony with respectful reminiscence and admitting that she had learned much of lasting value from the Church, even though she had long since lapsed from practicing Catholicism. This voice characterized many other authors on the same theme, culminating in Christopher Durang's play *Sister Mary Ignatius Explains It All for You* (1981), a black comedy in which a nun and parochial school teacher, from a family of twenty-seven brothers and sisters, is driven to madness and murder by taking her Catholic Church's teachings literally. The conventions of the literature include the idea that going to confession as a child necessitates years of psychotherapy in later life, that fasting creates gluttons, that chastity stokes up the libido, and that intense self-sacrifice stimulates hedonism.

This literature depended on the great contrast between pre- and postconciliar American Catholicism. Authors in the genre needed their readers to be able to remember the old Church and to agree that it had been full of strange customs and bizarre ideas. The authors were not necessarily anti-Catholic, nor even lapsed, but they had at least to be able to see the funny side of things that had once appeared completely serious, particularly the repressive sexual teachings and the cultivation of morbid guilt. The fact that they were willing to hold up parts of their earlier lives to public scrutiny also showed a degree of self-confidence. "Ghetto" Catholics of the earlier twentieth century would have closed ranks against exposure to any hint of ridicule.

The importance of Vatican II for Catholicism, both worldwide and in America, would be hard to exaggerate. It brought to an end the long era of mutual Protestant-Catholic tensions in America, quickly curtailed Catholics' perceived standoffishness, and affected the way Catholics approached each other, their leaders, and the social problems of their rapidly changing society. The council's encouragement of Catholics to become involved in worldly problem solving coincided with a new resolve among liberal Protestants to struggle against injustice in the "secular city." These combined influences, accordingly, brought an array of white Protestant ministers, Catholic priests, and nuns to Selma, Alabama, in March 1965, to join civil rights demonstrators in a tense confrontation with city officials. Their joint prayer services there, in the midst of the African American evangelical clergy and in the face of angry lines of prosegregation police, marked the dawn of a new era not just in American race relations but in American ecumenical relations too. In the ensuing decades, American Catholics challenged their own leaders (on such questions as contraception) and participated in national debates (about such issues as abortion, nuclear weapons, and refugee policy), learning in the process new skills in alliance building across religious lines. To Catholics born and raised after the council, religion meant something entirely different than it had to their parents.

Chapter 5

Shaking the Foundations: 1963–1972

American Judaism

Hannah Arendt's *Eichmann in Jerusalem* (1963) is not, at first glance, a religious book. It describes how Israeli agents discovered the former Nazi death camp organizer Adolf Eichmann in South America, transported him back to Israel, put him on trial for crimes against humanity, found him guilty, and executed him by hanging. It goes on to describe several dismaying aspects of the Holocaust, among them the way in which Jewish authorities in many European cities cooperated with the Nazis in the hope that their good conduct would secure them better treatment, and the lack of resistance to the Nazis' policy of extermination, not only among other Germans but among Jews themselves. The book's subtitle was *On the Banality of Evil*. Eichmann on trial defended himself with the claim that he had just followed orders, just tried to do a good job, as required of him by his superiors. Arendt agreed that Eichmann was not the kind of evil monster you meet in legend and folklore. He was something worse: a dull, everyday, methodical, efficient, unimaginative mass killer. Such, she concluded, was the nature of evil in the mechanized twentieth century.

The Holocaust was not widely studied in the twenty years after World War II nor widely perceived as a historical event with religious resonances. The

outlines of the story, and its magnitude, were certainly well known; many survivors and displaced persons (refugees) had come to America immediately
after the war. Jews who were children in that era remember, however, that
their families would avoid the topic or hush it up if it was raised at home.
Brooks Susman said that in his Pittsburgh family, "our parents hid it from us.
They didn't want us to be injured or brutalized by it." Yitz Greenberg in
Brooklyn had the same experience at school: "The subject of the Holocaust
did not come up at the Brooklyn Talmudical Academy." So did Marcia Lee
Goldberg, who recalled that the subject "was passed over in my religious
school in St. Louis shortly after the war," with the result that she "thought of it
as something like the Queen Esther story."[1] Children who did hear about it or
who saw the horrifying newsreel footage often reacted with shame; one
recalled that "I was embarrassed that these people who marched to their
deaths without fighting were my people. I was a tough kid, and if somebody
tried to do something to me I fought back" (125). As late as 1966 a *Commentary* magazine survey of Jewish beliefs contained no questions about the Holocaust, and the Jewish writers participating rarely mentioned it in their
responses. As sociologist Nathan Glazer wrote, "Before 1967 young radical
Jews were quite capable of using the term 'genocide' to describe what was happening to American Negroes or Vietnamese, with no self-consciousness of the
fact that their own people had truly been subject, and recently, to a not wholly
unsuccessful effort to kill them all."[2] Arendt's book, however, helped to inaugurate a Holocaust literature, theological and historical, which eventually
grew to giant proportions. By 1975 (unlike 1955 or 1965), ideas about and
memories of the Holocaust had become an inseparable part of being an American Jew.

Despite the shadow of the Holocaust, the postwar decades were, in many
ways, a miniature golden age for American Jews. The children and grandchil-
dren of immigrants, Jews had been among the most successful in achieving
upward social mobility and in moving into a prominent place in American
business, the professions, and artistic and intellectual life. Outstandingly successful academically, they had begun to win professorships in university facul-
ties that had previously been composed of white Anglo-Saxon Protestants
(WASPs), and by the 1960s a cadre of brilliantly talented Jewish social scientists
led by Daniel Bell, Seymour Martin Lipset, and Nathan Glazer made the running in American sociology. Many of America's leading creative figures were
Jewish too, including the novelists Philip Roth, Saul Bellow, and Norman
Mailer and the musicians Leonard Bernstein and Andre Previn.

The American Jewish community was divided into three branches, Orthodox, Conservative, and Reform, each with a distinct history of its own. Reform
Judaism had come to America from urbane and assimilated German immigrants in the nineteenth century. Its leading figure, Isaac Meyer Wise

(1819–1900), had been eager to reorient Judaism away from its ghetto tradition and fierce adherence to the Bible and adapt it to the contemporary world. He emphasized ethical conduct more strongly than adherence to law, argued that Judaism was universal rather than particularistic, and dispensed with the *kashrut* dietary laws. Some Reform congregations even experimented with switching their Sabbath from Saturday to Sunday, in order to conform more nearly to the pattern of the Christian denominations. Already by the late 1940s, however, Reform was tempering its old iconoclasm and recovering an appreciation for tradition. Its Columbus Platform (summary of beliefs and self-definition) of 1937 admitted that Judaism was a people as well as a religion (something it had downplayed in the Pittsburgh Platform of 1885) and that its traditions, ceremonies, and rituals should be preserved and honored. It tended to attract the most successful and assimilated Jews, especially in the Midwest and the South.

The second branch, Conservative Judaism, had been created on American soil in the late nineteenth century and nurtured in the early twentieth under the leadership of a brilliant scholar and president of the Jewish Theological Seminary, Solomon Schechter (1847–1915). Conservative Jews tried to balance modernization with tradition and moved far more cautiously than Reform Jews did in discarding traditional ceremonies and customs. It had begun by combining a revolt against the aggressive modernizing of Reform with a recognition that immigrant Judaism, especially that coming from Eastern Europe at the turn of the century, must be Americanized, made dignified, and adapted to an advanced urban society. Conservative Judaism grew very rapidly in the years of religious revival after the Second World War because many of the new suburban communities selected it as a compromise between the Reform and Orthodox positions. Of the three branches, it had been, throughout the early twentieth century, the most dedicated to creating a Jewish homeland of Israel in the Middle East. Among the most innovative figures in the Conservative movement was another JTS professor, Mordecai Kaplan, whose book *Judaism as a Civilization* (1935) argued for the vitality of purely secular Jewish traditions and activities and later (despite his misgivings) became the foundation for another branch of American Judaism, Reconstructionism.

Orthodox Judaism was the form brought to America from Russia and Eastern Europe between about 1880 and the end of unrestricted immigration in the 1920s, and it was strongest in New York, New Jersey, and Philadelphia. Highly decentralized, often organized in synagogues with roots in particular Russian or Austro-Hungarian towns, it had tried to keep alive the full rigor of talmudic law and to make no concessions to changed circumstances. Such intentions could not be realized, however; the sheer fact of being in America side by side with the other branches of Judaism and in the midst of a predominantly Christian population caused Orthodoxy to develop with the passage of time. It was the least assimilation-minded branch, however, and preserved strict separation of men and women in the synagogue and strict adherence to the dietary laws, to keeping the Sabbath, and to talmudic laws governing all other aspects of daily life. Unlike Conservatism, whose scholars undertook historical-critical study of the Bible, it had an absolutist approach to the Torah (the first five books of the Bible), regarding it as divinely inspired and as having been delivered to Moses once and for all at Sinai. Many Orthodox rabbis denied the legitimacy of the other branches and were sharply opposed to their congregants' intermarriage with Reform and Conservative Jews, let alone with Christians. Nearly all affirmed that Judaism was a people as well as a religion, and nearly all supported the creation of Israel.

The New York–New Jersey area remained, as it had been throughout the early twentieth century, the center of American Judaism, and its more than three million Jewish inhabitants made New York the most Jewish city in the world. Fine class and ethnic distinctions were possible within the Jewish community, and varying degrees of adaptation to American conditions. To be sure, not everyone was religiously observant; rabbis from all branches of Judaism lamented how many Jews failed to attend synagogue services or to observe the law; attendance figures were consistently lower than those among Christians. Numerous memoirs, meanwhile, describe how *baseball* began to replace the synagogue as an object of reverence. The novelist Philip Roth, for example, recalls that when he was a ten-year-old in Newark, New Jersey, his baseball mitt, bat, and ball were virtually sacred. "The solace that my Orthodox grandfather doubtless took in the familiar leathery odor of the flesh-worn straps of the old phylacteries in which he wrapped himself each morning, I derived from the smell of my mitt, which I ritualistically donned every day to work a little on my pocket." He adds that his love of baseball was the decisive sign of his being American, enjoying "membership in a great secular nationalistic church from which nobody had ever seemed to suggest that Jews should be excluded."[3] In his story "The Conversion of the Jews," a group of bored and restless Jewish boys sit grudgingly through Hebrew school classes, longing to be out on the baseball diamond. Similarly, Irv Saposnik recalled that there was a religious dimension to being a Dodgers fan in the 1950s, since they always lost out to the "victorious goyim," the Yankees. "Having pain and defeat as part of our inheritance, this was easy to understand. And they played into our messianic hope, our looking into the future. The Jews were waiting for next year in Jerusalem. The Dodgers were waiting for next year to win the World Series. We saw baseball in a Judaic context and followed it with religious fervor."[4]

From being a predominantly urban population, however, American Jews, even those in New York, were becoming suburbanized as more of them prospered. The move to the suburbs, where "dilution" in the wider American population was a danger, prompted many American Jews to become more religiously observant than they had been in the crowded urban immigrant ghettos, and to send their children to Jewish schools. As a result, Judaism shared in the postwar American religious revival. Most of the major American cities developed one or more predominantly Jewish suburbs in which a new Jewish way of life emerged. Brooks Susman recalled that the Squirrel Hill district of Pittsburgh, where he was raised, was divided into a wealthy German-Jewish and Reform area and a humbler area, Stanton Heights, inhabited primarily by Eastern European and Orthodox Jews. "And to me there was one Judaism: Reform. Conservative and Orthodox Judaism did not exist. I never saw a tallit [prayer shawl] or a yarmulke" (69).

In addition to urban and suburban Jewish communities, smaller numbers of Jews lived in the American provinces, sometimes in little clusters, occasionally alone in an otherwise entirely gentile population. Southern Jewish families, for example, often lived isolated lives as they ran rural or small-town businesses. Rachel Shilsky's father, a former rabbi, had a store that was patronized mainly by the black people of Suffolk, Virginia, and she recalled the loneliness of her childhood as one of the town's few Jews. "You know, a Jew living in Suffolk when I was coming up could be lonely even if there were fifteen of them standing in the room, I don't know why; it's that feeling that nobody likes you; that's how I felt, living in the South." She added that her family's business further depressed their status: "The Jews in Suffolk did stick together but even among Jews my family was low because we dealt with *shvartses* [black people]."[5]

As the civil rights movement gathered force in the late 1950s and 1960s, all but a minority of Southern Jews sided with the defenders of segregation, often from fear that they would be victimized if they advocated radical social change. Nevertheless, the pro-integration campaigns of Northern Jewish organizations often led Southern whites to see Jews in general as dangerous, and the era witnessed a succession of segregationist attacks on Southern synagogues. A handful of Southern rabbis broke the mold by energetically supporting the civil rights movement. Perry Nussbaum of Jackson, Mississippi, for example, suffered the bombing first of his synagogue, then of his family home in 1967 because of his outspoken support of the movement. Among the friends who came to sympathize with Nussbaum was a local Baptist minister, who condemned the bombing but then added, "Isn't it a shame that the rabbi doesn't know Jesus!"[6]

In all parts of the country, religious activities maintained Jews' sense of distinctiveness. The structure of the week itself differentiated Jews from all their neighbors. Sabbath (Shabbos) began with the lighting of Sabbath candles at nightfall on Friday and persisted until nightfall on Saturday, usually punctuated by visits to the synagogue on Friday night and Saturday morning. Observant families prepared for the onset of Sabbath by cleaning the house and ensuring that all preparations had been made, so that no work would have to be done during the day of rest. Some Orthodox families took the injunction against Sabbath-breaking with great seriousness. They were not allowed to light fires on the Sabbath, and their rabbis interpreted this rule to mean that neither could they turn electric lights on or off. Instead they would tape over the light switches once they had been set in the appropriate "on" or "off" position. The injunction against fires also prohibited them from driving cars (which rely on the fire of spark plugs to ignite the fuel). Conservative rabbis in the 1950s decided to make an exception to this rule and permit driving to services, since their congregations were scattered in the new suburbs, sometimes miles from the synagogue. Orthodox rabbis, by contrast, refused the concession, with the result that strongly Orthodox residential neighborhoods developed, with members living close enough to the synagogue that they could walk. Such neighborhoods also developed the institutions necessary to Orthodox life—kosher butchers and bakers, yeshiva schools, and sometimes the *mikvah* ritual bath, in which community women cleansed themselves meticulously at the end of their menstrual periods.

The most extreme example of this intensive neighborhood development pattern came in the Hasidic communities of Brooklyn, which opposed all assimilation into mainstream American life and maintained sharp boundaries against outsiders. Hasidic Jews, often recent immigrants from remote areas of Eastern Europe, sought guidance in the details of everyday life from their charismatic rebbes. Hasidic men wore distinctive black clothes, beards, and curled earlocks, while the women, once married, shaved their heads and wore only wigs. Elaborate taboos governed their daily conduct, marriages were usually arranged, and spouses were forbidden even to touch one another before marriage. Encountering them could be an unnerving experience even for other Jews. Shalom Goldman recalled that after an early-childhood experience of middle-class suburban Judaism in Connecticut he was taken to see the Satmar Chasidim in Williamsburg. "Here I was, a typical-looking American Jewish kid surrounded by all these Chasidic kids, nasty little boys who were tweaking my cheeks and screaming at me in Yiddish, 'Und vee iz doner payess?' [and where are your earlocks?]."[7]

The Hasidim were willing to sacrifice economic opportunity for the sake of maintaining a close and nurturing community. Even the more adaptable "modern Orthodox," however, were diligent boundary guardians. Observing a different Sabbath than the Christians sometimes imposed on them also a heavy economic burden. In 1961, for example, the Supreme Court adjudicated the case of *Braunfeld v. Brown*. Abraham Braunfeld, a furniture-store owner, was forced to close on Sunday in accordance with Pennsylvania state law, but he also closed on Saturday because he was an Orthodox Jew. He claimed that the state's Sunday-closing law abridged his First Amendment right of free exercise and that he was being forced to choose between his business and his religion.

The Court denied his claim, arguing that a genuine public interest was served by the law and that it was not primarily religious in nature.

Not only the days of the week but also the religious festivals of the year marked the distinction between Jews and gentiles, and they structured the passing of the seasons. Rosh Hashanah, the Jewish New Year, an autumn event, is an occasion for self-examination and repentance. Some people undertake *tashlich*, throwing fragments of bread, each of which represents one of their sins, into the water. The Days of Awe that follow are marked by the sounding of a *shofar*, made from a ram's horn. Yom Kippur, ten days after Rosh Hashanah, is the Day of Atonement, on which participants fast until sundown, then ask for forgiveness for their sins before winning the assurance of God's mercy. Sukkoth, later in the fall, is a harvest festival in which people build flimsy shelters (*sukkahs*) in their backyards and sleep there if the weather is not too harsh, in conformity to the biblical injunction "You shall live in huts seven days: all citizens of Israel shall live in huts in order that future generations may know that I made the Israelite people live in huts when I brought them out of the land of Egypt" (Leviticus 23:42–43). Simhat Torah witnesses a processional dance of thanksgiving for the gift of the law itself. Passover, an eight-day spring festival to commemorate Moses' deliverance of the Children of Israel from slavery in Egypt, includes a succession of ritual "seder" meals with symbolic foods and a chair left empty in the hope that the prophet Elijah may appear to take his place at the feast.

Jewish children in America knew from early in their lives that they belonged to a minority population. No season of the year brought that point home more sharply than Christmas, when nearby Christian families indulged themselves in an orgy of consumerism. Is Crystal, growing up in the small Jewish community of Duluth, Minnesota, recalled that "a Jewish friend from a wealthier family" teased him that "if we hung up stockings, they'd get filled with toys and other presents. We tried it, but all we got was coal and orange peels and potatoes. That was our parents' way of telling us Christmas wasn't our holiday."[8] Some Jews acquiesced to their children's clamor and joined in the Christmas celebration, remarking that for many people the festival had largely been secularized in any case. A rabbi from White Plains, New York, told a 1949 conference: "The pull of the Christian environment is very powerful. Every Christmas presents a crisis in our school. There are scores of homes in which children experience a Christmas tree and parents argue with the rabbi whether it is a national or religious holiday."[9] Many American Jews reacted to the annual Christmas ordeal by giving a new importance to the Jewish festival of Chanukah, which in earlier times and other places had been a comparatively minor celebration. Chanukah commemorates the victory of Judas Maccabeus and his brothers over a Hellenizing ruler, Antiochus Epiphanes, in 165 B.C.E. An eight-day cycle of gift giving and the introduction of "Chanukah-bushes" reconciled many Jewish children to the absence of Christmas presents and the

Christmas tree. It, like the other festivals, served to create a succession of reminders of Jewish identity and Jewish history throughout the year.

Life-cycle events as well as seasonal festivals punctuated Jewish existence. On the eighth day after their birth, Jewish boys were circumcised, usually in the synagogue, by a *mohel*, a surgical operation that symbolized in the most vivid physiological way their entrance into the community. Jewish boys were also expected to undergo a rite of passage, the bar mitzvah, that symbolically brought them into the adult male community at the age of about thirteen. With some variation depending on the branch of Judaism to which he belonged, the boy was required to learn scriptural passages in Hebrew and to recite them from the *bimah* (lectern) on the designated day, after which his family threw a lavish party. A parallel tradition for girls, the bat mitzvah, began in the 1920s but was not popularized until the 1950s. It was one of the many ritual innovations developed by Mordecai Kaplan, the founder of Reconstructionist Judaism, and first undertaken by his daughters. The bar mitzvah had historically marked the moment at which a Jewish youth joined the men and began his religious life in earnest. Ironically, in many midcentury families, it took on the opposite function, of being the *last* time at which systematic study of the Torah and the Hebrew language were required of him.

Finally, a special approach to food made Jews different from the Christian majority. "Keeping kosher" meant different things to different Jews, and there were widely varying degrees of strictness. Many Jews avoided pork as a *treyf* (nonkosher) food, but fewer had separate sets of plates and kitchen sinks for meat and dairy dishes, and fewer still would decline to eat socially with non-Jewish friends. A common midcentury compromise was "kosher-style" eating, described here by Elizabeth Ehrlich as an element of her Detroit childhood:

> For a long time we children thought we were kosher. . . . We never drank milk with meat, or ate anything made with cheese or cream at the same meal as chicken or lamb or cow. The chickens, lambs, and cows were killed according to Jewish law. There never was pork in the house, never hindquarters, never a cut of meat called butt or rump or loin. . . . Strictly speaking, though, our *kashrut* was a fiction. We had only one set of dishes, not two. Shrimp came home now and again and I knew no sense of transgression. . . . In restaurants, we ate what we wanted. I accepted unquestioningly, as have so many others, the schizophrenic distinction between "eating home" and "eating out." Shifting tables, one became a different person.[10]

As Ehrlich added, to keep kosher strictly limited one's choices severely, but "in midcentury America, that's what the good life was all about—choice" (179).

In the affluent society of the 1950s and 1960s some Jewish commentators expressed their fear that a people that had endured centuries of persecution, never losing its corporate sense of identity, might now dissolve benignly into the general American population; in 1964 *Look* magazine picked up the idea and

ran a story on "the vanishing American Jew." Nathan Glazer had already noted
in his 1957 history of American Judaism that full observance of the law, which
had once been a defining characteristic of all Jews, was now the preserve only
of the Orthodox. "This creates a more serious break in the continuity of Jewish
history than the murder of six million Jews. Jewish history has known, and
Judaism has been prepared for, massacre; Jewish history has not known, nor is
Judaism prepared for, the abandonment of the law."[11] Nevertheless, he noted
something equally significant: "It is that the Jews have not stopped being Jews.
. . . They still *choose* to be Jews [and] do not cast off the yoke or burden of the
Jewish heritage" (141). Ironically, he concluded, "It is because of this negative
characteristic, this refusal to become non-Jews, that we see today a flourishing
of Jewish religious institutions" (142). It may be halfhearted, it may be just
"kosher-style," but, he concluded, the identity persists.

Part of this persistence was based on opposition to anti-Semitism. Fear,
hatred, and persecution had followed Jews throughout their history. Anti-Semitism in America was far less intense than it had been in most other places, and
it declined rapidly after the Second World War. Returning servicemen of all
faiths who had mixed with and cooperated with one another under fire were
often less prejudiced than their elders. Still, anti-Semitism remained a source
of anxiety and concern, and several Jewish organizations were dedicated to
identifying and opposing it. A best-selling novel on the issue, Laura Hobson's
Gentleman's Agreement (1947), became an Oscar-winning film. It starred Gregory Peck as a gentile who pretends to be Jewish to expose and denounce middle-class bigotry and prejudice. The reality of "genteel anti-Semitism" included
the exclusion of Jews from prestigious country clubs, resorts, and residential
neighborhoods (which were legally permitted to exclude people by race or ethnicity up to the early 1960s). Jews, despite exceptional educational achievements, found it more difficult to enter the upper ranks of many professions,
while Jewish students were denied entrance to professional schools at higher
rates than Christian applicants. Moreover, Christian educational literature still
created a negative stereotype in young students' minds by asserting that "the
Jews" were collectively to blame for the death of Jesus. Leonard Dinnerstein, a
historian of anti-Semitism, found that Christian adult literature in the 1950s
and 1960s was also saturated with anti-Jewish remarks and assumptions. The
Church of the Nazarene's *Bible School Journal*, for example, described Judaism
as "a religion that is inadequate, based on ignorance and prejudice, non-satis-
fying, and providing no solutions to the problems of sin and death."[12] Anti-Semitism tended to flare up during crises, and Jews still sometimes became scape-
goats for community tensions. The attempt of two Jewish families to move into
a Chicago suburban neighborhood in 1950, for example, set off days of anti-
Jewish demonstrations, during which protesters threw rocks at the Jews' houses
while police officers stood idly by. And, as we have seen, attacks on Southern

synagogues during the civil rights movement bore witness to segregationists' scapegoating of Jews for the era's racial upheavals.

One sure sign of the decline of anti-Semitism, however, was the rise of inter-marriage between Jews and gentiles, which increased rapidly after midcentury (9 percent in 1964, 25 percent in 1974, 44 percent in 1984, and more than half by 1990). That process in turn caused intra-Jewish anxieties. Intermarriage could be interpreted optimistically as a way of bringing more recruits *into* Judaism, or it could be interpreted more pessimistically as further evidence of community breakdown and loss.

Some trends, such as the increased rate of intermarriage, continued through the postwar decades. In other respects the social upheavals of the 1960s created shocks of dislocation. The first of these shocks was the sundering of American Jews from their long-standing alliance with African Americans. Radicalized young Jews were prominent in the civil rights movement in the late 1950s and early 1960s. Some were "red diaper babies" whose parents had been Commu-nists or Socialists in the 1930s. Others came from religious families but attrib-uted their activism to a displaced form of religious expression. For example, Murray Polner, a Jewish activist, told an interviewer:

> When to the horror of our parents and grandparents many of us fled from their ritualistic Orthodoxy looking for a larger world, we carried along their humanism, their quest for peace, their sense of commitment, caring, and charity, that is bedrocked in Jewish life. . . . For many Jews I knew this notion of doing for oth-ers emerged in left-wing activities.[13]

But by 1966 and 1967 strains were showing. Martin Luther King's nonviolent, integrationist message was being pushed aside by a generation of younger, less religiously motivated activists who preferred Malcolm X's brand of black mili-tancy. Stokely Carmichael wanted more "black power" and less Christian turn-ing of the other cheek.

Jewish radicals went along with the turn to a more radical posture at first, but they could not be happy with a broadening streak of anti-Semitism in black mil-itants' rhetoric. The urban riots of the mid-sixties' "long hot summers" often tar-geted Jewish-owned stores, and black militants began to single out Jewish land-lords and store owners as a chief source of their troubles. At a meeting of the Mount Vernon, New York, school board in February 1966 to discuss desegre-gation, tempers rose between black and Jewish citizens until a black activist and Congress of Racial Equality (CORE) official named Clifford Brown shouted: "Hitler made a mistake when he didn't kill enough of you."[14] After the assassi-nation of King in April 1968, black demonstrators invaded and severely van-dalized a Cincinnati synagogue. Black militants in Boston threatened another synagogue board that the same fate would befall their building (situated in an area that was changing residentially from Jewish to black) if they did not hand it over free of charge. "Put the temple in the hands of the black community or we'll burn it down with Jews in it," declared one of their threatening letters. The synagogue board hastened to comply (215). No wonder such confrontations created a gulf between African American and Jewish activists.

A second and even greater shock for American Jews was the Six-Day War in 1967. Ever since its creation in 1948, Israel had been at war against neighboring Arab countries that refused to accept its existence. This permanent state of conflict, punctuated by regular border incidents, had heated up into open fighting in 1956. In May 1967 Egypt and Syria tried to coordinate attacks on Israel, hoping to overwhelm and destroy it once and for all, but Israeli intelligence was well prepared. Israeli forces struck first, destroyed the Egyptian air force before it even got off the ground, and won a series of overwhelming victories. Within a week Israel expanded its territorial boundaries south and east while battering its enemies into submission.

How did these events affect America? The American Jewish community had played a central role in Israel's survival right from the start. Heavy lobbying had assured a consistently favorable view of Israel from Capitol Hill and the White House. Contributions from American Jews had assured the new state's solvency, and a steady flow of Jewish migrants from America had brought some highly educated, prosperous, and idealistic settlers. Even so, before 1967 a surprising number of American Jews were lukewarm about Israel and many had decided against migrating there—where they would enjoy a much lower standard of living and chronic insecurity. Highly secularized and satisfied with their position in America, they felt little temptation to identify closely with Israel; in fact, a few—from Reform communities on the left to ultra-Orthodox Hasidim on the right—had actually opposed its creation. Reform opposition was based on the fear that Israel would create a suspicion of dual loyalty and undermine their achievement of assimilation. Hasidic opposition was based on the belief that the Jewish people ought not to be gathered in Israel until the coming of the Messiah. A Hasidic rabbi in Chaim Potok's novel *The Chosen* (set in the mid-1940s) flies into a rage when he hears from his son, the narrator, about plans for an Israeli state, because he regards David Ben Gurion and the other secularized Jews who are to lead it as contaminated "goyish" Jews:

> "Who are these people?" he shouted in Yiddish, and the words went through me like knives. "Apikorsim! Goyim! Ben Gurion and his goyim will build Eretz Yisroel? They will build for us a Jewish land? They will bring Torah into this land? Goyishkeit they will bring into the land, not Torah! . . . The land of Abraham, Isaac and Jacob should be built by Jewish goyim, by contaminated men? . . . Never! Not while I live!"[15]

Once Israel had been established and had fought for its survival, however, such opposition had diminished. But now the Six-Day War showed all American

Jews how vulnerable Israel could be. What if it had been taken unawares? The result could have been a massacre, a renewal of the Holocaust, this time at Arab hands.

In the war's aftermath, American contributions to Israel soared and continued to climb into the 1970s, as did American Jews' migration to Israel. The war also encouraged a generation of young, often secular, Jews to meditate on their origins. In the following years many moved to an explicitly religious position and away from a heavy involvement in left-wing politics and the counterculture. The Jewish chaplain at Yale University, Richard J. Israel, wrote in 1967 that the war had prompted a strong shift among Jewish students toward greater religious observance and away from the "oppressive religious conventionalism of their parents."[16]

The assertion of "black power" in 1965 and 1966 was beginning to squeeze Jewish activists out of the civil rights movement, but at the same time, paradoxically, it offered them the model for a new way of thinking about themselves as Jews. In the late 1960s and early 1970s African Americans, then Hispanics, then Native Americans, each declared pride in their distinctiveness and their determination to reject the ideal of bland assimilation into the American mainstream. Michael Novak's *The Rise of the Unmeltable Ethnics* (1972) made the same claim on behalf of Poles, Italians, Greeks, and Slavs (using as a badge of honor the acronym "PIGS," which angry demonstrators often chanted at police and nationalistic blue-collar workers in the Vietnam era). By then the American-ness of all these groups was not in doubt; they belonged to the third and fourth generations beyond immigration, so that asserting distinctive elements of their ethnicity (rather than trying to get away from it, as from a prison) had come to seem attractive.

Some Jews drew the same conclusion and began to express their Judaism in public (by the wearing of yarmulkes, for example, or by more open celebration of the Jewish holidays) rather than confining it to home and synagogue. The Modern Orthodox movement, which developed rapidly in the 1970s, exemplified this trend. "They were demonstrating," says historian Samuel Heilman, "that the new Orthodoxy was no longer simply the result of having been born into and remaining locked in an insular ethnic community of the observant but was now a matter of informed religious choice."[17] Michael Berger (b. 1962) grew up in this atmosphere. He recalled that his Brooklyn neighborhood became increasingly Orthodox in the late 1960s and 1970s, and that his generation, unlike that of his parents, *was* systematically educated about the Holocaust and the vital importance of Israel.

My growing up, 1973–1980, was the period of transition in talking about the Holocaust. Elie Wiesel became a really prominent figure — we read *Night, Gates of the Forest, Beyond the Wall,* and so on. There were only a limited number of films on the Holocaust in those days . . . gory . . . the bodies being bulldozed, and so on, the emaciated bodies. It was important for us to understand the history of it. In eleventh grade we did a whole yearlong course on it. It was the same culture as Yad Vashem in Israel—the national shrine memorial to the victims. But it was also the time of a new cultural incarnation which is called the "March of the Living." Students go to Poland, spend Holocaust Commemoration Day in Auschwitz, and then a week later go to Israel. It's didactic: "Here's what happens in diaspora, and this is why we need sanctuary." It wasn't meant to condemn Christians so much as Nazis, but Christians clearly fell into the category either of bystanders or perpetrators. There weren't too many protectors whose names we knew.[18]

For people raised in this environment, the taboo on intermarriage was powerful, but a Modern Orthodox upbringing was not meant to marginalize its beneficiaries—they could still undertake careers in the American business and professional mainstream. Berger himself, after two years' intensive yeshiva study in Israel, went to Princeton and from there to a secular academic career, while many of his contemporaries prospered in business, law, and medicine.

By the 1970s, accordingly, an unexpected development had taken place. Some Jews continued to follow the minimalist trajectory of the preceding years, "disappearing" into the general American population, while another group, smaller but self-conscious and articulate, created a more visible, structured, and distinctive model of Judaism. The middle group, those who had been attracted to Conservative Judaism in the earlier decades of the twentieth century, began to decline in numbers and vitality—a problem Samuel Heilman referred to as "the shrinking middle": "In the polarizing atmosphere of the sixties and seventies, a world where one either took Jewish life and Judaism more seriously and actively engaged it, or where one let meaningless rituals and old traditions fade, the middle level was hard to justify or sustain."[19]

The dilemma of whether to remain true to a distinct Jewish identity or to move into the American mainstream was explored by Chaim Potok (1929–2002), whose novel *The Chosen* I mentioned above. The question of divided loyalties as they affected an artistic temperament—such as Potok's own—was brilliantly illuminated in another of his novels, *My Name Is Asher Lev* (1972). Its protagonist and narrator, Asher Lev, is the only child of a Hasidic couple in Brooklyn, followers of the "Ladover Rebbe." The boy's father travels for the rebbe, attempting to secure the release of Hasidic Jews from the Soviet Union (the setting is the 1950s), to keep Judaism alive behind the Iron Curtain, and to revive Hasidic life in Western Europe. Asher himself is gifted as an artist but finds no acknowledgment of, or interest in, his gift in the tight-knit community. His father describes the boy's endless drawing as mere "foolishness" and urges him on to more important studies, particularly the Torah and the Talmud. Asher will not be deterred, and eventually the rebbe asks an established American artist, himself a nonpracticing Jew, to train the boy.

This teacher, Jacob Kahn, points out to Asher that in becoming one of the geniuses of Western art, he is entering a tradition for which two of the most important art forms are the nude and the crucifixion. Asher is at first aghast at the idea of breaking strong community taboos, and his mother warns him against copying paintings of Jesus that he finds in the museum: "Do you know how much Jewish blood has been spilled because of him, Asher? How could you spend your precious time doing this?"[20] Despite such warnings from home, he cannot resist the challenge that these artistic forms present. The novel comes to a climax when he exhibits two paintings, titled *Brooklyn Crucifixion I* and *Brooklyn Crucifixion II*. Critics acclaim them as masterpieces, assuring Lev a place in the great tradition as well as great commercial success, but his parents, both of whom are depicted in the paintings, are horrified beyond words. Asher never meant to hurt them and has remained an observant Jew, but the logic of his artistic development has placed him permanently outside the boundaries of the community. Throughout he has had to struggle against his father's fear that his art is not a gift from God but something demonic. He reflects at the end that this might in fact be true:

> I looked at my right hand, the hand with which I painted. There was power in that hand. Power to create and destroy. Power to bring pleasure and pain. Power to amuse and horrify. There was in that hand the demonic and the divine at one and the same time. The demonic and the divine were two aspects of the same force. (367)

Potok was presenting here, in a highly charged form, the dilemma common to many creative Jews who found their American prospects to be in tension with their religious tradition.

Vietnam, Part II

The Vietnam War created sharp divisions in almost every area of American life during the 1960s, and religion was no exception. At first the broad anti-Communist consensus of the last twenty years seemed to justify intervention in aid of the South, to prevent the spread of Communism. We saw earlier how a Catholic doctor, Tom Dooley, had sanctified the cause of Vietnam for many American Christians in the mid-fifties. Fundamentalist anti-Communists like Carl McIntire and Billy James Hargis were equally enthusiastic about the war in the sixties. McIntire described the war as "a righteous and holy cause."[21] In "How to Win the War" (1967) Hargis wrote: "The war in Vietnam is being fought against an aggressor, fought for freedom, fought for the security and protection of the United States" (163). Fundamentalists were annoyed with President Johnson not because he had committed American troops to the war but because he seemed not to want a decisive victory. "It is inconceivable that we would send so many thousands of our fine young men to Vietnam and not put them in a position to win, or even let them win," wrote one indignant fundamentalist, Wallace Malone, in *Christian Crusade* (165n). Conservative evangelicals like Billy Graham and Carl Henry also supported the war but more as a necessary evil, a patriotic duty in the long, hard struggle against Communism. Some liberal Protestants, including the distinguished Princeton ethicist Paul Ramsay, took the same view at first. America's premier Catholic leader, Cardinal Spellman of New York, who was also military vicar of the U.S. armed forces, went off to Vietnam to spend Christmas with the troops at the end of 1965 and to reassure them that they were fighting in a righteous cause.

As in former wars, chaplains from the major denominations accompanied the troops, trying to maintain their morale and comfort the wounded. Chaplain Lieutenant Philip Kahal of the United Church of Christ was in Da Nang in 1965 and was horrified by the sight of some of the first heavy American casualties of the war. "To see young lads with torn, broken, and bleeding bodies is not an experience from which one can derive any satisfaction" he wrote,

> yet it is an experience and duty which cannot be shirked, for there is a vital and necessary work to be performed at the Marine Field Hospital. Not only does the chaplain serve God in the service of men, but his own life is enriched by the experience, for he too is forced to search for the strength and courage of God deep within the recesses of his own life.[22]

The corruption and tyranny of the South Vietnamese regime, its unpopularity, and its own soldiers' reluctance to fight, quite apart from the sheer remoteness of Vietnam, led growing numbers of Americans to doubt their government's policy. So did the fact that in this guerrilla war, civilian bystanders were as often the victims of gunfire and bombing as were enemy soldiers.

As the American presence escalated, religious opposition to the war spread. Pope Paul VI visited New York in October 1965 and spoke in favor of world peace, first at the United Nations and then in a huge candlelit rally at Yankee Stadium. He did not go into specifics about Vietnam, but observers noted that his speech, delivered in the diocese of Cardinal Spellman, was an implicit rebuke. A month later Roger LaPorte set fire to himself on the steps of the United Nations in New York and died to protest America's role in the war. That December, a group of Catholic, Protestant, and Jewish antiwar activists united to form a new organization, Clergy Concerned About Vietnam (soon amended to Clergy and Laity Concerned About Vietnam, hence its acronym, CALCAV). Taking advantage of the era's climate of ecumenism, Richard Neuhaus, a radical Lutheran pastor, Rabbi Abraham Heschel, and Daniel Berrigan, a Jesuit priest, agreed that their organization could work across the lines of old religious

divisions for the common purpose of peace in Vietnam. The group's first organizational meeting was held at the home of John Bennett, a distinguished
mainline Protestant leader and president of Union Theological Seminary in
New York. Right from the beginning, it had friends in high places. The
National Council of Churches gave CALCAV office space, and William
Sloane Coffin, chaplain of Yale University, organized a telephone campaign to
create chapters throughout the country. Donations poured in from liberal Jews
and Christians, and within a year the group was holding large-scale demonstrations.

In January 1967 CALCAV held a two-day event in Washington, D.C., with
an antiwar liturgy at the New York Avenue Presbyterian Church and a series of
workshops. Coffin, already a veteran of the civil rights movement and one of the
liberal Protestant celebrities of the era, recalled that outside the church,

> with his small army of pickets, was the ever-faithful Carl McIntyre [*sic*], the pro-
> war fundamentalist preacher. I'm sorry to say this but I'm afraid it's true: only
> among religious folk could a man of such limited intellect raise so large a follow-
> ing and so much money. McIntyre is for those who want an answer to life with-
> out daring to search for it themselves. Not surprisingly, the pickets, when I ques-
> tioned them, had only the vaguest idea of who we were and what we repre-
> sented.[23]

Coffin was among the members of a CALCAV delegation that visited Secretary
of Defense Robert McNamara just after this event; the climax of the meeting
was a passionate antiwar harangue from Rabbi Heschel. CALCAV members
and leaders often let their emotions run away with them and demonized their
opponents. For example, Daniel Berrigan declared in one speech that "to wage
war in modern times as it is being waged in Vietnam is forbidden. . . . In such
a war, man stands outside the blessing of God. He stands, in fact, under His
curse."[24]

CALCAV was delighted to feature Martin Luther King Jr. as principal
speaker at one of its next major antiwar rallies, on April 4, 1967, in New York's
Riverside Church. King had become convinced that the war was wrong by
1966 but had held back from public comment lest he harm the desegregation
work of the Southern Christian Leadership Conference (SCLC). Since he was
a Nobel Peace Prize winner and one of the three or four most famous people
in America, his public statements carried enormous moral weight. He told a
packed congregation of three thousand that night that the American government had become "the greatest purveyor of violence in the world today."[25] To
anxious colleagues King said that he was determined to live up to the demands
of his Christian conscience, even if prudence dictated keeping quiet about the
war. Clergy Concerned welcomed him as cochairman of their organization.
Much of the press, at that point still guardedly in favor of the American role in

Vietnam, was critical and said King had undermined his important civil rights work by involving himself with a controversy he did not properly understand. Another veteran of the civil rights movement, the Reverend James Bevel, joined King in the antiwar movement, and when asked whether it was a left-wing movement, answered: "We're going to get left of Karl Marx and left of Lenin. We're going to get way out there, up on that cross with Jesus."[26]

Religious protests against the war intensified. Jesuit Daniel Berrigan worked not only with Clergy Concerned but also as a student chaplain at Cornell University, trying to stir up the university community on behalf of the pacifist cause. To be a real Christian, he insisted, was to be an uncompromising pacifist, just as Jesus had been. Therefore it was obscene that so many Catholics should be following their bishops in support of the war as though such a posture were perfectly normal. It was as if Jesus himself had been taken as a prisoner of war. His brother Philip Berrigan, a priest in the Josephite order, gave antiwar protest a theatrical turn without precedent in American Catholic history. With three friends in November 1967, dressed in his clerical black, he entered the offices of the Baltimore Selective Service draft board, the place where the drafting of young men into military service was organized, and threw pints of his own and his friends' blood over the files. The act symbolized the bloodletting of the war itself and represented a superb antiwar photo opportunity for the group of journalists Berrigan had alerted earlier.

Berrigan and the "Baltimore Four" were arrested peacefully at the scene of their action. The following May, before going on trial for the first incident, they attacked another draft board, this time joined by Philip's brother Daniel, who had meanwhile scandalized prowar Americans by taking part in a peace-mission visit to the enemy capital of Hanoi. Their target this time was the draft office in the Baltimore suburb of Catonsville, Maryland. They seized more files from surprised secretaries, took them to the parking lot (where press photographers again stood ready) and set fire to them with homemade napalm, a facsimile of the sticky burning agent dropped by U.S. aircraft in Vietnam, which caused horrible burn wounds on those it touched.

Daniel Berrigan, writing his memoirs twenty years later, continued to see the Catonsville raid as a turning point in his own life, in the course of the war, and as an event of religious significance:

> For the remainder of our lives, the fires would burn and burn, in hearts and minds, in draft boards, in prisons and courts. A new fire, new as Pentecost, flared up in eyes deadened and hopeless, the noble powers of soul given over to the "powers of the upper air." . . . We had removed an abomination from the Earth.[27]

Arrested as before, the demonstrators were tried and convicted.

Rather than surrender himself for imprisonment when his appeals were exhausted, Daniel Berrigan disappeared into the thriving antiwar "underground" that protected deserters and draft resisters. Sympathizers passed him along for more than a year, beyond the reach of police and FBI, but while underground he struggled with feelings of loneliness and despair. "I remember only an ache, a void, as though of a breath indrawn and held, until it hurt. God was absence. Not nothing, but Someone who had withdrawn for the duration" (250). A book he began writing while in hiding, *Dark Night of the Resistance*, was based on a great Catholic spiritual classic, Saint John of the Cross's *Dark Night of the Soul*, which explored this terrifying sense of spiritual emptiness. One of his most daring acts was his appearance at a suburban Philadelphia church pastored by sympathetic clergy to give an unannounced sermon one Sunday morning. The event was filmed and became the basis of a documentary film, *Holy Outlaw*. Even more remarkable, a play he had written, *The Trial of the Catonsville Nine*, opened in Los Angeles while he was still in hiding, to enthusiastic reviews, and became one of the most widely distributed literary works of the antiwar movement. Berrigan kept ahead of the law for most of a year, granted interviews to TV and journalists, and became the religious poster boy of the antiwar movement before finally being caught and arrested on Block Island, Rhode Island, in August 1970 and sent to prison in Danbury. He and his brother Philip, in and out of prison, would continue to dedicate themselves to the cause of Christian pacifism and to play a prominent role, ten years later, in the antinuclear movement.

Patriotic fundamentalists remained loyal to the war and looked on antiwar protests as aids to the Communist foe. "Let no one take wartime as an excuse to be a rebel against government and thus a rebel against God," wrote one, John Rice.[28] They were not surprised to see that liberal Protestants and Catholics—in their view, unbiblical people—were prominent in the antiwar movement. "The sad spectacle," wrote another, "is that in some cases church leaders—clergymen—who have long since departed from the authority of the Bible as God's Word, are leading in this rebellion against the laws of our land" (173n). They held their own Washington demonstration, Churchmen for Victory, in January 1967.

Army morale in Vietnam suffered from the soldiers' knowledge that the war was becoming unpopular at home, from the difficulty of identifying and destroying the enemy, and from the fact many of them were reluctant conscripts, draftees rather than volunteers. Chaplains had to counsel men who received rejection letters from girlfriends at home and letters critical of the work they were doing in this unpopular war. To make matters worse, American forces suffered high casualties. One murderous spot was the isolated hill outpost of Khe Sanh, near the Laotian border, besieged and bombarded by the enemy in early 1968 until three-quarters of the Americans there had been killed or wounded. "Living, as everyone was, under the threat of violent death from the skies," says a chaplains' history of the siege, "the level of spiritual discussion and activity was deep. Many marines sought Baptism and the Eucharist."²⁹ A Catholic chaplain, Robert Brett, who had been saying mass ten times a day in dugouts and field hospitals, was killed there, in a mortar round explosion on February 22, 1968. When the siege was finally lifted, one of his colleagues could still draw spiritual consolation from the episode:

> Can one ever forget the . . . pale bodies and ashen faces of the 26th Marines after the Khe Sanh siege? But there are those who begin to look at the meaning of life or death in a new light. "I've discovered that God wants the man here as well as hereafter," is the way one young sergeant expressed it. It's ironic that so many leave "churchy" America with her temples and cathedrals, only to make Life's Greatest Discovery beside a paddie or on a bridge or in a bunker half a world away. But there's joy in heaven whenever and wherever it happens. And many find God in Vietnam. (164)

His colleague Michael O'Neil, a Catholic chaplain, witnessed the men's morale dropping as the possibility of working toward a decisive victory in the war ebbed away. "When a 'no-win' policy is formulated, how in the name of God can you expect individual men of the Armed Forces to feel great or even have decent morale?" (165).

Opinion back in America continued to turn against the war, especially after the Tet (New Year) Offensive of 1968. What else could churches do to show their abhorrence for the war? William Sloane Coffin organized church services at which draft-age men turned in their draft cards to him, a rabbi, and a Catholic priest, for which he was arrested and put on trial for conspiracy. He and the other CALCAV leaders recognized that they were in a position to win over influential parts of the American middle-class, church- and synagogue-goers who would never have responded to the call of the radical left but who took notice when ministers, in clerical black or shirt and tie, denounced the war in moderate and reasonable terms.

One of their strategies was to encourage churches to turn themselves into sanctuaries for draft resisters and deserters. They recalled that in the Middle Ages European churches had been safe havens against violence and arrest (though the fate of Thomas à Becket suggested that church sanctuary was never entirely reliable). The Unitarian-Universalists of Natick-Wellesley, Massachu-setts, were among the congregations that voted to make their church a sanctu-ary in June 1968. Richard Scott, an army deserter, arrived in the company of members of the New England Resistance, an antiwar group. A gaggle of press reporters interviewed and photographed him, but then federal agents arrested him and took him away, ignoring his plea for sanctuary.

Church members, local citizens, then crowds of children and curiosity seek-ers gathered at the church over the next few days while sympathizers sent food, clothes, and blankets, in preparation for the next arrival. Resistance workers gave seminars in nonviolence and a "teach-in" about the war itself. Then a group of angry (prowar) local youths broke into the church, looking for trouble.

> The youths grabbed a Resistance member and started slapping his face back and forth, finally shoving him against a wall. One of the youths spat at a Committee member, tore off the Resistance button he had been wearing, and threw him against the wall. The committee member asked the boy whether he had ever been in the service or in a war, the answer to which was "No, have you?" When the Committee member responded that he had indeed served in World War II, the youth asked, "Well, what are a bunch of square guys like you doing with this bunch of — homos?" "We're trying to keep boys like you from getting killed," the Committee member answered. At this point one of the Resistance members arrived with some eggs which were thrown around the room. . . . One boy was thrown down the stairs, but was caught before being injured. Upon hearing the approach of the police the youths ran for their car.[30]

A second deserter arrived, but the sanctuary, which minister Robert Gardiner had expected to be decorous and symbolic, continued to deteriorate into a shambles of spitting, brawling, obscenity, and recriminations. "The situation was extremely volatile and dangerous," he wrote. "A number of fist fights broke out, and rocks were thrown at and into the building. The police arrived (22 squad cars full) just in time to avert what might have otherwise been a major riot" (529). A government health inspector warned that the ever-growing group of people milling about inside the church buildings day and night were breaking the law because the church did not have a license to run a boardinghouse. After nineteen days the Resistance, the ministry, and the police collaborated in clearing the church and bringing the event to an end. The minister resigned in dismay, concluding that the event, designed to arouse local consciousness against the war, had actually turned people *against* the demonstrators and in favor of the police.

The war ground on inexorably through the late 1960s, and although after Tet a majority of Americans were looking for what would today be called an "exit strategy," most were still eager to leave with at least the feeling that an independent South Vietnam was secure. Ray Abrams, whose classic indictment of churchmen at war, *Preachers Present Arms*, had first appeared in 1929, issued a fortieth-anniversary edition in 1969, including an epilogue on the current Vietnam situation. He noted the surprising number of churches and leading religious personalities who now were against the war, but added:

> Our society is not geared to accept those who take the teachings of Jesus this seriously; at least, they would not be trusted in public office. Hence, unless the religious community can change the current feeling about war objectors, or bring Jesus down to earth as a human being (not just a Savior and the Son of God in the clouds), there is no hope that pacifism or resistance to war has any chance of being anything in the social milieu but playing the role of a gadfly to the government.[31]

Collectively, despite moments of discouragement, the religious opposition was turning more and more respectable mainstream figures against the war. Several of the Methodist ministers of Evanston, Illinois, were willing to accommodate in their churches several hundred members of the Weather Underground, a faction of Students for a Democratic Society that advocated violent resistance against the war and gathered in Chicago in October 1969 to undertake their armed "days of rage."

If tempers were souring in America, how much worse was the situation in Vietnam itself? Draftees smoked marijuana and injected themselves with heroin, both of which were easily obtainable. Overzealous officers were killed, "fragged," by their own men. A supposedly desegregated military found itself constantly dealing with racial bigotry in the ranks. Efforts to help the local Vietnamese population broke down because of suspicion that they were aiding the guerrillas. Captain John Zoller, a United Methodist chaplain, wrote a gloomy assessment of the situation among his Marines in October 1969, especially of the horrifying fragging incidents.

> My own thinking about this . . . suggests the dearth of any real inner sense of right and wrong within the perpetrator, a lack of moral development, a moral cripple. Second, prolonged exposure to participation in a combat environment where violence and killing are commonplace will condition some individuals to consider violence as normal and acceptable. Third, weapons are readily available and knowledge of their use is widespread. Fourth, a frustrating, perhaps threatening situation, such as an order to return to the bush, confronts an individual. A simple, direct solution may seem to be the elimination of the source of frustration or threat by "blowing him away." Add to this the possibility of racial overtones and/or the deterioration of inner inhibitions through the use of drugs or alcohol. Also, the exterior restraints and controls of family and society are largely non-existent in this combat setting. Judgement becomes warped, moral values distorted and the individual may react with animal-like fury and directness and, sometimes, cunning.[32]

The number of draft resisters and deserters continued to rise as the war dragged on, many of them claiming that although they did not belong to the historic "peace churches," they were opposed to this particular war. By 1970 nearly everyone agreed that the Americans would have to leave Vietnam — President Nixon won the 1968 election partly on his promise of a secret plan to end the war.

Catholic Challenges to Church Discipline

Meanwhile, in 1968, America's Catholics broke into open argument over an issue that was, to them, as divisive as Vietnam: birth control. In that year Pope Paul VI issued an encyclical letter, *Humanae Vitae*, upholding his church's teaching about contraceptives. The letter stated that every act of sexual intercourse (an activity properly confined to married couples) must be open to the transmission of life. In other words, contraceptives were forbidden. His letter upheld a position that the Catholic Church had held throughout the twentieth century, but in the circumstances of 1968, Catholics, so soon after Vatican II had given them a taste for experimentation, were less willing than before to accept it. To make matters worse, the editors of a reform-oriented Catholic newspaper, the *National Catholic Reporter*, had learned that a majority of the members of a pontifical commission reviewing the issue in Rome had written a report that advocated changing the rules.

During the second half of the twentieth century, a series of technological and biological advances had enabled scientific researchers to create highly effective methods of birth control. For the first time it was possible for families to plan when they would like to have children, without having to travel the heroic high road of sexual abstinence. Catholic families from the 1930s through the mid-1960s had shunned artificial contraception, and in the mid-twentieth century the big Catholic family was a familiar sight. It could even be a point of competition, as Kathleen Joyce (b. 1964) recalled of her own family:

> My father had a brother who had eight children, my mother's sister had nine, and it always bothered her that while she had eight her sister had nine, especially since two of the nine were twins, so that the number of pregnancies was the same. . . . I think that for my parents it was a show of affluence — they could afford to have eight children and didn't want to be shown up by their relatives.[33]

Ironically, a Catholic doctor, John Rock, had played a major role in developing "the Pill," one of the most effective new methods of contraception. He had hoped that the Catholic Church would permit its members to use the Pill since, unlike condoms and diaphragms, it did not actually obstruct passage of sperm to egg in intercourse.

One of the intellectual fads of the late 1960s was the idea of world overpopulation. Alarmist books like Paul Ehrlich's *The Population Bomb* (1968) declared that unless drastic population control programs were instituted at once, the world would soon enter a period of crisis in which millions would die of starvation. In his view, and the view of many less-hectic observers, the big Catholic family, hallmark of the preceding decades, must go, to be replaced by small families that, at most, duplicated the current population and prevented further expansion.

To a generation of well-educated Catholics the argument was appealing. For several decades now, some married Catholics had struggled to come to terms with their own excessive fertility. In the early 1960s a spate of Catholic books with titles like *The Experience of Marriage* had overcome the old taboo against discussing sex. In the pages of such books, couples explained their attempts to restrict their families' size without violating Church teaching. Back in 1952

Pope Pius XII had, illogically, expressed his approval for the rhythm method of contraception, in which an attentive couple, taking regular temperature tests and mucus readings to locate the infertile period of the woman's menstrual cycle, could hope that their carefully timed acts of intercourse would not always result in a pregnancy. Pius had regarded the method as acceptable because there was no actual physical obstacle or pharmaceutical effect inhibiting the possibility of conception. To deliberately separate sex from procreation, he had said, was to turn your back on God's gift of life. "Vatican Roulette" was the laity's nickname for this method, which, ironically, required a great deal of technical gear and some expertise, and did not always work. One bitter joke of the era went like this: Q. "What do you call people who use the rhythm method?" A. "Parents." Paul VI, in issuing *Humanae Vitae*, permitted the rhythm method, as before, but otherwise upheld the traditional teaching.

Another phenomenon of the 1960s was the sexual revolution. For the first time in American history the idea gained currency that sex outside of marriage—equally for women and for men—was not necessarily disgraceful. Popular versions of Freudian psychology had for three or four decades been spreading the idea that "repression" was potentially dangerous. An affluent, expressive, relatively carefree generation of youths, the maturing baby boomers, were experimenting in this as in many other areas of their lives. Good Catholics shied away from arguing in favor of pre- or extramarital sex, but they could not help being aware that discussion of sex and sexually explicit films, books, and advertising were suddenly all around them, and that sexual censorship was declining fast (with a push from Earl Warren's permissive Supreme Court).

What made *Humanae Vitae* so galling to many American Catholics was the fact that it seemed to contradict the spirit of Vatican II. Was not the church now "the People of God" rather than an autocracy? Was it not supposed to draw on its members' experience and expertise? If so, who could possibly have less experience in sexual matters than a celibate clergy, and who could have more expertise than married Catholics, involved with these sexual and family issues in their everyday lives? Among the members of the commission whose advice Paul VI had decided to reject was John Noonan, an American legal scholar who had recently published *Contraception*, a huge book on the history of Catholic teaching about sex and contraception. It showed, among other things, that the Church's teaching had gone through many different stages, reacting to medical and technical changes through the centuries, and that the present teaching was not a once-and-for-all position, as some Vatican conservatives asserted. When the pope discarded his commission's majority report and rejected the idea of a development of the doctrine, he seemed to many Americans to be acting in the bad old pre-conciliar, autocratic way.

Publication of the encyclical set off a storm of protests. Charles Curran, professor of theology at the Catholic University of America, in Washington, D.C., summoned a press conference the following day, at which he denied that the letter was binding on Catholics. It showed, he said, an "inadequate awareness of the natural law" and an "overemphasis on the biological aspects of conjugal relations as ethically normative." Worse, it showed "an almost total disregard for the dignity of millions of human beings brought into the world without the slightest possibility of being fed and educated decently."[34] In the following weeks six hundred other priests, professors, and theologians joined Curran by signing a protest he had drafted against the encyclical.

Sociologists who subsequently studied the issue discovered that most American Catholics before 1968 had tried hard to uphold the old teaching, fully expecting that their difficult days were coming to an end. When the pope told them to carry on as before, however, they demurred and began using contraceptives anyway, acting on what they had *hoped* the letter would say rather than on what it did say. By the late 1970s Catholics (with the exception of a small traditionalist minority) used contraceptives with the same frequency as all other American population groups, their once distinctive behavior in this area having disappeared rapidly and completely.

The late 1960s were perhaps especially stressful for Catholics because the rapid transformation of their church after Vatican II coincided with profound changes in American society. Nuns and priests had, for centuries, been educated in obedience, self-denial, and self-discipline. Now, in the spirit of Vatican II, they began to challenge the rules. Some orders of nuns decided to abandon their traditional habit. It was impractical for them in their teaching and nursing work, they said, and it drew an artificial barrier between them and people in the outside world. Many of them wanted to branch out into other forms of work. A few had marched at Selma for civil rights and wanted to carry on working for civil rights and against urban poverty. Others took up the psychology of self-fulfillment in place of the old disciplines of self-denial and began to question their vocations. Large numbers decided to leave the convent or the priesthood, and by the early 1970s every Catholic had a story about the ex-priest who had just married an ex-nun.

Catholic colleges went through upheavals during the same years. Since the late nineteenth century the Catholic Church had built more than a hundred colleges and universities, but not according to any logical pattern. Rival orders of priests and sisters often sited several in the same area so that they competed for the limited pool of Catholic students and staggered along from one financial crisis to the next. Bankruptcies and closings were common. In 1955 the Catholic historian John Tracy Ellis had caused a furor by complaining that the intellectual standards prevailing in nearly all of these schools were low. The education they offered, he asserted, was defensive, censorious, distracted by sports, and hamstrung by Vatican censorship. Don't blame the Protestants, he added—it is our own fault.

Ellis's article set off a debate whose temperature rose sharply after Vatican II. Lay professors at St. John's University in New York went on strike in 1965, saying that they were denied academic freedom and decent salaries by the Vincentians, the order that ran the university, and lacked the structured tenure system of America's secular colleges and universities. Educators throughout America sympathized with them and helped ensure the success of their strike. Administrators at America's other Catholic colleges took note. Father Theodore Hesburgh, the president of Notre Dame, for example, arranged for his, the most famous American Catholic university, to be taken out of the control of the Holy Cross Fathers and placed in the hands of lay trustees. Many other schools followed suit after a conference to discuss the process, chaired by Hesburgh, at Land o' Lakes, Wisconsin, in 1967.

African American Religion After King

Martin Luther King Jr. had developed a successful strategy for social change in the late 1950s and early 1960s, and had done as much as anyone to promote important civil rights legislation in 1964 and 1965. The Nobel Peace Prize (1964) had made him world-famous. By the mid-1960s, however, younger African Americans were becoming dissatisfied by the pace of change and were unwilling to be the victims of racist violence without fighting back, as King's nonviolent philosophy required. The magnetic rhetoric of Malcolm X, Stokely Carmichael's call for Black Power, the rise of the Black Panthers, and a spate of inner-city riots after 1964, all presented challenges to King's vision of a peaceful, Christian road to integration and equality.

In 1966 a group of black clergymen gathered in Harlem to form the National Committee of Negro Churchmen (subsequently the National Conference of Black Churchmen, or NCBC). Influenced by the young civil rights workers' more confrontational rhetoric, they wrote the "Black Power Statement" and published it as a full-page advertisement in the *New York Times* on July 31, 1966. It implicitly criticized King's nonviolent approach by saying that among powerless blacks, the movement's dependence on the transforming power of Christian love was unhealthy. It was "a distorted form of love, which in the absence of justice becomes chaotic self-surrender." Only when black Americans had power commensurate with that of whites could appeals to Christian love lead to justice.

> From the point of view of the Christian faith, there is nothing necessarily wrong with concern for power. At the heart of the Protestant Reformation is the belief that ultimate power belongs to God alone and that men become most inhuman when concentrations of power lead to the conviction—overt or covert—that any nation, race, or organization can rival God in this regard.[35]

To oppose the whites' monopoly of power—which gave them godlike delusions—simply with love was "a blind and dangerous illusion," and it contributed to the black churches' tendency to give up on this world altogether, looking for the Kingdom of God in heaven rather than on earth. Against that view the NCBC aimed to show that "Jesus Christ reigns in the 'here' and 'now' as well as in the future he brings in upon us" (27).

This declaration was soon followed by some black writers' attempts to reconceptualize Jesus and to find him a new role; he must no longer be the endlessly forgiving and self-sacrificing figure portrayed by King. Some writers placed a new emphasis on Jesus as outcast and as warrior for justice. In 1967, for example, Vincent Harding argued that black Americans had for too long been pacified and intimidated by the idea that Christ was a genteel white man. Now they were beginning to realize that this was a false image, foisted on them by whites, and was quite unlike "the Jesus who shared all he had, even his life, with the poor . . . the Suffering Servant of God."[36] Albert Cleage, minister of the Shrine of the Black Madonna in Detroit, went further in *The Black Messiah* (1968), an anthology of sermons: "For nearly 500 years," he wrote, "the illusion that Jesus was white dominated the world only because white Europeans dominated the world. Now with the emergence of the nationalist movements of the world's colored majority, the historical truth is finally beginning to emerge—that Jesus was the non-white leader of a non-white people, struggling for national liberation against the rule of a white nation, Rome. . . . Jesus was a revolutionary black leader, a Zealot, seeking to lead a Black Nation to freedom."[37]

These militant Christians were as dismayed as their nonviolent brethren by the assassination of Martin Luther King Jr. on April 4, 1968, in Memphis, but it did not lead them to a change of direction. King's death triggered riots in Washington and other inner cities, which intensified their view that black access to power and wealth was indispensable to a proper settlement of the nation's racial crisis. In 1969 the Interreligious Foundation for Community Organization (IFCO) commissioned James Forman (b. 1928), a former Student Nonviolent Coordinating Committee (SNCC) organizer, to write a report on the black community and the responsibilities of white churches. The resulting document, "The Black Manifesto," was strongly worded and could not get the unanimous endorsement even of its own sponsoring agency. Liberally sprinkled with revolutionary Marxist rhetoric, it demanded "reparations" of half a billion dollars ("fifteen dollars per nigger"), to be paid by white churches and synagogues to the black community in compensation for centuries of oppression in which they had participated, and it threatened chaos if they didn't pay up.[38]

The public debut of "The Black Manifesto" created a storm, not only because of its contents but also because of Forman's theatrical method of presenting it. On Sunday morning, May 4, 1969, he interrupted a service in New

York's Riverside Church (the church where King had spoken for CALCAV against the Vietnam War two years earlier) just after the opening hymn. A striking figure with a big Afro haircut, Forman read out his list of threats and demands from the chancel step. "Our fight is against racism, capitalism, and imperialism," he declared, "and we are dedicated to building a socialist society inside the U.S. where the total means of production and distribution are in the hands of the state, and that must be led by black people, by revolutionary blacks who are concerned about the total humanity of this world. . . . We work the chief industries in this country and we could cripple the economy while the brothers fought guerrilla warfare in the streets" (82–83). The Riverside churchgoers, bewildered at this unexpected interruption and at the revolutionary intensity of the charges made against them, never resumed the service. Forman also posted his demands on the front door of the Lutheran Church in America's New York headquarters nearby (a deliberate evocation of Martin Luther himself posting his ninety-five theses at Wittenberg) and delivered them at a board meeting of the ecumenical National Council of Churches. The NCC, just across the street from Riverside Church, responded with sympathetic noises but also called the police to forestall a rumored occupation of their building.

Reactions were mixed. New York's Catholic archdiocese rejected the manifesto, as did the Synagogue Council of America. IFCO president Marc Tanenbaum distanced himself from it in a personal statement, deploring its "revolutionary ideology and racist rhetoric" and the disruption of a church service. Bayard Rustin, who had organized the 1963 March on Washington, said, "The idea of reparations is ridiculous," and *Christian Century*, the mainstream Protestant journal, cautioned that "disruption of worship is a mean game which any number can play, including segregationists and fascists."[39] On the other hand, the Jesuit journal *America* admitted that the manifesto had "by its very violence and unreasonableness" forced Jesuits to pay attention to the glaring economic disparities between blacks and whites, and speculated that "it may force not only the churches but the whole nation to come up with a better strategy for remedying that national injustice."[40]

Issues like the nurturing of black pride, overcoming poverty, and gaining power were by then more important to many black churchmen than was the bloodless goal of integration. These themes, along with a blistering denunciation of white Christians' racism, marked the work of a strong new theological voice, that of James Cone (b. 1938), whose polemical debut, *Black Theology and Black Power* (1968) caused a sensation. A dazzling phrasemaker, Cone knew how to shock black and white readers with unexpected images.

> Where does Christ lead his people? Where indeed if not in the ghetto. He meets the blacks where they are and becomes one of them. We see him there with his black face and big black hands lounging on a streetcorner. "Oh but surely Christ

is above race." But society is not raceless, any more than when God became a despised Jew. . . . For whites to find him with big lips and kinky hair is as offensive as it was for the Pharisees to find him partying with tax-collectors. But whether whites want to hear it or not, Christ is black, baby, with all of the features which are so detestable to white society.[41]

Cone was equally cutting in his condemnation of the white churches for their racism and the traditional black churches for their otherworldliness and political passivity. Gayraud Wilmore, an original member of the NCBC, wrote that after reading this book by the thirty-year-old Cone in one sitting and rejoicing in its power and cogency, he "whooped for joy." Cone quickly became the "resident theologian" of the NCBC because "no-one had severed the Gordian knot which tied us to the old theology more cleanly than he."[42]

Cone, showing a marked preference for Malcolm X over Martin Luther King Jr. and impressed by the appeal to Black Power, followed up with *A Black Theology of Liberation* (1970). Theology, he declared, was not a meditation on the nature of God, or an explanation of how faith remained possible in a secular and rationalist world, as whites seemed to think. Instead, it was an instrument of liberation, which grew out of the experience of oppressed people. Its vantage point was decidedly partial, not universal. Cone did not pretend that it was written for everyone; by older criteria it did not look like theological writing at all. "What we need is the divine love as expressed in black power, which is the power of blacks to destroy their oppressors, here and now, by any means at their disposal. . . . Unless God is participating in this holy activity, we must reject God's love."[43] He repeated that even God was subordinate to the cause of black liberation: "Black theology refuses to accept a God who is not identified totally with the goals of the black community. If God is not for us and against white people, then he is a murderer, and we had better kill him."[44]

Ironically, despite a venomous hostility to white Christianity (at least rhetorically), he accepted a faculty position at Union Theological Seminary in New York, the most coveted post a liberal Protestant academic could achieve. This was in fact the audience he was speaking to, even though he wrote of it with nothing but contempt. He was lionized by white theologians and graduate students far more than by black community leaders, and he wrote his denunciations of whites in books crammed with references to Karl Barth, Paul Tillich, and Dietrich Bonhoeffer, the (white) German theological greats of the early and mid-twentieth century. Disdaining white critics' attacks, he was willing to submit to the chiding of other black theologians such as Deotis Roberts, Major Jones, and Preston Williams, who urged on him a deeper appreciation of historic American black culture, and the role the black church had played in preserving it through the hard years of slavery and segregation. His subsequent work in the 1970s and 1980s, books that maintained his preeminence among black liberation theologians, investigated and interpreted this cultural legacy with far more sympathy than he had shown in his harsh early jibes at the black church.

James Cone was a powerful intellectual but had no popular following comparable to King's or Malcolm X's, and was not—like each of them—a charismatic preacher. White Christianity increasingly suffered from a split between the intellectuals and the spellbinding preachers; Reinhold Niebuhr was perhaps the last person who could excel in both roles. The same was now true among African Americans as well. After King's death the intellectual task fell to Cone and other writers, while the preaching and politics went to Jesse Jackson, King's legatee, and Louis Farrakhan, Elijah Muhammad's successor in the Nation of Islam.

Chapter 6

ALTERNATIVE RELIGIOUS WORLDS: 1967–1982

Space Travel

Jews and Christians had for centuries believed that heaven was literally above them, up there in the sky. Even when advances in astronomy had made the idea of "heaven above" more problematical, there was still a hint of the supernatural about the possibility of flying through the air. The idea of visitors from other worlds arriving in spaceships, or of men journeying out to the stars in their own ships, became staples of science fiction after 1900. Immense strides in aviation technology had put mankind on the brink of space travel by the middle of the century, and the "space race" heated up in the 1950s. Meanwhile, the first "flying saucer" was sighted in 1947 by aviator Kenneth Arnold in the state of Washington. From then on, "UFOlogists" suspected that the federal government knew more than it was letting on about visitors from outer space. Some believed that the government had captured aliens, or at least their remains, for secret study, at "Area 51" near Roswell, New Mexico.

There is nothing necessarily religious about believing that alien spaceships are visiting Earth. Throughout the Cold War, however, years when many suspicious objects were flying through the air, a stream of witnesses came forward with the claim that they had been visited by aliens from spaceships and received some form of higher wisdom from them. Usually the aliens brought a message of cosmic peace and urged the humans to turn away from their war-like ways. As historian J. Gordon Melton observes, UFOlogists, who wanted scientific rather than metaphysical explanations, scorned these early con-tactees, especially those who remembered under hypnosis that they had been abducted by the aliens for scientific tests or even sexual impregnation. But "to the contactee fellowship," says Melton, "there was no question about the objects' identity and purpose; they were flying saucers piloted here by 'Space Brothers' to warn us of the consequences of our evil ways. What the contactees created was a space age version of an occult visionary religion, with roots in theosophy, the I AM movement, and other supernatural belief systems in which wise extraterrestrials played a role."[1]

One distinctive characteristic of the mid- and late twentieth century in America was that religious experiments nearly always attracted academic onlookers. Anthropologists, sociologists, historians, and psychologists wel-comed the chance to study religious groups: the more eccentric the group, the more avid their interest. The social sciences, though many of them had origi-nated among clergy, religious social workers, and missionaries, had developed austere, secular, and this-worldly methods by 1945. In most cases they rejected out of hand the possibility that God really was acting in history or that super-intelligent space aliens really were sending occult messages through "chan-nels" or landing to talk with the humans.

Leon Festinger, for example, a University of Minnesota social psychologist, studied the question of how religious groups react when their prophecies fail. American history provided plenty of examples of confident prophecies that were falsified when the great day came, but records usually lacked the kind of details he coveted. In the early 1950s, however, he was delighted to discover a cult/UFO group awaiting the imminent end of the world, as disclosed to them by space aliens. Festinger and his colleagues at once arranged to infiltrate the group as participant observers so that they could watch members' reactions when (as they assumed) the prophecy did not come true. Their experiences formed the basis for *When Prophecy Fails* (1956).

The central figure in Festinger's account was "Mrs. Marian Keech," who had dabbled in theosophy, dianetics, and I AM (an occult movement founded in Chicago in the 1930s), become interested in flying saucers, and then started to receive messages by automatic writing from her dead father. Other beings on the "astral plane" also got in touch with her, including one named Sananda, who revealed himself as the spirit of the former Earth-man Jesus. He warned her that the war-torn world would soon be destroyed in a flood but that those who had gained enlightenment could expect to be taken away from the disas-ter in a flying saucer to visit planets on a higher plane. Another group member, Bertha, periodically channeled "the Creator" and spoke with his voice to con-firm these prophecies. Faith in these messages sustained the group in the face of mockery from neighbors and the press. They prepared themselves for their voyage by giving up alcohol and coffee and, for a time, living on a diet of nothing but nuts. They also removed all metal items from their clothes so as to be ready for the flight, ripping off buttons and tearing out zippers that might impede the smooth working of the flying saucer.

When a long December vigil in the Minnesota snow did not lead to the promised saucer landing on any of the four days they had been told to expect it, the members reacted in two different ways. People who had joined only recently, had had doubts about the whole thing, or were living apart from the main group, drifted away disillusioned. But those most committed to the group and physically present every day, who had given up their jobs or severed relationships for its sake, intensified their commitment. They were still being prepared and tested, they reasoned, and they interpreted every "disconfirmation" as evidence of the eventual confirmation of their faith. One member told a participant observer: "I've had to go a long way. I've given up just about everything. I've cut every tie: I've burned every bridge. I've turned my back on the world. I can't afford to doubt. I have to believe."[2] This core of committed believers even received a message explaining why the saucers had not come: The faith of the group was so radiant that God had decided not to send the flood after all. "Not since the beginning of time upon this Earth has there been such a force of Good and light as now floods this room and that which has been loosed within this room now floods the entire Earth" (169). The group made this consoling message the basis of a press release.

Festinger concluded by pointing out the power of the social group for maintaining faith, an insight now widely shared by historians and sociologists of religion. As he said, "The Lake City people, who had social support, were able to accept the rationalization [for the flying saucer's failure to appear], thus reducing the dissonance somewhat, and they regained confidence in their original beliefs. The presence of supporting co-believers would seem to be an indispensable requirement for recovery from such extreme disconfirmation" (229).

Festinger's insightful and entertaining book was a source for Alison Lurie's even more entertaining novel *Invisible Friends* (1967). It is told from the point of view of an assistant professor of sociology, Roger Zimmern, helping his colleague, Professor Tom McMann, gather data on the Truth Seekers, a cult group that seeks wisdom from aliens. "I liked the outer-space aspect of it," says Roger, "the idea that science now dominated the culture to the point where people were sitting round a table conjuring up ectoplasmic ray guns and little green men instead of ladies in white veils."[3] The fictional sociologists, like Festinger's real academic group, join the cult while covertly gathering data about the members' ideas and actions. The principal alien, Ro of Varna, whose ideas are relayed to the others by a delectable nineteen-year-old beauty, Verena Roberts, requires them to submit to various forms of self-abasement, such as burning all clothes made from natural fibers and wearing only synthetics. Itching and irritable in his all-nylon outfit, and careful to stay in the background lest he change the group's dynamics by his presence, Zimmern feels his status diminishing. On campus he is a man of some importance, but here he is only "stupid Roger." The experiment goes wrong, the cult members become convinced that Professor McMann is the embodiment of the alien leader Ro, and he comes to believe it too, ending up in the state mental hospital. Lurie's book nicely skewers the social scientists as well as the cultists. They are, she shows, self-justifying busybodies who can become Truth Seekers only by being perpetual liars and eventually self-deceivers too.

UFOlogy and flying saucer cults generated a vigorous controversial literature throughout the following years. Visitation from hyper-intelligent spacemen remained a Hollywood staple too, sometimes in sinister garb (*Invasion of the Body Snatchers*), sometimes sentimental (*E.T.*), sometimes humorous (*Men in Black*), and often didactically P.C. (*Close Encounters of the Third Kind*). Blockbusters like the *Star Wars* series (beginning in 1977) were drenched in Christian imagery and apocalyptic battles between good and evil. Anyone who, like me, grew up hearing the words "the Lord be with you" every Sunday in church, felt a shock of recognition at hearing Obi-Wan Kenobi's blessing of Luke Skywalker: "May the Force be with you"!

Meanwhile, a real space program carried the first humans out to the "final frontier" and raised religious questions of its own. The novelist Norman Mailer, covering the first Moon landing (1969) in a brilliantly eccentric series of articles for *Life* magazine (later published in book form), speculated that the WASP (white Anglo-Saxon Protestant) "had emerged from human history in order to take us to the stars. How else to account for that strong, severe, Christian, missionary, hell-raising, hypocritical, ideologically simple, patriotic, stingy, greedy, God-fearing, nature-despoiling, sense-destroying, logic-making, technology-deploying, brave human machine of a WASP. It was a thought with which to begin to look at astronauts."[4] Witnessing the Saturn V rocket that would take Apollo 11 to the Moon, floodlit at night and awaiting takeoff, Mailer experienced a Catholic image: "In the distance she glowed for all the world like some white stone Madonna in the mountains, welcoming footsore travelers at dusk" (59). He speculated on the "psychology of machines" and the fact that rockets' behavior was so unpredictable that they seemed almost to need propitiatory sacrifices, like ancient deities, in return for their good behavior. "Rocket engineers could have been forgiven for daubing the blood of a virgin goat on the orifice of the firing chamber" (168).

The space program generated religious excitement among its participants too. Frank Borman, commander of Apollo 8, read aloud from his Bible on Christmas Eve 1968 while orbiting the Moon. He and his crew were the first people ever to look back and see Earth from that vantage point, which added poignancy to his words:

> In the beginning God created the heaven and the Earth. And the Earth was without form, and void; and darkness was upon the face of the deep. And the spirit of God moved upon the face of the waters. And God said, let there be light; and there was light.[5]

Buzz Aldrin, one of the two astronauts to land with Apollo 11 on the Moon the following summer (both white men, both Protestants), smuggled onto the mission a consecrated communion wafer and a little communion wine along with his Bible. He wanted to announce to the world that he was taking communion on the Moon—it was a Sunday. NASA told him not to because Madalyn Murray O'Hair, "America's most famous atheist," had sued them over Borman's Bible reading, claiming that these religious observances in a government-financed program violated the First Amendment. Aldrin had to content himself with a moment of silence and then a request for peace and for Earth's people "to recognize that we are all one mankind under God." On the way back, however, he did read aloud over the radio a passage from Psalm 8: "When I consider the heavens, the work of thy fingers, the moon and the stars, which thou hast ordained; what is man, that thou art mindful of him?"[6]

The American religious press reacted to the Moon landing in various ways. The journal that Reinhold Niebuhr had founded, *Christianity and Crisis*, regarded it as a wonderful ritual event of transcendent significance:

> We might compare the Apollo mission with the medieval cathedral which also aspired to reach beyond Earth, both physically (in its soaring gothic arches) and theologically. The cathedral was in its time a technological achievement in stone and glass, but as in the case of Apollo ritual needs dictated its priority.[7]

The evangelical *Christianity Today* was also impressed by the achievement but disappointed that the astronauts had not given explicit thanks to God for their safe arrival. Of Armstrong's first words—"That's one small step for man, one giant leap for mankind"—it wrote that the sentence had "humanistic overtones" that would be "debated in ecclesiastical and theological circles for many years."[8] When President Nixon, welcoming the astronauts back on board the U.S.S. *Hornet*, gushed, "This is the greatest week since the beginning of the world, the Creation." CT's editors demurred: "We want to emphasize that the greatest week in history was the week in which Jesus Christ went to Jerusalem to die for the sins of the world and to be raised again as victor over sin and death and hell."[9] The liberal *Christian Century* was even less moved by the whole affair, arguing that the space program was ruinously expensive and had drained away money that ought to have been used to solve pressing social problems here on Earth.

Several of the men who orbited Earth and walked on the Moon, men who had been chosen for their military experience, cool nerves, and unromantic hardheadedness, were spiritually transformed by the experience and devoted much of their later lives to religious quests. Two of America's twelve Moon-walkers, James Irwin and Charles Duke, became Christian ministers after leaving NASA. Irwin was a biblical fundamentalist and founder of the High Flight Foundation, an organization that financed expeditions to Turkey's Mount Ararat to search for the remains of Noah's Ark, which, according to the Book of Genesis, had come to rest there. The seventeen-thousand-foot mountain, covered in ice and snow, was a tough physical challenge, and Irwin, in a serious fall, was nearly killed on his first ascent. Undeterred, he returned five more times, even after a severe heart attack, telling well-wishers, "I just feel like the Lord has given me a lot of information and opportunity to look for the ark."[10] Another expedition was accompanied by a clairvoyant who told Irwin he had met Noah in a vision and that the Ark's logbook had been preserved in leaves and oil. Irwin died in 1991 with the Ark's whereabouts still unresolved.

Another astronaut, Edgar Mitchell, began to explore the mysterious links between scientific and religious knowledge after a personal epiphany on his way back from the Moon. In his autobiography, Mitchell wrote:

> What I experienced during that three-day trip home was nothing short of an overwhelming sense of universal *connectedness*. I actually felt what has been described as an ecstasy of unity. It occurred to me that the molecules of my body and the molecules of the spacecraft itself were manufactured long ago in the furnace of one of the ancient stars that burned in the heavens about me. And there was the sense that our presence as space travelers, and the existence of the universe itself, was not accidental but that there was an intelligent process at work. I perceived the universe as in some way conscious.[11]

He created the Institute of Noetic Sciences in 1972 and searched for connections between the great mystical traditions (Lao-tzu, Buddha, Jesus, and Muhammad) and quantum mechanics, the theory of relativity, and subatomic physics, convinced that the habitual dualism in Western thought (mind against matter) should be reconceived as *dyadic*, with apparent opposites being reconceptualized as different aspects of the same phenomenon. Resisting the idea that he was the guru of a new faith (while admitting that he often had to fend off disciples), Mitchell was willing to entertain evidence from psychics, telekineticists (like Uri Geller, who could bend forks without touching them), and UFOlogists. In the 1970s and 1980s, meanwhile, space travel became almost routine—until the jarring shock of the *Challenger* disaster in 1987, when a shuttle carrying the first schoolteacher into space exploded a few minutes after takeoff and killed everyone on board.

Feminism and Ministry

Many social and religious movements born in the 1960s disappeared within a few years. Others were here to stay, and among them, none had a greater impact than feminism. Women had long been the majority of American church members, but in many denominations they had been closed out of the leadership, or else they played subordinate roles to the minister's, such as taking care of religious education and music programs. The women's liberation movement of the late 1960s and early 1970s challenged women's inferior position in society and led to controversy in the churches. Should women be ordained as ministers, priests, and rabbis? Just because Adam, Abraham, Moses, the prophets, Jesus, and his disciples were all men, did that mean their successors had to be? What about God "himself"? Did God have a gender, and if not, how should people think about him, or her? Everyone agreed, at least in theory, that God was not just a big old man in the sky with flowing gray hair and a beard, but the early days of the new feminism prompted much more self-consciousness about how to think of the Almighty.

Advocates of male-only leadership found plenty of support in Scripture. The highly patriarchal world-view of the Hebrew Bible was sustained through much of the New Testament. Paul's letters were full of strictures against women:

> During instruction a woman should be quiet and respectful. I give no permission for a woman to teach or to have authority over a man. A woman ought to be quiet, because Adam was formed first and Eve afterwards, and it was not Adam who was led astray but the woman who was led astray and fell into sin. Nevertheless she will be saved by child-bearing provided she lives a sensible life and is constant in faith and love and holiness. (1 Timothy 2:11–12)

Despite such discouraging Scriptures, some Christian groups already accepted the ordination of women, at least in principle. America's first female Congregationalist minister, Antoinette Brown, had been ordained back in 1853, permitted to take this unusual step because her male contemporaries recognized her as a "prophetic" figure chosen by God. Earlier still, women who believed that God had singled them out had led Christian groups in the colonial era (Anne Hutchinson) and in the Revolutionary era (Shaker founder Mother Ann Lee). Women had played a major role in developing Protestant overseas missions in the nineteenth century and, as ministers' wives, had often done vital community work too. Inspired by their American founder, Evangeline Booth, Salvation Army women had been leaders from the beginning. In the early twentieth century, likewise, the Pentecostal churches had recognized the possibility of charismatic female leadership and at least one minister in this tradition, Aimee Semple McPherson (1890–1944), had become a household name in the 1920s for her antics at the Foursquare Gospel Church near the

Hollywood movie studios. (Her reputation for up-to-the-minute evangelism had taken a beating in 1926 when she tried to cover up an amorous tryst with an employee by claiming to have been kidnapped and to have made a miraculous escape from the Mexican desert.) Female leadership was, however, still the exception rather than the rule in midcentury America, especially in the mainstream denominations. The Presbyterian Church accepted the principle of women's ordination in 1955, and the first minister, Margaret Towner, was ordained the next year, but only a handful of women followed her example.

The women's movement transformed the situation. Late-sixties feminists argued against the common assumption that women's primary role should be as wives and mothers; they deplored the unequal gender structure of society. The civil rights movement had established that discriminating against people by accident of birth violated American principles of democracy and equality. The principle was written into the sixties' civil rights laws, which prohibited discrimination for reasons of sex as well as those of race. Churches were exempted from the legislation, but it created a legal environment in which the *presumption* was against, rather than in favor of, denying candidates for ministry because of their gender.

Broader social forces as well as feminist arguments nudged the churches toward accepting female ministers. First, the growth of the population since World War II, especially in the suburbs, had led to a rapid rise in the number of churches and synagogues that needed ministers and rabbis—they were in short supply, and women could potentially make up the numbers. Second, more women were highly educated than at any point in the nation's history, some of them in subjects suitable to ministry, such as religion, pastoral counseling, and Hebrew. Third, America honored the idea of professionalism: that possession of the right credentials and the ability to do a job well were more important than the appearance or background of the person doing it.

Churches in the liberal Protestant tradition, along with Reform Judaism, were disposed to change. For every conservative biblical quotation invoked against women's participation, they could find offsetting pro-women passages, not the least of them Paul's declaration in Galatians 3:38: "There is no such thing as Jew or Greek, slave and freeman, male and female, for you are all one in Christ Jesus." American Lutheran women gained the right of ordination in 1970, Reform Jews in 1972, and Episcopalians in 1976.

Even when the disposition to change was present, however, the reality of making the change could be stressful, for there was rarely a unanimous vote for reform. Episcopalian women had been admitted to their denomination's divinity schools since the late 1950s; ten years later an articulate group of them, led by Suzanne Hiatt, was lobbying hard for ordination. Traditionalists among the Episcopal bishops, who still believed in a male-only priesthood, dragged their feet and were able to use procedural tactics to vote down changes at their annual convention, despite growing approval for the idea of women priests among junior clergy and laity. Eventually, in 1974, three retired Episcopal bishops who believed in the need for change, Edward Welles, Daniel Corrigan, and Robert Dewitt, precipitated a crisis by ordaining eleven women at a euphoric service in Philadelphia in front of a congregation of nearly two thousand. An angry male priest in attendance, who disapproved, shook his fist and shouted: "You will never again be called bishops, for today you violate the law of God that says *his* priests shall be called *Father*."[12]

The Episcopal House of Bishops gathered in emergency session in Chicago to condemn the trio and to declare the ordinations sacramentally invalid. Theological experts in favor of the women countered by upholding the validity of the ordinations; theological experts against them rebutted that the maleness of Christ was a vital element of the characteristics necessary in his priesthood. Finally in 1976 the General Convention, meeting in Minneapolis, accepted the fait accompli, and the jubilant women found their ordinations validated. One of them, Peggy Boysmer, returned from the convention to Little Rock, Arkansas, to find a welcoming committee at the airport:

> A huge crowd of people were there with iced champagne and a huge sign, ALLELUIA, that went all across the front of the terminal. The whole lobby was just packed with people; Episcopalians cheering, and Roman Catholics too. Someone told us the Roman Catholic nuns had been praying for us all through the convention. Everybody in the airplane was going, "Wow, look at that! What's happening?" And we said: "The Episcopal Church just voted to ordain women." (190)

The defeated bishops were able to legislate that they would not be forced to violate their consciences by ordaining women if they had opposed it earlier. Presiding bishop John Allin remarked grudgingly: "Women can no more be priests than they can become husbands and fathers."[13] On the other side Norene Carter, a supporter of women priests, wrote that comments like Allin's revealed "the core of sexual panic and misogyny" that lay behind the opponents' remarks (369). A handful of Episcopal congregations felt so strongly about the issue that they split off from the denomination and created a small organization of their own, the Anglican Church of North America.

The ordination of women in Reform Jewry was less traumatic, though it, too, came after considerable delay. Earlier in the twentieth century, scattered women, often the widows of rabbis, had led congregations by standing in for their late husbands. One, Paula Ackerman, of Meridian, Mississippi, had served in that capacity between 1951 and 1954. She was widely admired and provided a valuable precedent for other Reform Jews when a long period of debate finally ended. Sally Priesand, scheduled to become the first Reform rabbi ordained in

America, studied at Hebrew Union College in Cincinnati and became the center of press interest in the two or three years before completing her seminary course. Often interviewed by TV and newspaper reporters, and invited to give speeches to Jewish groups in the Cincinnati area, she realized her importance as a pioneer, was tactful, dressed modestly, avoided controversial statements, spoke guardedly in favor of feminism but not of "women's lib," and cooperated with the seminary's leaders. In consequence she won overwhelming support from her teachers and fellow students and proceeded on schedule to ordination in 1972.

Two years later the first Reconstructionist female rabbi, Sandy Eisenberg Sasso, was ordained, after which both of these more liberal branches of Judaism began to ordain other women. The Rabbinical Assembly voted against ordaining women as Conservative rabbis in 1973 but changed its mind a decade later. As the historian Ellen Umansky pointed out, these women rabbis had had to overcome not only institutional barriers in taking up leadership roles but also the assumptions with which they had grown up.

> Psychologically it became difficult for women to think of themselves as leaders. Socially, legally, and religiously they were inferior to men. They were always dependent, first on their fathers and later on their husbands. In marriage, divorce, matters of inheritance and within the courts, women's rights were severely limited. Family responsibilities exempted them from many of the 613 commandments that Jews were obligated to fulfil, including the obligation to study and pray three times a day.[14]

Episcopalian woman echoed this view, agreeing that they too had had to overcome internal as well as external obstacles before their leadership could be effective.

Women who did become rabbis or ministers often reconceptualized the leadership role, sometimes arguing that the traditional female nurturing virtues were particularly appropriate to their new status. One observer of female Episcopal priests noted how their presence transformed the significance of the Eucharist (Holy Communion, sharing of bread and wine). Suddenly, "motifs of feeding and nurturing are more prominent, the sacrament is perceived as more 'embodied,' women experience greater connectedness and self-affirmation . . . and women's blood and suffering are correlated with Christ's."[15] Another noted that women "are characterized as more compassionate, more sensitive, more caring. . . . In fact, those kinds of qualities are described as not only appropriate but as constituting a 'special gift' that women can bring."[16] Women clergy were often enthusiastic, too, about changing the sexist language common in most denominations' prayers, and about trying to avoid always using "he" as the pronoun for God.

Women in almost every denomination could be found in support of reform, but churches that placed more emphasis on tradition were slower to change and sometimes refused outright. The Catholic Church, for example, insisted on the equality of men and women but regarded it as an equality based on complementary differences rather than an interchangeable equality. *Gaudium et Spes* (1965), one of the Vatican II documents, declared that "every type of discrimination, whether social or cultural, whether based on sex, race, color, social condition, language, or religion, is to be overcome and eradicated as contrary to God's intent. . . . Such is the case of a woman who is denied the right and freedom to choose a husband, to embrace a state of life, or to acquire an education or cultural benefits equal to those recognized for men."[17] So far so good, but that did *not* mean women could be priests. Why not? Because, in the view of the Vatican authorities, it could not be a coincidence that Jesus himself, the incarnation of God, and all twelve of his apostles, had been men, nor that almost the whole weight of Catholic tradition, two thousand years of it, opposed women's ordination. Catholicism, moreover, offered women the option of becoming nuns, the time-honored female vocation, and that had long been a vocation within which opportunities for leadership (albeit of a segregated all-female community) had been possible.

American nuns themselves were experiencing sweeping changes in the late 1960s and early 1970s, partly as a result of the era's general cultural upheaval and partly because Vatican II (which opened with no women present but finally admitted twenty-two as "auditrices," none of whom was allowed to speak or vote) had led to a profound reconsideration of the religious life. Nuns who had earlier learned to suppress their emotions and discipline their will were now being encouraged to explore their inner lives and express themselves. Large numbers expressed themselves by leaving the religious life altogether so that they could marry and accept career opportunities that were opening up to them in the wider society. Those who stayed took a more independent line in deciding on their social role and work; many threw off the restrictive traditional dress, gained higher degrees, and dedicated themselves to issues of social justice as well as education, nursing, and charity. One group organized the Leadership Conference of Women Religious, endorsed the feminist outlook, and declared, in two resolutions of 1974, that it believed "all ministries in the Church [should] be open to women and men as the Spirit calls them" and that "women [should] have active participation in all decision-making bodies in the Church."[18] Its pamphlet *Nuns and the Women's Movement*, issued the following year, added that in its treatment of women "the mainstream of tradition within the Catholic Church . . . is one of the most oppressive of all religious superstructures" (376).

Conferences, an outpouring of scholarship in justification of women's ordination, and petitioning of bishops and the Vatican followed. The Vatican responded with its *Declaration on the Question of the Admission of Women to the Ministerial Priesthood* in 1977, denying the proposed reform and repeating that there was an intrinsic link between Christ, maleness, and priesthood. Before Vatican II, a statement of this kind would have brought debate to an end, but the Catholic laity were no longer the docile working-class immigrant people they had been in the early twentieth century. Now mainly well educated and middle class, inspired by the spirit of Vatican II, American Catholic laity regarded themselves as fully entitled to rebut the Vatican's arguments and did so. Letters of protest and objection poured in from aspiring women priests but also from male theologians and religious teachers, including the whole faculty of the Jesuit seminary at Berkeley. "Never," wrote the theologian Rosemary Ruether, "has an official Vatican declaration been so roundly rejected and even ridiculed by both theological authorities and the general populace" (381). She noted that a Gallup poll on the question led to a sharp *increase* in support for women's ordination among Catholics after the papal statement. The Vatican had still not reversed itself by the end of the century, even though male vocations to the priesthood were diminishing. Canon law permitted women to work as "parish administrators," positions in which they took on nearly all the duties of priests except administration of the actual sacraments, but the Vatican reiterated its ban on female priests in 1994 and the following year underlined the point by declaring that this was an *infallible* Catholic teaching.

Feminist Theology

Growing numbers of women, whether or not they belonged to churches that ordained women, began writing on questions of theology and spirituality. They became familiar figures, first as divinity school students and then as faculty. An almost entirely new undertaking, feminist theology, developed in the 1970s and rapidly became a staple part of the theology curriculum. It began as a branch of liberation theology. The term "liberation theology" was coined in 1968 by Gustavo Gutierrez, a Latin American theologian who wanted the Catholic Church in Central and South America to separate itself from the area's ruling elite and to voice a "preferential option for the poor." It took as its starting point the experiences of the suffering poor, and drew not only on biblical themes but also on Marxist social theory. Before long, African American theologians (such as James Cone, whom we met in chapter 5 above) had borrowed some of its principal ideas, especially the existential starting point, and developed a liberation theology based on their own marginal situation. In the 1970s women followed suit.

Feminist theology took various forms, but central in nearly every case was the task of displacing androcentrism (male-centeredness) and finding the deeper truths in Christianity that centuries of patriarchy (male domination) and misogyny (woman-hating) had obscured. Rosemary Ruether, one of the most distinguished first-generation feminist theologians, wrote that they had to dislodge the tenacious assumption that the *male* case in humanity was normative (which made the female either a deviation from the norm or a mere afterthought).

> This exclusion of women and its justifications result in a systematic distortion of all the symbols of Christian theology by patriarchal bias. The imagery and under-standing of God, Christ, human nature, sin, salvation, church, and ministry were all shaped by a male-centered, misogynist worldview that subordinated women and rendered them non-normative and invisible. . . . For example, God is not only imaged almost exclusively in male terms but also in terms of patriarchal power roles, such as patriarchal father, king, warrior, and lord.[19]

Only after exposing these old biases and distortions could women begin using Christian, or Judeo-Christian, materials to create a non-sexist theology.

Ruether *did* believe that a non-sexist Christian theology was possible. She located a prophetic Old Testament tradition of denouncing patriarchal power, and Jesus' continuation of this mission when he cleansed the temple in Jerusalem. But could feminists still look to Jesus, a man, as their liberator? Yes, she said, because the role of feminists was not to make women dominant *over* men but rather to achieve full humanity for all. "Jesus proclaims an iconoclas-tic reversal of the system of religious status: The last shall be first and the first last." This was not an attempt to invert the social order but rather to create "a new reality in which hierarchy and dominance are overcome as principles of social relations."[20]

One element of feminist theological method relied on the reinterpretation of familiar biblical stories using the "hermeneutics of suspicion." In other words, readers were encouraged to approach the old stories—especially those involving women—cautiously, ridding themselves of conventional interpreta-tions and exposing the social and political assumptions that lay behind them. Phyllis Trible, another pioneer feminist theologian, became an accomplished practitioner of this method. In her view the Bible teaches liberation, patriarchy is not liberating, therefore patriarchy is incidental rather than central in the Bible and can be overcome through more rigorous analysis. On one occasion, which has become a classic of feminist analysis, Trible took the Adam and Eve story, broke it down to the Hebrew words from which it was constructed, and reconfigured it to look completely different from the traditional tale of how female inferiority can be traced right back to the Creation. As she tells it, God did not create "Adam," a man in the recognizable sense, but rather a creature out of the earth (she justifies this translation of the relevant Hebrew words). Only when God *divided* this creature in making the first woman did the first man come into being.

> In the very act of distinguishing female from male, the earth creature describes her as "bone of my bone and flesh of my flesh." These words speak unity, solidar-

ity, mutuality, and equality. Accordingly in this poem the man does not depict himself as either prior to or superior to the woman. His sexual identity depends on her even as hers depends upon him.[21]

The emphasis, she argued, is not on Eve's inferiority to Adam, or her status as an afterthought, but rather on mutuality in partnership, each dependent on the other, and this is the lesson we should learn.

Trible kept a sharp eye on Bible translators, aware that they sometimes wrote their own assumptions into the text rather than giving an accurate rendering of ambiguous or unexpected Hebrew gender language. She drew readers' attention to passages in the Psalms where female rather than male imagery is used in describing God, and she interpreted Deuteronomy 32:18 to mean that God is like a woman in labor, giving birth. "We need to accent the striking portrayal of God as a woman in labor pains, for the Hebrew verb has exclusively this meaning. . . . Over the centuries, however, translators and commentators have ignored such female imagery, with disastrous results for God, man and woman. To reclaim the image of God female is to become aware of the male idolatry that has long infested faith."[22]

The early feminist theologians, mostly white, middle-class, and affluent, were aware that although they had been marginalized in a male-dominated society this marginalization was far milder than that of the desperately impoverished peasants of Latin America or the hard-pressed black communities of decaying American inner cities. They acknowledged, too, that using their own experiences as the starting point for theology imposed on them the obligation to grant the same right to other women, the poor, black, Asian, and Hispanic. Before long, accordingly, further variants of feminist theology emerged. Black women theologians used the term "womanist" to differentiate themselves from both white women and black men, while Latin American women selected "mujerist" for their own variant. In each case, personal experience, particularly the experience of oppression by the other gender or other races, provided the foundation on which the theology was constructed. The editors of a feminist theology anthology, *Weaving the Visions* (1989), noted that to their contributors, drawn from a wide variety of oppressed female groups, the patriarchal Judeo-Christian tradition "is not simply sexist but racist, imperialist, ethnocentric, and heterosexist as well."[23]

Womanist theology—the term was invented by the novelist Alice Walker—took the experience of African American slavery and segregation as its starting point, and found analogies in biblical slave stories. Whereas white feminists had been interested in Sarah, Abraham's wife, for example, the womanist theologian Delores Williams singled out Abraham's slave-concubine Hagar, the mother of Ishmael, for sympathetic attention. Hagar suffered slavery, rape, sexual exploitation, violence, class oppression (when Sarah forced Abraham to evict her), and homelessness (like many African American women, Williams noted), but she was also resourceful, defiant in the face of adversity, and won a promise of God's blessing and protection. She therefore becomes a scriptural role model for black women, who need not share the traditional Judeo-Christian attention to Abraham, Sarah, and Isaac. Alice Walker's novel *The Color Purple* (1982) itself became a womanist classic, especially a conversation between Shug and Celie, two central characters, over the question of how to think about God. Celie at first says that God is "big and old and tall and graybearded and white" and that he "wear white robes and go barefooted." Shug retorts, "That's the one in the white folks' white Bible." She urges her friend to stop thinking of God as "he" and to get rid of this vision—it is in effect an internalized image of her racial oppression. Instead she should recognize that "God is inside you and inside everybody else. . . . Don't look like nothing. It ain't something you can look at apart from everything else. . . . I believe God is everything . . . that feeling of being part of everything, not separate at all." She adds that God does not condemn even her sexual feelings. "God love all them feelings. That's some of the best stuff God did. And when you know God loves 'em you enjoys 'em a lot more."[24] The book takes its title from Shug's conclusion that the color purple itself is an extraordinary manifestation and signal of God's presence in the world, one that can liberate her and Celie from the oppressive images they have hitherto held about God.

While one group of feminist theologians looked for ways to reconfigure the Judeo-Christian tradition in ways empowering to women, another group concluded that its whole structure was so distorted in favor of men that it could never provide women with a sense of liberation or fulfillment. None was more colorful or controversial than Mary Daly. In 1968, after gaining a theology doctorate in Germany, she published *The Church and the Second Sex*, skewering the inferior position of women in the Catholic Church and what seemed to her to be a centuries-long history of misogyny. In 1971 she became the first woman to preach at Harvard Divinity School, an occasion that she devoted to arguing that women should create an "exodus community" as they abandoned the Christian churches. By then she had concluded that Christianity was inherently repressive of women, an idea that she elaborated in *Beyond God the Father* (1973). It ended with the brilliantly insightful and playful idea that the sacramental work of Christian priests was a spiritualized version of ordinary women's work, which further denigrated an already subordinate female sex:

> Graciously they [the priests] lifted from women the onerous power of childbirth, christening it "baptism." Thus they brought the lowly material function of birth, incompetently and even grudgingly performed by females, to a higher and more spiritual level. Recognizing the ineptitude of females in performing even the

humble "feminine" tasks assigned to them by the Divine Plan, [they] raised these functions to the supernatural level in which they alone had competence. Feeding was elevated to become Holy Communion. Washing achieved dignity in Baptism and Penance. Strengthening became known as Confirmation, and the function of consolation, which the unstable nature of females caused them to perform so inadequately, was raised to a spiritual level and called Extreme Unction. . . . [They] made it a rule that their members should wear skirts. . . . They thus became revered models of spiritual transsexualism.[25]

As Daly told it, all the power inherent in women had been stolen by men ("these anointed male mothers who naturally are called Fathers" [196]) and sanctified by the leaders of the Judeo-Christian religions, from whose grip women must rescue themselves. It was, she thought, a hopeless task to look for the feminine within the Christian God because the tradition had made it impossibly difficult for women even to know themselves.

Daly was not only a writer but also a professor, in the theology department of a Jesuit-run university, Boston College. The college tried to deny her tenure in 1969 because what she was teaching was nothing like the conventional version of Catholic theology. She threatened to sue, claiming that her record of publication and good teaching, examined side by side with the achievements of comparable men, entitled her to tenure. A petition signed by 2,500 (male) students supported Daly, and the college relented, granting her tenure later that year. In 1972, by which time BC had become coeducational, Daly decided not to allow men into her courses on feminism (though she did agree to teach them in a separate group). The college grudgingly accepted this arrangement. Flareups between Daly and the Jesuits persisted through the next twenty-seven years, however, until her retirement (again amid threats of litigation) in 1999.

In her later books, *Gyn-Ecology* and *Pure Lust*, Daly, always a marvelously imaginative writer, as well as one who made a fine art of biting sarcasm, took wordplay further than any contemporary. Obsessive and brilliant with puns, she could twist language to invert its original meanings, keeping the reader perpetually off guard. She loved to take old insults against women (crones, witches, hags) and turn them into badges of honor. Look at the back cover of *Gyn-Ecology* (1978), for example, whose blurb, "Mary Daly is a Revolting Hag," is meant to convey high praise. It was time, she declared in this book, for "letting out the bunnies, the bitches, the beavers, the squirrels, the chicks, the pussycats, the cows, the nags, the foxy ladies, the old bats and biddies."[26] They must find their own sense of history ("Crone-ology"), their own sense of time (getting away from "Old Father Time"), and their own divinity. Was not the Holy Trinity of Father, Son, and Holy Ghost, she asked, "the perfect all-male marriage, the ideal all-male family, the best boys' club?" It was an invention "excluding all female mythic presence, denying female reality in the cosmos" (38).

The idea that an ancient women's religion had been suppressed and paved over by "patriarchy" caught many imaginations in the 1970s and contributed to the Goddess movement. Practitioners insisted that they were not *inventing* it but reviving it. Maybe, but the thing they "revived" certainly bore strong traces of the 1960s and 1970s counterculture. One link to ancient tradition was use of the word "witchcraft." Its devotees argued that the centuries-long persecution and execution of witches in Europe and America was really a form of patriarchal domination over remnants of the Goddess religion. Charlene Spretnak, one early enthusiast, found liberation in witchcraft as opposed to oppression under the Judeo-Christian God, Yahweh, whom she described as a "distant, judgmental, manipulative figure of power who holds us all in a state of terror."[27] Another self-appointed witch, Starhawk (née Miriam Simos), had been raised Jewish but rejected Judaism in the same way Spretnak had rejected Christianity. She tried to make of witchcraft an ethically responsible form of feminist spirituality, as different as possible from the horror-movie type, and many of her injunctions were mild reminders about the importance of honesty, decency, and even the need to pick up litter. Her description of the early "history" of the Goddess religion, on the other hand, is wildly romantic, her rhetoric a cross between the Bible and Tolkien. As patriarchal invaders long ago swept across ancient Europe, she wrote,

> the Faeries, breeding cattle in the stony hills and living in turf-covered round huts, preserved the Old Religion. Clan mothers, called "Queen of Elphame," which means Elfland, led the covens, together with the priest, the Sacred King, who embodied the dying God, and underwent a ritualized mock death at the end of his term of office. They celebrated the eight feasts of the wheel with wild processions on horseback, singing, chanting, and the lighting of ritual fires. . . . The covens, who preserved the knowledge of the subtle forces, were called *Wicca* or *Wicce*, from the Anglo-Saxon root word meaning "to bend or shape." They were those who could shape the unseen to their will. Healers, teachers, poets, and midwives, they were central figures in every community.[28]

Her summary history of the world went on to show that all the suffering had been caused by patriarchy and war, all the love and healing by surviving vestiges of the old matriarchy.

Feminism, for Starhawk, now marked an opportunity for the revival of the long-suppressed power. "Only in this century have Witches been able to 'come out of the broom closet,' so to speak" (7). Witchcraft, she added, was highly intuitive, poetic rather than rational, emotional, mystical, yet powerful withal. Like popular fiction versions, it *did* include spells and magical totems; her book *The Spiral Dance* (1979) ended with a set of how-to instructions for casting them, depending on whether the witch wanted love, money, healing, justice, or protection. If she wanted to win a court case, she should act as follows: "Use a square of blue cloth, filled with bay laurel, High Joan the Conqueress Root, St. Joan's Wort and vervain. If you are being persecuted by an enemy, add a pine nut or part of a cone, some tobacco, and some mustard seed. Put in a small picture of an open eye, so that justice will look favorably on you. Tie with a purple thread" (124). With this charm and with the help of a sympathetic coven (how to form ritual circles and perfrom magical dances is also described), the jury would find in your favor.

Goddess religion was influenced not only by the feminist movement but also by the environmental movement, which was developing during the same years (1968–1980). Some enthusiasts speculated that women had an intrinsic affinity for the earth itself and for peace, just as men had an intrinsic drive to dominate the earth and to make war against one another, victimizing and raping women and the earth alike. Goddess advocate Carol Christ (pronounced with a short *i*) argued for an organic unity of women with the earth. "For me the divine / Goddess / God / Earth / Life / It symbolizes the whole of which we are a part. This whole is the earth and sky, the ground on which we stand, and all the animals, plants, and other beings to which we are related."[29] Christ herself believed that the Greek goddess Aphrodite had been one manifestation of the Great Goddess, and her book *The Laughter of Aphrodite* (1987) described her visits to Greece, in which she tried to locate the ancient sites of Aphrodite worship. With another woman on the Aegean island of Lesbos she decided to dedicate herself to the goddess at an old, abandoned temple, as she recovered from a wounding love affair. She bought a new dress for the occasion: "I would go to Aphrodite's temple in white, symbolizing my desire to be initiated into her mysteries. The golden shawl would honor her goldenness and my own."[30] In the temple "we found womblike spirals and vaginal roses carved in stone" and built an altar on one of the old ruined stone columns. "I sat between the trees opening my body to the midday sun. I anointed myself with milk and honey and poured milk and honey into my shells. The sun warmed and transformed my body. Alone with the Goddess in her sacred space, I felt myself opening, becoming whole. I became Aphrodite" (191).

New Religions, "Cults," and Their Critics

The familiar forms of the Judeo-Christian tradition proved unsatisfactory to others besides feminists, particularly young people, such that the late 1960s and 1970s saw the flowering of numerous new religions. Some were old wine in new bottles, such as the counterculture and hippie versions of Christianity. Others were adaptations of Asian religions with long histories of their own elsewhere but new to the American setting.

The Jesus People or "Jesus Freaks" grew out of the hippie movement, shared much of its philosophy, and argued that Jesus, like them, had been a long-haired wanderer in comfortable, loose-fitting clothes who rejected the shallow materialistic conventions of his own society in favor of something more authentic. (A Jesus like that was the star of Andrew Lloyd-Webber and Tim Rice's 1971 musical show *Jesus Christ Superstar*, which shows how rapidly the ideas of the Jesus People were domesticated and commercialized.) The hippies became a media sensation in 1967, especially when journalists began to explore San Francisco's Haight-Ashbury community, Berkeley's Telegraph Avenue, and other Bay Area enclaves. Beginning with the promise of peace, free love, mind expansion through the use of LSD, and a complete rejection of violence, exploitation, and materialism, the hippies offered young people a chance to live in community, at odds with America's competitive individualism.

Native American groups had long used peyote to induce religious ecstasy, so it was not difficult to make a link between drugs and religion. The novelist Aldous Huxley had taken mescaline in 1953 as part of a psychological experiment, and the drug had intensified his awareness to such an extent that he was suddenly able to grasp what mystics had meant when they wrote about the beatific vision. About a previously unremarkable vase of flowers on his table he wrote that under the influence of the drug it became an object of almost unbearable fascination: "I was not looking now at an unusual flower arrangement. I was seeing what Adam had seen on the morning of creation—the miracle, moment by moment, of naked existence."[31] His book on the experience, *The Doors of Perception* (1963), became a central text of the next generation's encounter with drugs.

Students and scholars of religion were, accordingly, quick to see the spiritual side of the hippies in the 1960s and to find historical parallels. Michael Novak, then a religion professor at Stanford, wrote that the hippie communities were doing today what the early Benedictine monks had done in the Dark Ages, becoming the inspirational centers of a new society. "The gentleness and nonviolence of the hippies are a token of high spiritual achievement and are a hopeful forerunner of the future," he wrote. Their drugs might have a benign spiritual function. "The Creator may have graced his creation with drugs which, discovered in due time, might be instrumental in preparing people to understand the gentleness, brotherhood and peace of the gospels."[32] Warren Hinckle, who wrote an influential article for *Ramparts* about the hippies in 1967, noted that LSD was a drug to be *shared* and that Ken Kesey, its early advocate and popularizer (when it was still legal), "handed LSD around like the Eucharist."[33]

Unfortunately the reality of hippie life was not all peace and love; it soon developed a seamy underside. Teenage runaways were vulnerable to sexual exploitation, the drugs were sometimes contaminated, hunger, malnutrition, and hepatitis began to spread in the hippie districts, and by late 1967 disillusioned refugees from the "summer of love" were already looking for alternatives, or just for shelter. An energetic group of Christians sympathetic to the hippie outlook responded. The Haight-Ashbury Living Room, a storefront ministry and coffeehouse run by evangelist Ted Wise, where hippies could "rap about Jesus," provided a widely emulated model. Wise and many other young ministers admired the counterculture's values as genuinely superior to those of mainstream society and actually more like Jesus' own. They tried to shape a Christian version of hippie life. Another was a Berkeley Episcopal priest, Richard York, who held a Christian Hippie Happening on the Feast of the Blessed Virgin Mary, at which a thousand hippies enjoyed free food, elaborate Episcopal rituals, rock music, foot washing, and a shower of balloons labeled "love," "peace" and "Mary."

A third hippie-oriented minister was Arthur Blessitt, a Los Angeles Baptist preacher with showbiz flair, who tried to get teenagers off their drug addiction and preached that Jesus was "life's greatest trip." A handsome twenty-seven-year-old in 1967, originally from Mississippi, he had come to save wayward teenagers on Sunset Strip, Hollywood, which was dominated by topless bars, sex clubs, and massage parlors. After preaching for a while at a music club, Hollywood-a-Go-Go, he opened His Place, which he described as a "gospel nightclub," where young people could go for comfort, food, shelter, Christian rock music, and some intense preaching in hippie idiom. Prayer was "turning on to Jesus Christ" and salvation was "tripping on Jesus." When anxious, lonely, or despairing teenagers came in, converts from earlier sessions would lay their hands on them and pray for their conversion. Blessitt himself and a growing group of assistants also offered counseling and Bible study groups. The club featured psychedelic light shows and Bibles printed on Day-Glo psychedelic paper. After an evening of preaching, when his powerful rhetoric and the collective emotion had stimulated teens to turn their lives to Jesus, Blessitt would hold "toilet services" in which they flushed away their remaining drug supplies and promised to mend their ways. Blessitt's colorful books about his exploits are peppered with stories about souls he saved—tales that lose nothing in the telling:

> The first time I met Linda she was stoned out of her head with acid. She had ridden with a San Antonio and Houston motorcycle gang and then with Hell's Angels. . . . Now working on our staff full time Linda is beautiful in her dedication to Christ. Her witness is really something else. When guys on bikes come over and ask her to split with them, she hops right on the chopper and takes off. When they stop she lays the Word of the Lord on them. Her witnessing almost freaks them out![34]

As for himself, "I'm naturally stoned and Jesus puts it together forever" (30). He wore open-necked flowery shirts, beads, bell-bottoms, and sandals rather than clerical dress and did what he could to avoid scaring away young visitors.

Blessitt's activities on the Strip roused other business owners there into opposition. The sex industry discovered that his fervent evangelizing gave its customers a bad conscience and so was bad for business; twice, building owners decided (under pressure) not to renew his lease. After the second incident, in June 1969, he found that no one else would rent to him either. Rather than abandon the mission, he staged a street drama to draw attention to his cause, chaining himself to a massive cross on the sidewalk and swearing to stay there, fasting, until God showed him a way out of the dilemma. "The chain felt wonderful, each link binding me to Christ."[35] Some police were critical, but others sympathized because they knew his work against drug addiction could be effective. After a month, during which he performed sidewalk hippie weddings, lost thirty-five pounds, and became the focus of media fanfare, another local businessman finally agreed to rent him a building on the Strip. Later he moved his ministry to the equally sinful Times Square in New York, after walking across the country, dragging the great cross with him.

The Jesus movement consisted of dozens of such ministries in areas where young, rootless people gathered; observers were impressed by the transformation wrought in their lives and their enthusiasm for learning (often memorizing) Scripture. These ministries were mostly autonomous and knew little about one another, usually coalescing around charismatic ministers like Blessitt in Los Angeles, George Bogle in Detroit, David Berg in Orange County, and Jack Sparks in Berkeley, who created drug-free and sex-free places for teenagers to live in sobriety and safety, while proselytizing on the street for more converts. Several ran Christian underground newspapers (the *Oracle*, the *Hollywood Free Paper*, *Right On*) or wrote "hip" translations of the Bible, like this paraphrase of 1 John 2:15–17 from Sparks's *Letters to Street Christians*:

> Don't get hooked on the ego-tripping world system. Anybody who loves that system doesn't really love God. For this whole gig—the craze for sex, the desire to have everything that looks good, and the false security of believing you can take care of yourself—doesn't come from our Father, but from the evil world system itself. . . . Dig it! This whole plastic bag is exactly what Jesus liberated us from.[36]

Others ran Christian communes, again borrowing from a popular theme in the counterculture (sharing everything in a form of primitive communism) but disciplined by strong male leadership and evangelical Christian ethics.

Jack Sparks, leader of the Christian World Liberation Front in Berkeley, often parodied the Third World Liberation Front, which was then popular on the University of California campus. Political leftists regarded the "God Squad" as an annoying distraction and accused Sparks (a Ph.D. and former statistics professor at Penn State) of being on the payroll of right-wing organizations. Sparks replied: "If what you're into contributes to the build up of a violent revolution, then you're a revolutionary. But we're talking with people about love and peace and a relationship with God. And that's counter-revolutionary. . . . So they're right when they call us that."[37] His group, like most of the Jesus People, had little interest in the era's stormy politics; it followed the twentieth-century's long evangelical tradition of working for the transformation of individual souls rather than the transformation of society.

Relations between the Jesus groups and the conventional churches were sometimes strained. Methodists, Presbyterians, and Episcopalians all helped underwrite the Jesus People's centers, coffeehouses, and publications but found few of the new converts willing to attend their services. The young converts explained that conventional Christianity was too stiff and staid, no longer fervent and "biblical," and that churchgoing on Sunday morning did not constitute living the Christian life. Jesus People were more enthusiastic than their elders about speaking in tongues, about the omnipresence of Satanic forces, the need for exorcisms, and the imminence of Christ's Second Coming, and were reluctant to take time away from evangelizing to work in everyday jobs. They were often experience- and emotion-based almost to the exclusion of having any real theological system, but made up in charismatic ardor what they lacked in intellectual depth.

Observers feared that some Jesus People's separatism, single-mindedness, and devotion to charismatic leaders were sinister, cultlike. The religious journalist Hiley Ward, for example, deplored the narrowness of the Bible education offered in the Local Church movement, founded by two Chinese evangelists, Watchman Nee and Witness Lee. Members were expected to shout out a handful of Bible verses again and again but were stridently anti-intellectual and reluctant to talk about the consequences of conversion or the meaning of complex passages of Scripture. Similarly, Ronald Enroth and his colleagues, evangelical sociologists who researched and wrote an early study of the phenomenon, expressed misgivings about the Children of God, a Southern California and Texas group, for their lockstep evangelism, their leader David Berg's authoritarian style, and their harsh criticism of the established churches. Even more alarmed were the parents of some Children of God recruits. They formed the Parents' Committee to Save Our Sons and Daughters from the Children of God Organization. Their children had been kidnapped and brainwashed, they alleged; the judiciary should intervene.

The most explosive Christian cult of the 1970s, which amply justified such parental fears, was the People's Temple, whose entire membership, more than nine hundred people, eventually took poison and died in a mass suicide ritual. This event, without parallel in American history, shocked the world. The first response, from the press and media, was to regard it as an outbreak of insanity or mass hysteria—it certainly intensified a growing anti-cult sentiment in 1970s America and made life difficult for members of other new religious groups.

Jim Jones, leader of the People's Temple, was one in a long line of American charismatic religious leaders who, in the preceding two hundred years, had won passionate followers and equally passionate enemies. An Indiana native born in 1931, he blended the intense spiritual commitment of Pentecostal Christianity with a liberal social agenda and was an outspoken Christian critic of racism. Unlike the Jesus People, Jones was not content just to offer spiritual consolation to suffering souls and miraculous healing to suffering bodies; in addition he wanted to reform an unjust society. He preached some of his first spellbinding sermons to the Wings of Deliverance Church in Indianapolis in the early 1950s and won admiring recruits among the city's poor, black and white.

His People's Temple Full Gospel Church, founded in 1955 and affiliated with the Disciples of Christ, built the first interracial congregation in Indianapolis, a city where Ku Klux Klan membership was strong and race relations tense. It included a soup kitchen, a free grocery store, and a clothing exchange, all of which Jones saw as consistent with his faith in what he called Apostolic Socialism. Despite the obsessive anti-Communism of the early and mid-1950s, Jones was strongly attracted to communism, both as a way of living and as the antidote to capitalism, which, he believed, oppressed the poor. The Indianapolis city government, recognizing Jones's influence over his flock and dedication to his mission, appointed him to its Human Rights Commission to help integrate the city's agencies in the early sixties.

In those crisis years, however—when Christians debated "bomb shelter ethics" as they prepared for an atomic Armageddon—Jones became convinced that nuclear war was imminent and that he must find a place where he and his followers could survive it. He considered a retreat to the Amazon jungle in Brazil but eventually decided on a rural American site. In 1964, he therefore moved the most committed members of his congregation, about 150 in all, to Ukiah, in Redwood Valley, California. There they lived a close communal life, building a complex of homes, churches, and recreational facilities known as Happy Acres. They sent traveling missions out by bus (Jones had acquired a fleet of eleven used Greyhound buses) and recruited new members in San Francisco, while drawing into their orbit former members of Father Divine's Peace Mission, an earlier utopian and antiracist commune.

As his movement grew in the late 1960s and early 1970s, Jones began to make more extravagant claims for himself: that he could raise the dead, that he was the embodiment of God, and that he was going to solve all the world's great problems of poverty, suffering, racism, and war. He opened a church in San Francisco and again recruited heavily in poor black districts. Three-quarters of his members were black and about two-thirds of them women. He also attracted a minority of well-educated, middle-class whites, some of whom, led by Timothy and Grace Stoen, later defected to become outspoken critics. They described how Jones had claimed to have raised forty-three people from the dead, how he sometimes preached and ranted for five or six hours at a time, how he faked faith healings, producing pieces of rotten meat and claiming that these were the actual cancers that he had extracted from sufferers' bodies, how he had forced men and women alike to have sex with him, how he had seduced new members into handing over all their property and pay to the church, and how, when members protested, he had ordered them severely beaten or publicly humiliated.

On the basis of these allegations, first the *San Francisco Examiner* and later *New West* magazine ran a series of articles describing Jones as an authoritarian dictator and brainwasher who merely posed as a Christian humanitarian. The articles also asserted that his claim of sexual rights over the female commune members had led to his fathering several of their children. Even then his proven ability to rescue drug addicts and reform alcoholics, and his eager cooperation with Democratic politicians, made Jones as attractive to important figures in San Francisco's government as he had been earlier to those in Indianapolis. Mayor George Moscone appointed him chair of the city's housing authority in 1976, and his organization continued to grow.

Jones, however, had become discouraged by the slowness of a corrupt society to change its ways and to acknowledge his messianic presence. He also became convinced that he was endangered by treacherous former disciples and an unsympathetic press, and that his movement was in danger of persecution. In 1977, pursued by allegations of fraud and intimidation, he made the fateful decision to abandon America altogether and move to Guyana, on the northern coast of South America. He had been considering the move since 1973, had bought land there, and had a sent a corps of pioneers to clear land, build a village (Jonestown), and prepare it for the whole church.

The sudden arrival of almost a thousand members and their rapid organization of workable farms and dormitories demonstrated that the People's Temple was well disciplined. In the view of the Committee of Concerned Relatives, an anti-cult group consisting of former members and the anxious parents of current members, this discipline was maintained by violence, coercion, and torture. They urged the federal government to investigate and to repatriate their family members. California congressman Leo Ryan led a delegation of these Concerned Relatives to Guyana in November 1978, and its arrival precipitated the final scene in Jones's strange drama. After inspecting Jonestown, Ryan tried to leave, taking with him fourteen People's Temple members who said they wanted to return to America. Jones reacted by having five of the group, including Ryan and three journalists, ambushed and shot. The same day, he mixed containers of cyanide into bowls of Kool-Aid and prepared everyone for death. The People's Temple, whose fear of persecution had been mounting steadily over the preceding year, had practiced this mass suicide ritual and now carried it out in a frighteningly orderly way on November 18, 1978.

Explanations for why it had happened have varied. The Soviet press declared that it was emblematic of the way life in America drove people to despair and self-immolation, while the Japanese press saw the primarily black victims as casualties of America's unresolved racial crisis. Shiva Naipaul, an influential West Indian writer, described it as the ultimate outcome of an over-permissive society whose members, deformed by utopian promises, seek purpose in their lives by abandoning themselves to charismatic leaders. By contrast John Ross Hall, the most searching scholar on Jonestown, argues that the suicide needs to be understood (even by those who find it revolting) as a form of collective martyrdom, congruent with those of the Jewish resistance at Masada in 73 c.e., or the communities of early Christians who accepted collective annihilation in the name of their faith. It was, Hall adds, an end that brought no collective hope for the future but at least vindicated the honor of the group's members, who had aimed to establish an ideal, racially integrated community beyond the reach of its persecutors. Ironically, Jones had had to become increasingly repressive in order to try to maintain the boundaries between those inside his utopia and those in the threatening outside world. The constant breaching of these boundaries finally made the end inevitable. Hall argues: "Rather than successfully establishing the other-worldly sanctuary of a promised land, [Jones] could only denounce the web of 'evil' powers in which he was ensnared and search with chiliastic expectation for the imminent cataclysm that would affirm the integrity of his cause."[38]

Asian Spirituality in American Dress

Asian religions, or American adaptations of them, also flourished in the Vietnam and Watergate era among people whose rejection of mainstream American values led them to look for exotic alternatives. The most famous popular musicians of the mid-1960s, the Beatles, were among the first Western celebrities to travel to India in search of spiritual enlightenment, and they claimed that they had found it at the feet of Maharishi Mahesh Yogi, the avatar of Transcendental Meditation. With long robes, a white beard, and a jolly smile, the Maharishi seemed almost to be the parody of an Eastern holy man and was featured widely in the news media and magazines. American celebrities including the actresses Mia Farrow and Jane Fonda followed the Beatles' lead and claimed that meditation with the Maharishi had brought them serenity and confidence.

Transcendental Meditation became popular in America partly because it was relatively easy to get started, required none of the heroic asceticism associated with some forms of Asian spirituality, and enjoyed good publicity because the Maharishi opposed drugs. In exchange for a week's pay, aspirants were given a mantra, a Sanskrit word or phrase that they were expected to repeat in their twice-daily twenty-minute meditation sessions. Maharishi ordered his followers to keep their mantras secret and explained that his initiators (instructors) knew how to assess a candidate for the appropriate mantra. It should "resonate to the pulse of his thought and as it resonates, create an increasingly soothing influence."[39] He claimed that the Spiritual Regeneration Movement he had started in 1958 blended the best insights of Hindu meditative tradition and modern science (he had a degree in physics from the University of Allahabad) and that its outcome would be a happier population, collectively approaching a state of bliss.

Gurus were rare in America before the 1960s but not completely unknown. At the World's Parliament of Religions, back in 1893, the Swami Vivekenanda had made impressive speeches that turned him into America's first Hindu celebrity; he then toured the United States for several months as the guest of admiring American ladies. He had founded the Vedanta Society, which survived through the twentieth century as a sedate and Americanized version of Hinduism. Similarly, Thomas Merton, the Columbia University student who later became a Trappist monk, had ardent discussions with Doctor Bramachari, a Hindu holy man, in New York during the late 1930s. The scale of Asian-derived religions in the 1960s and 1970s was, however, something new, not least because as the baby boom generation moved into early adulthood, the sheer number of "seekers" was so large and alienation from "straight" American institutions was so widespread. This time, moreover, the interest was as much in the actual practice of Asian religions as in theorizing about them.

By the mid-1970s a wide array of Asian religions was available to the American consumer. Harvey Cox, the liberal Protestant theologian and Harvard professor who had celebrated the "secular city" ten years earlier, surveyed his hometown of Cambridge, Massachusetts, and found more than forty Asian religions represented there, including TM, Zen and Tibetan Buddhism, Sufi dancing, Ananda Marga, Hare Krishna, Divine Light, Sikhs, Sri Chinmoy, and an array of Yoga and Tai Chi centers. "When one adds them together," he observed, "the picture of Cambridge as an intellectually prim university town fades as the image of a hive of neo-Oriental religious fervor begins to take its place."[40] He doubted their value at first because they tended to be inward-looking rather than socially activist, but before long he, like thousands in his generation, had begun to study them and to become a participant observer, finding out firsthand what the disciplines felt like, and discovering through experience and conversation why people joined them.

He experimented with the sitting meditation of Soto Zen, and spent a week or two trying to solve the notorious riddle of Rinzai Zen, "What is the sound of one hand clapping?" The experience was alien to anyone raised in the Western religious tradition.

> One who comes to Zen with the desire to "experience" anything, including satori, or enlightenment, will eventually discover that Zen neither promises nor produces an experience of anything. Through its demanding disciplines one learns that all a person really needs to experience is the experience that one needs to experience nothing. Here then is a practical philosophy that manages to belittle both religious doctrine and religious experience, that provides no stated rituals, no heaven or hell, no God (and no "no-God") and that offers no obvious ethic, since it sees such categories as "good" and "evil" as imposed and deceptive. (24–25)

He stuck with it anyway, struck by the opportunity for reflection that meditation afforded him, and eventually incorporated a Tibetan style of meditation into his daily life, without attempting to accept all the philosophy that went with it.

Buddhism, like Hinduism, was attractive to Cox and to many countercultural Americans because it appeared to be antimaterialist and peaceful, representing the antithesis of what they now considered a sick and warlike American society. It had begun to attract white seekers in the 1950s. D. T. Suzuki (1870–1966), a Japanese immigrant, had popularized Zen Buddhism after World War II and taught it in an idiom Americans could grasp. Allen Ginsberg and Jack Kerouac, the Beat writers, heard Suzuki lecturing at Columbia University in the late 1940s, and his influence is apparent in their work. In *The Dharma Bums* (1958), for example, Kerouac used Buddhism to argue that a life of simplicity and wandering provides greater tranquillity and satisfaction than the conventional American route to wealth and possessions. The book's hero, Japhy Ryder (a thinly fictionalized version of Kerouac's friend Gary Snyder, who studied Zen Buddhism in Japan), has a vision of America transformed by Zen seekers:

> I see a vision of a great rucksack revolution thousands or even millions of young Americans wandering around with rucksacks, going up to mountains to pray, making children laugh and old men glad, making young girls happy and old girls happier, all of 'em Zen lunatics who go about writing poems that happen to appear in their heads for no reason and also by being kind and also by strange unexpected acts keep giving visions of eternal freedom to everybody and to all living creatures.[41]

The Dharma Bums also teaches the lesson that human striving is futile. As the narrator gazes in awe at a mountain he and his friend are about to climb, the wise Japhy tells him: "To me a mountain is a Buddha. Think of the patience, hundreds of thousands of years just sitting there bein' perfectly perfectly silent and like praying for all living creatures in that silence and just waiting for us to stop all our frettin' and foolin'" (67).

One of the Beats' friendly critics was Alan Watts (1915–1973), whose book *Beat Zen, Square Zen, and Zen* (1959) reproached them for dabbling in Zen concepts rather than struggling to master them. Watts himself (who elsewhere admitted that he was a dabbler too) was an immigrant from England. He had studied Suzuki's writings and pioneered his own eclectic brand of Buddhism. He believed that the insights of Buddhism and Christianity could be reconciled, and had seen no contradiction in training for the Episcopalian priesthood in the 1940s. A chaplain to students at Northwestern University until his bishop ejected him for sexual misconduct, Watts had moved to California in 1950 and become a member of the American Academy of Asian Studies. Watts loved the paradoxical side of Buddhism and was a wonderful debunker of religious solemnity. Fascinated by the hippie movement, himself an LSD experimenter in the days when it was still legal, and a playful critic of acquisitive materialism, he remained an accessible interpreter of Buddhist ideas to society rather than an academic. He was also a brilliant public speaker whose regular radio spot through the late fifties and sixties made him a familiar figure—and to some people a guru—in the Bay Area. He died in 1973 but left a body of accessible writings on Zen and a marvelous autobiography, *In My Own Way* (1972).

Buddhism as a religious option developed rapidly. Zen meditation centers had opened in Los Angeles in 1956, San Francisco in 1959, and Rochester, New York, in 1966. This last center was the creation of Philip Kapleau, an American who had spent the previous thirteen years in Japan, studying the Zen discipline at a monastery, an experience he encapsulated in *The Three Pillars of Zen* (1965). Kapleau argued that it was right to adapt Zen to American conditions, just as in earlier generations it had been adapted from Chinese to Japanese conditions. He therefore encouraged students to keep their ordinary Western clothes rather than adopt Japanese robes and to use English rather than Japanese. Tibetan as well as Japanese Buddhists introduced new forms in the 1970s, including the Rocky Mountain Dharma Center, founded by Chogyam Trungpa (1970) in Boulder, Colorado. Thomas Merton spent much of the 1960s studying the similarities between Christian and Buddhist monasticism. His premature death occurred in an electrical accident when he was attending a 1968 conference on comparative monasticism in Thailand.

These various Americanized Buddhist enterprises differed markedly from their Asian counterparts because many of their students were American laity seeking some education and some opportunity for meditation rather than monks seeking complete seclusion from the world, and because at least half the participants were women (whereas in Asia Buddhist meditation was a males-only affair). Indeed, one Buddhist Center, Shasta Abbey, was founded and run by a woman, Jiyu Kennett (like Alan Watts a British immigrant). This contrast in participants' makeup and purpose, and the fact that each teacher or monastery existed side by side with dozens of others, helped transform the meaning of Buddhism in America, making it, in effect, one more choice available to religious "consumers." The number of Americans who *became* Buddhists was never large, but so many highly educated people experimented with it and learned about it, and it informed so much study of comparative religion, that it acquired a considerable cultural influence. Buddhist references are scattered through countercultural literature of the era after Kerouac, nowhere more popular than in Robert Pirsig's best-selling novel *Zen and the Art of Motorcycle Maintenance* (1974).

American Buddhists managed to avoid the accusation of cult behavior, even in the years when fallout from the People's Temple mass suicide made the devotees of all unusual religions objects of suspicion. Other Asian imports were not so lucky, especially those that required of members a radically transformed way of life. "Cult" was itself a pejorative term, usually denoting the observer's belief that a group discouraged independent thought, that it was led by greedy and dictatorial figures who took all their members' money and property, and that it "brainwashed" them, making them powerless to quit. "From the perspective of outsiders," wrote one interpreter, "especially parents, the perception that their children are being financially exploited is seen as one of the most pernicious and malevolent aspects of the group."[42] Members of the new religions, by contrast, often told interviewers that they welcomed the life *because* it offered a highly structured round of daily tasks and a clearly defined pattern of beliefs. They found a sense of purpose and spiritual satisfaction that had hitherto been missing in their lives, along with a community of welcoming and supportive people who shared these beliefs.

Despite "cult" members' claims of contentment, an anti-cult movement grew rapidly in the 1970s, of which the Jonestown Concerned Relatives group was just one part. Families believed their children had been robbed of free will and were, in effect, prisoners of the cults rather than voluntary members. Two sensational books advanced this idea, Ted Patrick and Tom Dulack's *Let Our Children Go* (1976) and F. Conway and J. Siegelman's *Snapping: America's Epidemic of Sudden Personality Change* (1978). Eminent psychological writers too, such as Robert Jay Lifton, endorsed the idea that group pressure could lead a cult member to surrender his or her ego entirely to the group. Patrick, who had experimentally "infiltrated" the Children of God and felt group programming sapping even his ability to think independently, said the answer to this threat lay in "deprogramming," by which he meant seizing cult members, carrying them off to a secret place, and subjecting them for several days to intense mental stimuli that would undermine the cult group's lessons. Deprogramming would enable them to recover the capacity for independent thought and reunite them with family, friends, and the ordinary world. He established the Citizens' Freedom Foundation in 1974 (later the Cult Awareness Network) to promote the idea of deprogramming.

Anti-cult activists petitioned state governments to pass anti-cult laws, but when it came to the point, legislators found it very difficult to define where

"respectable" religion stopped and cult activity started. After all, ecstatic healing services sometimes took place in Baptist churches; even some Episcopalians held Pentecostal meetings in which spirit-filled members cried out in
unknown tongues. Was that kind of thing "cultish"? Might they be liable to
prosecution under these proposed new laws, and if so, of what use was the First
Amendment? Besides, American churches enjoy tax exemption, and even
those whose members disliked fringe religious activity were reluctant to see
other religious groups lose this cherished benefit, lest the precedent bite them
later. No laws were passed.

One of the deprogrammers' targets was ISKCON (International Society for
Krishna Consciousness). Its members, usually referred to as the Hare Krishnas,
belonged to a branch of Hinduism, dressed in saffron robes, shaved their heads,
and practiced ecstatic dancing and chanting. Introduced to America in 1965
and popularized by Beatle George Harrison's 1971 song "My Sweet Lord,"
whose chorus included the chant "Hare Krishna, Hare Rama," ISKCON
required of its members self-discipline, surrender of material goods, a simple
vegetarian diet, and sexual self-denial. Throughout the 1970s, airports and city
street corners resounded to the repetitive chorus "Hare Krishna, Hare Rama,"
and the group pressed every passerby to join them, accept a copy of the Bhagavad Gita, and contribute generously. The Krishna movement, like the Jesus
People, was successful in turning its many ex-hippie members off drugs, but the
seeming narrowness of the new way of life alarmed some members' parents and
led to recurrent legal troubles.

In 1979 a Hare Krishna devotee, Rebecca Foster, was seized by deprogram-
mer Ted Patrick at ISKCON's Los Angeles temple, driven to Lake Tahoe in
Northern California, and subjected to his intensive program to break the
"cult's" grip on her mind. Patrick had been hired by Ms. Foster's family, who
were convinced that the Krishnas had turned her into a "mindless robot." After
three days she collapsed in tears, declared she was no longer enthralled by the
cult, and had returned to normal. As it turned out, however, she was faking. She
had no sooner gotten away from Patrick than she returned to the Krishna temple, then sued her parents for kidnapping, false imprisonment, and conspiracy.
The family was acquitted after a 1981 trial in Santa Monica, but the sequence
of events exposed the ambiguities of the deprogrammers' position. Some
observers argued that *they* were cultlike in their obsession and in the doubtful
legality of their tactics. Harvey Cox condemned deprogramming as "plainly
illegal and unconstitutional" and a "frightening" violation of the First Amendment's guarantee of religious freedom. "Some psychiatrists have even been
known to lend support to the incarceration of the devotees of the Krishna Consciousness movement . . . because they think that anyone who chooses a life of
prayer and worship instead of a career must obviously be mentally disturbed."[43]

Other forms of legal trouble also dogged new religions. The Bhagwan Shree Rajneesh (1931–1990) enjoyed a few years' notoriety in America before drawing the unwelcome attention of the legal system. An Indian from the Jain tradition and a former professor of philosophy, he created an ashram (spiritual center) at Poona, India, at which he encouraged "*sannyasins*" not to renounce the material world but to seek holiness within it through a combination of meditation and ritual dancing. His followers wore orange robes, a "*mala*," or string of 108 wooden beads, and carried copies of the Bhagwan's picture. He came to the United States in 1981 and bought a 64,000-acre ranch near the Oregon town of Antelope, which he named Rajneeshpuram. Before long, five thousand orange-clothed enthusiasts, mostly Americans, had joined him there and were working hard to build a community that blended spiritual and hedonistic fulfillment. The Bhagwan treated himself as a near-divine figure and was ostentatious about his wealth and possessions, which included ninety-three Rolls-Royces. He also encouraged beggars and street people from other parts of America to settle there, which inflamed an already anxious local population. At their instigation, government agencies began to investigate and arrested the Bhagwan in 1985 for immigration fraud. He accepted a plea bargain and was deported, with the result that Rajneeshpuram, lacking his magnetic presence, went into a rapid decline.

Like the Hare Krishnas and the Rajneeshis, the Unification Church ("the Moonies") also fell afoul of the law. Its leader, the Reverend Sun Myung Moon, was a Korean Christian whose book *The Divine Principle* (1957) foresaw the coming of the "Lord of the Second Advent." Central to Moon's vision was the family. In his view, the world's first family, Adam and Eve's, had been wrecked by Satan, while Jesus himself had erred in not marrying and producing a new perfect family. Now it was time for him, Moon, to build the perfect family. His own wife, Hak Ja Han, was called the Bride of Christ by Unification Church members, and many of them assumed that Moon himself was the Lord of the Second Advent. Hostile observers regarded him as another brainwasher—they noted with horror that he decided which of his members should marry one another and that he had organized a mass wedding of eight hundred couples one day in 1975. Deprogrammers and concerned parents lobbied for a government investigation and, after an escalating series of confrontations, Moon was arrested and convicted of tax evasion in 1982. He, like the Bhagwan, was forced to leave the country, though his influence persisted, among a few thousand American supporters and through his newspaper, the *Washington Times*.

The new religions of the 1970s prospered only if they found ways to pass their vision on to new generations (children, as well as recruits from outside) and only if they were able to accommodate to America's broad social principles. The more exclusive and intolerant they were, the more they required eccentric dress, behavior, and beliefs, the less likely they were to thrive beyond the early years of their mushroom growth. Buddhism and Hinduism thrived among Asian immigrant communities, for whom they were *not* exotic, and among small white, middle-class groups who became serious scholars and practitioners of religions to which they had first been attracted by their novelty.

Chapter 7

EVANGELICALS AND POLITICS: 1976–1990

Jimmy Carter and the Evangelical Presidency

Jimmy Carter defeated President Ford in the election of 1976 and became the thirty-ninth president. He was a surprising winner, first because he had no prior experience of Washington politics (he had been governor of Georgia) and second because he was an avowed "born-again" Christian and Baptist Sunday school teacher. But 1976, the nation's bicentennial, was no ordinary election year. Ford had become president only with the resignation of President Nixon, disgraced and shamed out of office by the Watergate scandal (1972–1974). Carter's grinning godly goodliness attracted voters in a way it might not have done in other years, and they took seriously his promise of a foreign policy based on Christian decency and respect for human rights. On inauguration day he swore his oath of office on a Bible given him by his mother, open to the Book of Micah, which he quoted in his inaugural address: "He hath showed thee, O man, what is good; and what doth the Lord require of thee, but to do justly, and to love mercy, and to walk humbly with thy God."[1]

Carter came from the Southwest Georgia town of Plains, where he had grown up in the Southern Baptist Church. An Annapolis graduate and former submariner, he had taken over the family's peanut business in the 1950s and was among the first white Georgians to take a principled stand in favor of racial inte-

148

gration. He had been the only white businessman to refuse to join the White Citizens' Council in his county after the Supreme Court's decision in the *Brown* case of 1954 and had made a point of doing business with a racially integrated Christian farm-training center, Koinonia, in the Plains-Americus area. As a state senator in 1966 he volunteered to sponsor a racially integrated Billy Graham outreach program in Americus when all the local white clergy had refused.

Carter was more openly and actively religious than any other twentieth-century president, not just as a parishioner but as a Sunday school teacher and evangelist. He came from an evangelical but not fundamentalist tradition, and his reading of Reinhold Niebuhr's sermons and essays in 1965 enabled him to reconcile some of the most puzzling questions about the connection between practical politics and Jesus' difficult teachings. He later told Bill Gunter, the minister who had suggested he read them, that a book of Niebuhr's essays on politics was his "political Bible." His biographer Peter Bourne argues that "he conceptualized politics as a vehicle for advancing God's kingdom on earth by alleviating human suffering and despair on a scale that infinitely magnified what one individual could do alone. His most frequent prayer was that his life be meaningful in the enhancement of God's will and in the lives of fellow human beings."[2] Even when campaigning for the governorship of Georgia in the late 1960s he found time to work with the Baptist Home Missions movement, spending weeks in Pennsylvania and Massachusetts going door to door and trying to win converts to Christ.

As a presidential candidate Carter was sometimes naive in his responses to curious journalists probing the religious issue. By contrast with the Watergate era's abusive cynicism, his Christian simplicity seemed like a breath of fresh air, but aides despaired of his unguarded remarks. In an interview with Robert Scheer printed in *Playboy*, for example, honesty prompted him to make admissions that could have damaged his campaign:

> Christ set some impossible standards for us. Christ said, "I tell you that anyone who looks on a woman with lust has already committed adultery." I have looked on a lot of women with lust; I've committed adultery in my heart many times. This is something God recognizes I will do—and I have done it—and God forgives me for it. But that does not mean I condemn someone who not only looks on a woman with lust but leaves his wife and shacks up with somebody out of wedlock.[3]

The interview caused a furor, with some Southern clergymen condemning him for agreeing to speak to *Playboy* at all and others deploring his use of such slang phrases of the sexual revolution as "shacking up." Carter, in other ways a shrewd and accomplished politician, was able to repair the temporary damage this interview did to his cause, and went on to win in the November 1976 election.

The most lasting achievement of his presidency was the Camp David peace accord he brokered between Israel and Egypt in 1978. Menachem Begin, the

Israeli prime minister, and Anwar Sadat, the Egyptian president, each faced opposition in his own country for making the necessary compromises and concessions. Sadat later paid for it with his life when he was assassinated by a Muslim extremist. Nevertheless, the negotiations enabled one of the most important Muslim nations in the world to accept the continuing existence of the world's only Jewish nation after thirty years of continuous hostilities. The Christian president guided the two leaders through countless apparent deadlocks and was able at last to preside while the Muslim and the Jew established a durable agreement, prelude to a treaty.

Carter, like most late-twentieth-century presidents, was a staunch supporter of Israel, but in his case it was a support that sprang as much from religious as political convictions. As a child he had studied maps of the Holy Land and identified the sites of Bible stories. "By the time he was ten years old," writes Bourne, "he had a greater knowledge about Palestine than he did about the rest of America" (32). In his autobiography Carter confirmed the point: "I considered this homeland for the Jews to be compatible with the teachings of the Bible, hence ordained by God."[4] He did not scant Palestinian or Arab claims, however, and he believed deeply in the need for peace, with the result that he was able to develop strong personal friendships with both Begin and Sadat.

Carter, despite this Camp David triumph, was unlucky. He faced troubles at home and worse troubles abroad. First was stagflation, a combination of economic stagnation and price inflation that defied orthodox economic theory. High prices and high unemployment worsened in 1979 because of an immense rise in imported oil prices. Abroad, while Egypt was showing a new willingness to compromise with Israel, Islam elsewhere in the Middle East was becoming more militant than ever. In 1979 Shi'ite Muslims overthrew the Shah of Iran and installed a fanatical theocratic regime, which ruled according to the harshest interpretation of Islamic law. The Ayatollah Khomeini, an imam (Islamic holy man) exiled by the Shah's regime in the 1960s, returned to Iran in triumph. He approved a militant student takeover of the American embassy in the capital city, Teheran, and the capture of the sixty-six American "devils" inside. The last year of the Carter administration was devoted to finding ways to extricate them. A military rescue attempt failed, and Khomeini added insult to injury by releasing them only on the day Carter relinquished the White House to his successor, Ronald Reagan. Reagan magnanimously appointed Carter as his representative to greet them.

The New Christian Right and the Reagan Campaign

Although Carter was the twentieth century's first avowed evangelical president, by 1980 many other evangelicals were openly campaigning against him, and they contributed to his downfall. The New Christian Right, a network of conservative evangelical ministers and lobbyists, took shape in the late 1970s, made up of men and women dismayed by what they saw as a tide of immorality sweeping across the nation. The sexual revolution, feminism, legalized abortion, easily accessible pornography, the homosexual rights movement, church-state separation, high rates of violent crime, and declining standards of public and political morality—all these things they interpreted as signs of a national moral crisis, which they believed President Carter had done too little to oppose.

Among the most eloquent and energetic figures in the New Christian Right was Jerry Falwell (b. 1933), a Baptist minister from Lynchburg, Virginia. A young hell-raiser, son of a drunk (who died of cirrhosis of the liver when Jerry was fifteen), Falwell had transformed his life when he was born again as a teenager. Just after graduating from Bible Baptist College (Missouri) in 1956, he and thirty-five dissidents from a local Southern Baptist church had rented a Donald Duck Cola Bottling Company warehouse and set up an independent Baptist congregation. Almost at once, the boundlessly energetic Falwell had begun a radio ministry, preached four times every Sunday, and swelled the ranks of his congregation to 864 in the first year. He had also set up an all-white Christian high school, a college (Liberty Baptist), and ministries for children, teenagers, the elderly, the deaf, the retarded, and prisoners.

Soon he was televising services too, and he bought his own TV cameras in 1968. Changes in Federal Communications Commission rules eased his way. In the early decades of religious television, the 1950s and 1960s, mainstream Protestant ministers and Catholic priests had dominated the small screen—one of the Catholics, Bishop Fulton Sheen, had run a spectacularly successful show, *Life Is Worth Living*, in the mid-1950s. In the 1970s, by contrast, the FCC permitted all religious groups to bid for airtime, such that by 1980 90 percent of religious broadcasting was by evangelical and fundamentalist ministers, who paid for it by issuing fund-raising appeals on the air.

Falwell's television ministry, the *Old-Time Gospel Hour* (whose title paid tribute to Charles Fuller's *Old-Fashioned Revival Hour*, which he had heard on the radio as a boy), was broadcasting to an estimated four million people every week by 1980, and showed how skillfully he had adapted to the era's most popular broadcast medium. Like Billy Graham and other evangelical predecessors, he mixed his "old-time" biblical message with a shrewd use of contemporary technology. His ally in the New Christian Right leadership, Richard Viguerie, editor of the *Conservative Digest*, was equally adept in the use of direct-mail techniques, trawling for contributions from evangelicals throughout the country.

In the early years of his ministry Falwell had adhered to the traditional Baptist principle of separating religion from politics. In 1965 he had preached: "Believing the Bible as I do, I would find it impossible to stop preaching the pure saving gospel of Jesus Christ and begin doing anything else—including fighting Communism, or participating in Civil Rights reforms."[5] The perceived moral deterioration of the nation in the following years seemed to him so severe, however, that he changed his mind, and he became a founding member of Moral Majority in 1979. Moral Majority was an interfaith conservative pressure group dedicated to restoring Judeo-Christian morality in American life. It declared war on the philosophy that appeared to be guiding society, "secular humanism," and did not shy away from the military rhetoric that goes with war. Falwell told his congregation:

> The local church is an organized army equipped for battle, ready to charge the enemy. The Sunday School is the attacking squad. The church should be a disciplined, charging army. Christians, like slaves and soldiers, ask no questions. . . . It is important to bombard the territory, to move out near the coast and shell the enemy. . . . But ultimately some Marines have to march in, encounter the enemy face-to-face, and put the flag up. I'm speaking of Marines who have been called by God to move in past the shelling . . . encounter the enemy face-to-face and one-on-one bring them under submission to the gospel of Christ, move them into the household of God, put up the flag and call it secured. You and I are called to occupy it until He comes.[6]

Visitors to Falwell's Thomas Road Baptist Church in Lynchburg noted the paradox that, in person, Falwell was affable and well-to-do, living comfortably in a gentle, small-town setting, largely immune from daily trauma, yet he kept up in his preaching and writing this rhetoric of war, setting himself and his congregation sharply at odds with what he depicted as a sinister outside world.

The New Christian Right, with Moral Majority as one of its central elements, believed that President Carter had not lived up to his promises. As a Baptist, for example, Carter was personally opposed to abortion but had not worked against the Democratic Party's pro-choice position. Similarly, the Carter government had done nothing to dismantle the court-sanctioned wall of separation between church and state, which cut off public school children from their nation's religious heritage. Should religion and politics be mixed? Falwell, eschewing his earlier belief in keeping the two separate, now answered with a confident yes. "What else would you expect? One's religious convictions impact on every area of one's life. If a man is religious, it's him. It's part of him. It's all of him."[7] He campaigned vigorously against Carter, claiming in one speech (falsely) that he had met Carter in the Oval Office and that Carter had told him he had to hire homosexual advisers because of the homosexual constituency in the Democratic Party.

Democratic Party policy seemed to the New Christian Right to threaten the integrity of the traditional family. Paul Weyrich, another leader, emphasized the importance of family to their concerns in a 1980 interview:

> What is behind the thrust against the traditional family values? Well, first of all, from our point of view, this is really the most significant battle of the age-old con-

flict between good and evil, between the forces of God and forces against God,
that we have seen in our country. We see the anti-family movement as an attempt
to prevent souls from reaching eternal salvation, and as such we feel not just a
political commitment to change this situation, but a moral and, if you will, a religious commitment to battle these forces.[8]

Among the forces threatening the family, according to this view, in addition to
homosexuality, were the Equal Rights Amendment for women, elective abortion, and pornography.

As the 1980 campaign gathered momentum, critical observers began to
wonder whether this new political activism on the right was as inclusive as its
leaders claimed. Moral Majority itself was careful to insist that its leadership
included Catholics and Jews, but at a Dallas meeting of the Religious Round-
table in August 1980, where many of the Protestant leaders (and Republican
candidate Reagan) spoke, the president of the Southern Baptist Convention,
Bailey Smith, declared: "My friend God Almighty does not hear the prayer of a
Jew. For how in the world can God hear the prayer of a man who says that Jesus
Christ is not the true Messiah. It is blasphemy. It may be politically expedient,
but no one can pray unless he prays through the name of Jesus Christ."[9] Falwell
himself was apparently sympathetic to Smith's view but recognized that his
move into the national political arena made such declarations unwise. The
American Jewish Committee, whose observer at the conference had been
shocked and dismayed at this declaration of religious exclusivity, publicized the
remark nationwide. AJC's director of interreligious affairs, Rabbi Marc Tanenbaum, met with Falwell to craft a statement distancing Moral Majority from
Smith's exclusivist position. God is a "respecter of all persons" who "loves
everyone alike and hears the cry of any sincere person who calls on Him," it
read (165). Smith insisted that he was a supporter of Israel and a friend to the
Jews, but reiterated that he could not better express his friendship than by bringing them, if possible, to the light of Christian truth.

Not all evangelicals were willing to conciliate Catholics and Jews for the
sake of political viability. Bob Jones Jr., president of Bob Jones University in
South Carolina, for example, stuck to the separatist principles that had inspired
his father to found the university in 1927. He condemned Falwell as "the most
dangerous man in America today as far as Biblical Christianity is concerned,"
adding in his journal *Faith for the Family* that Moral Majority was "one of
Satan's devices to build the world church of Antichrist."[10] Jones had previously
refused to have anything to do with Billy Graham's crusades because they were
too inclusive, and he was involved in federal litigation because his university
(which had admitted black students only since 1975) forbade interracial dating.
Of a 1981 assassination attempt on Pope John Paul II, he commented: "This
could be God's way of answering the prayers of his people" (98), and when Sec-

retary of State Alexander Haig denied a visa to the inflammatory Northern Irish politician, the Reverend Ian Paisley, Jones told a university audience: "I hope you'll pray that the Lord will smite him [Haig] hip and thigh, bone and marrow, heart and lungs . . . that he shall destroy him utterly and quickly" (97). Falwell, and the other evangelicals entering politics to rescue the nation from secular humanism, understood that they must create an emphatic gap between themselves and the intolerant, polemical side of their tradition that Jones represented.

"Born-again" Christians were suddenly much in the news. The phrase referred to the feeling that, if one turned wholeheartedly to God, the burden of one's sins was lifted and a better life in Christ could begin. Ezra Graley, a roofing contractor in the town of Nitro, West Virginia, gives a classic and heartfelt description of the experience:

> You feel the weight of the whole sins of the world is lifted off of you, whereas you had a heavy heart burdened down with sin, and now you feel that them sins is all been pardoned and you're—they're gone and you're just free—just seem like you could fly through the air almost. It's an experience that anybody'd have to experience theirself. . . . I went to an altar when the minister gave the invitation for those who wanted to accept Christ to come forth. And I prayed but I didn't feel like I was really borned again or converted. My sins I didn't feel like had got a complete job, and then I come home after the church service and prayed, and probably two o'clock in the morning it seemed like the whole weight of the world lifted off of me. The burden of sin was gone and then I walked in newness of light.[11]

As we have seen, there was nothing new to the 1970s about emotional, born-again Christians. Billy Graham and other evangelical preachers had worked unflaggingly since the 1940s to win new converts. What was new was their flexing of political muscles after half a century of relative withdrawal from public life since the Scopes Monkey Trial of 1925. The fact that nearly a quarter of the entire population, fifty million people, told pollsters in 1976 that they were born-again Christians showed that they were, latently, a political force of the first magnitude.

The New Christian Right's favored candidate in 1980 was, oddly enough, the Republican conservative and former governor of California Ronald Reagan. Although Reagan had no clear religious affiliation, was divorced, admitted to having experimented with drugs, and had spent much of his working life in Hollywood (which many Christian conservatives viewed as a den of iniquity), he had built his political career since the early 1960s as an uncompromising anti-Communist and as a defender of social conservatism against Berkeley radicals, hippies, the counterculture, and the New Left. His first run for president, back in 1968, had fizzled early, but he had done much better in 1976 and now he dominated the Republican primaries.

The jubilant New Christian Right claimed much of the credit for his victory over Carter in 1980. Academics and journalists, probably the two most secular professional groups in the nation, were amazed and alarmed. Would the "Reagan Revolution" reverse the social trends of the sixties and seventies, outlaw abortion, bring church-state separation to an end, and make America a Christian theocratic version of Khomeini's Iran?

The answer to all these questions was no, but a glance at some of the more exotic elements of the New Christian Right helps to explain the critics' alarm. For example, the New Christian Right included numerous dispensational premillennialists, fundamentalists who interpreted the Bible to mean that, just as each previous era of the earth's history had ended in catastrophe (expulsion from the Garden of Eden, Noah's flood, the Tower of Babel, the crucifixion, and so on), so would this one. Seven years of catastrophic war, culminating in the Battle of Armageddon, would devastate the earth, after which Jesus would return and preside over a thousand-year era of peace. Reagan's first secretary of the interior, James Watt, shared the premillennialist outlook, and early in his administration the president himself also expressed an interest. He told a lobbyist for Israel:

> You know, I turn back to your ancient prophets in the Old Testament and the signs foretelling Armageddon, and I find myself wondering if we're the generation that's going to see that come about. I don't know if you've noted any of those prophecies lately but, believe me, they certainly describe the times we're going through.[12]

He also referred to the Soviet Union as the "Evil Empire," a phrase calculated to make premillennialists think of the Book of Revelation and Antichrist's empire of the end times. After 1986 some of them speculated that the distinctive birthmark on Soviet leader Mikhail Gorbachev's forehead was "the sign of the beast," also foretold in Revelation.

If the world was about to come to an end, did it matter who was president and whether America's nuclear arsenal was adequate to withstand the Soviet threat? And what was the use of Christian academies and all the rest of the fundamentalist subculture since those whom God has chosen would be raptured (seized out of the world suddenly by Jesus) before the seven-year Tribulation? Such considerations had previously tended to keep fundamentalists out of politics. The sense of living in the end times was widespread in the late 1970s and early 1980s—America's best-selling book of the 1970s was Hal Lindsey's gory premillennialist classic *The Late, Great Planet Earth* (1970). Fundamentalist authors and artists inspired by Lindsey imagined the chaos on American highways when dozens of drivers were suddenly raptured, leaving their fast-moving cars driverless.

Evangelical movie director Donald W. Thompson's *A Thief in the Night*

(1972) made a dramatic visual presentation on the same theme. The film begins with a woman awakening and hearing on her alarm-clock radio the following bulletin:

> To say that the world is in a state of shock this morning would be to understate the situation. . . . Suddenly and without warning literally thousands, perhaps millions of people just disappeared. The few eyewitness accounts of these disappearances have not been clear, but one thing is certainly sure: Millions who were living on this earth last night are not here this morning.[13]

She gets up to consult her husband but finds only his electric razor, still buzzing in the bathroom. She screams in horror as she realizes what it means. He's been raptured and she's been left behind! Thompson estimated that between a quarter and a half of the entire American population had seen the film by 1980 and that it had led hundreds of thousands to turn to Jesus. He followed up with a series of films about the horrors of life for those left behind to suffer the Tribulation: A *Distant Thunder, Image of the Beast,* and *Prodigal Planet.* Historian Randall Balmer asked Thompson's partner Russell Doughten whether these films were *scaring* people into joining the church. Doughten answered: "Anybody who seriously reads the prophetic books or Revelation . . . will be scared. There's some pretty heavy stuff in those prophecies. If you take seriously what's being said there, it's frightening. And it ought to be." He added, "If they get into the kingdom through being scared, that's better than not making it at all" (63).

However, preparation for the Rapture and belief that the end times were imminent was only one aspect of the New Christian Right. Another element of growing importance drew on the ideas of the theologian Francis Schaeffer (1912–1984), who urged evangelicals to concentrate on rescuing their world from moral decay rather than dwelling on apocalyptic fantasies about its end. According to Schaeffer, evangelicals had neglected their country and permitted it to fall into the hands of God's enemies:

> Sixty years ago could we have imagined that unborn children would be killed by the millions here in our own country? Or that we would have *no freedom of speech* when it comes to speaking of God and biblical truth in our public schools? Or that every form of sexual perversion would be promoted by the entertainment media? Or that marriage, raising children, and family life would be objects of attack? Sadly we must say that very few Christians have understood the battle that we are in. Very few have taken a strong and courageous stand against the world spirit of this age as it destroys our culture and the Christian ethos that once shaped our country.[14]

Schaeffer's wide-ranging analysis of the corrupt modern world, and how it got that way, became holy writ to many fundamentalists as they reentered the political arena.

Schaeffer had been trained by, and regarded himself as a successor to, J. Gresham Machen, the theorist of fundamentalism who, in the interwar years, had split from the Presbyterian Church when it temporized on the question of biblical inerrancy, and had written the most intellectually distinguished defense of the fundamentalist position. By the 1970s Schaeffer lived in Switzerland; his home, L'Abri, became a kind of Protestant pilgrimage site for young evangelicals, who went in search of the long-haired, grizzled, and bearded guru. He was a controversial figure; skeptical about Billy Graham–style revivalism, which he regarded as anti-intellectual and too emotional, dismissive of evangelical attempts to use the theological insights of Karl Barth, the great German-language theorist of neo-orthodoxy, and an unflinching advocate of absolute biblical inerrancy. Some evangelical scholars winced at his confrontational style and denigrated his scholarly attainments, but all acknowledged his importance to the political reemergence of fundamentalism.

Schaeffer's breakthrough to widespread influence over American evangelicals, including Jerry Falwell, came with his film series and book titled *How Should We Then Live* (1976), a sweeping survey of the history of civilization from the evangelical perspective. It was, in effect, an answer to Kenneth Clark's *Civilization* (1969) and Jacob Bronowski's *The Ascent of Man* (1973), two upbeat television series from the same era about the development of humanity and civilization. Schaeffer, like Clark and Bronowski, took an interest in every aspect of society: art, architecture, intellectual life, popular music, literature, and even the current drug scene. He told his audience that as evangelical Christians they must often condemn the decadent things they found but they must not retreat into pietism, freezing out the contaminations of the world and so letting the world degenerate further. It was the absence of vigorous Christian protests that had led to the secularization of law (a baleful lineage from Oliver Wendell Holmes to the Supreme Court of *Roe v. Wade*, which legalized abortion) and science (in an equally distressing line from Darwin to Carl Sagan).

A confident dealer in sweeping generalizations, Schaeffer argued that the decline of Christian society could be traced back to the Renaissance and the Enlightenment, from which had sprung the false religion of humanism and which the Reformation, for all its grandeur, had been unable fully to prevent. Secular humanists, said Schaeffer (and a growing array of his American popularizers, such as Tim LaHaye), now occupied crucial positions in government, schools, and the media, from which they spread an essentially anti-Christian and anti-family message. With no higher beliefs to restrain them, unelected representatives of the elite, such as the Supreme Court justices, could manipulate popular opinion and change society in decisive (and dangerous) ways, as the school prayer decisions and *Roe v. Wade* had shown. "Secular humanism" became, with Schaeffer's guidance, the religious right's catchphrase for a wide range of its ideological adversaries.

He approved of Moral Majority's decision to bring evangelical Christians out of their self-imposed political exile and back into the fray, because they were battling for a fundamentally accurate vision of the world against one that was false and destructive. This was the message of his *Christian Manifesto* (1981), written as a deliberate parallel to Marx and Engels's *Communist Manifesto* (1848) and to the *Humanist Manifesto* (multiple authors, 1973). "The Moral Majority has drawn a line between the one total view of reality and the other total view of reality and the results this brings forth in government and law," he wrote. "All Christians have got to do the same kind of thing, or you are simply not showing the Lordship of Christ in the totality of life."[15]

Despite all the excitement that surrounded the emergence of evangelicals and fundamentalists as political activists in 1980, actual changes of political direction were slight when the new government got under way in 1981. The controversy over Bailey Smith and the "prayers of a Jew" had provided a premonition that there would be no sweeping change. Even if there was no secular humanist conspiracy of the kind Schaeffer feared, American politics was in fact highly secularized and pragmatic, with rules of its own. High-minded and indignant individuals entering the political arena with definite Christian objectives soon found that politics was a realm not of idealism but of compromise, concession, horse trading, and equivocation. It was all very well to pay lip service to religion in general—virtually all politicians did so. It was, however, a very different matter to press a specific religious position in national politics; Moral Majority had discovered at once that it must either distance itself from Smith or face accusations of intolerance, prejudice, and hostility to the First Amendment.

These lessons were not learned all at once, but the religious right began to feel disillusioned as the Reagan presidency progressed. Reagan favored pro-family policies in a general way, and he appointed Francis Schaeffer's friend and colleague Everett Koop to the position of surgeon general. On the other hand, he favored *reducing* the size and intrusiveness of the federal government, whereas Moral Majority's proposed pro-family legislation would have required a big and complicated federal enforcement apparatus. Hardheaded Republican Party professionals warned Reagan that it was unwise to invest too deeply in anti-abortion politics, a vital issue for Moral Majority, because opinions did not line up with party loyalties; millions of Republican voters were pro-choice, just as millions of Democrats were pro-life (Reagan's own first nominee for the Supreme Court, Sandra Day O'Connor, 1981, was herself a pro-choice Republican). Neither did the issue of restoring prayer in public schools—another key concern for Moral Majority—follow party lines. Reagan therefore contented himself with speaking frequently and vigorously to Christian conservative groups while taking few practical steps to enact their program.

Political pollsters, meanwhile, noticed that in the late 1970s and early 1980s religious participation in politics was taking on a new character. Growing numbers of well-funded, "single-issue" organizations were lobbying for legislation about particular moral concerns, but they were no longer narrowly identified with any particular church. Instead, conservative Catholics and Orthodox Jews were joining conservative evangelical Protestants in the campaigns against abortion, feminism, and secular humanism and for school prayer. On the other side of the ideological barricades, liberal Catholics and Reform Jews often found that they had much more in common with liberal Protestants than with conservative members of their own faiths. This new alignment, which in an important 1988 book with the same title the sociologist Robert Wuthnow described as "the restructuring of American religion," would persist in the ensuing decades.

The Abortion Controversy

How had abortion become one of the bitterest sources of division in American society, religion, and politics? In 1973 the Supreme Court's decision in *Roe v. Wade* had effectively legalized abortion in the first trimester of pregnancy. A decision that surprised supporters and detractors alike, it had overturned laws in all fifty states. Some doctors had been campaigning for abortion law reform over the preceding decade because they considered most state abortion laws too vague. The feminist movement had intensified the call for reform in the name of women's autonomy and reproductive freedom, and the idea was popular in other parts of society because of the widely shared belief that the world was over-populated and that drastic measures were needed to reduce numbers.

At first only a handful of Americans, nearly all of them Catholics, resisted abortion law reform. America's first anti-abortion demonstration was a quixotic affair, led by the editors of an ultra-orthodox Catholic magazine, *Triumph*, in June 1970. They marched against a Washington, D.C., clinic carrying cruci-fixes and wearing red berets, borrowed from the Spanish Civil War–era monar-chist faction they admired, and chanting, "Viva Cristo Rey" (Long live Christ the King). Police, as they arrested and dragged away the leaders for smashing clinic windows, mistook them for left-wing admirers of Che Guevara.

Even before *Roe v. Wade*, however, mainstream Catholic organizations, including the bishops, were becoming concerned at the progress of campaigns to legalize abortion, and eager to counteract them. In 1971 a Catholic doctor, Jack Willke, founded the first anti-abortion counseling center for pregnant women in Cincinnati. "Crisis pregnancy advisers" there, and in the three thou-sand other such centers that opened across America in the following years, advised unexpectedly pregnant women about prenatal care and helped those who decided to keep their children or to give them up for adoption. They were horrified by the Supreme Court's decision since, in their view, it legitimated the killing of children at the most vulnerable moment of life. Their belief that the fetus was a human being from the moment of conception—a belief their adversaries did not share—at once explains the intensity of their feeling. It seemed incredible to them that a democratic nation that prided itself on being the defender of the free world and the harbinger of human rights to oppressed peoples should in effect legalize the killing of children at their mothers' discretion.

Other religious groups, by contrast, notably liberal Protestants and Reform Jews, welcomed the Supreme Court's finding in *Roe v. Wade* since it gave women the chance to choose for themselves, even after becoming pregnant, whether to become mothers, and it seemed like a logical next step down the feminist road to personal autonomy. The Quakers, for example, whose consistent pacifist ethic gave them high moral standing on human rights issues, declared that they supported "a woman's right to follow her conscience concerning childbearing, abortion, and sterilization. . . . That choice must be made free of coercion, including the coercion of poverty [and] racial discrimination."[16] The Central Conference of American Rabbis (Reform Jewish) issued a 1975 statement that declared: "We believe that the proper locus for formulating the religious and moral criteria [relating to an abortion] and for making this decision must be the individual family or woman, and not the state or other external agency."[17] Unitarians, the United Church of Christ, Episcopalians, Lutherans, the United Methodists, the Disciples of Christ, Presbyterians, and the Mormons all made statements in the years after *Roe v. Wade* in which they accepted that the decision about whether to have an abortion could be seen, after mature deliberation, as one of individual choice. Even the socially and theologically conservative Southern Baptist Convention was amenable to the idea at first.

The most important and persuasive anti-abortion theorist in America was Berkeley law professor John T. Noonan, a Catholic layman. Already an established authority among Catholics for his scholarship on the history of religion and contraception (he had advised the Vatican to approve the use of artificial contraceptives in the mid-1960s), he developed a series of powerful arguments in support of the pro-life position. The intensity of his opposition to abortion sprang from his religious beliefs, but he argued that the humanity of the fetus could also be justified on purely secular grounds. Some participants in the debate about when a human life begins suggested that "viability" was the logical point, i.e., the time after which the child could survive outside the womb in the event of a premature birth. The problem with this criterion, said Noonan, was that neonatal technology was improving so rapidly that the moment of viability, far from being an objective moment on which scientific opinion could agree, was being pushed further and further back from year to year. Instead he argued that *conception* was the only objective moment at which a new human life could be said to have begun. After all, conception is the moment when a new individual is fully genetically encoded by the bringing together of the two discrete sets of genetic material, male and female, neither of which alone would ever have developed into a human being. Once conceived, however, the fetus needs no further genetic input, and it has an 80 percent chance of reaching the moment of birth. Conception, then, is a moment of objective *discontinuity* between the existence of mere organic tissue on the one hand and a distinct human life on the other, the most objectively convincing moment to say—here is a human life.

Noonan also traced the American legal tradition relating to unborn children. He noted that before *Roe v. Wade* the legal protections afforded to the unborn had been getting steadily stronger. In one 1967 case, for example, a pregnant Jehovah's Witness had been ordered by a court to permit her unborn child to have a blood transfusion to save its life. The woman had objected on First Amendment grounds (her religion opposed blood transfusions), but even this potent First Amendment right had been set aside by the need to save the baby—vivid evidence, said Noonan, of the court's assumption that the unborn child deserved the full protection of the law.

He also used two powerful analogies. The first was with slavery. In the infamous *Dred Scott* decision of 1857 (in which a slave had been denied standing to sue), he noted, the Supreme Court had denied an entire category of people citizenship rights because of their race. Now an entire category of people was being excluded on grounds of their age. Worse, they were being killed, which led to his second analogy, with Nazi Germany. The Nazis had exterminated more than six million people, not because of what they had *done* but because of what they *were*. Now America was permitting the same thing to happen—creating a situation in which (by the mid-1970s) more than a million people each year were killed, not for anything they had done but simply for being unwanted, without any consideration of their rights or interests.

These arguments had their effect, as did the sheer fact that abortion, once legalized, proliferated so rapidly. Early Catholic anti-abortion activists like John Kavanaugh O'Keefe came out of the Catholic left. After his brother was killed in Vietnam, O'Keefe, an undergraduate at Harvard, had sought conscientious objector status. His anti-abortion work in the 1970s, including some early sit-ins at abortion clinics, borrowed techniques, rhetoric, and hymns from Martin Luther King Jr., the civil rights movement, and the nonviolent branches of the anti-Vietnam movement. O'Keefe believed there was an absolute continuity between stopping the killing of war and stopping the killing of abortion. He found relatively little support on the left, however. Recruits to the anti-abortion movement more often came from the Catholic right, like James McFadden, founding editor of the movement's journal, the *Human Life Review*. McFadden described his reading of the *Roe v. Wade* decision in the *New York Times* as his own road to Damascus, a galvanizing event that led him to change the direction of his life (until then he had worked for William F. Buckley Jr.'s conservative journal, *National Review*).

In the late 1970s and early 1980s most grassroots opponents of abortion were Catholic housewives. The sociologist Kristin Luker, having studied activists on both sides of the abortion controversy in the early 1980s, showed that one of the critical differences between them was their ideas about motherhood. Pro-choice women would speak of an "unwanted" pregnancy, whereas pro-life women spoke of unplanned pregnancies as "surprise" or "unexpected." This choice of words was revealing. For the pro-lifers, in other words, motherhood was their primary role in life, to which other roles should be subordinated. For the pro-choicers, by contrast, motherhood was simply one of the roles they might fulfill, and if the prospect of giving birth intruded upon other ambitions, they felt entitled to end the pregnancy. The pro-choice women were more afflu-ent and much more likely to have careers. "Perhaps the single most dramatic difference between the two groups," Luker added, "is in the role that religion plays in their lives."[18] Three-quarters of the pro-choice women she studied never went to church, whereas 69 percent of the pro-lifers said that religion was important in their lives and that they attended church at least once every week, sometimes more often.

Luker's activists worked within the law, writing letters to congressional rep-resentatives, sometimes appearing before state legislatures to protest. In the late 1970s and early 1980s, however, a more confrontational style of anti-abortion activism developed, with chanting demonstrations outside abortion clinics, designed to disrupt the abortion providers and scare away women seeking the procedure. The first leader in this phase was another Catholic, Joseph Schei-dler, who understood how to use inflammatory rhetoric to draw media attention to the issue. Scheidler organized demonstrations in Chicago in the early 1980s and wrote a pamphlet, *Closed!* (1985), on effective techniques of disrupting clinics, which included injecting glue into door locks, blockading doorways with old cars and concrete slabs, and padlocking one's own body to the doors or to the machinery inside. It was Scheidler who first used the term "rescue" rather than "sit-in," because he wanted to emphasize that his actions at clinics were not just symbolic but were designed to prevent abortions from taking place and, with luck, to rescue children from death. He also harangued doctors and developed the idea of "sidewalk counseling," by which some of his volun-teers would try to discourage women arriving at the clinic from going through with the procedure.

Scheidler's Pro-Life Action League, like the civil rights movement of the 1950s and 1960s, sought to get its members arrested in order that their incar-ceration and trials could create more publicity for the movement (though he himself, unlike Martin Luther King Jr., was reluctant to suffer arrest). Impris-onment for the cause became a badge of honor rather than of shame, and the movement's fame spread rapidly. Scheidler even got two invitations to meet President Reagan at the White House, and Reagan himself indicated his approval of the movement (if not all its tactics) by permitting an anti-abortion book (*Abortion: the Conscience of a Nation*) to be published under his name just before the 1984 election.

The most uncompromising anti-abortion activist of all was Joan Andrews (b. 1948), a Catholic woman who was repeatedly arrested at clinic demonstrations, at which she did everything she could to destroy the abortion machinery. She had learned militant religion at an early age, being a member of the only Catholic family in a rural Tennessee farm district and having to stand up for her faith at school. In 1960, when she was twelve, she had held in her hands the fetal child that her mother had miscarried. Convicted in 1986 for trying to destroy a suction machine in a Pensacola, Florida, clinic, Andrews was sentenced to a five-year prison term because she refused to promise to stop picketing the clinic. Denying the legitimacy of her imprisonment, she then refused to cooperate in any way with prison authorities. She would not even walk, but instead went limp and had to be carried from place to place by guards. Noncooperation led to incarceration in a tough women's prison, Broward Correctional Institution, where she suffered strip searches and then two and a half years of solitary confinement. She sustained herself with prayer, writing in 1987: "I don't know what I'd do without the great blessing of prayer. . . . How I love my rosary, the wonderful devotionals people have sent me, and our rescue hymns and Marian hymns."[19]

Throughout Andrews's ordeal her case got little attention from the national mainstream media (the *New York Times*, the *Washington Post*, *Time*, *Newsweek*, and so on), whose editorial position was uniformly pro-choice. The evangelical television stations, by contrast, such as Jim and Tammy Bakker's *PTL* and Pat Robertson's *700 Club*, carried news of her pro-life martyrdom to a mass Protestant audience, even though she was a Catholic. As a result of the efforts of Atlanta businessman Peter Lennox, a fundamentalist, a massive letter-writing campaign to the governor of Florida was mounted on her behalf, along with a spate of demonstrations in Tallahassee, the state capital. Florida's state government finally bowed to this pressure and released Joan Andrews in October 1988. Unbroken, she at once began to participate in anti-abortion protests elsewhere. Her autobiography, *I Will Never Forget You*, shows her to be an artless, single-minded, ascetic personality, willing to suffer any penalty, including, apparently, a Christian martyr's death, on behalf of the unborn.

In 1987 the creation of Operation Rescue (OR) marked the emergence of evangelicals in anti-abortion leadership and their strengthening partnership with conservative Catholics. OR brought together Protestants, Catholics, and Jews under the leadership of Randall Terry, an evangelical preacher from Binghamton, New York, who had learned his techniques from Joe Scheidler and now aimed to get supporters arrested by the hundreds instead of the dozens. Large numbers of volunteers, trained in nonviolence, would appear suddenly outside a clinic and block all its entrances, trying to make it impossible for women seeking abortions to enter. Trained sidewalk counselors would urge the women to reconsider and direct them to centers where they could arrange to give birth and have their babies adopted. When police responded to the blockades by arresting OR activists, they went limp, their comrades singing or praying as they were carried to waiting police vans. In their first big New York demonstration, in early 1988, ecumenical harmony was assured when the Catholic members agreed not to pray the rosary and the Pentecostalist members agreed not to speak in tongues. Operation Rescue came to wide public notice with that demonstration, at which Austin Vaughan, auxiliary Catholic bishop of New York, was arrested, along with Mark Bavaro, a Catholic football star with the New York Giants. The next big OR demonstration, in Atlanta that summer, was timed to coincide with the Democratic National Convention, when much of the national media had concentrated there. Tense confrontations with police and pro-choice counterdemonstrators made the rescues noisy and turbulent. One hundred thirty-four people were arrested on the first day in Atlanta, hoping to pack the jails as vivid, living testimony to their sense of horror at the killing. They carried no identification, and when asked their names they answered simply "Baby Doe."

Some leading local churchmen, however, including Atlanta's most important Baptist minister, Charles Stanley, declined to endorse the movement because of its mass-arrest strategy and its potential for lawless chaos. Other clergy also kept it at arm's length. In the 1970s the American Catholic bishops, after a bold initial stand against *Roe v. Wade* that appeared to authorize civil disobedience, had drawn back from fear that direct involvement in this political issue might lead to challenges to the Catholic Church's tax-exempt status (as it was, they became embroiled in a ten-year challenge to their exemption). Similarly, Jerry Falwell, who appeared in Atlanta and handed Randall Terry a tenthousand-dollar check, later distanced himself from OR when pro-choice groups mounted a massive legal counteroffensive, charging it with racketeering, intimidation, and conspiracy. These legal maneuvers were successful in ensuring that after its peak year of 1989 Operation Rescue was never again able to match its New York and Atlanta mass protests. Terry himself, imprisoned in Atlanta, suffered a nervous breakdown in prison while his lieutenants on the outside feuded, and OR collapsed in 1991, almost as rapidly as it had arisen.

Wives and Mothers

Throughout the 1970s and 1980s abortion and gender questions unsettled nearly all religious groups. As we have seen, some groups hastened to adapt themselves to changing social mores by ordaining women into their ministry, while others resisted the change in the name of tradition. Meanwhile, the National Organization of Women and other feminist groups had revived the

Equal Rights Amendment to the Constitution, first introduced into Congress in 1923. It finally passed through Congress in 1972 and was sent to the state assemblies for ratification by the necessary three-quarters of them. Its aim was to eliminate invidious discrimination against women, particularly in matters of employment and constitutional protection. As with abortion, so with the ERA, the liberal churches endorsed it enthusiastically and anticipated its easy passage through the state assemblies.

Conservative religious women, on the other hand, led the opposition against the ERA's ratification. Phyllis Schlafly, their leader, was a devout Catholic from St. Louis who was horrified by the implications of the amendment. In her view, it violated natural realities, by trying to organize society as though God-given gender differences did not exist. She regarded women not as victims of discrimination but as the bearers of privileges that feminism threatened. The ERA, she predicted, would put women into unisex bathrooms at home and military combat overseas while denying them the legal protections as wives and mothers that they had long enjoyed. Organizing an effective coalition of grassroots demonstrators named StopERA, she arranged demonstrations outside state assembly buildings when the issue came up for ratification. At first, state assemblies had scrambled to ratify the ERA and its passage seemed assured, but as the 1970s progressed and Schlafly's movement gathered strength, states began to vote the other way. Several, under intense pressure, even withdrew their ratification. The amendment never became a part of the Constitution.

Women and men in the more conservative churches felt the need to respond to issues raised by the sexual revolution and the feminist movement. In doing so they drew a quite different picture of gender relations—as they were and as they should be—than did the feminists. They agreed with feminists that gender relations were not right in contemporary America but disagreed as to the reasons and the potential solution. Evangelicals were guided by such scriptural passages as Paul's decree "Wives, be subject to your husbands, as to the Lord. For the husband is the head of the wife as Christ is the head of the church. . . . As the church is subject to Christ, so let wives also be subject in everything to their husbands" (Ephesians 4:22–25). In their view, feminist striving undermined husbands' authority and worsened an already unhealthy situation. They also believed, however, that the giving of authority to husbands was not a matter of submitting to arbitrary power. After all, Paul had also in the same place ordered men: "Husbands, love your wives as Christ loved the church and gave himself up for her," and he added elsewhere: "Live considerately with your wives, bestowing honor on the woman as the weaker sex, since you are joint heirs of the grace of life" (1 Peter 3:7).

Evangelicals were, accordingly, eager to refute the feminist claim that there was something inherently repressive of women in traditional marriage and the nuclear family. Beverly LaHaye, wife of Tim LaHaye, one of Moral Majority's founders, collaborated with her husband on an evangelical manual, *The Act of Marriage* (1976). It was far more sexually explicit than previous evangelical literature on the topic, having been influenced by the sexual revolution even while constituting part of the counterattack. So long as sex took place within marriage, the LaHayes argued, a vigorous and pleasurable sex life was good, as was the use of contraceptives in family planning. "Modern research has made it abundantly clear that all married women are capable of orgasmic ecstasy. No Christian woman should settle for less," they wrote, adding that "your heavenly father placed it [your clitoris] there for your enjoyment."[20] Beverly LaHaye went on to write a string of evangelical women's advice books, such as the best-selling *The Spirit-Controlled Woman* (1976), which counseled women to find strength and confidence in their faith. The *reason* to develop this confidence was not to challenge what secular feminists described as patriarchal domination but to become a more fulfilled wife and mother. The nuclear family model remained, in LaHaye's telling, a divinely sanctioned principle of social organization, satisfying to men and women alike, and necessary in the struggle against secular humanism and the corrupt popular culture.

In addition to a busy writing schedule, Beverly LaHaye founded Concerned Women for America, a conservative Christian women's lobby that claimed half a million members by the late 1980s. The women who ran its chapters embodied the same contradictions as Phyllis Schlafly: they counseled wifely submission, nurture, and domesticity while demonstrating that they themselves were powerful and effective in politics. Indeed, the way they described submissiveness showed it to be a power stragegy. Maxine Sielman, head of an Iowa branch of CWA, told historian Randall Balmer:

> I think women are the key to turning this nation around. I firmly believe that this is why Satan went to Eve, not Adam. . . . I firmly believe the role of a woman today is to nurture our next generation. She has the power within her hands to either make or break a nation. . . . The secret to a woman's role, I believe, is authority and being submissive. And I feel that just as God asked the woman to bear children because He knew that she wouldn't want to put up with a pregnant man for nine months or He knew that a man could not tolerate the pain of having a child, God also asked her to be submissive, which is one of the hardest things that a woman is asked to do. But therein comes real peace. As we submit to God and become all we can be under God's authority, we find fulfillment. There's no limit to what women can do today.[21]

Other students of gender relations in theory and practice came to the same conclusion: The appearance of subordination and submission could be a highly energizing and powerful approach to both politics and everyday life.

Other evangelical theorists echoed LaHaye. In a tightly argued six-hundred-page study, *Man and Woman in Christ* (1980), replete with biblical chapter and verse, Stephen Clark wrote that Christians must preserve the family and, within it, the complementarity of the sexes. "There is room for some flexibility in deciding which tasks are the man's and which are the woman's [but] there is no room for the type of flexibility which undermines the distinct line between male and female spheres of responsibility."[22] Clark argued that modern technological society not only threatened the family as the primary unit of society, it also eroded the dignified status women had held in earlier ages and simpler societies, such as that depicted in the Bible. Ours was an oversexualized society. Christians, in reaction against it, "should relate to one another primarily as brothers and sisters in the Lord and not as members of the opposite sex" (599). Meanwhile, men should take responsibility for bringing up boys, and women should take responsibility for bringing up girls, with less reliance on the peer group and maximum opportunity for cross-generational contacts.

LaHaye and Clark agreed that gender differences were ineradicable and that a well-ordered Christian society required a benign form of hierarchy. Folksy Edward Hindson, a friend and fellow minister of TV evangelist Jerry Falwell, explained in *The Total Family* that the husband's superiority imposed on him duties and responsibilities:

> The Bible clearly states that the wife is to submit to her husband's leadership and help him fulfill God's will for his life. . . . She is to submit to him just as she would submit to him as her Lord. This places the responsibility of leadership upon the husband, where it belongs. In a sense, submission is learning to duck, so God can hit your husband! He will never realize his responsibility to the family as long as you take it. . . . The same passages that command the wife to obey her husband, command the husband to love his wife! Being a leader is not being a dictator, but a loving motivator, who, in turn, is appreciated and respected by his family. Dad, God wants you to be the loving heartbeat of your home by building the lives of your family through teaching and discipline.[23]

Who could object to having a benign and loving male motivator in the home, especially if he didn't smoke, drink, beat his wife, or tyrannize the kids? And yet the phrasing and the assumptions could hardly have been better calculated to enrage secular feminists!

Jewish as well as Christian commentators argued over proper gender relations. While Reform, Reconstructionist, and eventually Conservative congregations all accepted the idea of ordaining women as rabbis, the Orthodox community refused. The legal code governing Orthodox Jews' lives, the halakah, prohibited it. Some Orthodox women, such as the writer Blu Greenberg, who was influenced by feminism but determined to remain loyal to her Orthodox community, looked for ways to increase women's rights and enhance their role without violating halakhic principles. In 1981 she wrote: "Though the truth is painful to those of us who live by Halakah, honesty bids us acknowledge that Jewish women, particularly in the more traditional community, face inequality in the synagogue and participation in prayer, in halakhic education, in the religious courts, and in areas of communal leadership."[24] She proposed ways in which women could be given greater roles in worship, better education, and full legal equality without violating the tradition. At the same time she criticized aspects of the feminist assault on the traditional family and its denigration of genuine biological differences between men and women, insisting that the family was "the primary source of strength and support [for Jews] in coping with an often dangerous and hostile world" (12).

Other Orthodox Jews found nothing to praise in feminist ideas and argued that traditional Orthodoxy was the best safeguard of their interests as women. During the 1970s and 1980s, in fact, the ultra-Orthodox Hasidic community was growing rapidly, maintaining the loyalty of its female members and drawing in, as new recruits, discontented women from other branches of Judaism. When the journalist Lis Harris studied the Lubavitcher Hasidim in the mid-1980s her principal informant, Sheina, described her migration to Hasidim from a more assimilated Jewish life and rejoiced in it. To her the role of wife and mother was dignified and fulfilling, and she argued that she and her husband, in their common dedication of their lives to God, suffered no conflict in living up to very different gender expectations. Impressed despite her initial skepticism, Harris admitted that this way of life had its attractions:

> Moshe and Sheina have rejected most of the values of that society [the secular world around them] and, buttressed on all sides by like-minded fellow Hasidim, they serve God in a spirit of dedicated communality. They present to the world not only a counterculture but a counterreality, which turns most modern notions of sexual politics, self-expression and cultural adaptation upside down.[25]

Sheina went on to say that she had no objection to being segregated behind a women's screen in the synagogue; that too was part of a tradition worked out over thousands of years. "We are not striving for togetherness in shul. My relationship to God is private. It's not where I sit that counts but the spirit of my prayer" (134). Other defenders of Orthodox tradition, likewise, denied that the secular wisdom of the era regarding women's roles was adequate to displace the traditional wisdom about men's and women's roles.

Feminist and anti-feminist ideas about women's role in society and religion did not move toward reconciliation in the late twentieth century. Each group could provide convincing scriptural and practical reasons for its own point of view, and each thought the worst of the other. Certain realities affecting both groups, however, were gradually shifting the terms of the debate. Women's participation in the American workforce was continuing to increase; family incomes were increasing in real terms, but individual incomes were not. The

1950s ideal of Dad at work and Mom at home with the kids could no longer be realized by most families in the 1980s and 1990s. The rhetoric of gender-conservative women, accordingly, shifted to accommodate the fact that many of them would have to work outside the home, even as it held fast to the ideal of biblically sanctioned complementary differences.

Chapter 8

THE CHRISTIAN QUEST FOR JUSTICE AND WISDOM: 1980–1995

The 1980s were an activist decade among Christian groups on the right and the left, which aimed to correct injustices and bring America into line with the gospel. A sharply divided Christian community, however, held different opinions about which aspects of American life violated the Christian message. For those on the political left it was the nation's continuing dependence on nuclear weapons for its defense, its support for oppressive right-wing regimes in Latin America, and its exclusion of refugees fleeing from them. For Christians on the political right, by contrast, it was the power of secular humanism. We have already seen how the New Christian Right mobilized against abortion, which it interpreted as the horrible outcome of secular humanism. In this chapter we will consider conservative evangelicals' campaigns against the teaching of cultural relativism and evolution in public schools. Neither side of the religious/political divide felt satisfied at the outcome of its campaigns. The Christian left was unable to change the direction of American defense and foreign policy. The Christian right, despite scattered victories against what it saw as objectionable textbooks, was unable to prohibit the teaching of evolution or restore school prayer. It reacted in part by creating independent Christian schools and in part by forsaking schools of any kind, making a switch to home schooling.

The Antinuclear Movement

Before Vietnam nearly all Americans were anti-Communists. The war punctured most of the old anti-Communist verities. It showed, first, that the domino theory was false. Just because one country falls to Communism does not necessarily mean that all those around it will follow suit. Second, by 1975 when Saigon fell, it had become impossible to believe that Communists always acted in concert and were all parts of a worldwide Red conspiracy. The Soviet Union had aided the North Vietnamese, but the Chinese (whom the Vietnamese had hated for centuries) had not. President Nixon himself had realized that he could gain diplomatic leverage against Russia by befriending China, the insight that led to his visit to China—the great diplomatic coup of 1972.

The most harrowing discovery of the late sixties and early seventies for idealistic Americans was that their country's foreign policy might sometimes be no more virtuous than that of their great adversary. Radical opponents of the war got so carried away with this notion that some of them even carried Vietcong flags at demonstrations, and attributed to Ho Chi Minh all the virtues they thought Lyndon Johnson and Richard Nixon lacked. The grisly aftermath of the war, in which the conquerors exterminated or imprisoned thousands of South Vietnamese who had collaborated with the Americans, while thousands more made desperate efforts to escape the new regime in unseaworthy boats, soon shattered that idea. Even so, the era of anti-Communist consensus was at an end.

After Vietnam the biggest foreign policy question among American religious groups was how to think about nuclear weapons. An earlier surge of popular concern about nuclear proliferation had been displaced by the Vietnam crisis but had never disappeared. Now it revived, especially in light of the Senate's failure to endorse the 1978 Strategic Arms Limitation Treaty (SALT II) and the Reagan administration's apparent belief that it could fight and win "limited" nuclear wars. Reagan believed that America, "God's country," was not doing enough to win the Cold War and that it should undertake its world-saving mission with new vigor. He therefore authorized development and deployment of a new generation of nuclear missiles, including space-based defense systems (nicknamed Star Wars, after the 1977 movie) while bringing many older weapons, even battleships, back into commission. In his first administration the Department of Defense and the armed forces grew by leaps and bounds, as did their political clout.

He and many of his supporters in the New Religious Right maintained the old view that American possession of nuclear weapons targeted on Russian cities deterred Soviet aggression and was therefore morally acceptable. A growing chorus of voices in the liberal churches disagreed and began to organize demonstrations to protest a policy based on the threat of massive, indiscriminate annihilation of civilians. The fact that America's Catholic bishops joined in this protest was, at first glance, surprising. In the first two decades of the Cold War, the Catholic Church, as much as any group in America, had stood squarely behind a nuclear deterrence policy. Their most eloquent spokesman of that era, John Courtney Murray, S.J., had worked out a theological defense of nuclear weapons in the Cold War context. By 1981, however, the men in office as Catholic bishops and in seminaries as Catholic theologians were very different people from their predecessors. The new men, appointed after Vatican II, were enthusiasts for the council's invitation to get involved with worldly matters. Less socially and politically conservative than their predecessors, and distraught at the catastrophic vision of the post-nuclear-war world depicted in books like Jonathan Schell's *The Fate of the Earth* (1982), they decided to write a pastoral letter on nuclear weapons.

To draft their letter the bishops chose J. Bryan Hehir, an austere and brilliant priest with an encyclopedic knowledge of the political, military, and ethical issues at stake. In keeping with Vatican II's democratic tone the bishops deliberated in the open, rather than behind closed doors as of old, and did not try to disguise the fact that some of them (such as Raymond Hunthausen of Seattle) were absolute pacifists while others (such as John O'Connor of New York) were old-style Cold Warriors. Each of the three drafts of their letter was published and debated, and all interested parties—not just Catholics—were invited to join in the debate. In its final form (May 1983) the pastoral letter, *The Challenge of Peace: God's Promise and Our Response*, took a highly critical view of nuclear weapons as currently deployed by the American military, deplored deterrence theory, and condemned altogether the targeting of cities.

Catholic conservatives, sympathetic to the Reagan administration and to the effectiveness of deterrence policy, worked vigorously against the near-pacifist tone of the letter. Among these critics were William Simon, President Reagan's secretary of the treasury; William F. Buckley Jr., founder and editor of *National Review*; and Michael Novak, a former Catholic leftist who had emerged in the 1970s as a leading neoconservative intellectual. In their view the bishops' letter was misguided. It represented, they said, a form of defeatism, the mood of "the Vietnam syndrome" dressed up in Catholic rhetoric.

Both the bishops and their adversaries wrote in the language of the Catholic "just war" theory, a theory that had evolved in the Middle Ages to limit the destructiveness of war but one that was increasingly difficult to reconcile with the conditions and technologies of modern war. Among the requirements for a just war was the consideration of "proportionality"—that the destruction done by war was more than outweighed by the achievement of good. Novak's book-length answer to the bishops' letter, *Moral Clarity in the Nuclear Age* (1983), argued that nuclear weapons fulfilled the proportionality criterion. They were *used*, he said, by sitting in their silos and deterring Soviet aggression. They killed no one so long as they stayed put, but at the same time they were immensely effective instruments of national security. In this paradoxical but not unreasonable view, he argued that the way to *use* a nuclear weapon was to *avoid* actually sending it against the enemy. To deepen the paradox, he acknowledged that the enemy was deterred only by the knowledge that, if it came to the point, America *would* fire its missiles. Accordingly, the best way to avoid firing them was to maintain the continual threat of doing so. In this way tens of millions of lives were safeguarded. Given the instability of the world, and the magnitude of the Communist threat, this safeguard was religiously and ethically defensible.

Other churches joined the Catholics in making statements about nuclear weapons. The bishops of the United Methodist Church, one of the largest Protestant denominations, issued a pastoral letter of their own in 1982, asking that it be read aloud in all their denomination's churches. Similar in tone to the Catholic bishops' letter, it admitted the difficulty of negotiating with the Soviet Union in a Cold War atmosphere of profound mistrust but saw arms reduction and eventual abolition as a moral necessity for Christians. Bishop John Warman of Harrisburg, Pennsylvania, a signatory, added: "You cannot boil seven million human beings in their own juices and then speak of Christian love. It would be far better for us to trust the God of the Resurrection and suffer death than to use such a weapon."[1] The American Baptist Churches, the Disciples of Christ, the United Presbyterians, the Episcopalians, and many other Protestant churches made comparable declarations in the early 1980s. By contrast, a motion to support the "nuclear freeze" movement among Southern Baptists, a denomination 13.5 million strong, was defeated. The Southern Baptist Convention instead blended an appeal for mutual disarmament negotiations with a reminder about the imperative need for a strong and effective defense.

The net result of this great outpouring of religious debate and statement making from 1980 to 1984 was, from the churches' point of view, disappointingly slight. The Reagan administration was certainly concerned at the sight and sound of so much outspoken religious criticism (and grateful for scattered statements of religious support), but it did not, on that account, change its policies. The government, Congress, the armed forces, and the manufacturers of nuclear weapons employed tens of thousands of people who belonged to the churches that condemned America's nuclear defense policy, but these church statements did not lead to mutinies, strikes, or mass resignations.

Here again appears the paradox of emphatic secularity side by side with vigorous religiosity. It can be explained partly by the fact that the ordinary churchgoer was remote, geographically and in outlook, from his or her church's national policymakers. The churches' full-time employees, especially those staffing national offices, were more familiar with one another and with national political affairs than with the bread-and-butter concerns of their denominations' local parishioners. An ordinary churchgoer might hear an ardent sermon against nuclear weapons or the reading of a denominational statement, might briefly entertain the priest's or minister's view that the nation was embroiled in a form of collective and un-Christian madness, but might later in the day read newspaper stories and see television reports on the Soviet arms buildup and Soviet aggression in Afghanistan. The churches had no monopoly on information or its interpretation, ministers were sometimes politically naive, and their occasional calls for a defiant impracticality faced constant discredit from other information sources.

Sanctuary

President Reagan not only maintained and escalated the nuclear confrontation. He also authorized covert American aid to anti-Communist wars around the world, notably by aiding the Contra guerrillas in Nicaragua as they tried to overturn the Soviet-backed Sandinista regime. At the same time he aided right-wing regimes in El Salvador and Guatemala—nominally civilian but heavily dependent on military force—as they tried to forestall leftist revolution. His support for El Salvador, where tens of thousands of civilians had recently been displaced and many more tortured and killed, caused controversy right from the start of his administration. In March 1980 Oscar Romero, the Catholic archbishop of San Salvador, who had angered the regime by criticizing its human rights abuses, had been gunned down in his cathedral, probably by a right-wing assassin. A few weeks after Reagan's election three American Maryknoll nuns and a Catholic laywoman, radicalized against the regime by what they had witnessed in El Salvador, were kidnapped, raped, and killed. Amnesty International and other human rights groups confirmed that the Salvadoran regime was not a democracy and that it ruled by terror, torture, and execution.

Growing numbers of American Christians protested against their government's support of such a regime on human rights grounds. Those sympathetic to the political left looked at the issue through the lens of liberation theology, which had become popular in American divinity schools during the 1970s and had underlain the development of black and women's theologies. Since an epoch-making meeting at Medellín, Colombia, in 1968, Latin America's Catholic bishops and theologians had argued that the crucial division of the world lay not between the capitalist West and the Communist East, as in the orthodox Cold War view, but between the rich "north" (America and Western Europe) and the impoverished "south" (Africa, Latin America, and South Asia). Much of Latin America, they had written, bore witness to "a situation of injustice that must be recognized as institutionalized violence, because the existing social structures violate people's basic rights; a situation which calls for far-reaching, daring, urgent, and profoundly innovative change."[2] Jesus, they added, came to save not just the souls of the poor but also their bodies; Christian witness must be a social and political as well as a spiritual venture, and could even justify participation in revolutionary violence. God's "preferential option for the poor," an idea central to liberation theology, characterized the work of the leading liberationists, Leonardo Boff and Gustavo Gutierrez. It became a first principle for U.S. Christians who sympathized with the Central American struggle against poverty and oppression, and shaped the work of the Sanctuary movement.

The wars generated refugees, many of whom fled in fear for their lives. Like nearly all political refugees of the twentieth century who were able to do so, these Guatemalans and Salvadorans headed for the United States, often arriving after exhausting and dangerous journeys across Mexico and the Sonoran Desert. In one notorious incident of 1980 twenty-six Salvadorans were abandoned in the desert by their Mexican "coyotes" (border-crossing smugglers), and half of them died of heatstroke before help arrived. The survivors, and hundreds more like them, were captured by the U.S. Border Patrol. The Immigration and Naturalization Service (INS) in the Cold War era usually granted refugee status and political asylum to people fleeing from regimes hostile to the United States. Cubans since 1960 and Vietnamese since 1975, for example, had found it relatively easy to obtain asylum. Salvadorans and Guatemalans in the Reagan era, conversely, found it almost impossible. Many were promptly sent back despite their terrified claims that they had been targeted by death squads, without even having their right to apply for asylum properly explained. Many, lacking any understanding of English, did not realize that a paper they were asked to sign was a waiver of their right to a hearing.

Learning of this state of affairs, a group of Christian activists in the Tucson, Arizona, area organized to help the refugees. Jim Corbett, a Harvard-educated Quaker who now raised goats in the area, and John Fife, a Presbyterian minister (with a civil rights background—he had marched with Martin Luther King Jr. at Selma, Alabama, in 1965), began raising money to bail Salvadorans out of jail pending deportation hearings, hired lawyers for these hearings, and publicized the refugees' plight. Fife and other sympathizers also took refugees awaiting hearings into their homes. Aware that the INS preferred to do its work inconspicuously, he drew national media attention in March 1982 with the announcement that he was turning his church, Tucson's Southside Presbyterian, into a sanctuary where illegal Salvadorans would be protected. After a heart-wrenching five-hour meeting his congregation had voted 59–4 in favor of the idea, despite the fact that harboring illegal immigrants was punishable by imprisonment. In a statement read out to journalists and TV cameras before the church, Fife declared:

> We believe that justice and mercy require that people of conscience actively assert our God-given right to aid anyone fleeing from persecution and murder. . . . [My

congregation] declared sanctuary because they determined after Bible study, prayer and agonizing reflection that they could not remain faithful to the God of the Exodus and prophets and do anything less. It was for us a question of faith.[3]

Sanctuary was a time-honored tradition in the Judeo-Christian religions. Moses, according to the Book of Numbers, designated a sanctuary city, where fugitives were safe from pursuit; the Roman emperor Constantine, when he converted to Christianity, had made all churches sanctuaries; and the tradition had persisted in medieval Europe. We saw (in chapter 5 above) that the experiment had been tried (unsuccessfully) to protect draft resisters and deserters in the Vietnam era.

Sanctuary was not a legally binding concept in American law, but, as Fife had hoped, it was certainly newsworthy and brought publicity, and new recruits, to the cause. Ministers around America began to join in. Gus Schultz, a radical Lutheran pastor in Berkeley, California, was one, and he organized other clergy in the city on behalf of Sanctuary. The refugees themselves—nearly all Catholics—were often baffled to find themselves sheltering inside Protestant churches devoid of statues of the saints they venerated, but they welcomed the protection afforded them by these influential and dedicated gringos. The movement spread quickly along the huge U.S.-Mexican border and far into the American heartland.

The Sanctuary movement's next step was to organize safer border crossings for Salvadorans and Guatemalans than those provided by the predatory coyotes. Corbett, fluent in Spanish, explored the refugees' routes through Mexico and created a network of volunteers on both sides of the border to help them get into the United States. He compared the group to one of the base communities (*comunidades de base*) that were central to liberation theology: grassroots clusters of people for whom religion was not merely a set of ideas but a set of practices, growing out of the circumstances and events of their lives. Latin American base communities were usually all-Catholic, whereas the Sanctuary community was interfaith. Corbett wrote: "Our joint practice is grafting the people that is the church into the people that is Israel; we are—Christian and Jew—affirming in practice that we are formed by the same Covenant. . . . Sanctuary is the needle's eye through which congregations composed of the beneficiaries of violence are entering into active community with the violated."[4]

The Reagan government denied that the Salvadorans' lives were in danger; it saw them as seekers of economic opportunity rather than as genuine political refugees and denied that there was any hard evidence of persecution against those who had been arrested and repatriated. Elliott Abrams, an assistant secretary of state, told a Sanctuary conference that "many of the people organizing the Sanctuary Movement are . . . using some of the Salvadorans and others as pawns in their efforts to attack Administration policy in Central America."[5] Nevertheless, government agents hesitated at first to take refugees out of Sanctuary churches, even though they were legally entitled to do so, from fear of adverse publicity.

Before long, Fife, Corbett, and their assistants had organized an updated version of the "underground railroad" that had smuggled escaping slaves to free territory before the Civil War. They helped refugees to cross from Mexico to the United States, then carried them away from the border, where they were most likely to be arrested, dispersing them to church groups around the country where they could be sheltered and given legal support and temporary employment. Not only young radicals but also liberal Christians from many denominations and all age groups joined in. Innocent-looking middle-aged women volunteered for such dangerous assignments as meeting refugee groups just inside the border and driving them to places of relative safety, sheltering, and feeding them. Many of these politically moderate Sanctuary workers, and their supporters, contradicting press claims that they were romantic religious lawbreakers, insisted that the *government* was breaking the law by not following the asylum procedures Congress had specified and that they, as citizens, had merely taken the initiative to uphold the relevant statutes. Even the highly respectable Catholic archbishop of Milwaukee, Rembert Weakland, harbored eight Salvadorans in his home.

By 1982 more than one hundred American churches were involved (the number would eventually reach more than four hundred). Twenty-two cities, including Los Angeles and New York, and three states, including the border state of New Mexico, declared themselves sanctuaries, ordering their law enforcement officers not to pursue illegal Salvadorans and Guatemalans. The Sanctuary movement itself enjoyed royal treatment from the media. Print and television journalists were far more ready to trace a direct line from the civil rights movement to Sanctuary than they had been to trace one from the civil rights movement to the anti-abortion movement (which made the same claim). Ed Bradley, of the CBS news show *60 Minutes*, along with a film crew, accompanied Corbett on a cross-border venture to help a Salvadoran family get into the country, and the successful mission was shown on nationwide television.

Tensions arose within the rapidly growing movement over how centralized its leadership should be, how openly political it should be, and how selective it ought to be in its identification of suitable refugees for sanctuary. The Chicago Religious Task Force, largely Catholic in membership, favored a well-developed structure to avoid duplication of work, and selectivity to keep track of affiliated groups and their actions. The group clearly had a political as well as a religious agenda; part of its Statement of Faith read:

The sanctuary movement seeks to uncover and name the connections between the US government and the Salvadoran death squads, and the connection between US business interests and the denial of human and economic rights of the vast majority of people. We believe that to stop short of this is to betray the Central American people and the refugees we now harbor.[6]

Corbett's Quaker instincts, by contrast, led him to prefer a sprawling, decentralized, and nonselective approach, and he bridled at the idea that there should be a political criterion to his selection of refugees for help.

Eventually the INS was forced to react, lest its border policy and respect for immigration law collapse altogether. It repeated its claim that the movement was politically motivated, not humanitarian, and that many of the refugees were simply seeking economic opportunity. Having infiltrated the movement early on with bogus "volunteers" assigned to gathering information, it knew what was happening and could identify the leading spirits. In January 1985 it arrested fifty-eight refugees and sixteen Sanctuary organizers, charging them with the transportation of illegal aliens. Those arrested included Fife and Corbett, as well as three Catholic nuns, two Catholic priests, and two Methodists. The arrests enraged Sanctuary activists, one of whom, another nun, wrote:

> It is not these people of faith who should be indicted. It is the United States government that should be indicted on charges of inducing refugees to flee El Salvador and Guatemala by sending millions of dollars of military aid to those oppressive governments. The US government should be indicted on charges of deporting tens of thousands of refugees back to harassment, torture, and possible death.[7]

Stacy Lynn Merkt, a Texas woman who had been arrested and convicted earlier, was adopted by Amnesty International as a prisoner of conscience, further eroding the government's position in the public relations confrontation.

Press coverage of the trial that followed dramatized it as a confrontation between church and state, conscience and citizenship. As anthropologist Hilary Cunningham noted:

> This coverage of Sanctuary established a structure of polar oppositions between Southside [Presbyterian Church] and the U.S. government—church versus state, religion versus politics, conscience versus the law, humanitarian values versus national security, refugees versus economic migrants—that prepared the public for a dramatic confrontation, a "shoot-out" as it were, between church and state.[8]

Sympathy for the movement enabled the defendants to raise an effective team of attorneys. Ham-fisted tactics by the prosecution, on the other hand, the untrustworthiness of its informer, Jesus Cruz (whom the defense was able to paint in the likeness of Judas Iscariot), and the fact that the INS had authorized numerous information-gathering break-ins at Sanctuary churches over the preceding year, all contributed to embarrassing the government and aiding the defendants' cause. Among the defendants was a charismatic nun, Sister Darlene Nicgorski, who became one of the movement's great stars. She had worked as a teacher in Guatemala and witnessed the persecution of peasants by the military, leaving the country only after the murder of a priest she knew and threats that she and her fellow nuns would be next. As Sanctuary historian Ann Crittenden wrote:

> Sister Darlene had attracted a devoted retinue of nuns, many of whom had also served in Latin America and who were in constant attendance at the trial. She as much as the others had become instant folk heroes of the left, which had few enough in the Age of Reagan, as the trial became a magnet for journalists, film-makers and activists hoping for a replay of the great civil disobedience scenes of the 1960s.[9]

Most of the defendants were found guilty, but the judge, after receiving hundreds of letters appealing for clemency, including one from Arizona senator Dennis DeConcini, who had nominated him for his position on the bench, gave them suspended sentences rather than sending them to prison.

Sanctuary work continued, but with an enhanced emphasis on the legality, rather than the illegality, of what its members were doing. Breaching the border remained unlawful, but the movement was careful to select individuals who had a good claim to refugee status according to criteria laid down by Congress and the United Nations. Once they were inside the country—no matter how they had arrived—they could make formal application for political asylum. A Supreme Court decision in 1987 helped the movement by broadening the conditions under which a foreigner in America was allowed to apply for asylum. The movement itself, increasingly riven with political differences, split. Even in Tucson, where it had begun, a splinter group, El Puente, split off from Corbett and Fife's Tucson Refugee Support Group because of its dissatisfaction with what it saw as the coercive outcome of TRSG's Quaker-derived form of consensus building.

The gradual return of political stability in Latin America made the Sanctuary movement less newsworthy after 1988. Like the antinuclear movement, it had created publicity and called attention to controversial policies but had been unable to reorient national priorities in either Latin America or refugee policy. Its work had *influenced* politicians, prompting many to ask for leniency in the sentencing of Sanctuary workers, but it had not persuaded either a congressional majority or the administration's immigration and foreign policy executives that they must reform their approach to Latin American affairs. Its work on the religious/political left was no more successful in creating a national change of direction than the anti-abortion movement's comparable work on the right. Members of both movements followed a religious imperative to help their fellow humans, and the most highly motivated members of both showed themselves willing to suffer prosecution and imprisonment on behalf of their causes. Neither, however, was able to duplicate the achievement of the civil rights movement on which they modeled themselves, because they could not build decisive *national* majorities behind their own interpretation of events. Segregation as an intellectually respectable option had virtually collapsed by 1960, even if a preference for it lived on — shamefaced — in white popular culture. Freedom of choice about abortion, on the other hand, continued to benefit from the work of tenacious intellectual and political defenders, as did the need to forestall Marxist revolution in Latin America and to safeguard national boundaries against unchecked immigration.

Creationism and Evolution

While liberal Christians in the early 1980s worked against nuclear weapons and for Salvadoran refugees, conservative Christians continued their struggle against secular humanism. Although its practitioners rarely called themselves secular humanists, they were recognizable by their ideas. They favored excluding prayers from public schools while including Darwinian evolution in the biology curriculum, they regarded homosexuality as a lifestyle rather than a sin, and they favored a woman's right to choose abortion. Conservative Christians conducted campaigns against these preferences even though the New Christian Right was learning, to its sorrow, that President Reagan was not quite the wholehearted leader they had anticipated. Among its campaigns of the early 1980s was an effort to promote creation science in the public schools.

Creation science, said its advocates, was a scientific theory that explained the creation of the world, its current condition, and the existence of all the species in it. It agreed with the first chapters of Genesis not only as a matter of faith but as a matter of verifiable science, and stood in stark opposition to the theory of evolution. Ever since publication of Charles Lyell's *Principles of Geology* (1830–1833) and Charles Darwin's *On the Origin of Species* (1859), Christians and Jews, scientists and ministers, had struggled to come to terms with scientific theories that were at odds with the Bible. Lyell's evidence suggested that the Earth was millions of years older than most interpreters had previously believed, and that nearly all its geological processes took place gradually. Darwin's picture of life on this ancient planet was bleak. Species survived, he argued, not because a benevolent God had created them all at once and given each of them its own little niche in the natural world, but because the fittest members of each species had seized and adapted to available niches, fighting off all competitors in a perpetual war of predation within species and between them. Hundreds of creatures died for every one that lived. Species developed over the course of millions of years by random mutation rather than according to a purposeful plan; they had not been created all at once, and each of them was destined, sooner or later, for extinction.

These geological and biological theories were so persuasive, and fit so well with the accumulating physical evidence, that they had won over most scientists by 1900. A few, like Louis Agassiz in America and Philip Gosse in England, continued to hold out against evolution because it contradicted Genesis. Gosse even suggested that the fossils of creatures no longer in existence, which were an important part of Darwin's evidence for evolution, had been placed in the rock strata by God to make evolutionary theory *seem* plausible and thus strengthen men's faith in the Bible in the face of contrary temptation!

In the early twentieth century the fundamentalist movement organized around a cluster of basic Christian beliefs, one of which was the inerrancy of Scripture. After all, said the early fundamentalists, if one part of the Bible (the Genesis Creation story) is discarded as inaccurate, other parts will follow, and men, rather than God, will become the judges and arbiters of truth. George McCready Price, a Seventh-day Adventist and self-taught geologist, claimed in *The New Geology* (1923) that the pattern of the Earth's rock strata was the consequence not of processes taking place over aeons but of the upheavals that accompanied Noah's flood. William Jennings Bryan (1860–1925), the most famous fundamentalist of his day, believed Price had resolved the apparent contradiction between Scripture and science. He also believed that the Darwinian vision of the world—and, even worse, the social Darwinism derived from it—was utterly heartless and immoral, and that society could not hold together if it lost its biblical foundations. He volunteered to join in the prosecution of John Scopes, a Tennessee schoolteacher who broke state law in 1925 by teaching evolution. He won his case in court but found he had suffered a propaganda defeat at the hands of a pro-evolution national media. The case was later fictionalized in a play, *Inherit the Wind* (1955), which unfairly depicted Bryan and his fundamentalist cohorts as sinister bigots.

Tennessee's anti-evolution law stayed on the statute books, and the issue continued to simmer through midcentury. Cartoons and jokes about humans' chimpanzee ancestors became standard fare whenever creation and evolution were at issue. Tennessee and many other states, especially in the South, continued *not* teaching evolution right into the 1960s. Publishers, who had gradually introduced evolutionary ideas into their high school biology textbooks between 1900 and 1925, quietly removed them again. Only in 1968 when the Supreme Court upheld an Arkansas judgment in the case *Epperson v. Arkansas* were anti-evolution laws overturned. By then America was trying to revamp its science education curriculum because an early Russian victory in the space race (the orbital flight of *Sputnik* in 1957) had convinced American politicians and educators that they were losing the Cold War on the classroom front.

Other Supreme Court decisions of the early 1960s, prohibiting prayer and

Bible reading in public schools, showed fundamentalists that efforts to continue teaching biblical Creation in the old way would now, after *Epperson*, be interpreted as a violation of the First Amendment. Partly to overcome this new legal difficulty and partly in the hope of giving their beliefs a genuine scientific pedigree, a group of fundamentalist scientists developed "creation science." The first recognizable work in the genre was *The Genesis Flood* (1961) by Henry Morris, a Ph.D. and professor of hydraulic engineering at Virginia Polytechnic Institute, in collaboration with theologian John Whitcomb. It updated George McCready Price's work, again explaining the Earth's geological strata as the result of Noah's flood, rather than as the outcome of sedimentation and geological forces acting over millions of years.

In the following years, stimulated by educational and legal developments, creation scientists themselves split into two camps; old-Earth creationists, who were willing to admit geological and evolutionary evidence for everything but humans, and hard-line young-Earth creationists, who insisted on the literal historical accuracy of the Genesis account right down to the last detail. Both groups agreed, despite this difference, that human beings, made in God's image, were not a mere evolutionary phenomenon and were not closely related to the rest of the animal kingdom. Duane Gish, a leading creationist and a faculty member of the Institute for Creation Research in San Diego, which Henry Morris had helped to found in 1972, got right to the point: "There is no evidence, either in the present world or in the world of the past, that Man has arisen from some 'lower' creature. He stands alone as a separate and distinct created type, or basic morphological design, endowed with qualities that set him far above all other living creatures."[10]

Gish and his seven ICR colleagues, all holders of doctoral degrees in the sciences (though not, in most cases, biologists or geologists), devoted themselves more to publicizing their cause than to conducting original research. Morris's son began an archaeological search in Turkey for traces of the all-important Noah's Ark, which, he realized, must have been a truly magnificent vessel and a great engineering feat, because it would have had to be big enough to contain—along with everything else—two of each of the dinosaurs and enough food to keep them going for a year. ICR books, tapes, and seminars aimed to convince people nationwide, especially schoolteachers and state assembly members, that creationism was *scientifically* defensible and could therefore be used in schools without violating the First Amendment. They pointed out numerous mistakes that had been made by scientific evolutionists, such as their acceptance of fraudulent fossil remains like Piltdown Man. They also argued that if, as evolutionists believed, new species evolve bit by bit out of older ones, there would be more examples of intermediate species in the world. They implied, falsely, that every problem confronted by evolutionists was evidence in favor of their own theory. They neglected to mention that evolutionary scientists, by systematically going over the evidence, had themselves spotted various frauds and had worked to explain anomalies in the general theory of evolution. Meanwhile, members of the scientific establishment, notably the Harvard biologist Stephen Jay Gould, launched repeated and furious counterattacks against what they regarded as the creationists' bogus reasoning. Liberal ministers, Protestant and Catholic, stayed out of the dispute. Most of them believed that an intelligent Christianity could be reconciled with evolution as a natural process, but one over which God presided.

In the early 1980s Arkansas and Louisiana passed laws that required science teachers in their public schools to devote equal time to the two theories, evolution and creation. The Arkansas assemblymen called theirs the Balanced Treatment law, a title that gave a nice impression of pluralism and evenhandedness. Nevertheless, the American Civil Liberties Union sued Arkansas in 1981, claiming that the state was covertly introducing religious content into its science curriculum and thus violating the Establishment Clause of the First Amendment. To support its case, the ACLU asked not just a group of scientists but also a liberal theologian, Langdon Gilkey, and a prominent religious historian, George Marsden, to testify against the law. The state gathered expert witnesses of its own in hopes of making the case that creationism was science, not religion. It avoided the ICR spokesmen from San Diego because their evangelical objectives were too well known. It did include a fundamentalist professor from Dallas, Norman Geisler, but he provoked laughter in the courtroom when he declared that unidentified flying objects were instruments of Satan. Sure enough, the judge ruled for the ACLU, finding that the law violated the First Amendment.

With one victory under its belt, the ACLU at once sued Louisiana. The wording of the Louisiana statute was less specific than that of the Arkansas law and made no mention of God. Could it therefore evade condemnation? No. The judge made a summary judgment in favor of the plaintiffs, noting that the Arkansas verdict had established the relevant precedent. The state also lost on appeal, but doggedly took its case to the U.S. Supreme Court. Seventy-two Nobel Prize winners in the natural sciences signed an amicus curiae brief against the law, condemning creation science, and were vindicated when, in *Edwards v. Aguillard* (1987), Louisiana lost for a third time in the nation's highest court of appeal by a vote of seven to two. Dissenting, Justice Antonin Scalia pointed out that students were being denied the chance to decide the issue for themselves after hearing evidence on both sides, which meant that the decision abridged their academic freedom.

These two decisive victories should have meant an end to creationism in schools. Actually the issue was not so clear-cut. New Christian Right activists, sympathetic to the creationist view, often campaigned for seats on local school boards and influenced the choice of teachers, curriculum, and textbooks in their communities. At the level of higher education, when Jerry Falwell's Liberty University (formerly Liberty Baptist College) faced de-accreditation from the state of Virginia if it continued to teach creation science in its biology courses, it came up with an ingenious solution. In the revised syllabus, under "Biology" the professors taught the theory of evolution, but then, under "Philosophy" the same professors taught creationism, with considerably greater gusto. The biology professors also signed a "statement of faith" declaring that "no professor was ever asked to teach anything as a proven fact that violated his or her religious convictions."[11]

The creation-evolution dispute continued a trend in American education. School curriculum had become a battleground for fundamentalists in the early 1970s and was one of the issues that prompted the political emergence of the New Religious Right. Mel and Norma Gabler of Longview, Texas, had become specialists in lobbying for and against school textbooks, depending on their conformity to fundamentalist values. Once every five years the Texas Board of Education decided which sets of texts it would approve for the whole state. Textbook companies had learned not to provoke the Gablers, lest they draw a condemnation and lose the lucrative state contract. The Gablers' influence, indeed, extended beyond Texas, because most manufacturers could not afford to produce separate editions for each state and so tended to offer all states only books that the Texans would accept. In 1974 the Gablers acted as consultants to the evangelical citizens of Kanawha County, West Virginia, in a protest against Interaction, a new range of textbooks from Houghton Mifflin that their school board had adopted. Alice Moore, an evangelical minister's wife and a school board member since 1970, began the protest, having become convinced that the books were part of a Communist conspiracy. Other evangelical and fundamentalist Christians, including a group of militant ministers, soon joined the ranks. The series, they alleged, was too sympathetic to "alternative lifestyles," did not condemn crime with sufficient emphasis, had too much detail about sex, too many swear words, too much street language, and in general scanted Christian values.

Other religious groups—the mainstream churches—approved of the books. The local Episcopal clergy, along with a group of ten ministers from other churches, including Methodists, Presbyterians, Catholics, and Jews, issued a letter supporting the series, on the grounds that it introduced students to important problems in their world. "We know of no way to stimulate the growth of our youth if we insulate them from the real issues. We feel this program will help our students to think intelligently about their lives and our society."[12]

Energetic publicity against the series led to widespread school boycotts that fall when the academic year began. Local coal miners refused to go to work if their children were subjected to these books, despite the orders of their union, the United Mine Workers. They picketed the schools and intimidated parents who tried to bring in their children. James Moffett, general editor of the Inter-action series and later the author of a book about the whole affair, describes what happened next. "Violence escalated during the second week of school, and the number of wildcat mine strikes reached eight to ten thousand over several counties. Two men were wounded by gunfire at picket points and another was badly beaten. . . . A CBS television crew was roughed up at one place, and car windows were smashed at others" (19). The superintendent closed all the schools to prevent further confrontations, but while they were closed two elementary schools were destroyed by dynamite bombs, and most of the fleet of school buses was vandalized. In April 1975, as a chaotic school year neared its end, one of the fundamentalist ministers, Marvin Horan, was convicted of conspiracy to bomb the churches and sent to prison for three years.

The Appalachian coal towns have a history of conflict and bloodshed, along with a tradition of singing about their woes. Moffett, revisiting Kanawha County a few years later, collected several songs written during the bloody textbook controversy, including this one:

Kanawha County gave them a surprise!
They never figured we'd ever uprise.
We were still willing to compromise.
But our little children will never read those lies.
When the police arrested Graley, Horan, Hill
They figured prison would soon break their will
But he will perish who takes up the sword.
(91)

Moffett also noted that since the Kanawha conflict "no publisher has dared offer to schools any textbooks of a comparable range of subjects and ideas and points of view to those the protesters vilified and crippled on the market" (26).

Christian Academies and Home Schooling

Isolated victories like that in Kanawha County did not change evangelicals' belief that they were losing their war against secular humanism in the public schools. Their failure to establish creationism in the curriculum and their inability to restore prayer were among the issues that stimulated the growth of private Christian academies, where the Establishment Clause did not apply. The 1970s and 1980s witnessed a boom in the size and number of these schools, which were designed as places in which the parents' ideas about Christianity, patriotism, and morality, far from being challenged, would be woven into the curriculum their children followed.

The immediate predecessors of such academies were built in the late 1950s and early 1960s, partly as a way of giving Southern white parents a means of avoiding public school desegregation. Historian Raymond Wolters describes the scene in Prince Edward County, Virginia, in 1958, when the county's whole public school system closed down rather than desegregate. White parents began building alternative schools with their own hands, in an atmosphere of exhilaration akin to that of a revival meeting. When Southern "massive resistance" to desegregation petered out in the early 1960s, such schools, in Prince Edward County and throughout the South, survived because the shock of the Supreme Court's desegregation rulings was closely followed by the shock of its rulings against prayer and Bible reading. They were not explicitly religious schools, but Youth for Christ was usually an active campus presence.

In the 1960s and 1970s, purpose-built evangelical academies continued to develop rapidly around the country, at an average rate of two *per day*, and were educating more than a million children per year by the mid-1980s. In 1972 the American Association of Christian Schools was founded; it and the Association of Christian Schools International (1978) became lobbies on behalf of these schools, working to ensure favorable state and federal legislation, to monitor tax and accreditation regulations, facilitate teacher training and transfers, and to keep the schools apprised of each other's activities. Organizations like Accelerated Christian Education (ACE) sold ready-made curriculum packages to start-up schools.

Not being subject to state educational bureaucracies, the schools took many different forms, depending on the type of church sponsoring them and the interests of the parents whose payments kept them afloat. Families' motives for turning to them were also varied. For some the lack of prayer and the teaching of evolution in public schools were key issues; for others it was dismay at the public schools' low educational levels, along with students' vulnerability to drugs, gangs, and other students' sexual precocity. George Ballweg, a doctoral student in education, surveyed Christian schoolchildren's parents in 1980 and found that more than half of them had enrolled their children in these schools more because of their commitment to firm discipline, educational "basics," and wholesome morality than for strictly religious reasons.

Nevertheless, religion and religion-related activities played a prominent part in the daily activities of most. Christine Stolba (b. 1973) recalled that at the Keswick Christian School in St. Petersburg, Florida, in the early 1980s, each day began with the pledge of allegiance to the American flag and was followed by a pledge to the Christian flag: "I pledge allegiance to the Christian flag and to the Savior, for whose Kingdom it stands. One Savior, crucified, risen, and coming again, with life and liberty for all who believe."[13] In the school chapel students would hear conversion testimony from former sinners who had turned to Jesus (including tattooed bikers and former convicts) and then undertake "Sword Drill."

> We would raise our Bibles in our right hands and wait with great anticipation for the principal to say a Bible reference — "Romans 4:32," for example — whereupon you'd hear a collective WHUMP as students brought their Bibles into their laps and began furiously thumbing through the pages for the verse. Competition was fierce, and the student who found the verse first would stand up. . . . The nimble-fingered student would then read the verse out loud. Ostensibly this exercise encouraged us to memorize the order of the books of the Bible (something we had to do for Bible class as well — and which I still remember since it was drilled into my head so many times). In reality it was an opportunity for school-wide competition. Those of us with regular Bibles were often outmaneuvered by students who owned "deluxe" Bibles with tabs marking each separate book.[14]

Once a year they also went to a weeklong seminar called "Walk Through the Bible." Motivational speakers led them through the central events of the Old and New Testaments and taught them to recite the whole sequence in an intensely compressed form, complete with synchronized hand gestures.

> By the end of the week, when asked, "Can you walk through the Bible?" the entire student body would respond "YES," whereupon we'd leap up from our seats and begin chanting and motioning the lengthy litany we'd learned: "Creation, Fall, Flood, Nations, Four thousand years, Ur, Persian Gulf, SALT — Sarah, Abraham, Lot, Tara — Tigris, Euphrates, Heron, Tara dies, Sea of Galilee, Jordan River, Dead Sea . . . " and on and on (my favorite marker was the one for Moses when he tangled with Pharaoh, which was "Let my people go!" "NO!"). During the rest of the year we performed the "Walk" weekly in Bible class.[15]

The school's theology was premillennialist. After watching the *Thief in the Night* movies about the Rapture (see above, chapter 7) and grisly scenes of the end times (torture, beheadings), students were encouraged to rededicate their lives to Christ so as to be sure that, when the moment came, they would not be "left behind."

Catherine Remick (b. 1972), another student at the school, recalled that students were assembled one day to learn about rock music,

> and how it promoted devil worship. [The demonstrator] set up this whole stereo system on the stage and proceeded to talk about song lyrics and how, when played backwards, it was the Devil trying to get you to join his ranks. He would play several well-known heavy metal records backwards and then say things like: "Did you hear that? It said: 'Smoke Marijuana.' Here, I'll play it again so you can hear it." I remember trying not to laugh because it didn't sound like anything at all — and it definitely didn't sound like the Devil telling me to do drugs.[16]

(Children at this and similar schools were forbidden to dance. Even as a parallel "Christian rock music" subculture flourished, kids in their audiences might sway, click fingers, and tap feet, but they must not give way to the eroticism of dance! There was no school prom, just a farewell banquet.)

Sociologist Susan Rose studied a contrasting pair of evangelical academies in upstate New York in the early 1980s. She discovered that their curricula corresponded closely to the religious principles of their founders and that they reflected the class and social attitudes of the churches to which they were attached. A charismatic community in a middle-class district, "Covenant," many of whose members had come out of the Jesus movement of the 1970s, for example, drew on Montessori philosophy and encouraged their children's self-expression. The school was intellectually rigorous; its handbook explained how all the secular disciplines, necessary and valuable in themselves, could be learned in a Christian context:

> *Mathematics*: In light of the order God has produced in the material universe and its set relationships in space and time, we cannot overlook mathematics as being an instrument for teaching our students concepts of order and logic that Creation itself portrays as a very attribute of God. Mathematics is an exact science and in this present age of "relative truth" it affords the Christian school an excellent opportunity to teach each student how to comprehend the orderly world around him, created by God who presents Himself as Absolute Truth (John 14:6).[17]

Teachers encouraged students to cooperate, to love God through love of one another, and to relate all their learning to their faith; parent-teacher conferences would sometimes include a joint prayer.

At a second school, "Lakewood," in a nearby working-class district, by contrast, Rose found a more authoritarian model in operation and a more anti-intellectual atmosphere, fewer teachers, and reliance for curriculum on a package bought from ACE. This curriculum, designed with cash-starved communities in mind, enabled a small number of "monitors" (not trained teachers) to supervise the learning of a large number of students. The principal told Rose that although he certainly wanted the students to learn all they could, his highest priority was "to produce students who are all born-again, saved by grace and working on being the best Christians they can be" (120). A rigorously fundamentalist atmosphere and stern discipline prevailed. Rose also noticed a twelfth-grade lesson that taught that Jews and Roman Catholics "deny the power of the living God" and "lack the inner power to live a truly Biblical, and therefore a truly free life" (127).

Keeping such schools going was a financial burden, especially for poorer communities like Lakewood. Parents complained that they had to pay Christian school fees while still paying taxes for the support of the public schools they despised. Would it not be just, they argued, for the IRS to offer private school tuition tax credits? Or perhaps local government should issue vouchers to all parents, to be redeemed at whatever schools, private or public, the parents chose? Catholics, with their massive school system, had long favored such plans. President Reagan spoke in favor of both alternatives, but, as with so many of these religio-political issues, never actually threw much of his weight behind legislative reforms. Tuition tax credits and the voucher system remained perennial items on the Christian schools' wish list throughout the century's later decades. The argument against them, made by such organizations as Americans United for Separation of Church and State, was that the voucher system would accelerate the breaking up of the entire educational community into mutually estranged groups, and even permit fringe cults to create their own schools. A 1990 editorial in its journal *Church and State* argued: "It takes little imagination to expect the Rev. Louis Farrakhan and the Nation of Islam to create Moslem schools. And how about the Rev. Sun Myung Moon and his Unification Church?"[18]

For some evangelical parents, even the Christian academies were not good enough. After all, they still brought children, for long periods of time, into the company of their peers, which increased the danger of contamination by the era's degenerate popular culture. A more decisive alternative was home schooling, and in the 1980s and 1990s growing numbers of evangelicals took this route. As sociologist Mitchell Stevens has shown, an odd alliance advanced the cause of home schooling: on the one hand, evangelicals, for whom public schools were godless and licentious; on the other hand, social radicals, for whom schools were training grounds of repressive conformity.

States varied in the requirements they imposed on home schoolers; at first some parents were prosecuted for withholding their children. A Nebraska Christian couple, Lester and Dixie Rice, for example, spent more than ten thousand dollars in legal costs defending their right to home-school their child in the early 1980s, before finally winning vindication from the state's supreme court. Theirs was one of a number of lawsuits that generally ended in victory for the parents, on First Amendment free-exercise grounds. Parents who chose home schooling were enthusiastic about its superiority over the public schools, and regarded it as the more "biblical" approach. One couple, Peter and Char Yarema, told a journalist in 1983:

> Deuteronomy 6 is very clear . . . that *we* are to teach our children what they need for living—not someone else. Proverbs speaks again and again about fathers and mothers instructing their offspring. Even if there were a Christian school down the block we wouldn't send our children there. Teaching them is *our* job.[19]

The Bible and American tradition could both be cited in support of home schooling, since such distinguished citizens as Abraham Lincoln, Thomas Alva Edison, and Franklin Roosevelt were examples of home-schooling success stories.

To strengthen their legal, social, and educational position, enthusiasts created information and lobbying networks, support groups, and then a conference circuit and curriculum options to help others follow them into home schooling. Certain books advocating home schools, such as John Holt's *Instead of Education* (1976) and the more religious Raymond and Dorothy Moore's *Home-Grown Kids* (1981) and *Home-Spun Schools* (1982), became essential reading, and home schoolers could subscribe to a growing array of newsletters aimed at home-school families. The Moores, Seventh-day Adventists who ran a home-schooling foundation, referred to the dependence of American children on their peer groups (often used as an argument against home schooling) as a form of "social cancer."[20] The Home Schools Legal Defense Association, under the leadership of Michael P. Farris (formerly Washington State's Moral Majority director), developed effective lobbying techniques and was able to get an exemption for home-school families from federal legislation requiring the certification of all elementary and secondary teachers.

Although social radicals like John Holt had played an important part in creating the movement, it was not long before they became the minority partner. In their view the schools suffered from being far too structured and from squelching the children's individuality. Christians, the big majority of home schoolers, more often took the opposite view: that the schools were not sufficiently disciplined and did not live up to biblical ideals of benign hierarchy. Nine out of every ten home-schooling families had religious motives; a 1995 survey found that "eighty-four percent agreed that the Bible is the inspired word of God and literally true; 81 percent agreed that eternal life is a gift of God, predicated on belief in Jesus Christ; and 93 percent agreed that Satan is currently working in the world."[21]

Mail-order curriculums, like those in the Christian schools, wove religious elements into lessons on ostensibly secular subjects. For example, the A Beka Book mathematics curriculum included a budgeting component in which seventh graders were asked to include church tithing as a principal element of their monthly expenditures. Another curriculum was based entirely on Jesus' Sermon on the Mount, breaking it down verse by verse and investigating its significance in the light of science, mathematics, public health, and the English language. Most teaching and supervision was done by women; in fact, home schooling often obliged mothers to give up their careers and entailed financial hardships, since the family then lived solely on the father's pay. In one sense this division of labor fit traditional evangelicals' ideas of appropriate gender roles. If Mother was a teacher, she was extending her role as nurturer. In another way, however, it showed how even families eager to resist such modern phenomena as feminism were moving with the times. The woman who blended her traditional housekeeping tasks with the immense responsibility of home-educating several children was taking on a role akin to that of the fabled feminist superwoman.

Figure 14. Sally Priesand, America's first female rabbi (Reform), in 1974. (AP)

Figure 15. Mary Daly, radical feminist theologian. The biographical line on the cover of her book *Gyn-Ecology* (1978) reads: "Mary Daly is a Revolting Hag." (AP)

Figure 16.   Jim Jones, leader of the People's Temple and organizer of its collective suicide in Guyana, 1978. (AP)

Figure 17. Jerry Falwell, Baptist minister and Moral Majority leader, on NBC's *Tomorrow* show, February 5, 1981. (AP)

Figure 18. Randall Terry, minister and founder of the anti-abortion group Operation Rescue. (AP)

Figure 19. Phyllis Schlafly, in 1977, during the campaign she led to prevent states' ratification of the Equal Rights Amendment for women. (AP)

Figure 20. Jim and Tammy Bakker, TV evangelists, at the height of their success, in 1986. (AP)

Figure 21.   Nation of Islam leader Louis Farrakhan in Chicago, February 23, 1997. (AP)

Figure 22.   Mona Banawan, an American Muslim, studies the Quran before a prayer service, October 12, 2001, in Charlotte, North Carolina. (AP)

Figure 23.   Bill McCartney, founder of Promise Keepers, at the organization's "Stand in the Gap" rally on the Washington Mall, October 4, 1997. (AP)

Figure 24. A mural of Elian Gonzalez being miraculously rescued from drowning, painted by Humberto Gonzalez (no relation), April 2000. Notice the crowd of symbolic figures, including Jesus, the Virgin Mary, Saint Michael, Pope John Paul II, President Bill Clinton, and the Statue of Liberty. (AP)

Figure 25. New York firefighters and police officers at a memorial service for the victims of the attack on the World Trade Center, in St. Paul's Chapel, New York, on Good Friday, March 2002. Many observers treated the old church's survival as a miracle. (AP)

Chapter 9

PROFITS, PROFLIGATES, AND PROPHETS: 1987–1995

The Evangelical Scandals

The religious and political struggles of the early 1980s, over nuclear weapons, sanctuary, creationism, school prayer, and textbooks, were grim affairs. Religious news took an unexpectedly humorous turn in the late eighties with a pair of sex and money scandals. Sex and religion have always been explosive partners, prime material for novelists and for truths-stranger-than-fiction. For entertaining novels on the theme, try Sinclair Lewis's *Elmer Gantry* (1927) with its sultry, seductive prophetess Sharon Falconer and the lecherous minister of its title, or John Updike's *A Month of Sundays* (1975), told from the point of view of a sexually promiscuous minister who just can't resist his lady parishioners. Among true stories it would be hard to match those of Jim Bakker and Jimmy Swaggart, two evangelical superstars who came to grief in 1987.

Jim Bakker and his wife, Tammy, were every satirist's delight. Small, wholesome, and energetic, Pentecostalist Protestants attached to the Assemblies of God, they began their public careers as youth directors in Minnesota's Evangelical Auditorium. Later they appeared on evangelist Pat Robertson's Christian Broadcasting Network, where Tammy ran a highly successful biblical puppet show for children and Jim conducted a chat show, *The 700 Club*, seeing himself as the evangelical equivalent of Johnny Carson. That was in the late 1960s when evangelical TV was just getting started and Robertson, son of a U.S. senator, was starting to build his evangelical empire in Virginia Beach, Virginia.

One main theme of the Bakkers' feel-good preaching was that money, comfort, and success are all signs of God's favor. If God likes you and you trust him, you will get rich. "Beloved, I wish above all things that thou mayest prosper and be in good health, even as thy soul prospereth" (3 John, verse 2). The first stage in "prosperity theology," however, is willingness to give generously as a sign of faith, for which the biblical support is Luke 6:38: "Give, that it may be given to you." Bakker discovered that by disclosing a real financial crisis at the network, or manufacturing the appearance of one, he could persuade TV viewers to send in more money than if he gave the impression that everything was under control. In an early CBN telethon he experimented by weeping on-camera, declaring that the ministry was nearly broke and in danger of going off the air. CBN enjoyed an overwhelming response in money donations from viewers. "From the moment that I stepped before a television camera at CBN God began to anoint me to raise money for Christian television. I realized it the night I wept during the first '700 Club' telethon. Many times since then, God similarly anointed me."[1]

Bakker became convinced that God was calling him and his wife to create an evangelical kingdom of their own, so they parted from Robertson in 1972. After a couple of years at Paul Crouch's Trinity Broadcasting Network in California, they moved to Charlotte, North Carolina, and began to work for another start-up television ministry, Praise the Lord. They rose to leadership positions after discovering and revealing the financial incompetence of its original managers. In the following years they enlarged the ministry by buying cheap morning airtime from dozens of television stations around America. In 1978 they built their own satellite station and were able to broadcast directly to affiliates twenty-four hours a day. PTL offered counseling and prayer to phone-in sufferers and paid its bills from donations sent in by eager viewers, many of whom claimed that the prayer had had miraculous healing effects.

The Bakkers' blend of storytelling, preaching, and folksy Christian chat shows was intoxicating; even people who should have known better found themselves powerless to switch channels when the magnetic couple was on the air. "The truth was that the Bakkers were enormously gifted television performers who turned the program into a real-life soap opera about their own lives and the life of the ministry itself," wrote TV historian Quentin Schultze.[2] Tammy had the gift of being able to weep at will and sometimes, appearing to be emotionally transported by her interviews with born-again guests, let the tears flow freely. Her mascara was so heavy that it mixed with the tears and flowed down her cheeks, creating a Gothic web of black tracks. Nothing made her weep more than a falling-off in donations, and nothing seemed so well calculated to bring forth more cash than another bout of sobbing.

Heritage USA, in Fort Mill, South Carolina, was the Bakkers' 2,300-acre evangelical theme park, an ambitious yet godly version of Disneyland, with a mixture of hotels, time-share condominiums, pools, shops, a water park, a home for single mothers, conference centers, chapels, an amphitheater, and rides for the kids. It proved that Christianity could be fun, and in the early 1980s it was attracting several million visitors a year.

Building and running Heritage USA, however, proved unexpectedly costly. So did living in fine style, with fur coats, houseboats, Rolls-Royces, and princely dwellings throughout the United States. The money poured in to PTL, but so did the bills. Record keeping was slapdash and did not keep pace with the rapid growth. Bakker found he was unable to follow through on a promise to extend his ministry to South Korea and Brazil. Two journalists, Charles Shepard of the *Charlotte Observer* and Hunter James of the *Atlanta Journal-Constitution*, convinced that the Bakkers were defrauding viewers to subsidize their lavish way of life, began to investigate the sources and destination of PTL's funds. Embarrassing stories in both papers, which the Bakkers themselves interpreted as the work of Satan, were soon picked up nationwide. Two further embarrassments followed in quick succession: first it was discovered that Tammy had been treated at the Betty Ford Clinic for drug addiction, and second, that Jim had, a few years earlier, had a sexual affair with a nineteen-year-old church secretary named Jessica Hahn.

To salvage a worsening situation, Bakker called on another evangelical TV star, Jerry Falwell, to intervene and take over PTL ministries temporarily. Falwell came from the Baptist fundamentalist tradition and did not always see eye to eye with Bakker's emotional Pentecostalism. Nevertheless he felt that thousands of well-meaning, Bible-believing people would be disillusioned if PTL collapsed. He stepped in, began to investigate the mess, and was horrified to discover its extent. Dozens of projects had to be frozen and assets sold. Then another televangelist, Jimmy Swaggart of Baton Rouge, Louisiana, announced that the Jessica Hahn incident had not been isolated. He alleged that she had had sex with several PTL clergymen and had since received more than $200,000 to keep quiet about it. Next, allegations began to circulate that Bakker had also been visiting prostitutes and that he had had homosexual encounters too.

Falwell may have been exaggerating when he said, "It is doubtful that the cause of Jesus Christ has ever suffered a greater tragedy than during the past several weeks," but his alarm was understandable.[3] Despite the heroic selflessness of PTL viewers, who continued to send in $7 million per month to keep the ministry afloat, it was forced into bankruptcy three months after Falwell's intervention. By then its debts amounted to $70 million. Jim and Tammy Bakker never seemed adequately to appreciate the seriousness of their predicament and, despite the accumulating scandals, plotted a comeback. Federal prosecutors cut short their hopes, and Jim went on trial for wire fraud, mail fraud, and conspiracy. About to be convicted, he suddenly fell to pieces.

> Trembling and sobbing, he had to be placed in handcuffs and leg shackles after a psychiatrist and his defense lawyer testified that he had been hallucinating and cowering in a fetal position on the floor of his lawyer's office. Still sobbing, bent and broken, Bakker was led by federal marshals from the courtroom to a car, where he again curled up in a fetal position in the backseat, to be driven to a psychiatric ward in the federal prison in Butner, North Carolina.[4]

He had been sentenced to forty-five years' imprisonment (but was actually released after just six).

Jesus said: "Let he that is without spot of sin cast the first stone." At least one stone-caster (and broadcaster), Jimmy Swaggart, had a sinful spot or two of his own. His name, the perfect blending of "swagger" and "braggart," was well adapted to his manner and preaching style, but he too had an immense and devoted television audience, a Christian school and college, and broadcast arrangements in more than a hundred foreign countries. He claimed that half the population of the entire world had access to his broadcasts and that his worldwide audience was five hundred million. His offices, which had their own zip code, received more mail than any other address in the whole state of Louisiana, and in the mid-1980s money was rolling in at the rate of half a million dollars per day. Here is the journalist Lawrence Wright's vivid description:

> He has called homosexuality "the worst sin in the world" and has said, "I'm sick to death of words like *gay* being used to amass respect for people who don't deserve respect. Why don't we use words descriptive of their chosen lifestyle— such as *pervert*, *queer*, or *faggot*?" . . . These wild tirades are delivered as Swaggart waves his Bible overhead, his baritone voice rising into shrieks or falling into breathless whispers but always demanding, insinuating, taunting—an untamed, irresistible performance. He kneels, he struts, he dances, he sings, he bursts into tears; then he abruptly rains laughter on the thousands of worshipers waving their arms before him. Suddenly he breaks into the incantatory language of the Holy Spirit: "*Hun da sheek kulaba sone do roshay ketah do rotundai!*" he cries. "I speak in tongues every day of my life."[5]

Then he was photographed with a prostitute and crashed to the ground, as Bakker had crashed. By abasing himself and weeping before his congregation, confessing that he too was a sinner with feet of clay and begging for their forgiveness, he regained his pulpit, if not all of his influence. The Assemblies of God, the denomination with which he was affiliated, suspended him for only three months (rather than for a year, as was normal in such cases). They foresaw that his fall would ruin several hundred people whose careers and incomes depended on him. Meanwhile both the prostitute in the Swaggart case, Debbie Murphree, and Bakker's former church secretary, Jessica Hahn, followed up on these events in the same lucrative way: They took off their clothes and posed naked in *Playboy* and *Penthouse* magazines.

In some ways an equally spectacular moment in the evangelicals' catastrophic year, 1987, came when Oral Roberts, a Tulsa, Oklahoma, evangelist and faith healer with a television empire of his own, declared on the January 3 edition of his show, *Expect a Miracle*, that God was going to "call him home" (end his life) unless his supporters sent him a vitally needed eight million dollars. The money was required, he said, for fellowships at the Oral Roberts University medical school. Also on the air his wife, Evelyn, told him tearfully: "I certainly don't want the Lord to take you on March sixth" (the date was later changed to March 31). He went into isolation in the university's two-hundred-foot-tall steel-and-glass "prayer tower," fasting and praying to await the outcome. His son Richard, noting that the crisis was controversial and had inspired criticism, told journalists: "These people think we're out of our minds. Well, we are out of our minds, and into our spirits."[6]

Once again the crisis tactics worked, as they had worked for years at PTL. More than enough money ($9.1 million) rolled in, so that Roberts's life on earth might continue. He thanked viewers for their generosity but added that God had also told him that the same amount of money would have to be raised every year between then and the Second Coming of Christ. Some of the TV stations that ran his shows deplored the plea as a manipulative stunt in bad taste. Journalist Victoria Sackett, writing in the skeptical *New York Times*, quipped: "Others may ridicule or lament his entrepreneurship but I, for one, take off my hat to the man. Apart from giving new meaning to the word 'deadline' he has added a fresh dimension to a time-honored marketing technique — the threat. His contribution to the ploy is turning the threat against himself."[7] But, she added, it was a ploy that would work only once.

A Minister in the White House?

This combination of scandals and gimmicks knocked the wind out of evangelical sails, at least for a while, reminding believers and skeptics alike about the omnipresence of temptation and sin. Of course, far more evangelical churches, less in the spotlight and less lurid in their methods, continued to thrive under the guidance of blameless pastors. Evangelicalism's immense continuing influence was evident in the presidential election of 1988 when two ministers ran for the nation's highest office. One was Pat Robertson, the Bakkers' former boss, who ran for the Republican nomination. His colleagues at CBN, which by now had its own university, planned to take the revolution begun by Moral Majority in 1980 one step further. Robertson's CBN colleague Jerry Horner declared:

For too long we Christians have allowed everyone else to set standards for us. The
world sets standards regarding what we are to hear on the radio, what we are to
watch on our television screens, what we are to read, how we are to dress. The
world has been telling us how to measure success. And we've tolerated it too long.
It is time for us to set our own standards, to establish our own dominion, to bring
our exile in the land to an end.[8]

At first the campaign did well, and Robertson showed strongly in the Iowa cau-
cuses and the Michigan and Hawaii primaries.

Robertson's problem, as his campaign developed, was the fact that his career
had been built on miracles, faith healings, and speaking in tongues, activities
that repelled as many voters as they attracted. It was true that he had to some
extent "domesticated" faith healing, taking it out of the Billy Sunday revival
tent or the sweltering Oral Roberts meeting hall and into the cozy pseudo living room of his TV studio. Still, he, like many of his brethren, believed that the
Rapture and the Second Coming of Jesus were imminent and that the Apocalypse was at hand. In Concord, New Hampshire, during the primary campaign,
another premillennial minister pointed out the contradiction: "Wait a minute.
The next event on the eschatological clock is the return of Christ. Things in
society should get *worse* rather than better. If Christians worked to turn our
nation around, that would be a humanistic effort and delay Christ's return."[9]

Robertson tried to tone down the more breathless aspects of his religious
career during the campaign, but skeptical reporters, who had been having a
fine time dismembering evangelicals for the last couple of years, kept coming
back to them. These reporters discovered that Robertson's son—himself a *700
Club* broadcaster—had been born just ten weeks after his parents' wedding, a
revelation that shone a gaudy new light on Robertson's advocacy of premarital
chastity. The unfortunate son, Timothy, said that he "didn't exactly appreciate
having the story told on network television."[10]

Other discoveries about irregularities in Pat Robertson's past emerged. His
father, as a U.S. senator, had pulled strings to prevent Pat from being sent into
combat in the Korean War. Several of his business ventures had failed, and he
had been deceived by a con man on his first foray into television. Irregularities
in his ministry's finances appeared. They were not much by comparison with
the Bakker and Swaggart fiascos, but the accumulation of damaging stories
caused his star to wane. George Bush Sr., unnerved for a time by Robertson's
challenge, was a mild High Church Episcopalian, but he knew enough, when
campaigning in South Carolina, on the eve of the Super Tuesday primary, to
declaim the evangelical slogan: "Jesus Christ is my personal savior."[11] Bush
nailed down first the Republican nomination, then the November election.

Another ministerial contender for the presidency, in 1984 and again in 1988,
was Jesse Jackson, former lieutenant of Martin Luther King Jr. and the civil

rights leader's most widely known heir. King himself had lived and died by refusing to compromise and would have made a hopeless politician. Working deliberately outside the system, he had forced it to change by declining to accept its everyday reality. Politicians, on the other hand, talk morality but act pragmatic; they live to make deals, trade favors, and arrange compromises. Jackson, borrowing King's aura but highly attuned to political realities, was never sure which of these alternatives to adopt as his own. Partly as a result, he never fully enjoyed either the success of a professional politician or the reputation of a prophet, but was always stuck somewhere in between. As one academic observer noted: "Jackson aims to be a preacher and a politician in a society that says one can be a religious prophet or a practicing politician, but not both."[12] As with Robertson, moreover, Jackson's religious heritage and idiom were as sure to repel some voters as they were to attract others, and to raise doubts about his suitability in the highly practical, secular realm of American politics.

A native of Greenville, South Carolina, Jackson was illegitimate but knew that his biological father, Noah Robinson, was a preacher. Precocious and ambitious, he became a football star in college (at North Carolina A&T), then went to Chicago for training in the ministry. He guided King around the city in 1966 and took charge of Operation Breadbasket, an economic offshoot of the SCLC that negotiated with city businesses to increase black employment and threatened to boycott those that would not deal. He was in Memphis in April 1968, witnessed King's assassination, and returned hastily to Chicago to urge blacks not to riot there, as they did in Washington, D.C. Feuds with other civil rights ministers, many of whom vied with him for King's mantle, led Jackson to sever ties with the SCLC in 1971 and create in its place Operation PUSH (People United to Save Humanity). Legally enforced segregation was no longer an issue, so Jackson emphasized issues of economic opportunity rather than legal equality. He preached to black congregations a message of dignity, sobriety, no drugs, and the work ethic, a message that enabled him to strike up alliances with Chicago's mainstream Democrats.

By the early 1980s Jackson was strong enough, and nationally famous enough, to attract millions of Democratic voters to what he called the Rainbow Coalition, comprising poor blacks, poor whites, and members of other ethnic and racial minorities. He believed he was fulfilling a divine mission, telling reporters: "The main thing is that I do God's will to the best of my ability, if He can use me as an instrument of His peace, for some purpose."[13] His political speeches, like King's, had the cadence of sermons, and he had a wickedly effective sense of humor. In a speech to the Democratic National Convention in 1984, for example, he made fun of President Reagan's courting of the New Religious Right:

> Mr. Reagan will ask us to pray, and I believe in prayer. I have come this way by the power of prayer. But then, we must watch false prophecy. He cuts energy assis-

tance to the poor, cuts breakfast programs from children, cuts lunch programs from children, cuts job training from children, and then says to an empty table, "Let us pray." Apparently he is not familiar with the structure of prayer. You thank the Lord for the food that you are about to receive, not the food that just left! I think we should pray, but don't pray for the food that left. Pray for the man that took the food—to leave![14]

He was a persuasive speaker but had no electoral track record and was, in many voters' eyes, tainted by his association with Louis Farrakhan, the Nation of Islam's advocate of black racial purity. He found it difficult to live down an incident in which he and Farrakhan had referred to Jews as "Hymies." In the long run Jackson could not attract middle-class white voters in sufficient numbers and so could not hope to win a national election. First in 1984 and again in 1988, he campaigned unsuccessfully for the Democratic nomination, then watched while the men chosen over him, Walter Mondale (1984) and Michael Dukakis (1988), went down to resounding defeat.

The 1980s were a spectacular decade for American evangelicals, witnessing their powerful reentry into political life. But it was not an unqualified success. Evangelicals found the political system stoutly resistant to their plans for converting moral indignation into actual policies. Presidents Reagan and Bush, no less than candidates Robertson and Jackson, were grateful for evangelicals' hard work on behalf of their campaigns—their rhetoric showed that the evangelicals had changed the actual words politicians now had to use. Still, even the evangelicals' favorite presidents and members of Congress were careful not to promote moral policies unless their pollsters assured them they had majority support—which was rarely the case. A sign of the evangelicals' disappointment as the decade ended was Jerry Falwell's decision to disband Moral Majority. He made the announcement in Las Vegas, of all places, the hedonist's Mecca, in the summer of 1989 and, like all good politicians, dressed up defeat in the language of victory: "Our goal has been achieved. . . . The religious right is solidly in place and . . . religious conservatives in America are now in for the duration."[15] It was true that evangelical individuals and rhetoric would continue to influence political life into the next decade. The rise of another organization soon afterward to take Moral Majority's place—the Christian Coalition—suggested the belief of other conservative evangelicals that outside pressure on politicians would be as necessary in the nineties as it had been in the eighties. It also bore witness to the fact that much of Moral Majority's agenda was still unfulfilled.

American Islam

Jackson was reluctant to distance himself from Louis Farrakhan in 1988 because Farrakhan, a speaker almost as magnetic as Jackson himself, retained a powerful hold over the imaginations of African Americans. Farrakhan headed the Nation of Islam (NOI), but since Malcolm X's day it had divided, with a large part of its membership blending into America's rapidly growing, immigrant-based Islamic community.

Elijah Muhammad, the founder of the NOI, had died in 1975 and his mantle had passed to his son Wallace (Warith) Deen Muhammad. Almost at once Warith, calling himself Mujaddid (the renewer of the faith), disowned much of his father's teaching and led the Nation of Islam toward a more orthodox and nonracial Sunni Islam. He denied that white people were the devilish outcome of Dr. Yacub's mad experiment, as his father had claimed, and he urged black Muslims to join him in the study of Arabic and the Quran (he had made the hajj pilgrimage to Mecca in 1967). He also removed the seats from NOI temples, making them more like orthodox Muslim mosques, replaced anti-white slogans with Arabic decor, and denounced the old NOI gender code that subordinated women. In 1985 he disbanded the movement his father had founded altogether, encouraging its members to join mosques in their hometowns without regard to their racial and ethnic composition. Numerous middle-class Muslims accepted this direction and joined the mainstream Sunni Islamic communities. Warith also tried to overcome the black Muslims' tradition of estrangement from America, declaring that "the Constitution of the United States is basically a Quranic document" and that its principles had been "presented to the world over 1400 years ago by the Prophet Muhammad."[16]

Louis Farrakhan, on the other hand, dismayed by Warith's abandonment of his father's legacy, revived the name Nation of Islam in the late 1970s and breathed new life into its old teachings, gathering an estimated twenty thousand members to his cause. Born Louis E. Walcott in 1933 and raised as an Episcopalian in Boston, he was a talented violinist and had been making his living playing and singing calypso music in nightclubs when he encountered, and decided to join, the black Muslims in 1955. A handsome and always immaculately attired man with designer eyeglasses, dark blue suit, and bow tie, he upheld the NOI's tradition of powerful oratory. He also continued to recruit from the black underclass, not least in prisons, and to campaign against inner-city crises of drug dependency, gang warfare, teen pregnancy, and family fragmentation (a program outlined in his 1993 book, *A Torchlight for America*), with the result that he retained the respect of black politicians, even when his remarks crossed the boundaries of civic decency.

If anything, Nation of Islam teachings became more exotic than ever, as did Farrakhan's rhetorical provocation of whites in general, and Jews in particular. He claimed, for example, that Hitler was a great man and that the people who called themselves Jews in modern America were not the genuine article, but rather a degenerate group of Caucasians who practiced a "gutter religion." In a notorious 1994 speech at Kean College, New Jersey, his lieutenant Khalid Muhammad delivered a message to American Jews: "You're not the true Jew. . . . You are a European strain of people who crawled around on your all fours in the caves and hills of Europe, eating juniper roots and eating each other."[17] God's chosen people, on the contrary, were black, and the Hebrew Bible's stories of Jewish suffering and struggle referred to *their* tribulations. Farrakhan even put modern Jews in the role of Pharaoh and saw himself as the Moses who would lead his suffering, but chosen, black people out of bondage in their new "Egypt." These ideas were codified in *The Secret Relationship Between Blacks and Jews* (1992), published by the NOI, which also alleged that Jews had been the chief architects and practitioners of the American slave trade.

Farrakhan believed that he could commune with the spirit of Elijah Muhammad, the old leader, by entering an unidentified flying object (UFO), from a group of spacecraft in one of which, the *Mother Plane*, God lived. Seemingly unconnected phenomena were linked in his understanding of America in the 1980s:

> The imminent destruction of the present world order is directed from the *Mother Plane*. A nucleus of leading devils knows the wrath of God coming from out of space. This is why reports of UFOs are classified. This is why billions of dollars are invested in militarizing space and the science of astrology. The Strategic Defense Initiative continues to receive an enormous budget despite nuclear disarmament. This is because Star Wars was never intended as protection from the secular missiles of the Soviet Union but as a devil's shield against the holy missiles of divine retribution.[18]

Farrakhan also practiced numerology, believing that numbers in the outside world had a mystical connection to numbers in the Quran. He believed, for example, that the explosion of the space shuttle *Challenger* in 1986, which took place seventy-two seconds after takeoff, correlated to Surah [chapter] 72 of the Holy Quran, a prediction of "flaming fires" consuming anyone who pries into the secrets of heaven.

Farrakhan, a consistent supporter of racial separation, reached the height of his influence and popularity in 1995 by calling for a "Million Man March" on Washington. It provoked an immense response, making the event probably the single biggest human gathering in the entire history of the United States. The vast majority of the African American men present on the Mall that day were not Muslims, but they responded to his call for a reassertion of black manhood, pride, and dignity. The social element of Farrakhan's outlook was conservative, comparable in its emphasis on family and purity to that of many white fundamentalists during the same years.

Mainstream Islam, meanwhile, dwarfed Farrakhan's NOI and was growing rapidly in the United States. By 2000 there were probably more Muslims than

Jews in America, and certainly more of them than all of America's Quakers, Unitarians, Seventh-day Adventists, Mennonites, Jehovah's Witnesses, and Christian Scientists combined. Exact figures are hard to secure because the U.S. Census Bureau keeps no statistics on religion, but informed guesses placed the number of American Muslims at around six million by 2000. Early in the twentieth century a small-scale Muslim immigration had come from the Middle East. After the Second World War Muslim exiles from repressive regimes had swelled their numbers, but a greater surge of Muslim migration to America began after Congress passed color-blind immigration legislation in 1965. Muslim immigrants came from the Middle East (Lebanon, Saudi Arabia, Iran, Yemen), from India, Pakistan, Bangladesh, and Malaysia, and from a variety of partly Islamic countries of Africa, including Egypt, Senegal, Ghana, and Tanzania. They, like the Catholic and Jewish immigrants of the late nineteenth and early twentieth centuries, had to find ways to adapt to American life. In some respects the challenge was daunting—America's self-conception as a Judeo-Christian nation implicitly excluded them. On the other hand, Islam, right from the beginning, had been a crusading, expansionist religion, adapting to new lands and new cultures while bringing new populations into its orbit.

Some elements of Hebrew and Christian tradition are shared by Islam. Islam teaches that God revealed himself first to Adam, then to Abraham and the other patriarchs and prophets of the Hebrew Bible; that Jesus—born of the Virgin Mary—was among these prophets, but that the last and greatest of the prophets was Muhammad. Muhammad was a direct descendant of Abraham through Hagar's son, Ishmael. The Quran, first revealed to Muhammad in the year 610 C.E., when he was forty years old, as he meditated in a cave on Mount Hira, near Mecca, was the final, complete, and perfect book of God. It ought to be preserved in its original Arabic and not translated into any other language. Islam also teaches that a time of judgment will come on the Last Day, after which God will bring the righteous to paradise and cast the unrighteous into perpetual fire.

A good Muslim has to fulfill five commandments, the "five pillars" of Islam, and the punctilious must observe many additional religious duties. Some were easy enough to fulfill in the American context and fit nicely with national values, such as *zakat*, the imperative to be charitable; *shahada*, a belief in the unity of a monotheistic God; and *sawm*, the requirement of fasting until sundown during the holy month of Ramadan (which falls at a slightly different time every year because it is based on the lunar calendar). Fasting of various kinds was common in Judaism and Christianity too. The Islamic ban on eating pork and the requirement that food fulfill *halal* rules were analogous to Jewish *kashrut* regulations, and Muslims sometimes bought kosher food (which also excludes pork), then recited appropriate prayers over it to make it acceptable. The Islamic ban on the consumption of alcohol might be slightly awkward in some business hospitality settings but could be honored with a little self-discipline.

Other duties were more difficult. The commandment to make, at least once in one's lifetime, a hajj pilgrimage to Mecca in the twelfth month of the Islamic calendar, depended on possession of sufficient income (though the professional status of Muslim immigrants enabled growing numbers among them to fulfill it). Islam forbids lending or borrowing money at interest, which meant that strict observance would prevent Muslims from taking out mortgages to buy their houses or from making bank loans to build mosques. The fifth commandment, *salat*, presented the greatest difficulty of all: the requirement to pray in public five times every day, including once at midday. The constitutional guarantee of free exercise under the First Amendment meant that it ought to be honored, but there was little tradition among American employers or schools of interrupting the workday for such public prayers. Making it more difficult still was the requirement that special ablutions, including the ritual washing of the head, ears, neck, and feet, should precede prayer and that it should take place in a setting where no pictures were on display.

Islam, like other religions coming to America, gradually adapted to local conditions, even when it did so in the name of *not* compromising. Mosques, for example, which were built in most cities after 1970, often fell into the Christian pattern of providing collective prayer and schools for children on Sundays, even though Friday at midday was the traditional time for collective prayer. Without such a change working people could not attend, and without such schools children whose parents could not place them in full-time Muslim schools might never learn Arabic or develop a proper understanding and respect for their faith. The imam, or prayer leader, sometimes became, in the American context, more like a Protestant pastor, advising and counseling community members and helping them overcome problems with non-Islamic neighbors. One remarked that "the things I'm supposed to do here [America] are in no way comparable to what you have to do in the Middle East. It's like being a minister."[19]

Worshipers at collective prayer ceremonies (whether on Friday or Sunday) removed their shoes at the door of the mosque, performed the ritual ablutions, listened to the call to prayer (*adhan*) sung by the muezzin, and lined up shoulder to shoulder facing the imam. Then, with the men and women separated (women at the back or in a separate room), they knelt on prayer mats and went through a series of prostrations, touching their foreheads to the floor in a rhythm matched by Arabic verses of the Quran, all facing toward the holy city of Mecca. Major services would also include an address by the imam, on the nature of Islamic life.

Mosques sometimes doubled as community centers. In the 1980s and 1990s the Islamic Center of Southern California (ICSC), for example, offered a range of religious and practical services to Muslims in the Los Angeles area but also ran educational programs to advise Muslims of their political and legal rights and to correct outsiders' misconceptions about Islam. It invited non-Muslim religious leaders from the area to speak to its congregation, sent out Muslim speakers to schools and civic groups, and sometimes lobbied the local and state government. There were risks to taking on this public role, even when it was motivated by the desire to increase community understanding. "In times of international tension," writes sociologist Ron Kelley, "the Los Angeles center is usually the scapegoat for American hostility toward Islam, attracting crank phone-calls, hate mail, and occasional bomb threats."[20]

The status of women in Islam was one of many points of tension between Muslims and other Americans, and sometimes within Muslim communities. Muslims, like Christian fundamentalists, stressed that although men and women were equal before God, it was an equality of complementary differ-ences rather than interchangeable qualities—a point that many Western femi-nists disliked. Quranic inheritance principles gave twice as much to men as to women, and law courts weighed the testimony of one man as equal to that of two women. Islamic women reaching puberty were required, in many Islamic countries, to cover their hair or even their entire faces, lest their appearance arouse men's sexual desire. They attended separate schools and were segregated inside the mosque, and society was structured around the assumption that women were to be cared for, guarded, and protected by men.

The clothing issue could be difficult in the American context. In a society where every woman was covered, each particular woman would be inconspic-uous. In America, by contrast, where the practice was rare and where men and women intermixed in far more settings, a woman in *hejab* (head-covering) or *chador* (complete body covering) would stand out rather than blend in, thus defeating the purpose. A high school girl told sociologist Richard Wormser that her appearance with the *hejab* led to rumors that she was receiving chemother-apy for cancer and had lost all her hair. Other girls reported being teased and mocked. Some decided, in these circumstances, to go without the *hejab* since that was a more certain way of *not* standing out. Other women argued that *hejab* was liberating since it removed the temptation to turn oneself into a West-ern-style display object with provocative clothes and makeup. One, Hayat Alvi, argued that it allowed her to focus on "other important features in a person, such as morality and faith, intelligence, love, and care."[21] American customs also prompted some mosques to forgo the segregation of the sexes; in the ICSC women were encouraged to wear some kind of head-covering and to sit at the back, but were not required to veil or to pray in a different room.

Islamic women denied the common feminist complaint that their religion was misogynist or repressive. Muslims like Laila Al-Marayati, president of the Muslim Women's League, argued that in some Islamic countries repressive *cus-*

toms had restricted women but that these cultural accretions were not intrinsic to Islam. Asma Gull Hasan made the same point, in protesting that gender separation in the mosque was a cultural, not a Quranic, requirement. "If we are a community, let's be one and sit together. There is nothing in the Quran that solidly justifies such segregation. There is much in our native cultures that does, and we must move beyond that. We're Americans now, and Muslims, and must come together as such."[22]

How did American life appear to new Muslim immigrants? Many expressed ambivalence, half grateful at the religious liberty, civic order, education, and economic opportunities America provided, but half horrified at what seemed to them a plague of pornography, drugs, and immorality, constantly on display in the media. One immigrant told sociologist Kambiz GhaneaBassiri:

> I don't believe in economic depression. The depression they [the Americans] are suffering from is moral depression—prostitution, homosexuality, throwing children out of the home. . . . Here the dogs are in the homes, the children are in the streets. This nation, I would say every nation in Europe, is culturally retarded. I wish, if not Islam, if they were good Christians they wouldn't have these problems. They don't care about religion. . . . They believe money is everything.[23]

American-born Muslims like peppy Asma Hasan, on the other hand, were impatient with such complaints by "immigrants with more than their share of gray hairs," which were often accompanied by a false idealizing of their country of origin. She wrote that it was time for Muslim associations like the Islamic Society of North America to accept the fact that America was *home*. "My attitude is that I, and other Muslims, are figuring out how to live as Muslims *and* Americans, not one or the other." After all, there was so much to admire in America: "the emphasis on gender equality, an ethic of hard work, involvement and activism in the community."[24]

International conflicts in the late twentieth century repeatedly placed America and the world's Islamic nations on opposite sides, and these conflicts echoed painfully through America's Muslim communities. Anti-Islamic insults and attacks on American Muslims escalated at times of international crisis. The Jewish-Palestinian confrontation in Israel, more or less continuous in the second half of the century, the Iranian Revolution, hostage crisis, and Iran-Iraq war (1978–1981), the Gulf War (1990–1991), and the two attacks on the World Trade Center (1993 and 2001) all led to flaring American anger against Muslims.

As if being representatives of a widely hated faith were not enough, America's Muslims were often sharply at odds with one another. The Sunni majority and the Shi'a minority disagreed about interpretation of their faith, and their disputes were intensified in the 1980s after the Shi'a takeover in Iran and Saudi Arabian repression of Shi'a (which led to rioting and four hundred deaths in

Mecca in 1987). Even within the Sunni majority there were sometimes acute national conflicts, as between the traditionally adversarial Yemenis and Saudi Arabians. Each national group therefore had an incentive to create a mosque and a community life of its own, where old-country customs were still honored. Further complicating the picture, the Tableeghi Jamaat, a Pakistan-based organization, sent out its volunteers to recall all the faithful to their religious duty and a highly literal interpretation of the Quran.

A generally low level of knowledge about, and understanding of, Islam among other Americans exacerbated these tensions. A high school student, Mai Abdala, recalled a classroom confrontation in public school:

> I had a teacher who called my religion Mohammedanism. I corrected him and he got angry. He showed me a book in which the term was used. I said, "yes, but this book was written by a Western man a long time ago who didn't understand us. We don't worship Muhammad. He was a prophet, not a God. It offends us when somebody calls us Mohammadans." The teacher accepted the criticism but he wasn't happy about it.[25]

Offsetting these tensions and misunderstandings, the widespread American belief in religious freedom and mutual respect could work to support Muslims' obvious differences. Sohail Humayun Hashmi, an Indian immigrant raised in Statesboro, Georgia, reported that although his hometown was "very religious—Christian, Southern Baptist in particular," he had never experienced "any kind of hostility or tension or bigotry or prejudice. . . . In fact, our friends there were always interested in finding out more about Islam."[26] Another Muslim student, a high school girl, reported that she had been elected class president by her largely non-Muslim classmates "because they know that as a Muslim I don't lie, I don't cheat, and I can be trusted to keep my word," while a boy at the same school found that his non-Muslim friends tried to help him keep his Ramadan fast.[27]

Publicizing outbreaks of anti-Islamic prejudice could sometimes lead to an about-face, as communities realized their betrayal of America's tradition of religious freedom. When the Muslims of Northridge, California, planned to build a mosque of their own, for example, a suspicious city council at first laid down forty-four conditions and restrictions, even specifying that the building would have to be built in Spanish mission style to blend in with the neighborhood. But when a journalist from the *Los Angeles Times* took an interest in the case, everything changed. Mayor Tom Bradley spoke up on behalf of religious freedom and said the mosque could be built in a more suitable style and even have a minaret, if desired. A similar controversy over the building of a Saudi-funded Islamic school in Loudon County, Virginia, in the early 1990s was resolved in a similar way: Early local suspicions and objections were silenced when an American war hero, General Norman Schwarzkopf, reminded residents that "xenophobic protests go against the ideals we fought for in Operation Desert Storm."[28] Saudi Arabian money supported many Islamic initiatives in America, making use of an atmosphere of religious freedom not found in Saudi Arabia itself. The Dar al-Islam community in Abiquiu, New Mexico, for example, was a model village, complete with adobe mosque, founded in the early 1980s and built by an eminent Egyptian architect, Hassan Fathy. There, families and visitors from America's diverse Muslim traditions could meet, study, and practice their faith together, emphasizing the ideal interracial and interethnic character of Islam.

By 1990 nearly half of the American Muslim population was American-born, most being African Americans who had left NOI and entered mainstream Islam. Other African Americans joined for the first time. Steven Barboza, for example, who was raised Catholic, described his desperate (and unsuccessful) prayers to Jesus in a hospital chapel to save his mother's life, an event that "so shattered my already wavering [Christian] faith that I resolved to find a more effective way to pray to my Creator." He studied Islam, went through the conversion ceremony of reciting the *shahadah*, declaring that "there is no God but Allah, and Muhammad is His messenger," and tried to conform his work as a young executive to the Muslim commandments. At prayer times "I stole away to a stockroom in J. C. Penney's corporate headquarters, where alone I took off my shoes and recited the Quran, facing Mecca and prostrating myself on a flattened-out cardboard box."[29] Journalists and anthropologists discovered black and white converts from many other walks of life, including a former California congressman, Jim Bates, and a Catholic nun, Mary Froelich, who said she had left the convent after seven years when she began to doubt the divinity of Jesus, and found herself drawn to Islam after profound study of the Quran and the life of Malcolm X. Robert Dickson Crane, descended from seventeenth-century Puritan immigrants to Connecticut, a Harvard Law School graduate and former foreign policy adviser to President Nixon, became a Muslim in 1980 and was among the founders of the American Muslim Legal Defense Fund.

Immigrants and American-born Muslims alike faced the problem of ensuring transmission of their faith to the next generation. They, like Catholics and Jews before them (and like growing numbers of their Christian fundamentalist contemporaries), set about establishing schools of their own, in which they could be sure their religion was not merely accommodated and tolerated but honored. Arabic was central to the curriculum, in order that they could study the Quran, which, unlike the Bible, is not supposed to be translated into other languages. Muslim children sometimes welcomed the chance to go, since it delivered them from temptations that had surrounded them in public school. "In public schools," a sixteen-year-old boy told a researcher, "it seemed like everyone was into drugs, stuff like crack cocaine, reefer, booze. It was hard not to do that, especially when you were out with your buddies and everybody else was doing it. So I decided to go to a religious school."[30] Others found the schools restrictive, especially since they segregated the boys from the girls.

Earlier immigrant groups had struggled with the question of whom their children would be allowed to marry, and Muslim immigrants faced the same challenge. Just as the early twentieth century had witnessed bitter family quarrels over whether Jewish and Catholic sons and daughters could marry out of the faith or wed someone chosen by the individual for romantic reasons rather than by the parents in family negotiations, so the late twentieth century witnessed the same kind of fierce quarrels among Muslims. An extreme example of such conflict came when a Yemeni immigrant shot and killed his thirteen-year-old sister when she refused to abandon her social life, including dating, with the California teenagers around her.

America's fast-growing Muslim population in the closing years of the twentieth century found itself in the same situation as had many other religious groups before it. The majority were eager to adapt their religion to the American way of life, to find a way of pursuing business and professional success, making necessary practical concessions in their interpretation of older religious and cultural forms, while keeping the heart of the tradition alive. To them the small minority who endorsed foreign governments' anti-American views were an embarrassment that prevented full acceptance for all the rest.

The highly developed principles of "political correctness," by which expressions of dislike for another religion were taboo, worked in Muslims' favor in the 1980s and 1990s, even as a widespread fear of, and ignorance about, Islam among other Americans worked against them. Asma Hasan probably spoke for many Muslims, especially the native-born, when she made a pitch for America's having a "Judeo-Christian-Islamic tradition" on the grounds that all three faiths were monotheistic. Sohail Hashmi went further:

> The opportunity is greatest for American Muslims to really shape the course of Islam in the future because American Islam is a microcosm of Muslims from all over the world who have to find a way to live together. They have to come to a common understanding of what Islam means in this country, and moreover they're free from the kinds of cultural and political repression that are prevalent in Muslim countries.[31]

Paradoxical as it might seem, America, still the devil nation to Muslims abroad, could here be reconceptualized as the promised land.

Chapter 10

THE NEW WORLD ORDER: 1989–1999

End of the Cold War

The evangelical scandals of 1987 and the election of 1988 were overshadowed by the international events of 1989, which will be remembered as one of the four or five pivotal years of the entire twentieth century. The Soviet Union had been fighting for ten years in Afghanistan but with even less success than America had enjoyed in Vietnam. By 1989 troops from its constituent republics were in open mutiny. Russia's Eastern European client states, far poorer than the countries of Western Europe and dominated by repressive puppet regimes, were on the brink of revolt. Ten years of growing protest and disaffection in Poland had been nurtured by the work of Karol Wojtyla (Pope John Paul II) since 1978 and by the Catholic Church's support for the dissident trade union Solidarity. Now Czechs, East Germans, Poles, Rumanians, and Hungarians were clamoring for drastic reforms. The Russian economy, despite desperate reforms introduced by Mikhail Gorbachev since 1985, was foundering in the face of Western competition and its own dysfunction. In 1989 the whole chaotic system fell to pieces; cheering students tore down the Berlin Wall, families divided almost thirty years before were joyously reunited, and years of tyranny and antireligious coercion came to an end. Two years later the Soviet Union's own Communist Party state collapsed.

Americans were delighted by this successful end to the long Cold War, and religious groups did what they could to help the Russian and Eastern European transition to democracy and religious freedom. Billy Graham had visited the Soviet Union in 1982 and 1984 and had seen premonitions of change. By the time of his 1988 visit to celebrate the thousandth anniversary of Russian Christianity, the changes were unmistakable. Loudspeakers outside the churches where he spoke broadcast his message to a wider audience, as did TV cameras inside, and when he spoke at the Bolshoi Theater President Gorbachev came to listen. Graham was back in 1991 for an evangelists' training conference, and in 1992 for one of his massive crusades, which was held in the thirty-eight-thousand-seat Olympic Stadium and enjoyed a succession of capacity crowds. On the last night, with fifty thousand people squeezed inside and another twenty thousand outside, "the soaring voices of a magnificent men's chorus resounded through the huge, overflowing stadium, triumphantly echoing the familiar strains of one of America's best loved hymns of faith, the Battle Hymn of the Republic." Yet the singers were "the Russian Army Chorus, known for many decades as the Red Army Chorus—a group recognized all over the world not only for their musical talent but also for their role as one of the Soviet Union's chief propaganda tools."[1]

In the late 1980s the National Association of Evangelicals sponsored the emigration of thousands of Russian evangelical and Pentecostal Christians. But by 1990, as Graham's experience suggests, religious migration was becoming a two-way street. As the new government restored religious freedom, other enterprising American evangelicals began to flow into Russia, seizing the chance to harvest more souls for Christ. Baffling, and sometimes annoying to the Russian Orthodox clergy, who found them tough competition, the Americans—including student volunteers from Campus Crusade for Christ—distributed free Bibles, preached emotional sermons on street corners, led crowds of new enthusiasts in evangelical hymn singing, and showed subtitled versions of their videos about Jesus.

Mutual visiting flourished as the Cold War ended. America's Orthodox Christians—not just those from the Russian Orthodox Church but those from the Greek, Antiochan, Serbian, and Arabic branches as well—welcomed the Patriarch Aleksy II when he came from Russia in the fall of 1991 to visit President Bush and Orthodox congregations in New York and Pennsylvania. He appealed to them for funds to rebuild the faith in Russia and urged them to move toward a greater unity among themselves in place of their ethnic fragmentation in America.

American Jews, like Christians, acclaimed the collapse of the Soviet Union as the end of a long period of repression for their coreligionists. The New York–based Memorial Foundation for Jewish Culture had been smuggling Russian-language Bibles, copies of the Torah, religious videotapes, and even kosher cookbooks into Russia since the late 1960s and training émigré Jews as rabbis, in the hope that they could preserve the faith in Russia. Rabbis across America used high synagogue attendance at Rosh Hashanah and Yom Kippur in the fall of 1991 to organize a fund-raising drive to help cover the cost of the mass emigration of Soviet Jews into Israel. They also subsidized Soviet Jews coming to America and found that many, having been prevented from practicing their religion in Russia, knew little about it. For example, the Lurye family, who emigrated from Leningrad to Clifton, New Jersey, in 1990, were given an apartment, financial support, English lessons, and, for their son, a full scholarship to the Hillel Academy in Passaic by the local Jewish organizations. The Luryes attended synagogue regularly and enjoyed their first Passover services and seder as they struggled to learn new habits and a new language. A New York Hasidic rabbi, Yitzhak Kogen, traveled to Moscow in December 1991 and, side by side with a group of Russian Jews, lit a twenty-foot iron menorah in the building of the new Russian Parliament, which had just withstood an attempted countercoup, as a symbol of the country's new religious freedom.

After the initial euphoria, Americans had to face up to hard questions about the future of Eastern Europe and Russia. Would these nations manage to create and sustain Western-style democracies? Would the return of religious freedom lead to a new era of church growth, or would the end of repression send the churches into the same kind of decline as those in Western Europe had experienced? Pessimistic commentators feared that, having thrived on repression, the nations would now duplicate not the best of Western life—intellectual, political, and religious freedom—but the worst of it—pornography, crime, drugs, and decadence. Billy Graham's brother-in-law, Leighton Ford, who headed the Lausanne Committee for World Evangelization, warned: "If the East becomes just as materialistic as the West, this will not be the change we were looking for. If freedom means freedom to accumulate, not freedom to worship and serve, we have not succeeded."[2] Catholic philosopher Ralph McInerny agreed: "There are those who see what is happening in Eastern Europe as the desire for what is most loathsome in our own society."[3]

Whatever the verdict on Eastern Europe, America was now left as the world's one undisputed superpower, politically united and economically immense. Would it now police what President George Bush Sr. called "the New World Order" or would it draw back into the kind of isolationism that had characterized American foreign policy throughout most of the nation's history? The first test of its resolve came in 1990 when Saddam Hussein, Iraqi dictator, invaded Kuwait, Iraq's neighbor on the Arabian Gulf. President Bush reacted first by organizing United Nations sanctions, second with air strikes, and finally with a conventional military assault of overwhelming power. Iraq sustained massive casualties. American and UN losses were slight, but after the liberation of

Kuwait the campaign ended. Hussein remained in power in Iraq and, in the ensuing years, continued to brutalize populations under his control, especially the Kurds.

Religious Americans debated the rights and wrongs of the Gulf War. The president himself, an Episcopalian, wept in public as he recalled ordering the ground forces into battle, but he remained convinced the war was justified. He believed there was an obvious case to make in favor of intervention, first to protect the rights of small nations in general and Kuwait in particular, second to prevent the human rights abuses and terror methods by which Hussein ruled. "We fought for good versus evil. It was that clear to me; right versus wrong, dignity against oppression."[4] Other religious Americans made the same case and welcomed the president's decisiveness. George Weigel, an expert on Christian just war theory, argued in *Just War and the Gulf War* (1991) that the war had satisfied all the traditional criteria for a just war. Cardinal Bernard Law of Boston agreed, writing that the war was justified to deny "tyrants and aggressors an open field to achieve unjust ends."[5]

Others, by contrast, including some of Law's fellow Catholic bishops (such as Hunthausen of Seattle), criticized the war, feeling that their government's vigorous actions had been designed to protect American oil supplies more than to protect the lives of the oppressed, and that the cost of such a war stood in disgraceful contrast to the government's reduced social expenditures at home. Members of many denominations came together to express doubts about the war. William Sloane Coffin, for example, who had been one of the most energetic anti-Vietnam clergy, told a crowd of 350 people at a New York Unitarian church that "if we feel badly about Vietnam—and we do—we will feel even worse about this. . . . A gulf war is not politically or morally defensible in the least and would have to rank as one of the most stupid wars the U.S. has ever waged."[6] Riverside Church in Manhattan, where Martin Luther King Jr. had spoken out against Vietnam in 1967, led the antiwar forces again and offered itself as a sanctuary to soldiers who felt conscientious scruples about fighting in Kuwait. Jesse Jackson wrote that diplomatic methods and an embargo against Iraq were far better than the resort to force. Nevertheless, he said, "My prayers . . . go out to the young men and women whose lives are on the line in the desert."[7]

The war divided the American Muslim community, which endured one of its frequent periods of suspicion among other Americans. A few Muslims were dismayed at the prospect of fighting against other members of their faith. Others were willing because they regarded Saddam Hussein as an enemy of Islam, who merely posed cynically as its defender. Imam Talal Eid, religious leader of a New England mosque, told a journalist: "Every time political leaders like Saddam Hussein are in trouble, they hold up the banner of Islam, but most Muslims don't fall for this."[8] Kashim Ishmael Elijah Scott, a U.S. Marine on the ground in Kuwait, said he felt glad to be part of a force defending Saudi Arabia (America's ally in the war) because it was the birthplace and home of the prophet Muhammad. "I feel I have more of a purpose than the average marine. . . . I feel I am defending Mecca and Medina, which is sacred ground."[9] Army chaplains reported that the war experience had led "dozens" of the soldiers in their flock to convert to Islam.

In the early 1990s, the new world order faced new conflict flashpoints, in southeastern Europe (the former Yugoslavia, which was now broken into Bosnia, Macedonia, Croatia, and Serbia) and in parts of Africa (Rwanda, Burundi, Somalia). Both areas endured brutal civil wars, made worse by centuries-deep tribal and religious animosities, and both witnessed the hideous spectacle of "ethnic cleansing," in which tribal, ethnic, or religious groups exterminated entire categories of their rivals. Memories of the Holocaust (and a widespread belief that America had done too little, too late to save Europe's Jews) prompted many religious groups to urge American intervention to prevent further genocide. A coalition of religious leaders set aside a weekend in December 1992 as the "sabbath of Prayer and Petition." The National Council of Churches, the National Conference of Catholic Bishops, the Synagogue Council of America, and the National Council of Mosques all urged the American government "to promote an immediate and lasting end to the violence in both Somalia and the former Yugoslavia." Its members' conflicting anxieties— on the one hand of genocide, on the other of another Vietnam quagmire—were apparent in its caution that the United States "is not the policeman of the world" but that "the mass murder of innocents is unacceptable."[10] Government policy, like church opinion, was equivocal, involved but never fully committed in either region. Under both Bush and his White House successor, Bill Clinton, no signs of tailoring policies to church groups' appeals were evident. Church opinion was just one of the many public opinion components with which government had to deal.

Religion and Violence

Religion in late-twentieth-century America was never entirely separable from violence, at home as well as abroad, and the 1990s witnessed several religious episodes that ended violently. One was a federal government raid in 1992 against the Idaho mountaintop home of Randy Weaver, a Christian survivalist. He had been convinced by Christian Identity, a group blending racial-purity claims with Christian fundamentalism, that white Americans were the real descendants of the people described in the Old Testament, that Jews were agents of Satan, and that America was really run by "ZOG"—the Zionist Occupation Government. President Bush had meant his declaration of a new world order to be benign, but to Christian Identity it sounded like Antichrist's sinister organization for world domination. Anticipating the need to fight against "the Beast" during the coming end times, Christian Identity favored survivalism — learning to live without help from the rest of the world, being self-sufficient in food, medicine, and weapons. Weaver, with his wife and four children, found a congenial atmosphere among Idaho mountaineers who shared their suspicion of the federal government. They home-schooled the children rather than put them in government-run public schools. An agent from the Federal Bureau of Alcohol, Tobacco, and Firearms entrapped Weaver by persuading him to sell an illegal sawed-off shotgun. He hoped Weaver would bargain for leniency in return for information leading to the arrest of more important survivalists. Weaver refused, and ATF surveillance of his cabin erupted into sudden exchanges of gunfire in August 1992. A federal agent and Weaver's thirteen-year-old son were killed; the next day Mrs. Weaver also died in a hail of bullets. Weaver himself finally surrendered after an eleven-day standoff and was later found not guilty of murder (because ambiguous evidence suggested that the federal agent was killed in crossfire from his own side).

A second and much worse incident was the bloody end of the Branch David-ians, an offshoot of the Seventh-day Adventist Church. Independent since 1934, the group had been taken over in the late 1980s by David Koresh, a charismatic leader who gained absolute authority over more than a hundred followers and believed himself to be one of the figures foretold in the Book of Revelation. Koresh, like Weaver, was a posttribulationist. In other words, he agreed with contemporary fundamentalists like Jerry Falwell that the end times were imminent but did *not* agree that Christians could expect to be raptured before the seven years of war and suffering that would climax in Christ's Second Coming. Instead, he believed that true Christians would have to fight against Antichrist.

Evidence that he had assembled a formidable arsenal of weapons at his Mount Carmel compound near Waco, Texas, and rumors that he sexually abused children led to a raid in February 1993 by ATF agents. Koresh's follow-ers repelled the raiders with a volley of gunfire, killing four of the agents. The government responded with a large-scale seven-week siege, during which its representatives tried to reason with Koresh, bringing in a group of their own Bible experts to debate the meaning of Revelation. When negotiations stalled, the government forces tried to numb Koresh into psychological submission by illuminating Mount Carmel all night with powerful floodlights and by playing deafeningly loud rock music. Finally the FBI, with approval from the president and the attorney general, ordered an attack using riot-control gas and tanks. As they advanced, the buildings caught fire (which side set the fires is one of many points still in dispute), with the result that Koresh himself and an estimated 103 followers perished.

The heavy loss of life (seventeen of the dead were young children) led to great heart-searching after the event, especially when Timothy McVeigh, who destroyed the federal government building in Oklahoma City in 1995, described the denouement of the Waco siege as evidence that the federal government was at war against American citizens. Commentators noted that the government's anti-terrorism agents had not studied charismatic religious movements, were too willing to take advice from discredited "anti-cultists" who demonized the Branch Davidians, and had not adequately anticipated the way Koresh would interpret their conduct. One pointed out that the ATF and the FBI

> unwittingly played into his millenarian script. He wanted and needed their opposition, which they obligingly provided in the form of the initial assault, the nationally publicized siege, and the final tank and gas attack. . . . The government's actions almost certainly increased the resolve of those in the compound, subdued the doubters and raised Koresh's stature by in effect validating his predictions.[11]

A third conjunction of religion and violence in the same years marked the climax of the anti-abortion movement. Operation Rescue, working in an increasingly hostile legal environment, was unable to stage massive "rescues" after 1991. A handful of anti-abortion activists, determined not to give up, decided that they were religiously justified in killing abortion doctors, because by doing so they would be saving the lives of unborn children. The first attack was made by Michael Griffin, a thirty-one-year-old Pensacola activist, who shot and killed abortion doctor David Gunn in March 1993, in the belief that he was fulfilling a divine order. He had twice warned Gunn that he would kill him if he did not stop performing abortions, but Gunn had ignored the threats. News of the killing horrified the majority of pro-life activists, who had always confined themselves to peaceful protest, or at most to nonviolent civil disobedience. A handful, however, reacted by acclaiming Griffin's act. Collections for his legal defense poured in, and Randall Terry, former leader of Operation Rescue, wrote: "While we grieve for [Gunn] and his widow, we must also grieve for the thousands of children that he has murdered."[12]

Six months later Shelley Shannon, an Oregon housewife, made an attempt of her own. Shannon had already been inspired by other activists and had learned from an anti-abortion Army of God manual how to make firebombs to destroy clinics. She, like Griffin, had no doubt that she was working in a godly cause. After her first crime, bombing a clinic in Ashland, Oregon, she wrote in her diary that it was "a very powerful religious experience" (353). Some of her subsequent arson attacks failed, but she managed to destroy the Pregnancy Consultation Center in Sacramento, California, in November 1992. Recording the event on her computer, she wrote: "Glorious, glorious trip . . . didn't even care if I made it back, or care so much about getting caught or killed, just wanted to close the place. . . . It was supposed to be an early birthday present to

Jesus, early for expediency, but I found it was he who gave me a gift" (354). In an anonymous letter she warned a Milwaukee abortionist: "I will hunt you down like any other wild beast and kill you" but finally chose as her target Dr. George Tiller in Wichita, Kansas. She shot him as he drove out of his clinic, wounded him twice, but did not kill him, and said, on being arrested, that it was "the most holy, most righteous thing I've ever done" (356).

The next year, in June 1994, Paul Hill, a longtime extremist in the anti-abortion movement, ambushed John Britton, the doctor who had replaced David Gunn in Pensacola. Hill killed Britton with a shotgun, also killing James Barrett and wounding Barrett's wife, volunteers from a Pensacola Unitarian church who had agreed to drive Britton from the airport to the clinic. Both victims — aware of the hazards they faced — were wearing bulletproof vests, but both died anyway from head wounds. Six months later, that December, John C. Salvi III, a fourth violent activist, attacked two clinics in the Boston suburbs and one in Norfolk, Virginia, killing two receptionists and wounding five other employees before being arrested. Hill was sentenced to death in Florida, and Salvi, after being convicted and sentenced to life imprisonment, committed suicide in his cell. From her own jail cell, Shelley Shannon wrote that "for the Army of God, 1994 was a pretty great year. Paul Hill performed a termination procedure on an abortionist . . . and may be put to death for his obedience to God, a most honorable way for a Christian to die" (368).

This turn to violence was an act of desperation, not strength, and it at once weakened the anti-abortion movement. Traditions of civility and restraint were so deeply ingrained in most pro-life activists, as in most Americans of all kinds, that only a tiny minority, even of those who believed that their opponents were killing babies, were willing to cross over the line to violence.

Religious violence of a different kind — self-inflicted — marked America's most dramatic mass suicide since Jonestown when the Heaven's Gate community annihilated itself in 1997. Heaven's Gate was the creation of Marshall Applewhite and Betty Lu Nettles, who, during a prolonged car-camping trip to the far West in the 1970s, had become convinced that God had charged them with a special mission. They believed that they were the two lampstands mentioned in Revelation 11:3–13 and that they were charged with preparing themselves and others to move up to the "Next Level of Human Evolution." Known variously as "Guinea and Pig," "Bo and Peep," "Di and Ti," they sought out converts at New Age and metaphysical bookstores and conventions. At first they lived precariously; both were arrested for credit card fraud, and Applewhite spent six months in jail for renting a car in St. Louis and never bringing it back. They justified themselves biblically: "The Lord will be as a thief in the night." But when a group of affluent converts joined them and agreed to pay the costs of their daily life, they settled, first in Colorado, later in California. Applewhite and Nettles had visions of dying together and being resurrected in a blaze of light, but mundane realities intervened: Nettles died of liver cancer in 1985. Applewhite persisted, making videos to preach his gospel and, after 1995, running a Web page that warned of a coming world crisis. Members and ex-members agreed that he was a charismatic figure with high standards. "Shame and fear were your impetus to keep under control," one recalled. "You were trying to define yourself as a 'pure vessel' in the leader's mind. Your punishment was him denying you his approval."[13]

The group, which reached a maximum of two hundred members but sometimes shrank to a mere twenty-five, lived communally, shared all work and clothing (even underwear), designed Internet Web pages to pay the bills, and continued to develop its own quirky blend of science-fiction, New Age, and biblical ideas. The Kingdom of Heaven, they believed, nurtured gardens on other planets and introduced its higher wisdom to the inhabitants once they were ready. At a crucial moment in history, for example, the Kingdom had decided that Earth was ready for enlightenment, and so one member

> left behind His body in that Next Level (similar to putting it in a closet, like a suit of clothes that doesn't need to be worn for a while) came to Earth, and moved into (or incarnated into) an adult human body (or "vehicle") that had been "prepped" for this particular task. . . . That body (named Jesus) was tagged in its formative period to be the receptacle of a Next Level Representative, and even just that "tagging" gave that "vehicle" some unique awareness of its coming purpose.[14]

Jesus' purpose, said the Heaven's Gate Web page, had been to persuade people who had sufficiently awakened souls to abandon Earth and follow him to the Kingdom of Heaven. "Leaving behind this world includes: family, sensuality, selfish desires, your human mind, and even your human body if it be required of you—all mammalian ways of thinking and behavior." In other words, the human body is an encumbrance, tying the pure spirit down to the inferior Earth. Seven male members of the group found it difficult to resist sexual temptation but tried to live up to the ideal by having themselves surgically castrated.

The reason most of the American population failed to join Heaven's Gate, Applewhite argued, was because "discarnate spirits," space aliens or "Luciferians," had colonized the minds of the world's political leaders and dictated what was socially acceptable while discrediting the world's few real "angels." The lesson of the Luciferians was this: "Be married, a good parent, a reasonable church goer, buy a house, pay your mortgage, pay your insurance."[15] This propaganda had persuaded most ordinary folks, who thus remained trapped at the "mammalian" level.

In 1995 a dramatic fiery comet appeared in the heavens and was named after the amateur astronomers who had predicted and discovered it: Hale-Bopp. Thirty-nine members of the Heaven's Gate group, then living in a luxurious mansion in Rancho Santa Fe near San Diego, believed that a flying saucer was lurking behind the comet, that it was commanded by the spirit of "Ti" (formerly Ms. Nettles), with whom they had already been in contact, and that it had come to "take them home" to the Kingdom of Heaven. In order to get on board they shucked off their mortal bodies ("vehicles") by drinking lethal doses of alcohol and phenobarbitol, dying calmly in groups of fifteen, fifteen, and nine between March 26 and March 29, 1997, the days on which the comet made its closest approach to Earth. The sixty-five-year-old Applewhite left behind a farewell message on videotape. On the bodies, the police discovered rolls of quarters, as though the voyagers had expected to need loose change to board their starship.

Environmental Spirituality

Major social movements in postwar America usually developed a religious dimension, as we have seen throughout this book. Anti-Communism, civil rights, the counterculture, the women's movement, the antinuclear movement, and the anti-abortion movement all concerned issues that could be addressed simply on a secular plane, and often were, but each of them also had religious implications and found its own body of religious enthusiasts. The same was true again in the case of environmentalism. Arising first in a purely secular context during the 1960s, and sometimes sharply critical of the Judeo-Christian tradition, it struck religious chords and began to influence religious people's ideas about God, the relationship between the spiritual and natural worlds, and the possibility of extending notions of justice to the natural world. By the 1990s it had become a major preoccupation for some religious groups, giving rise to new forms of theology and new styles of preaching and liturgy.

The godfathers of American environmentalism are Henry David Thoreau (1817–1862), whose *Walden* (1854) lauded the simple life close to nature, and John Muir (1838–1914), who pioneered the preservation of American wilderness areas and thought of the great outdoors, rather than church, as the best place to look for God. Conservation of natural resources was an issue for American governments from the early twentieth century, but environmentalism in its modern form began in the 1960s. Rachel Carson's *Silent Spring* (1962), a surprise bestseller criticizing the indiscriminate use of chemical pesticides, was its first manifesto. The movement at first emphasized the danger of world overpopulation, of chemical hazards in the environment, of ugly urban sprawl, and the wastefulness of American consumer life. Lynn White Jr.'s influential article in *Science*, "The Religious Roots of Our Ecological Crisis" (1967), was an early attempt to link ecology and religion. White argued that Americans in the Judeo-Christian tradition overexploited the natural world partly because God had authorized Adam to "have dominion over the fish of the sea, over the birds of the air, and over every living thing" (Genesis 1:28) and had neglected to caution him against exploiting and degrading them. In the Judeo-Christian tradition, moreover, woods, rivers, hills, and the sky were not themselves deities, so Western civilization had felt far less restraint about manipulating the earth than, for example, Native Americans, for whom the earth itself was alive and spirit-filled.

The first Earth Day was celebrated on April 22, 1970, the same year that the Environmental Protection Agency became a department of the federal government. By then a few churches were hailing the insights of the "ecology movement" as appropriate to their constituencies and agreeing that they should work against pollution, waste, and overpopulation. The *Christian Century* devoted an entire issue (October 7, 1970) to the "environmental crisis." A predictable division took place among the Protestant churches. Some liberal Protestants embraced the idea of caring for the jeopardized environment as one more necessary duty, along with fighting poverty, racism, and the war in Vietnam. Many conservative or evangelical Protestants were indifferent or hostile at first, some because they had not yet reentered the political arena and preferred to confine themselves to questions of personal salvation, others because early environmentalists criticized the Christian tradition in a way that made them look like enemies. Even so, one of the most important evangelical writers, Francis Schaeffer, condemned indiscriminate industrial pollution as an affront to God. Catholics accepted the idea that America was a wasteful and dirty society but denied the assertion that overpopulation was a crisis—they were, after all, doctrinally averse not only to abortion but even to contraception, and still tended to have a lot of children. American Jews, overwhelmingly urban, found little to interest them at first in a movement much of whose energy was devoted to preserving wilderness areas. By contrast, ecology struck a sympathetic chord in the counterculture straightaway. Jack Kerouac's friend Gary Snyder, back in America after ten years in a Japanese Zen monastery, favored decentering humanity and bringing all of nature—worms, birds, fish, and all—into perfect equality. "What we must do is incorporate the other people . . . the creeping people, and the standing people, and the flying people and the swimming people . . . into the councils of government."[16]

Secular environmentalists often approached the issue with an evangelical intensity, and for some the imminent earth catastrophe appeared almost to be a substitute for the Christian Apocalypse. Their work, along with a series of incidents in the 1970s and 1980s, raised general levels of popular environmental awareness. Two temporary oil shortages (the "oil crises" of 1973 and 1979) demonstrated that America was heavily dependent on imported oil from the politically volatile Middle East and might profitably look for ways to economize. Rising oil prices stimulated a vogue for small cars and for energy conservation. The early promise of nuclear power as a safe, clean, efficient electricity source died with the Three Mile Island accident in 1979, in which operators lost control of a nuclear power station and briefly feared a catastrophic meltdown. By then the question of how to dispose of spent, but still radioactive, nuclear fuel rods had become a significant environmental problem too, and prompted a renewed interest in clean "green" power sources such as solar energy. The explosion of a Soviet nuclear power station at Chernobyl in 1986 devastated an area of Ukraine and made it uninhabitable, while the wreck of the supertanker *Exxon Valdez* on Good Friday of 1989 poured millions of gallons of crude oil into the coastal ecosystems of southern Alaska, killing wildlife and devastating an almost pristine coastline. Citizens became aware, also, that growing numbers of species faced extinction because their habitat was being destroyed by development projects.

The combined effect of these events was to raise the environmental awareness of nearly all Americans and oblige government and corporations to balance plans for economic growth against the potential environmental harm they might cause. For the first time, a major social movement opposed the idea that economic growth was necessarily a good thing. President Reagan's first secretary of the interior, James Watt, a premillennial fundamentalist who scorned environmentalists, soon proved ruinously unpopular not only among environmental activists but also within his own party, the GOP, which learned that it, no less than the Democrats, must at least appear to be environmentally sensitive from then on.

A spokesman for the environmental pressure group Friends of the Earth remarked in 1990 that "twenty years after the first Earth Day churches have barely touched on the subject [of the environment]. . . . The silence from the churches has been pretty deafening."[17] That was not quite fair. By then most American churches and synagogues had established national task forces on the environment and made statements endorsing environmental sensitivity, even if most ordinary men and women in the pews were still uninvolved. The pope devoted his New Year's message that January to the issue, urging Catholics to avoid indiscriminate industrial practices that contributed to global warming and ozone depletion. An interfaith group, the North American Conference on Religion and Ecology, founded the previous year, promoted 1990's Earth Day as a day when, "beginning at dawn, church bells will peal for the health of the planet, sermons will stress the urgency of responsible environmental practices and the faithful will be asked to sign conservation declarations, pledging to recycle products, save energy, and vote for ecology-minded public officials."[18]

The American Catholic bishops responded to this new wave of concern, and to the pope's lead, with a pastoral letter, "Renewing the Earth," and the United States Catholic Conference established an environmental justice program two years later. The Catholic leaders agreed that care for the environment ought to be part of everybody's religious duty, though their emphasis was on the human benefits; for people to be healthy they must have a clean environment. The bishops, hoping to "build bridges among the peace, justice and environmental agendas and constituencies," showed no interest in "biocentrism," the radical environmentalist idea that humans ought not to be privileged over other parts of the natural world. Their concern, rather, was with "the poor and powerless who most directly bear the burden of current environmental carelessness," and they argued that "solutions must be found that do not force us to choose between a decent environment and a decent life for workers."[19]

Liberal Protestant groups warmed to the theme of environmental concern too, and some tried to incorporate it in their liturgy as well as their social outreach. The Episcopal Cathedral of St. John the Divine in New York, for instance, ran programs on recycling and urban gardening but also celebrated an annual "Earth Mass" on the feast day of Saint Francis of Assisi (1182–1226), the medieval saint who loved animals, advocated radical voluntary poverty, and had been named patron saint of ecologists in 1980 by the pope. Parishioners were encouraged to bring their animals, and the sung liturgy "Missa Gaia/Earth Mass" was accompanied by wolf howls and the barking of dogs. Elephants, camels, llamas, and parakeets were included in the procession that climaxed the service. Paul Gorman, the cathedral's vice president for public affairs, explained the importance of the event:

> This is every bit as much a response to the greenhouse effect as efforts many of us make to reduce auto emissions. Until people understand that creation is truly sacred, we are going to continue to despoil it. . . . It's an enormous breakthrough for people to see animals in a sacred space like this. . . . They break down the idea that inside is holy, outside is profane.[20]

Environmental preaching was important too, and the same idea, of breaking down the church/world dichotomy, recurred. In advising other ministers how to preach effective environmental sermons, activist Richard Austin urged them to "get out of your study and into the woods" and learn to love God's handiwork at first hand. After all, "we cannot preach the gospel effectively until our own hearts have been touched and warmed."[21]

Jewish groups, indifferent at first, became interested in the environment— especially oil and energy policy—for political reasons after the Yom Kippur War (1973) but then for religious reasons in the late 1980s and the early 1990s. Ellen Bernstein, for example, founder of a Philadelphia Jewish environmental group, Shomrei Adamah (Keepers of the Earth), saw rituals like Sukkoth as a opportunity for environmental education. Sukkoth is the harvest festival in which families build simple shelters, give thanks for the abundance of the earth, and, ideally, eat and sleep out under the stars. Harry Kissileff of Teaneck, New Jersey, chaired Hug Tevah (Nature Circle) and argued that the entire structure of Jewish life was designed to emphasize human dependence not only on God but also on the environment. The Sinai revelation warned that a man should "not wrest from the soil or his fellow men more than he needs to survive" and the

Sabbath was the day on which God, after his work of creation, ceased manipulating the environment. "The Sabbath should be used as a time to reconnect not only with family and friends but with nature and teachings that help improve our relationships not only with each other but with our world." To destroy other species, he added, "is like tearing pages out of Scripture."[22] Michael Smart, a Jewish environmental educator, urged Jews to rethink the meaning of wilderness: "The Torah was given to us in the wilderness. . . . Wilderness is the place where Jews freed their hearts from slavery and prepared themselves for the promised land."[23]

Paul Gorman of New York's Trinity Episcopal Cathedral recalled in 1998 that when he first met a group of Jewish leaders to discuss environmental issues they said: "Look, we don't know from wetlands. . . . We have nothing to do with wilderness." Gorman amused them with his riposte, "I'm glad Moses didn't feel that way," and won their grudging respect. Some became involved in the National Religious Partnership for the Environment, an ecumenical group that Gorman founded in 1993 after recognizing that churches would be more likely to get involved if there were a more obvious human element in the movement's work. One of the Catholic bishops had asked him: "How come I never see any people in those environmental calendars?" and Gorman realized the significance of the question: "That's deeply provocative. For the religious community, environmentalism at that point was about the wildlife, wetlands, ozone depletion and endangered species. But where was the social and economic justice dimension which is deeply part of our tradition? Where were the people in all of this?"[24] He was also motivated by a letter sent to religious groups by thirty-two Nobel Prize–winning scientists, urging them to add a spiritual dimension to the cause of environmental protection. Under Gorman's skillful leadership the group soon included the major organizations of Jews, Catholics, liberal Protestants, Evangelicals, Greek and Russian Orthodox, and African American Christians. It distributed fifty thousand packets of materials on how to incorporate environmental themes in liturgy and preaching and how church members could become involved in useful environmental work. Its conferences and statements showed that America's many faith traditions could unite behind the environmental agenda. In 1996 the Center for the Study of World Religions at Harvard Divinity School began another ecumenical effort, a study of environmental ideas among ten world religions: Buddhism, Christianity, Confucianism, Hinduism, indigenous, Islam, Jainism, Judaism, Shinto, and Taoist. It looked for areas of common agreement and moral authority on the question and held a conference with Gorman's group in 1998 at the United Nations in New York.

Among the most influential twentieth-century writers on the environment was Aldo Leopold (1887–1948), whose essay "The Land Ethic" (1948) argued that the history of human ethics was one of a gradually widening circle of people who must be included in our moral considerations. Now the time had come, he said, to extend the circle beyond solely human beings to embrace the natural world also. Environmentally sensitive theologians picked up this insight and asked whether their work had to be "anthropocentric" (human-centered) or whether all of God's creation could be included. Admitting that people in the Judeo-Christian tradition had often assumed the right to dominate earth, they reinterpreted the Genesis Bible texts to mean that God had made mankind responsible *stewards* of his creation. Scattered theological writings on the issue had brought together the Faith-Man-Nature group, a branch of the National Council of Churches, between 1964 and 1974, whose members included Joseph Sittler, Paul Santmire, Richard Baer, and Philip Joranson. They emphasized that God *loved* his creation ("and saw that it was good"), that it had an intrinsic value in addition to its human usefulness, and that to disrupt it was to offend its creator.

Santmire, a Lutheran pastor and the most radical of the group, singled out the incarnational theologians in Christian history for special praise, writers like Saint Augustine and Martin Luther, who admired the whole of creation as a place to encounter God. By contrast, he denigrated the Gnostic and other theological traditions that despised the earthly side of life in favor of the spiritual. David Toolan, a Jesuit priest writing in the same spirit, elaborated on this distinction and tried to place Jesus firmly on the right (earthly) side of the divide: "In contrast to a Manichean or Gnostic spirituality that would have us despise the Earth and escape our prison-bodies, Jesus identifies with the Earth. And consecrates the Earth to new purposes. Of bread and wine he says, 'This is my body. Take and eat.'"[25]

Many Native American groups identified readily with these concerns because their own religious traditions often involved the propitiation of natural forces. At a 1990 conference at Middlebury College, Vermont, Audrey Shenandoah, an Onondaga Indian, asserted: "Human beings are not superior to the rest of creation. If human beings were to drop out of the cycle of life, the earth would heal itself and go on. But if any of the other elements would drop out—air, water, animal life or plant life—human beings and the earth itself would end."[26] Oren Lyons, from the same branch of the Iroquois people, went to Moscow that year to an international conference on religion and the environment. "Indians and other indigenous people have lived in nature, close to the Earth, and understand its wisdom and laws," he said. "Our ceremonies [are] ingrained as part of life. We celebrate the sacredness of the Earth in a year-round cycle of ceremonies expressing respect and gratitude for it."[27]

Eco-feminists borrowed themes and insights from ecological theology, feminism, and liberation theology. They argued that women, by their nature, have an intrinsic nurturing affinity with the earth, which is the opposite of men's instrumental, manipulative attitude toward it. The earth, like women, has been the victim of male domination. Women could overcome the cycle of domination and subordination only by breaking the ideas of patriarchy and hierarchy once and for all. That meant getting rid of the idea that God was a "Father" and even more the idea that "He" was a "King." Sallie McFague was among the leading eco-feminist theologians. In *Models of God* (1987) she argued that thinking of God as Lover, as Friend, or as Mother would have profound implications for the way we treated the earth. In *The Body of God* (1993) she added that there was no better way of understanding God's love for the Earth than to think of "the universe or world as God's body."[28] Using this idea, she reconceptualized "the poor" to mean nature itself, under assault by patriarchal society, and "sin" to mean environmental selfishness. She added: "The model of the world as God's body encourages us to dare to love bodies and find them valuable and wonderful—just that, nothing more. The 'God part' will take care of itself if we can love and value the bodies" (211). This striking idea, she believed, would also help to dislodge the old mind-body or spirit-body dualism that was so strong in traditional theology, usually with the implication that the body was the inferior half of the duality. Rosemary Ruether, an important figure in the development of feminist theology in the 1970s (see above, chapter 6), was equally important in the development of ecological feminist theology in the 1990s, notably with *Gaia and God* (1992). Whereas some of her elite feminist colleagues had abandoned Christianity altogether in favor of Goddess religion, Ruether argued for "WomanChurch," an environmentally sensitive and egalitarian women's community that was still in contact with Christianity. It could be purged of the old masculine characteristics of male domination over women and earth, and could learn reverence from the Gaia hypothesis (the idea that the earth itself was a semidivine superorganism) without turning the earth into a literal object of worship.

Creation spirituality, another religious outgrowth of environmentalism, drew from Christian, Native American, Buddhist, and eco-feminist sources. Despite the similarity of names, it was almost the exact opposite of creationism, the pseudoscientific defense of the Genesis Creation account (see above, chapter 8), because it welcomed the evolutionary account of creation and saw the process itself as something almost divine. Among its principal theorists was Thomas Berry (b. 1914), a Catholic priest and expert on comparative religion, who argued that his generation had been "the most destructive generation that ever struck the planet Earth." The science and technology that many twentieth-century people admired and celebrated seemed to Berry an unmitigated disaster that had resulted in a kind of spiritual deafness or autism. He expressed the hope, however, that a "new consciousness" was dawning, one that could foster "a more integral human relationship with the natural world, an ability to hear the voices." He dedicated *The Dream of the Earth* (1988) to "the Great Red Oak, beneath whose sheltering branches this book was written" and argued for

a "meta-religious transformation" that would sacralize the existence and transformation of the universe.[29] He regretted that so much Christian thought
scanted the earth and sought God elsewhere. To the contrary: "Earth needs to
be experienced as the primary mode of divine presence, just as it is the primary
educator, primary healer . . . for all that exists within this life community."[30]
Only a few scraps of traditional Christianity remained in Berry's theology; it
owed as much or more to Buddhism, whose "sense of compassion extends to
the natural world."[31]

Matthew Fox, like Berry a Catholic priest, tried to put creation spirituality
into action, partly with a journal *Creation* (founded 1985) and partly with a radical new form of worship, the Techno-Cosmic mass. Fox's writings included the
argument that the biblical Garden of Eden scene in which Eve ate from the
tree should be interpreted as a great moment in the Creation, an "Original
Blessing" rather than, as tradition had it, "Original Sin." He also believed that
a "cosmic Christ" presides over a continuous (rather than once-and-for-all)
process of creation, along with humans, his "co-creators," and that there is no
decisive distinction between humans and the many other forms of life. Fox, a
paradoxical, punning, and playful writer, tried to do for eco-theology what Mary
Daly had done for feminist theology. He argued that animals—not least his own
dog, Tristan—could be people's "spirit guides."

> Every galaxy is working, every star is working, all the grasses, the whales, the dogs,
> the animals, they're all doing their work. . . . The problem with our species is that
> we don't know who we are yet. Whereas Tristan is a dog—and he's good at it! He's
> close to the earth, he knows he's interdependent with it. He's kinda proud just to
> be here. These are all lessons he teaches me.[32]

Such notions, along with his invitation to the witch Starhawk to work at his
Institute of Creation Spirituality in Oakland, led to his suspension and finally
expulsion from the Dominican priesthood in 1993, after which he found a congenial home on the wilder shores of Episcopalianism.

Fox aroused strong feelings pro and con. A skeptical journalist who attended
one of his Techno-Cosmic masses in Houston described it as

> a two-and-a-half-hour four-part service that combines multimedia technology
> with music, dance and religious doctrine seemingly swiped from every corner of
> the globe. TCM is the brainchild of Matthew Fox, the California-based post-
> modern theologian who is trying to teach the world that praying isn't about get-
> ting down on bended knee and supplicating before a paternal God in humility
> and shame. He'd prefer you to shake your ass for the Almighty.[33]

An even more skeptical observer from the Episcopal Church, Doug Le Blanc,
described it as "a careless brew of paganism, manipulative imagery and an environmentalist hysteria unmatched by any apocalyptic street preacher."[34] Despite

such press, Fox was probably the leading popularizer of creation spirituality and eco-religious ideas through the 1980s and 1990s.

Fundamentalist Christians were dismissive not just of people like Matthew Fox but of environmentalism in general, fearing that it was a kind of pantheism that demoted human beings from their exclusive position as beings in the image of God. While eco-theologians and creation spirituality enthusiasts emphasized the similarity of humans to all other creatures, fundamentalists emphasized the differences. The weight of biblical evidence was probably on their side, and for them the Bible trumped all other arguments. The Old Testament insists repeatedly that the world is *not* sacred, and that nature worship—a constant temptation to the Children of Israel after their migration to the Promised Land—is wicked and will be punished. In the New Testament Jesus says little or nothing in support of the dignity of the natural world, and only special pleading could create an "environmentalist Jesus." In both testaments, "wilderness" is not something to be preserved and cherished. Rather, it is accursed land, where the Children of Israel have to wander for forty years and where Jesus has to overcome the devil's tempting. The historian Robert Fowler, in a fine study of Protestant ideas about the environment, summarized: "Evangelicals have no intention of aligning themselves with radical creation theology. For them the distinctions between human beings and God do not disappear in some mystical union. The earth is not Gaia, a divine goddess, nor is it God in any other way."[35]

The early 1990s, however, witnessed a change of emphasis in at least some fundamentalists' environmental views. As creationists they took literally the idea that God had created all the animals once and for all, and that he had saved at least one pair of each of them at the time of Noah's flood. Some of them now began to argue that it was their duty to carry on the work that Noah had begun, in preserving endangered species. The Endangered Species Act, passed by Congress in 1973, was a flashpoint for environmentalists and their adversaries through much of the later twentieth century because environmentalists often made use of it to obstruct building projects, claiming that land scheduled for development was the habitat of an endangered creature. Fundamentalists who had earlier scoffed at this use of the act, and of its tendency to brake economic growth, now began to change sides. Stan LeQuire, an evangelical minister, and Calvin DeWitt, a Wisconsin professor of environmental studies, founded the Evangelical Environmental Network in 1993 (affiliated with Evangelicals for Social Action), which they described as "America's Noah's Ark." By 1996 it was lobbying alongside other religious environmental groups to preserve tough endangered-species legislation. Evangelical college students handed out bumper stickers on Capitol Hill that read "God made it. We tend it. That settles it."[36] "We worship the creator, not creation," said LeQuire, to emphasize that his group had not been tempted into earth worship. He added: "This is not a fad. This is a way of expressing love for God's works. Our wakeup call comes from Scripture."[37]

The religious encounter with the environment was complicated. Reasonable people could, and did, disagree about the nature of the phenomenon. Some observers believed that radical environmentalists were too eager to hear bad news, too eager to demonize human activity in the world, and had worked themselves up into an apocalyptic frame of mind. The Interfaith Council for Environmental Stewardship, a neoconservative group, aimed to redress the balance. Its members, drawn from Protestant, Catholic, and Jewish communities, under the vigorous leadership of Rev. Robert Sirico, from the Acton Institute for the Study of Religion and Liberty, distinguished between genuine environmental hazards, such as poor sanitation, contaminated water, and smoke inhalation among Third World peoples, and what they thought of as false alarms, such as inflated claims about rapid species loss and human-induced global warming. Where biocentrists, neo-pagans, and devotees of creation spirituality looked on science and technology as forces that *harmed* the earth, Sirico's group continued to believe that, properly used, science and technology were essential to its welfare and progress. Their statement, the Cornwall Declaration (February 2000), blended concern for human welfare, political rights, free economies, and intelligent environmental stewardship:

> Human beings are called to be fruitful, to bring forth good things from the earth, to join with God in making provision for our temporal well-being, and to enhance the beauty and fruitfulness of the rest of the earth. Our call to fruitfulness, therefore, is not contrary to but mutually complementary with our call to steward God's gifts. This call implies a serious commitment to fostering the intellectual, moral, and religious habits and practices needed for free economies and genuine care for the environment.[38]

They noted that environmental sensitivity thrived in free economies, that pollution and disasters like Chernobyl had been far worse behind the Iron Curtain than in the capitalist West, and that serious concern for the environment presupposes prosperity, because desperately poor people are too busy procuring basic necessities to worry about the side effects of industrialization.

By the end of the century, environmentalism was integral to many religious groups' world-views. What to do with it remained in doubt. For tax reasons churches could not become directly involved in lobbying on environmental political issues. Even had they been so inclined, they would rarely have found consensus in their congregations. Many of the issues raised by the environmental movement were highly cerebral and depended on computer-based projections of possible future scenarios rather than tangible facts. For every exclamation of inevitable earth-doom from radical environmentalists, an offsetting murmur of reassurance emerged from anthropocentric neoconservatives; each could bring to his or her support a daunting array of scientific and religious specialists. It was difficult to know whom to believe. The environmental activities that ordinary churchgoers could undertake tended to be impersonal (clearing nearby polluted sites) or long-term (running sustainable "organic" fields and gardens) and lacked the human warmth of running a shelter or charity store, teaching children, or discussing the Bible. As a result, while occasional prayers, sermons, hymns, and group activities might have a "green" flavor, the environment rarely came to dominate the lives of ordinary religious communities. Its influence was more marked at the level of denominational leadership, theology, and divinity school education, but even there it was rarely decisive.

Megachurches

One way religious Americans responded to urban sprawl was by taking an interest in environmental issues. Another way was by doing some sprawling of their own. As Sunbelt cities expanded to ever-greater magnitudes—Miami, Atlanta, Dallas, Houston, Phoenix, Los Angeles, and San Diego—they began to sprout subsidiary urban centers, ten or twenty miles from the old downtown areas, and often organized around immense shopping malls. Mall-land was the setting for many of America's new megachurches, architecturally undistinguished worship and "Christian life" centers that could house thousands of worshipers at the same time, specializing in flashy, electrified, feel-good evangelicalism. They were designed not just to provide a setting for Sunday morning services but rather to provide an entire way of life, including schools, gymnasiums, dining halls, study group settings, therapy sessions, aerobics classes, bowling alleys, and sometimes even Christian-themed shopping.

Megachurch advocates, usually conservative evangelicals, believed that they answered a spiritual need among baby boom and younger Christians. Eager for new experiences, restless, less attached to a single denomination than their parents had been, they found spiritual satisfaction in the megachurches just as they found retail satisfaction at the big neighboring malls. "Adults born in the Fifties and Sixties don't carry the institutional loyalty of older generations" said Lyle Schaller, a megachurch planner. "People today expect to make choices about things—about a new TV, an automobile, what they eat, their housing," and the same was true with regard to church. "Denominations don't count much anymore. We see that clearly in the new congregations that don't carry any denominational affiliations, while the old-line denominations get a smaller and smaller slice of the pie."[39] A thirty-three-year-old recruit to Grace Fellowship, a Baltimore-area megachurch, echoed these claims as he described in 1994 what he liked about the congregation: "There were no religious symbols and no 500-year-old hymns. . . . Just an auditorium. The congregation was younger, like me. The pastor wasn't up there in a white robe with tassels and he didn't act like someone who has it all together—he shared his own struggles. It was very real."[40] A single mother from Phoenix said she loved her nearby megachurch,

Community Church of Joy, because "they don't make you feel you have to dress just so" and because "it was important to have a church the kids wanted to go to."[41]

Megachurches grew because of their ministers' charisma. Such men had to have the skill and allure to bring in thousands of worshipers (and contributors) every week. They and their staffs also had to make their fare entertaining, absorbing, and novel—prompting members to return, even if it meant a longer commute than to their local churches. Grace Fellowship minister Sandy Mason remarked that too many churches still relied on a 1950s idiom, "church-ianity," rather than up-to-date Christianity. He, by contrast, was "trying to get that out of the way so people can sit down and be with Jesus."[42] He and his fellow ministers understood that bigness had to be skillfully combined with intimacy, and that out of the massive worship arena members could move on to small-group encounters dealing with particular interests and needs. Pollster George Gallup told a 1991 conference on church growth that "at a time of acute loneliness and fragmented families in our society, small support groups serve as a powerful antidote to these social ills."[43] That insight became standard wisdom among entrepreneurial megachurch ministers.

By most accounts Willow Creek, in South Barrington, Illinois, was the greatest of them all. Founded in 1975 by the Reverend Bill Hybels, a newly graduated seminarian, it aimed to be bright, entertaining, and un-churchlike, and to offer age-appropriate services to each sector of its constituency. Hybels said he had turned to the Acts of the Apostles and tried to model his church on the very first Christian community:

> That was the vision passage for the church we wanted to build, where teaching God's word would transform lives, where people would share their property and possessions with each other so no one would have need, where the rich would care for the poor, where gender difference and racial differences would all be lowered and people would become like family.[44]

By 1995 Willow Creek was drawing between 15,000 and 20,000 people each weekend to its Saturday and Sunday services, had 260 employees and a $12.5 million annual budget. By 2000 the staff had grown to 500, along with 6,000 volunteers, and 17,000 members participating in small-group activities as varied as hairdressing, vacuum-cleaner repair, divorce counseling, and auto repair. Visitors sat in plush theater seats rather than pews, listened to an electric band and vocalists, and watched "interpretive dancers" accompanying the Christian songs in the vast auditorium, and could join in the songs by following the words flashed on massive overhead video screens. Spanish- and Mandarin-Chinese-speaking visitors had access to simultaneous translations of the preaching.

Inside Minister Hybels's office hung a sign: "What is our business? Who is our customer? What does the customer consider value?" The questions came from management expert Peter Drucker, whom Hybels had befriended, and it bore witness to his business-oriented approach to the job. A magnetic preacher, Hybels defended himself against accusations of worldliness by quoting Saint Paul to the effect that Christians should be in the world, but not of it. To be practical, he argued, was fine, so long as the motive was spreading the gospel. His job was to find what middle-class Americans actually wanted and actually responded to. That meant being realistic about current trends. Had not Jesus, the working carpenter of Nazareth, taken the same view? "For 30 of his 33 years he was in the construction business and knew how life in that world happened."[45]

Running megachurches needed a lot of managerial expertise. Historian John Wilson, visiting the 9,000-seat auditorium of Southeast Christian Church in Louisville, noted that "among paid staff and especially the elders and other volunteers are individuals who have had years of experience with the military, Federal Express and similar organizations. A church like Southeast could not have existed 100 years ago, because the managerial science it embodies was then just being born."[46]

Rivaling Willow Creek and Southeast in size and scope was Bellevue Baptist Church in Cordova, Tennessee (a suburb of Memphis), with 22,500 members in 1990 and a 7,000-seat auditorium-church on a 376-acre campus. Its minister, Adrian Rogers, was a former president of the Southern Baptist Convention, one of the theological conservatives who dominated the denomination in the 1980s and 1990s. He depended on the support of twenty-two assistant ministers and put on a spectacular show every Sunday. A visiting journalist wrote:

> His style might be characterized as laser-and-brimstone, considering the television cameras, the dramatic lighting and music, and the giant video monitors that project twin close-up images of Mr. Rogers high above the pulpit. The vast open space of the Bellevue sanctuary combined with Mr. Rogers' hard-driving message can be a bit disorienting to a first-time visitor accustomed to cozier churches.[47]

The services were broadcast on 1,600 television stations, too. Rogers understood the small-group imperative, however, and emphasized that his assistant ministers and numerous lay leaders balanced the big spectacle with intimate Bible-study and other groups. "Sometimes people have the idea that in a big church like this you might get lost in the woodwork. But the truth of the matter is we very carefully and prayerfully try to stay up with each individual" (ibid.).

The arrival of a megachurch was a mixed blessing to local dwellers, who suddenly faced massive, noisy building works and then an immense weekly influx of traffic. World Changers, for example, a megachurch in Atlanta, began building a sanctuary that its minister, Creflo Dollar, said would eventually hold 10,900 people at one time. Enraged neighborhood residents reported choked traffic every Sunday, flooded backyards from improperly built retention ponds, and a declining tax base for the area as the church took over an old shopping mall. Megachurches' rapid growth and enormous financial commitments also meant that congregational disillusionment could have rapid and drastic consequences; a minister's financial or sexual indiscretion could be the prelude to disaster. At Chapel Hill Harvester Cathedral, for example, another suburban Atlanta colossus, which President George Bush Sr. had identified as one of his "thousand points of light," cofounder Don Paulk Jr. and youth minister Duane Swilley, his nephew, both admitted to sexual indiscretions in 1992. Hundreds of the 12,000 members stayed away in disgust; donations fell sharply, and the church found itself unable to meet its weekly payments of $65,000 on a debt of nearly $20 million.

Even the untarnished megachurches, and those careful to maintain good community relations, faced criticism. Liberal Christians dismissed them as shallow, commercialized, and vulgar. Evangelicals, too, warned their megachurch brethren that they were in danger of creating a "McChurch" or "Church-lite" environment. David Wells's *No Place for Truth* (1993) was a sustained indictment, by an evangelical seminary professor, of trends in recent evangelicalism, megachurches included. Wells argued that they had become therapeutic places, emphasizing how to feel good rather than how to confess to one's sinfulness and face up to the stern teaching of the Bible.

Chapter 11

FEARS, THREATS, AND PROMISES: 1990–2000

Homosexuality and Religion

By the 1990s every religious group in America was aware, often uncomfortably aware, that some of its members were homosexual. Whether to welcome them, shun them, ordain them to ministry, or permit them to marry same-sex partners in church became questions of pressing concern and sundering disagreement. Ministers and congregation members held visceral feelings about the issue, and disagreements often led to conflict. How should they think about homosexuality? Should Scripture, tradition, church orthodoxy, doctrines of universal love, or current social opinion guide their decisions? While the churches were deciding what to do, religious homosexuals themselves had to decide whether their faith and their sexual orientation were compatible. Some gay activists told them that the whole idea of being a "gay Christian" or a "gay Jew" was a contradiction in terms.

John D'Emilio and other historians have shown that a gay subculture grew up in American cities after the Second World War. The war itself uprooted millions of young men and women from their homes and pushed them into same-sex groups for long periods of time, ideal conditions for lesbians and homosexual men to meet and develop relationships. The Kinsey Reports on human sexuality in 1948 (men) and 1953 (women) showed that homosexuality was

common in both sexes and across all social classes. A gradual change in scholarly and medical approaches to the issue led to its receiving progressively more
social tolerance with each passing decade and increasing the likelihood that gay
men and women would "come out of the closet." Stigmatized through most of
the 1960s, the gay community turned an important corner in 1969, the year of
the New York Stonewall Riot, in which police raids on gay bars were met not
by patrons' shamefaced flight but by their determined physical resistance. Gays'
fighting back was as important in this context as African Americans *not* fighting
back had been during the sit-ins and marches of the civil rights movement.

The gay liberation movement developed in the 1970s, following many of the
tactics of the black and women's movements. As gay women and men became
more outspoken on their own behalf, they argued that their sexual orientation
was innate and that it was not something of which they should be made to feel
ashamed. They, like activists in the earlier movements, claimed that they were
a victimized minority group whose human and civil rights were violated by the
majority. Among their objectives were civil and legal recognition of gay partners
as the equivalent of spouses, and legislation to prevent discrimination against
them in jobs and housing.

Their battle was harder and less conclusive than that of African Americans
against segregation. Although American psychologists abandoned their old
claim that homosexuality was a form of pathology in the early 1970s, many citizens continued to believe that it was a sickness, from which the "patient" might
recover. Others, in the Freudian tradition, argued that homosexuality was just
a phase individuals passed through on their way to a mature heterosexuality.
Most states decriminalized homosexual acts between consenting adults
between 1970 and 2000, and many cities passed laws against job discrimination,
but public opinion polls showed only a very slow trend away from condemnation of same-sex acts. In 1996, 56 percent of Americans still believed that such
acts were always wrong.

While doctors and state governments debated, religious conservatives—
Muslim, Jewish, and Christian alike—described homosexuality as a horrible
sin. The weight of evidence forced most of them to admit that homosexual
attraction was a reality, but that made no difference to their condemnation.
Central to their understanding of the world was that sin and temptation are
always among us. In their view, individuals who felt tempted to act on same-sex
attraction ought to resist the temptation rather than succumb and then ration-
alize their action. Catholic columnist Joseph Sobran, in a classic statement of
this approach, wrote in 1977 that it would be "a victory of humanity to undo the
damage of the gay rights movement by persuading its members, without humil-
iating them, that they need not pretend their vice is a virtue in order to belong
to the moral community. To put it another way, homosexuals should be encouraged to realize that homosexuality is unworthy of them."[1]

"Coming out" was the central rite of passage in gay liberation. Young men and women, having grown up uncertain about their same-sex attraction, and often ashamed, finally came to terms with it and declared it publicly to their families, friends, and each other. They then took on the responsibility of facing up to a society that regarded them as deviant, but they benefited from joining a vocal and supportive community of their peers. "Coming out" also referred to older practicing homosexuals' throwing off the veil of secrecy that they had drawn around their personal lives in the days when it was taboo. Individuals' descriptions of the experience often paralleled Christians' descriptions of the transformation that being "born again" had wrought in their lives. Suddenly they recognized what they were *really* like for the first time, having lived until then in a false or shadowy world full of deception and disappointment. One gay Christian man wrote: "When I was born again, it was a real experience. And the second time I was born again is when I came out at thirty-two, and it was a very similar experience. Except it was even more intense."[2] Another made a direct Christian comparison with the remark: "I can almost see it [coming out] as connected with the experiences the disciples might have had by becoming disciples of Christ; that to follow a path that you believe has most integrity for yourself sometimes puts you very much at odds with the prevailing society" (11).

One of the ironies of religious people's coming out was that it often estranged them from churches in which they had felt particularly welcome and "at home" as children. David Shallenberger, a writer on gay spirituality, noted that for such children, church was "a haven where the harsh rules of life [about] how to be an 'appropriate' boy or girl . . . did not apply," a place where boys could temporarily feel "free of masculine pressure" (10). Such children associated more readily with the gentle-faced Jesus in the stained-glass windows and Sunday school picture books than with their heterosexual contemporaries' sports heroes. Michael Warner, a gay adult reflecting on a Pentecostal childhood of this kind, wrote: "Jesus was my first boyfriend. He loved me, personally, and he told me I was his own." Even his clothing muted his gender identity. Warner added that "Anglo-American Christian culture has developed a rich and kinky iconography of Jesus," often showing him as an effeminate man "in a dress."[3]

Some gay people, after coming out, rejected the Judeo-Christian religions as incurably homophobic. Others declared that their life experiences made such a rejection impossible. In a classic essay on his life as a gay Catholic, the journalist Andrew Sullivan (editor of *The New Republic* in the 1990s) made further connections between faith and homosexuality:

> Like faith, one's sexuality is not simply a choice; it informs a whole way of being;
> but like faith, it involves choices—the choice to affirm or deny a central part of

one's being, the choice to live a life that does not deny but confronts reality. . . . It is, like faith, deeply mysterious, emerging clearly one day, only to disappear the next, taking different forms—of passion, of lust, of intimacy, of warmth, of fear. . . . And like faith, it points toward something other and more powerful than the self. The physical communion with the other in sexual life hints at the same kind of transcendence as the physical Communion with the Other that lies at the heart of the sacramental Catholic vision.[4]

It was in vain, said Sullivan, that the church's official statements condemned or tried to exclude him; the Catholic Church was the one he belonged to and he was there to stay. Far more bluntly, another gay Catholic told researchers Karla Jay and Allen Young: "Sucking a cock Saturday night and going to Communion Sunday morning doesn't seem out of line for me. Maybe I'm fooling myself but I honestly believe that God won't mind."[5]

A minority of churches and synagogues rallied in support of gay liberation in the late 1960s and early 1970s, convinced that gays were justified in comparing their situation to that of other minorities. Sympathetic clergy had already created the San Francisco Council on Religion and Homosexuality in 1964, the first organization of its kind in America. The United Church of Christ (UCC) issued a declaration in favor of full civil rights for homosexuals in 1969, and in the following years other liberal Protestant churches followed suit. When AIDS became a defining issue in the gay community after 1982, churches created AIDS awareness and support groups too. For gay Christians who preferred a church of their own, the Reverend Troy Perry, a former Pentecostalist minister, founded the Universal Fellowship of Metropolitan Community Churches in Los Angeles in 1968, branches of which grew in other urban areas in the following decades. It became a self-sustaining denomination, led by gay ministers and active in the gay rights and AIDS awareness movements, providing a space where the gay lifestyle was validated and where gay weddings could take place. It applied for admission to the National Council of Churches, first in 1983 and again in 1992. The NCC twice rejected its petitions, however, because it could not get "yes" votes from the necessary two-thirds of its member denominations.

Gay people not only built their own churches but also wrote their own theological literature to ground, explain, and justify the compatibility of their sexuality and their faith. Coming out of different traditions, from Orthodox Jewish and Christian fundamentalist to ultra-liberal, they disagreed on many points of emphasis. Their situation, however, like the situation of feminist theologians, encouraged them to adopt a hermeneutic of suspicion in their interpretation of the Bible. Many emphasized the idea of God's boundless love far more than his vengeful side, and developed the insight that a creator-God could hardly have created "waste" or "mistake" people, which they would be if their innate sexual situation somehow violated divinely created nature. Situations of *human* love gave them insight into divine love, they said, and some argued that moments with their lovers, far from estranging them from God, were premonitions of his still-greater love.

Integral to gay theology was a reinterpretation of biblical passages that traditionally had been used to condemn homosexuality, passages that anti-gay Jews and Christians were busily quoting against them. One of these passages (Genesis 18 and 19) tells the story of Sodom and Gomorrah, from which the term "sodomy" is drawn. According to the story, Lot was entertaining two of God's emissaries, angels, when the townspeople demanded that he give them up, so that they could "know" these strangers. Lot refused (though he did offer his daughters as substitutes), the townsmen tried to invade the house but were struck blind, and the next day God angrily destroyed the city. Theologian Derrick Sherwin Bailey argued that the story had little or nothing to do with homosexuality and everything to do with God punishing the townsmen for their lack of hospitality to strangers. Another gay writer, Toby Johnson, added that the anti-gay Christian Right of the 1990s should be seen as the inhospitable Sodomites, whereas the gay people—"fighting for health funding, volunteering as AIDS caregivers, reaching out to their suffering brethren in a true act of compassion, creating community in spite of adversity"—were playing the part of the angels.[6]

Other key Bible verses were Leviticus 18:22 and 20:13, literally translated as: "And with a male you shall not lie the lying down of a woman; it is a taboo" and "As for the man who lies with a male the lying down of a woman, they—the two of them—have committed a taboo; they shall certainly be put to death; their blood is upon them." Biblical scholar Saul Olyan, after a lengthy exegesis of the obscure provenance of these verses, noted that unlike most Hebrew rules governing sex, the rules set forth here occurred nowhere else in Scripture, and appeared to address the question of ritual purity rather than homosexuality. Homosexual actions other than anal intercourse between men were not mentioned, and neither were any homosexual actions between women. He concluded: "Did Israelites abhor male coupling, as has been generally assumed up to the present? Certainly the evidence of the Hebrew Bible is insufficient to support this view."[7] The verses provided ammunition for anti-gay Christian extremists who believed the death penalty was the appropriate response to homosexuality, but gay theologians rebutted that "Levitical prohibitions are part of Jewish purity law which the apostolic church rescinded in its entirety for Gentile converts."[8] Theologians were able, similarly, to contextualize apparently anti-gay passages from Paul's letters to the Romans and Corinthians, arguing that Paul was criticizing pagan exploitation of male prostitutes, rather than loving homosexual relationships among consenting Christians.

As the gay movement matured in the 1980s and 1990s, a second generation of more-radical gay theologians began to write a defiant brand of liberation theology, again borrowing insights from Latino, women's, and black theologies. Just as James Cone and Albert Cleage had insisted on a black Jesus, so radical "queer theologian" Robert Goss insisted on a "queer Jesus," and on a theology that made no claim to impartiality or objectivity. His work, he said, grew out of the suffering of ostracized gay people (hence his defiant use of a term previously used abusively against gays) and was usable only by them. He wrote: "If Jesus the Christ is not queer, then his . . . message of solidarity and justice is irrelevant. If the Christ is not queer, then the gospel is no longer good news but oppressive news for queers. If the Christ is not queer, then the incarnation has no meaning for our sexuality."[9] Whereas conservative Christians tried to subordinate themselves to the words of the Bible, gay liberation theologians like Goss, Marvin Ellison, and Richard Cleaver put the Bible itself on trial for homophobia and used or discarded its teaching only insofar as it affirmed their quest for liberation.

While liberal churches and synagogues offered support to religious gay and lesbian people, conservative churches and synagogues refused to endorse homosexuality as a permissible way of life, citing the traditional interpretation of the biblical passages cited above. The Southern Baptist Convention gathered a lot of angry adjectives in the same place when it resolved that "even the desire to engage in a homosexual relationship is always sinful, impure, degrading, shameful, unnatural, indecent, and perverted."[10] Other religious opponents began with a harsh condemnation but later moved to a more temperate view, recalling the old Christian injunction to hate the sin but love the sinner. *Christianity Today*, journalistic standard-bearer for evangelicals, argued in 1973 that it was morally wrong to "show compassion toward the homosexual" because it "confirms the sinner in his wicked ways."[11] By the end of the twentieth century, however, it had mellowed, and now condemned evangelical threats and insults against homosexuals: "Something is deeply wrong if a Christian suffers ostracism after admitting to struggles with same-sex attraction."[12] Few gay people would have been satisfied by *CT*'s solution, however, which was to urge such individuals to overcome the temptation to act on their homosexual inclinations. In the same vein, an Orthodox Jewish leader in Baltimore said that gay men ought not to be rabbis since their actions clearly violated Torah injunctions as a matter of religious law. At the same time Jews must not turn their backs on coreligionists who were gay or were suffering from AIDS: "Although Orthodox Jews would argue against a gay rabbi, Orthodoxy as a whole must stop allowing its beliefs to cloud its obligations to help fellow Jews in need."[13]

AIDS itself, first identified in 1981 and spreading rapidly, particularly in the gay population, appeared to some anti-gay religious figures as a form of divine punishment for sin. Jerry Falwell wrote in 1987 that "AIDS is a lethal judgment of God on the sin of homosexuality and it is also the judgment of God on America for endorsing this vulgar, perverted and reprobate lifestyle."[14] The extreme

lethality of AIDS did indeed give its appearance and spread an apocalyptic quality. It also provided a useful point of emphasis to Christians promoting teenage
sexual abstinence, supporting the conservative view that sex should be heterosexual only, and marital only.

The marriage bed alone was the place for sex. Conservative religious lobbyists, determined to prevent homosexuality from gradually coming to seem "normal," mixed their arguments for teen abstinence with lobbying against gay rights
legislation. The Christian Coalition, an umbrella organization of conservative
evangelical and Catholic groups, and the traditionalist Family Research Council (FRC), worked to ensure congressional passage of the Defense of Marriage
Act (1996), which specified that the word "marriage" in federal legislation
referred to "a union between one man and one woman." The importance of this
legislation, said FRC director Robert Knight, was to ensure that religious people
were not forced, in their working lives, to violate the teachings of their religions.
"If you are a devout Christian, Jew, or Muslim, or merely someone who believes
homosexuality is immoral and harmful, and the law declares homosexuality a
protected status, then your personal beliefs are outside civil law."[15]

Religious organizations, including those that supported gay civil rights, next
had to decide whether they would welcome active and open gay men and
women as their ministers, priests, and rabbis. The Episcopal Church, usually
well toward the liberal end of the spectrum on such matters, repeated its experience with women's ordination (see above, chapter 6) when idealistic members
violated an apparent prohibition and dragged the rest of the denomination along
behind them. In 1979 the Episcopal Church's General Convention had passed
a resolution against openly gay priests, but in 1990 Assistant Bishop Walter
Righter of Newark, New Jersey, ordained the openly gay Barry Stopfel as a deacon. His superior in the diocese, Bishop John Spong, endorsed Righter's action
and ordained Stopfel to the priesthood the following year. Spong was an enthusiastic supporter of gay Christians. He wrote, in *Rescuing the Bible from Fundamentalism* (1991), that Saint Paul himself had been a "self-loathing and
repressed gay male."[16] In 1994 he had circulated a document, "Koinonia," supporting the ordination of openly gay men and persuaded seventy-one other bishops to sign it. In 1995, however, conservative Episcopal bishops (led by a group
of ten traditionalists who had also opposed the ordination of women) gathered
the necessary seventy-six signatures to a petition summoning Spong's assistant
bishop, Walter Righter, to a heresy trial. The event generated a lot of publicity,
with Righter describing his prosecutors as "a narrow-minded, mean-spirited
bunch who are not in sync. with the rest of the church."[17] Gay Episcopalians
rejoiced at Righter's vindication in May 1996—the case was dismissed because
Episcopal *doctrine* did not specifically ban gay ordinations. These events showed
that the church was still anything but unanimous on the question, but from then
on it followed a policy of permitting each bishop to decide policy for his or her

own diocese. By then San Francisco, often regarded as the home of the gay rights movement, had an openly gay Episcopal bishop of its own, Otis Charles. Other religious groups, such as the Conservative Jews, were also willing to ordain all qualified candidates, gays included, to the rabbinate, but observation of what could happen when the issue was debated openly led them to urge rabbis to be quiet about their sexual orientation, noting that "publicly acknowledging one's homosexuality . . . can have grave professional consequences."[18]

No church faced the ordination question in a more acute or more paradoxical way than the Catholics. Their rule of clerical celibacy meant, in practice, that actively or latently gay men were often drawn to the all-male society of the priesthood. It was a not very well concealed secret that a gay culture thrived in many Catholic seminaries, even though a 1986 Vatican document (*On the Pastoral Care of Homosexual Persons*) had affirmed that homosexuality was an "objective disorder" and that homosexual acts were sinful. Non-gay men sometimes left in dismay when they realized that the vow of celibacy and the condemnation of homosexual activities were not always honored even among their fellow seminarians and teachers. As one commentator noted, "For Catholics to start asking questions about homosexuality in the priesthood is to risk finding out more than many Church members want to know."[19] A study of 101 admittedly gay priests in the 1990s found that many of them were sexually active with other priests and had convinced themselves that it was not sinful. "One man claimed that homosexuals made better priests—they were more sensitive counselors, more affectively attuned; they did not get into trouble with women and, since they could keep their liaisons within walls, were less likely to give scandal."[20] Stories of gay priests' activities surfaced periodically throughout the later twentieth century, as did stories of priests' sexual relationships with teenage boys, some of which were physically or mentally coercive. Early in the twenty-first century, indeed, the scandal was to break wide open, revealing extremely widespread child sexual abuse by priests.

As controversial as the ordination question was that of gay marriage. By the 1990s some employers were willing to extend spousal benefits to their employees' live-in partners of the same sex, while the state governments of Vermont and Hawaii effectively legalized gay marriage. Many churches considered whether they could solemnize such marriages, with the Reform Jews, the United Church of Christ, and the Episcopalians finding in favor. Most other denominations said no. Troy Perry, minister of the "gay denomination" (Universal Fellowship of Metropolitan Community Churches) held a ceremony in 1991 to give a blessing to 150 gay couples, and a gay march in Washington in April 2000 witnessed a similar ceremony on a larger scale (3,000 couples) at the Lincoln Memorial. Clergy elsewhere sometimes disregarded their denominations' rules against gay weddings and conducted them anyway. Mahan Siler, a North Carolina Baptist minister, agreed to officiate at a gay wedding in 1989 because individuals' sexual orientation was something they had not chosen and because it would be "cruel of the church to judge as an abomination what God has given in the creation of a person."[21] When the Reverend Jimmy Creech performed a lesbian marriage, also in North Carolina, in 1999, he was put on trial by the United Methodist Church's court and stripped of his ministerial credentials. In protest against his punishment, ninety-six other Methodist clergy gathered to celebrate another lesbian wedding in Sacramento, California.

Clergy found every aspect of the homosexuality debate difficult and dangerous. Outspokenly anti-gay clergy at one end of the spectrum and defiantly pro-gay clergy at the other were the minority. Far more, in all denominations, were uneasily aware that their own congregations included people with different opinions and that the issue was likely to cause heated disagreements. "Many clergy hesitate to speak about issues that have the potential to rip their congregations apart," wrote two social scientists observing the issue, "because to do so might threaten their job security. Of all contemporary political issues, homosexuality probably has the most potential to divide congregations."[22]

In an attempt to move beyond the exchange of angry polemics, a few writers tried to look at the debate from all sides. L. R. Holben, for example, though himself gay, showed in *What Christians Think About Homosexuality* (1999) that each group's arguments had strengths and weaknesses, including his own:

> It is no doubt satisfying on a certain level for gay liberation advocates to label all Christians who disagree with them as "homophobic" but such a charge disallows the clear evidence of Christian compassion and intellectual integrity on the part of many conservatives whose convictions are based not upon fear and loathing of homosexuals but upon their scriptural hermeneutic and their understanding of biblical inspiration.[23]

He and other researchers also discovered interesting gray areas. For example, ministers from the most anti-gay churches sometimes acted differently in private than they did in public. A gay man from a Southern Baptist background told sociologist James Sears that when he anxiously approached his minister for advice, the minister sympathized with his dilemma, told him to "get close to the Lord, find you a good lover, and be happy," but added that he would continue to preach against homosexuality from his pulpit.[24]

By the mid-1990s a spectrum of attitudes toward gay people could be drawn across American religious groups, with Unitarians, Reconstructionist Jews, and the United Church of Christ officially at the most sympathetic end and Southern Baptists, Jehovah's Witnesses, Mormons, Orthodox Jews, and Catholics at the most unsympathetic end. As the Catholic case suggests, however, the actual distribution of gay people through the population ensured that they were just as likely to come from any one of these traditions as from the others. Members of the unsympathetic churches did sometimes go "church shopping" in search of a church that validated them as practicing homosexuals, with the result that, for example, gay Catholics often came to rest in Episcopal or Quaker pews while gay African Americans often became Presbyterians or joined the UCC. Others resolved to stay and fight for a change in their churches of origin. They created denominational gay support groups such as Dignity (Catholic) and Affirmation (two groups used the same name, one Methodist, one Mormon). Unexpected recruits sometimes joined these groups when they discovered that their own family members were gay, jolting them out of conventional ways of looking at the issue. For example, a conservative Mormon bishop, David Hardy, on learning that his son was gay, found little practical help in the church. Despite its claim of compassion, it would accept his son only if he resolved never to act on his homosexual inclination. "We were forced to make a decision that no parent should be forced to make," said the anguished father, "to abandon one's child or one's faith."[25] In 1999 he and his wife began to operate a support group for gay Mormons and their families in Salt Lake City.

Interfaith gay religious groups developed too. One, Partners in Faith, was founded by Steven Baines, a Southern Baptist minister ejected from his South Carolina ministry in 1995 when his congregation's leaders discovered his sexual orientation. Another, Soulforce, was run by the Reverend Mel White, a former speechwriter for Pat Robertson and Jerry Falwell, who had come out of the closet in 1991. White published his memoir, *Stranger at the Gate: To Be Gay and Christian in America* in 1994. Soulforce, his grassroots pressure group, tried to stay in touch with prominent public figures who were opposed to gay rights, such as Falwell himself, in the belief that the only way to achieve wider social acceptance of gay people in America was through persuading religious leaders to modify their hostile attitudes and tone down their anti-gay rhetoric. He also speculated on the possibilities of boycotting crucial areas of religious life, telling journalist Shawn Zeller, "If all the gay organists quit playing one Sunday morning there would be silence in Christendom!"[26]

Memoirs make it clear that coming to terms with one's own homosexuality was rarely easy, especially for people raised in restrictive religious environments. Many people, convinced that they *were* gay, also continued to believe that it was *wrong* to be gay and took seriously their churches' injunctions not to act on their same-sex attractions. "Gerald," who had grown up in a fundamentalist environment, told David Shallenberger of his train of thought after his first homosexual experience:

> All my Christian upbringing told me that because of what I'd just done, I was going to burn in hell forever. If I stayed this way it was nothing but death for me. . . . I'd go around the house yelling at God, saying: "You were supposed to heal me of this. You were supposed to deliver me of this. I'm not supposed to be gay . . . so either you don't care, or you don't exist."[27]

While one set of support groups grew up to help gay Christians and Jews affirm each other and change their churches' attitudes, another set of groups arose to help reluctant gays overcome their temptation or to cure them of it once and for all. Courage was one such group, for gay Catholic priests and gay laity who were struggling to preserve their chastity. Transforming Congregations (Methodist) and the cross-denominational groups Homosexuals Anonymous, Day One, Desert Stream, and Liberation in Jesus Christ had the same objective. One of these pastoral groups, Exodus International, developed a spiritually based cure for homosexuality and in 1998 publicized it widely with full-page advertisements in the national media, including the *New York Times*, the *Los Angeles Times*, the *Chicago Tribune*, and the *Washington Post*. Its leader, Anne Paulk, described herself as an ex-lesbian and her husband, John, as a former transvestite; together they held out the promise of escape from an ungodly homosexual lifestyle. Therapists Elizabeth Moberly (*Homosexuality: A New Christian Ethic* [1983]) and Leanne Payne (*The Broken Image* [1981]) developed spiritual and psychological programs that aspiring ex-gays could use on their road to recovery.

Not surprisingly, in light of such trends, some nonreligious gay groups were indignant at the churches. Attempts by moderate gay organizations to improve their image among church folk, and attempts by gay Christians to improve their situation in the denominations, often led to a reaction from gays who were more militant. In 1998, for example, the Metropolitan Community Church (MCC) and the Human Rights Campaign announced a forthcoming Millennium March for Equality, emphasizing the themes of faith and family, rather than the more militant theme of radical social change and AIDS activism that had characterized previous gay national events. Troy Perry, founder of the MCC and one of the promoters, said: "At this march we want to show Middle America that we're mature people who work, just like them. This is our country and we pay our taxes. So we can't have men pulling their penises out at our demonstrations or our sisters removing their breasts from their blouses. Our fight is about much more than that."[28] More-radical gay organizations denounced the religious and pro-family image Perry was trying to promote, and his courtship of corporate sponsors. A spokesman for the Ad-Hoc Committee for an Open Process, leading critic of the march's planners, dismissed the event as "a marketing event in search of a political purpose."[29] Important groups— including the Gay and Lesbian Alliance Against Defamation, the National Gay and Lesbian Task Force, and Pride at Work—boycotted the march itself.

Promise Keepers

Marches and demonstrations in Washington were common in the 1990s among religious groups seeking to make a big statement and to generate good publicity. Eclipsing even Louis Farrakhan's Million Man March of 1995 and the gay Millennium March for Equality in 1998 was the Promise Keepers' Stand in the Gap event ("a Sacred Assembly of Men") of October 1997. Promise Keepers was the fastest-growing religious movement of the 1990s, a nondenominational organization for Christian men who believed that many of the nation's woes could be blamed on themselves for failing to play their biblically ordained role as strong husbands and fathers. Feminism, abortion, pro-family politics, and the gay rights movement had forced everyone to think about gender and social roles. Promise Keepers had conservative answers to the big gender questions and was routinely denounced by women's and gay organizations as sexist and homophobic. On the other hand, its white originators and organizers went to great lengths to show that it did not commit the other great contemporary sin—it was not racist.

Promise Keepers was the brainchild of Bill McCartney, and it is difficult to resist the conclusion that it began as a projection of his own demons onto a larger-than-life screen. McCartney was a lifelong football coach who had risen from high-school- to college-level jobs in the 1960s and 1970s, thanks to an unbroken record of victories. Taking over as head coach of the University of Colorado's Buffaloes in 1982, he led them from the Big Eight's basement to a national championship in 1990. The grateful university rewarded him lavishly, and by the early 1990s his annual salary was about $350,000. McCartney was, however, increasingly dissatisfied with the damage he had done to his family as his career thrived. He had succumbed to recurrent episodes of heavy drinking, had a workaholic's schedule that kept him away from home for weeks on end, and had had an extramarital sexual affair. His neglected family had taken a few missteps of its own. His unmarried teenage daughter gave birth to a son in 1989, whose father turned out to be none other than the Buffaloes' African American quarterback. Five years later, still unmarried, she gave birth to another son, this time fathered by a Samoan player on the squad. Meanwhile, poor Mrs. McCartney lost eighty pounds in a bout with bulimia.

McCartney, already renowned for passionate motivational speeches to his players before each game, in which he invoked God's aid for the team, and already an enthusiastic member of the Fellowship of Christian Athletes, founded Promise Keepers in 1990 and ran it full-time after resigning his coaching job in 1994. Its aim was to urge men to take their responsibilities to their wives and children more seriously, to beg forgiveness for their sins, and to regain control over their families' lives. As one early member noted, it filled a gaping hole in contemporary life: "As a man you get trained for your job, you get trained for athletics," but "who trains you to be a Christian man?"[30]

Promise Keepers' method was to hire stadiums and fill them with Christian men for two-day rallies that blended the old evangelical style of the traditional camp meeting with the high spirits, chanting, and cheering of a pregame pep rally. Its first success was an evangelical assembly at the University of Colorado basketball stadium in 1991, after which its membership grew by leaps and bounds. Participants in subsequent rallies (more than a million by 1996), attracted by imaginative advertising campaigns on Christian radio stations, billboards, and in-church notices, paid about fifty dollars to defray costs and spent the days listening to Christian motivational speakers, singing a mix of traditional hymns and modern Christian rock worship songs, praying publicly for forgiveness, high-fiving and even hugging one another. Reminiscent at times of Robert Bly's beat-the-drum "men's movement," it was incomparably more popular. The rousing chant of "Dee-fense" usually heard in these stadiums was displaced for a couple of days by euphoric chants of "Jee-zus" and sometimes "Thank God I'm a man." Jumbotron video screens showed preachers and musicians up close in place of their usual fare of slow-motion action replays.

McCartney himself spoke of faith in football-ish language: "You aren't going into the end zone without the Holy Spirit."[31] Men joining the movement signed on to the "Seven Promises," which required them to blend masculine strength and leadership with the more traditionally feminine virtues of nurturing, churchgoing, singing, and marital fidelity. One organizer told the *New York Times*'s Gustav Niebuhr, "I think it's an incredibly manly thing for a man to sing songs. This is not wimpy stuff, it's gutsy, real men singing praises to God."[32] McCartney hoped that participants, after these empowering events, would return to their home churches and create all-male support groups. By their example they would bring a stronger manly presence into churches, in many of which women members were a large majority. The idea was reminiscent of the Muscular Christianity and Men and Religion Forward movements from a hundred years earlier that had also tried to stem the feminization of American religion.

Rally observers noticed that the gatherings were racially integrated and that by 1996 many of the group's leaders were African American. McCartney believed racism was among America's worst collective sins and that it had to be overcome one individual at a time. Participants in Promise Keepers were charged with the responsibility of seeking out friends of a different race and confessing to them their sins of racism. At an Alabama branch meeting in the early 1990s a white man, Dale Layton, said the Holy Spirit had told him to wash the feet of one of the black men present, George Stewart, in imitation of Jesus' washing of his disciples' feet. Another of the black men present that day, a pastor, was alarmed at first but said that after this symbolically powerful act "the hostility left" the room and "I felt that God's spirit came in."[33] Nevertheless, the movement's racial integration did not proceed as quickly as McCartney had hoped. About 85 percent of the men at mid-1990s rallies were middle-class white men, most of them already from evangelical churches. The African American speakers and leaders, meanwhile, were not able to persuade large numbers from their denominations to join the group.

McCartney and the other leaders generally opposed feminism, especially insofar as it challenged conventional arrangements of family and work life. Men must lead their families, said PK speakers, but that did not mean they should be bullies or domestic tyrants. No—they must lead as Jesus led, through service. The National Organization of Women, unconvinced, condemned Promise Keepers. Patricia Ireland, its president in 1997, described the organization as "a feel-good form of male supremacy with dangerous political potential." She noted that McCartney had sponsored an anti–gay rights amendment in Colorado, had referred to lesbians and gays as "stark raving mad," had spoken at Operation Rescue meetings, and had urged PK men to "take back the nation for Christ."[34] Contradicting McCartney's claims that the movement was nonpolitical, she argued that any organization with a staff of 450 and a budget of "more than $97 million" could not plausibly claim to be a mere self-help group. Columnist Maureen Dowd joked that PK was "the evangelical equivalent of golf" because while the men were at rallies learning how to be sensitive, their wives were left behind as usual to do the housework and look after the kids. She added: "After all those years of making fun of women going to the bathroom in pairs, men can't seem to travel except in a convoy that requires 1,500 portable toilets."[35]

The group's mushroom growth in the early 1990s brought it a great deal of media attention. Billy Graham, Jerry Falwell, and Pat Robertson all endorsed it, which made it difficult for it to avoid being labeled politically as part of the religious right. McCartney and other leaders continued to insist that they had no political agenda, and that their principal concern was the moral reform and return to Christ of individual men. At a time when some denominations were reducing national staffs, PK built its headquarters in Denver and hired more than three hundred people to coordinate events.

In 1996 Promise Keepers held a rally especially for ministers (again male only) in the Atlanta Falcons' Georgia Dome. About forty thousand ministers attended, perhaps as many as a tenth of all the clergymen in America, with evangelicals predominating but including a big minority of liberal Protestant ministers and even a few Catholics. The Atlanta Symphony Orchestra, hired for the occasion, played traditional music before a Christian music band took over. Douglas DeCelle, pastor of an Ohio Presbyterian church, overcame his initial skepticism to attend, and found the event impressive and moving.

> On one afternoon the conference moved to ponder "The Pastor and His Family." A painful hush descended on the arena as the speaker articulated with devastating accuracy the impact that church careers have on spouses and children. As he spoke one could hear weeping—and not just from the charismatics. . . . This willingness of conference leaders to confess their own weaknesses is a PK hallmark . . . [and it] . . . lent a poignancy and power to the experience.[36]

He reflected that he, too, like Coach McCartney, had jeopardized his relationship with his own family in his eagerness to serve his flock.

A rally in Washington, D.C., the following year, 1997, called Stand in the Gap, was Promise Keepers' moment of greatest visibility. Unlike the stadium shows, this event was free (donations were voluntary). Buses, planes, and cars poured into the Washington area from all over America, and the Mall was so jammed that many enthusiasts were unable to reach the vast central area. The organizers, aware that estimated numbers often generate controversy, declined to offer a count, but experienced D.C. policemen reckoned it as even better attended than the Million Man March of two years before. The familiar mix of preaching, music, and public repentance characterized the rally, which (because of its reluctance to be pegged as part of the Christian Right) avoided political endorsements. McCartney, surveying the racially and religiously mixed crowd, declared: "We are being reunited. . . . This is diversity without dissension." He added: "We're going to spend all eternity together, but when we get up there we want to testify that we did it together. Can't no guy leave out of here a lone ranger."[37] He then challenged the men to look at pictures of their family members and admit in prayer that they had wronged them. A liberal Christian woman, skeptical at first, admitted:

> I have to say that hearing several hundred thousand men singing "A Mighty Fortress is Our God" does something even to the most detached observer. Likewise it was hard not to be genuinely moved when, at the bidding of speaker Bruce Fong, many of those same men prostrated themselves before wallet photos of their wives and children, praying quietly but audibly to be forgiven for sins of abuse and abandonment and for "sacrificing family on the altar of machismo, selfishness, power, pleasure, and personal ambition."[38]

Randy Phillips, an African American minister and the organization's president, spoke to reassure women that Promise Keepers worked in their interest too. "We have not come to demonstrate our power. . . . We have come to display our spiritual poverty. . . . No women should feel threatened by this gathering, because the ground is level at the foot of the cross."[39]

What did wives, mothers, girlfriends, and sisters do when the men went off to Promise Keepers? Some of them acted as ushers at the rallies; others stayed home in their "traditional" Christian roles. Before long, however, a string of regional women's auxiliary organizations was active, helping the Promise Keepers to keep their promises. Among them were Suitable Helpers, Heritage Keepers, Promise Reapers, Chosen Women, and Women of Promise. One PK wife at the 1997 rally was baffled to discover an anti-PK rally taking place at the same time, run by NOW members and by a group called Lesbian Avengers. "Promise Keepers is against pornography, cheating on wives and neglecting children. How could that possibly harm women?"[40]

Repeated assurances that the group was nonpolitical reassured neither feminist nor liberal groups, which continued to see Promise Keepers as an odious manifestation of the religious right. McCartney was on record opposing gay rights, and although he said he welcomed homosexuals to his rallies it was in the expectation that they were trying to transform themselves: "Those who practice homosexuality need a visitation of God in their lives."[41] Alfred Ross of Planned Parenthood, writing in *The Nation*, described PK as "the third wave of the religious right's assault on American democracy and values" after Moral Majority and the Christian Coalition.[42] Equal Partners in Faith was a Brooklyn-based group established in opposition to PK, and its founding document was endorsed by the moderator of the Unitarian-Universalist Church, the director of Catholics Speak Out, and the head of Americans United for Separation of Church and State. They too were afraid that this group "with so many overlays with religious right activists" might "become a political force."[43]

Could Promise Keepers maintain its momentum? No. The following year, 1998, it announced severe financial difficulties (partly because it had decided to abandon entrance fees for its stadium events) and laid off nearly all its 360 Denver-based employees. Among the apparent reasons for its decline was the repetitive nature of the rallies (few men kept going when they found each subsequent rally similar to their first), its dislike of denominationalism, which is central to American Protestantism, its theological feebleness (which some evangelical critics deplored), and its inability to build new constituency groups. After weathering this financial crisis, however, PK recovered its stability, resumed fee payment for events on a smaller scale, rehired nearly 200 staff, and persisted through the millennium and into the twenty-first century, gaining strength in such regions as the Northeast, where previously it had been weakest. As an organizer remarked at a rally in 2001, "I think a lot of men are [still] living lives of quiet desperation. We're looking for significance and meaning, and until we get hooked up with our creator we won't get significance."[44] For all its weaknesses and naiveté, it had struck a genuine chord among American Christian men, and their enthusiasm indicated the existence of a great collective need, which had certainly not been satisfied once and for all.

Millennial Expectation

In every generation since the Second World War, some Americans had felt themselves to be living in the end times. The approach of the year 2000 intensified the fervor, especially among evangelicals who believed they were witnessing many of the signs foretold in the Book of Revelation. An Associated Press poll in 1997 found that about twenty-six million American Christians (one in every four) expected to witness the return of Christ in their own lifetimes. Even nonreligious people got worked up about the "Y2K bug," a secular

transfiguration of the Grim Reaper, said to be intent on annihilating all computers at the stroke of the millennium. Jerry Falwell prepared a millennium
video that identified the Y2K bug as a possible prelude to the end times, "God's
instrument to shake this nation."[45] Arnold Schwarzenegger starred in *End of
Days*, a movie in which Satan hopes to use the exact hour of the millennium
to impregnate an innocent girl and conceive the Antichrist. After plenty of
explosions, car crashes, and a bloodbath or two, Arnold dies a sacrificial death
to save her virtue and the future of the Earth.

The biggest fictional phenomenon connected to the millennium was the
Left Behind series of novels, by Tim LaHaye and Jerry Jenkins, which sold tens
of millions of copies in the late twentieth and early twenty-first centuries.
LaHaye had been one of the founders of Moral Majority in 1979, and his wife,
Beverly, was the founder of the antifeminist group Concerned Women for
America. An earlier interpretation of the Rapture, the film *A Thief in the Night*
(1972), had been hugely successful among evangelicals, with its depiction of
Christians suddenly disappearing, or being raptured, before the end times (see
chapter 7 above). LaHaye and Jenkins, familiar with the film, realized there was
plenty more fictional mileage to be made of the Rapture—not that they were in
any way cynical about it—and that the approaching millennium had created
the ideal marketing environment.

Their hero, Rayford Steele, is an airline pilot whose devout wife and son
have mysteriously disappeared, along with millions of others. Steele realizes
what has happened and gradually convinces his skeptical daughter, Chloe, that
they have been left behind by the Rapture but that by turning to Christ, even
this late in the day, they can still be saved, though they must now endure the
catastrophic end times. They join "Tribulation Force," a plucky band of Christians who fight for good, and face plagues, earthquakes, and other natural catas-
trophes. Meanwhile, the Earth is gradually being taken over by a smooth-talk-
ing but evil Romanian politician, Nicolae Carpathia (Antichrist!), who uses the
United Nations to create a world government, a single currency, and a single
religion. Whereas most Christian fiction, like most Christian music, had
remained ghettoized, these novels (including a simplified series for children
and such spin-offs as "Don't Be Left Behind" T-shirts) crossed over to such
mainstream outlets as Kmart stores. Some readers, recognizing the books as fiction, simply enjoyed the adventure story, but many others saw them as a fictional transfiguration of real events that were, in fact, imminent. Other fictional
variants on the Rapture and the millennium included James BeauSeigneur's
Christ-Clone trilogy, in which a new Christ is cloned from blood cells scraped
off the Turin Shroud.

Many believers in an end to the wicked old world and the ushering in of a
new one at the stroke of the millennium expected the decisive events to take
place in Jerusalem. In 1998 and 1999, Jerusalem, flashpoint of Israeli-Arab ten-

sions for the past half century, became even more volatile as a gathering point for Christians from all over the world, many of them Americans, anticipating Earth-shattering events. About a hundred American Christians settled on the Mount of Olives, in the belief that it would be the exact place of Jesus' imminent reappearance. Meanwhile, Nazareth, home of Mary and Joseph and site of Jesus' childhood, witnessed an ugly conflict between Christians and Muslims over which group had the right to extend its religious buildings in the ancient village. Israel, pleased at the prospect of increased tourism but anxious about millennialist-inspired violence, struggled to keep the peace in both places.

Among those who saw a special significance in Jerusalem was a charismatic minister from Denver, Monte Kim Miller, who had been active in the anti-cult movement in the 1980s but then developed a powerful psychological grip over his own group of followers. He claimed to be in direct communication with God, who spoke through him, and he wielded immense influence over his followers (who numbered between one hundred and two hundred), arranging marriages among single members of his church, the Concerned Christians, and taking over all their wealth and property. He instructed them to give up their worldly possessions prior to a catastrophic earthquake on October 10, 1998, and follow him to Jerusalem. The earthquake did not take place, but the disappearance of about seventy-five members of the group caused a local sensation. The following month some of them turned up in Israel. Miller himself was not among them. He believed he was one of two prophets identified in Revelation 11 and foretold that his death in the streets of Jerusalem in 1999, followed by his resurrection three days later, would trigger the millennial catastrophe. Israel's police force monitored his followers closely, and when it learned that some of the Concerned Christians planned to provoke a gun battle in the streets of Jerusalem, they arrested and deported fourteen of them. Miller himself, however, never reappeared. Police also noted the spread of the "Jerusalem syndrome," by which ordinary tourists came to see themselves as biblical characters and wandered through the streets clad in bedsheets, declaiming Scripture or preaching ecstatically.

Millennialists who decided to stay in America also envisioned great changes, sometimes through the instrumentality of UFOs. A California sect, Morningland, believed that a flying saucer "as big as Texas" would bring Christ to Long Beach, California.[46] Its leader, Sri Patricia, claimed that she could foresee the future and that she could transform people's DNA with a wave of the hand, thereby (among other things) curing AIDS. God's Salvation Church, a Taiwanese American group in Garland, Texas, whose members wore white jogging suits and cowboy hats, also awaited a UFO. Its minister, "Teacher Chen," declared that God would appear on Channel 18 of every television in the world, then take over his (Chen's) body, before sending the big UFO to pick up the chosen people on the shores of Lake Michigan. Two institutes, the Millennium Watch Institute in Philadelphia and the Center for Millennial Studies at Boston University, kept track of these and dozens of other prophetic groups anticipating the end of the world.

American Jews had a calendar of their own and were much less likely to be drawn into religious ferment over the turning Christian millennium. December 31, 1999, fell on a Friday night, Sabbath. Muslims, too, observers of a third calendar, were relatively unconcerned, though the Christian millennium did fall during their holy month of Ramadan. Liberal Christians planned to celebrate but downplayed the millennium's apocalyptic aspect. The Evangelical Lutheran Church issued a pastoral letter of reassurance to its flock, "The Year of Our Lord, 2000." Tut-tutting about lurid millennialism, especially in the wake of the Heaven's Gate mass suicide of 1997, it emphasized the peaceful aspect of the Second Coming that all Christians awaited in hope but whose date none could foretell:

> Our Lord came to beat back the works of evil and establish a new order, a new time, a time of God's reign of peace. . . . His return, therefore, will not mean fearsome catastrophe but rather blessed completion; it will mean the end of the old time of sin and suffering and the beginning of the new, when God shall wipe away tears from every eye and death shall be no more.[47]

Many other denominations held worship services and processions or else seized on the occasion for its educational possibilities. An interdenominational march and rally at the Georgia Dome brought together members of Atlanta's many different faiths in the last week of 1999, during which participants were urged to find "millennium prayer partners" from other faiths. The Catacomb Project locked groups of Christian teenagers into churches and asked them to imagine that they, like the early Christians, had to testify on behalf of their faith even at risk to their own lives. Promise Keepers, back in 1997, had planned to hold rallies at every statehouse as the new millennium dawned, but then it occurred to them that a man should be with his family at such a time. Instead they promoted the idea that men should be "lighthouses," strong and steady supports to their families while shining the light of the gospel on their neighbors.

A story that began before the millennium and carried over into the new year shared the excitement of the millennial turn but also embodied many themes from the preceding fifty years: the persistence of intense religious experience in America, an eager searching for the supernatural, an intertwining of religion and politics, and even a threadbare remnant of the Cold War. In November 1999 a group of Cubans set sail in a small boat, in the hope of reaching America. Ever since Castro's revolution forty years before, the American and Cuban governments had demonized one another. Cuba was the arena for several of the starkest confrontations of the Cold War, when exchanges of nuclear weapons seemed imminent. A large Cuban exile community in Miami, passionately opposed to Castro, fed the flames of this confrontation, and a steady stream of boat people risking the treacherous ninety-mile crossing bore witness to native Cubans' hatred of their own regime. This boat, like many predecessors, sank in a storm, resulting in the deaths of ten among its passengers. Six-year-old Elian Gonzalez, however, somehow survived while his mother and stepfather died. He floated through the two-day storm on an inner tube and was picked up by fishermen on Thanksgiving Day, 1999, a few miles off Fort Lauderdale.

Relatives in Miami claimed him, and he went to live with one of them, twenty-one-year-old Marisleysis Gonzalez, his second cousin. She filed for custody, arguing that he would have a far better life if he stayed in the United States than if he were forced to return to Cuba to live with his father. If he went back, she said, Elian's mother would have died in vain. The boy's father, Juan Miguel Gonzalez, disagreed and demanded that Elian be returned to him in Cuba. An intense legal, political, diplomatic, and symbolic struggle ensued, involving both national governments, every level of the judiciary, every newspaper and TV station, and every pundit.

Elian himself, meanwhile, quickly became a cult figure, onto whose image Cuban exiles projected their religious and political concerns. Wherever he went in Miami, crowds gathered, not just to see the child who was the object of a news story but to see a harbinger of destiny. Zealous anti-Castro Cubans claimed that he was a divine messenger, an angel-child, whose miraculous survival on the hazardous passage to America had been guarded by an escort of dolphins, warding off shark attacks and keeping him from harm—even from sunburn. Elian, wrote Miami columnist José Marmol, was like the baby Moses in his basket, sent into the waters to save his life from a cruel tyrant. "The daughter of Pharaoh took in Moses and this changed the history of the Hebrews. . . . Moses lived to lead his people out of slavery in Egypt to the promised land of Israel, an exodus that lasted 40 years—about the same time as our exile from Cuba."[48] Artists' renderings of Elian emphasized the same theme. The painter Alexis Blanco depicted him "swaddled, like the baby Moses, in a blue blanket and nestled inside an inner tube. Three dolphins surround Elian as the hand of God manipulates puppet strings that lead the child away from a red background symbolizing Communism."[49] Old women strained forward through police barriers just to touch "*el niño milagro*"—the miracle boy. Now, they said, he held the fate of Cuba itself in his innocent young hands. They believed the rumor that Castro had consulted a "*santera*" (voodoo priestess) who had told him that if Elian returned his regime would survive, but if Elian stayed in America the regime would fall.

Crowds gathered in the Miami streets around the house where the boy was staying for daily demonstrations and prayer services. A local journalist wrote that the house looked more like a shrine:

A wooden rosary is draped across the front door and a picture of Elian, in the water with the dolphins and surrounded by an aura of light, sits next to the front door. A picture of Jesus is nearby. In March, when an image of what many believed to be the Virgin Mary suddenly appeared in the window of a Miami bank, Totalbank, it stopped traffic. Just blocks from the home where Elian was staying, the apparition was taken as confirmation that Elian was El Niño Milagro. People placed religious icons on the bank's front door.[50]

Eventually, however, the INS, the courts, and the Clinton administration agreed that they should honor Elian's father's wishes, even though it meant sending the boy back to Communist Cuba. To Miami Cubans, President Clinton was no better than Pontius Pilate, washing his hands of Jesus (Elian) and turning him over to Herod (Castro) for crucifixion. Nevertheless, the boy returned to Cuba in June of 2000. Like many episodes of the turning millennium, the story began prosaically, took on soaring supernatural overtones, but ultimately returned to Earth with a matter-of-fact political or judicial decision made in accordance with secular criteria.

Chapter 12

THE NEW MILLENNIUM: 2001

Religion at Ground Zero

The destruction of the World Trade Center and the partial destruction of the Pentagon on September 11, 2001, marked a traumatic moment in American history. The events themselves, and the nation's great outpouring of grief, anger, dread, and prayer, offer a glimpse of American religion at the opening of the twenty-first century. In some ways similar to citizens' reactions to great events in the Second World War, where we began, they were in other ways quite different, revealing a new landscape of religious groupings and new ideas about God, suffering, war, and the character of America itself.

The immediate reaction of most religious Americans was one of shock and grief as the extent of the destruction became clear. Clergy hurried to Ground Zero in New York and to the Pentagon in Washington, D.C., to say prayers over the dead, to offer last rites to the dying, and to comfort exhausted and traumatized disaster workers. Almost at once Father Mychal Judge, a Franciscan friar and chaplain to the New York City Fire Department, was killed by falling debris while saying last rites over a dying firefighter; his death certificate was the first to be filed officially. Other clergy found that many workers' only way to deal with the chaos was religiously. "There are no atheists at ground zero," said a Catholic priest, perhaps unconsciously echoing the World War II insight that "there are

252

no atheists in the foxholes." "Everyone has a spiritual life now. . . . This experience has moved the workers to a deeper sense of spirituality that they've never experienced before, me included."[1] Throughout America that morning people poured into churches and synagogues after hearing the news. "I was so glad to come over here," said an Atlanta woman at a downtown church nearly a thousand miles from Ground Zero. "Faith is the only thing we have to hold on to. I had to calm myself and say 'God is here. God is alive. God will get us through.'"[2]

September 11 raised theological issues, especially the theodicy question, in acute form. How could a benevolent God let such a horrible event take place? Doesn't it show either that there is no God or else that God exists but is indifferent to human suffering? One minister noted that after the disaster, "people became theologians for a little while and were thinking about the big questions."[3] Many police officers, firefighters, and relatives of the victims told reporters that the horror made them doubt God, at least for a time. Some Christians and Jews gave the orthodox answer that God, by giving man free will, enabled him to choose evil as well as to choose good, and that this was a horrifying example of sinful men choosing evil. "God does not intend evil to happen," said a Methodist chaplain and grief counselor at Ground Zero, but bad things happen "if people choose evil."[4] Others offered the idea of a vulnerable God. "People often ask 'Where is God in this?'" said an Episcopal priest. "I'll tell you where he is. He's in the rubble. He is with those who were in the stairs that collapsed in on each other when the towers came down."[5]

Jerry Falwell, the fundamentalist leader, took a different approach. Speaking on Pat Robertson's *700 Club* broadcast two days after the disaster, he suggested that it was a punishment sent by God against America, his chosen nation, for its sins, just as God once sent tribulations against His chosen Children of Israel. "God continues to lift the curtain and allow the enemies of America to give us probably what we deserve." He continued:

> The abortionists have got to bear some burden for this because God will not be mocked. And when we destroy 40 million little innocent babies, we make God mad. I really believe that the pagans and the abortionists, and the feminists, and the gays and the lesbians who are actively trying to make that an alternative lifestyle, the ACLU, People for the American Way—all of them who have tried to secularize America—I point the finger in their faces and say: "You helped this happen."

He, like everyone else, blamed the terrorists themselves for the outrage but argued that America had exposed itself to a hazard that, at other times, God might have prevented. Robertson agreed with him. "Jerry, that's my feeling. I think we've just seen the antechamber to terror."[6]

When these remarks were condemned in the mainstream media, however, Falwell and Robertson were forced to issue apologies for appearing insensitive at a time of national grieving. Falwell insisted that his comments had been taken out of context and that they were theological rather than political. A few days later a second group of evangelical leaders including Chuck Colson—the former Watergate conspirator turned prison ministry leader—and James Dobson—head of the evangelical group Focus on the Family—made a statement that appeared to agree with Falwell's diagnosis. It warned, "Our choices have consequences. Our rebellion has results. In many ways, the results of recent days are a reflection of the crumbling foundations of America," which could be put right only by "reclaiming the promises of God" in a national revival.[7]

Other fundamentalists speculated that the disaster was one of the oft-looked-for signs of the end times. One was James Merritt, president of the Southern Baptist Convention, who believed the attacks were "Satan's handiwork" and quoted Saint Paul's warning in 2 Timothy that "in the last days perilous times will come." According to Joe Van Koevering, a St. Petersburg, Florida, minister, an equally appropriate text was Matthew 24: "You will hear of wars and rumors of wars. . . . Nation will rise against nation, and kingdom against kingdom."[8]

Within a few days rescue workers, clergy, and volunteers at the disaster sites had begun to offset their sense of overwhelming tragedy by discerning what they thought of as small miracles. First, amid the debris they found a steel cross, fifteen feet high. It was a fragment of the World Trade Center's steel skeleton, standing stark and upright inside the ruins of a neighboring building after crashing through its glass roof. Rescue workers showed it to Rev. Brian Jordan, a Franciscan priest ministering at Ground Zero. He held a service beside it and a few days later had it brought out by crane and set up on a prominent site in the midst of the wreckage. He blessed it, workers scribbled messages on it ("God bless our fallen brothers"), and it presided over the cleanup from then on.[9] Witnessing it, an anguished Port Authority officer who at first had reacted to the disaster by doubting the existence of God, reflected: "I thought maybe there is something more here. . . . The Devil might have gotten away with this one but God is still here."[10]

Second, workers noticed that despite the immense impact of the falling Trade Center towers, only one church in the neighborhood had been destroyed. It was St. Nicholas's Greek Orthodox Church on Cedar Street. The Episcopal St. Paul's Chapel, nearby, ought to have been knocked flat too, yet it survived, coated with dust and soot but otherwise unscathed. St. Paul's was historically significant because it dated back to 1767 and was the place where George Washington himself had prayed on the day of his inauguration as America's first president in 1789. The prayer he made that day, "Almighty God we make our earnest prayer that thou wilt keep the United States in thy holy protection," was engraved on a bronze plaque there. Under the leadership of its rector, Lyndon Harris, St. Paul's now became an ecumenical sanctuary one block from Ground Zero, welcoming worshipers from all faiths every day, a feeding station for thousands of volunteers, a place where exhausted firefighters could sleep on cots, and a makeshift center for chiropractors, massage therapists, and podiatrists caring for the overworked rescuers. Harris himself said the chapel's survival was "a miracle, the fruit of some divine intervention." It had become "a beacon of hope and metaphor of good standing in the face of evil." New York's Mayor Rudi Giuliani agreed, describing it as the "miracle of September 11," adding that "standing defiant and serene amid the ruins, [it] sends an eloquent message about the strength and resilience of the people of New York City and the people of America."[11]

Miraculous in a more general way was the feeling of intense spiritual unity that many Americans experienced after the disaster. Volunteers drove or flew to the disaster sites from all over America, thousands lined up to give blood, and citizens gave more than a billion dollars to charity in the next three months. "No one of us is an independent man or woman," said Episcopal bishop Geralyn Wolf of Rhode Island, as she visited Ground Zero. "We all need each other, and the church at its best is a community of faith grounded in Christ, a real community of love."[12]

A series of memorial prayer services brought together members of nearly all faith communities, emphasizing their shared sense of loss but also their shared sense of a common destiny as Americans. At the National Cathedral in Washington, D.C., Billy Graham preached that the disaster had created an unprecedented sense of national unity. The terrorists' plan to shatter America had backfired because "we are more united than ever."[13] Two Sundays after the disaster an interfaith service at Yankee Stadium featured speeches from all points of the religious spectrum, along with musical offerings from such secular celebrities as Oprah Winfrey, Bette Midler, and Placido Domingo. Prayers were offered by the Catholic archbishop of New York, Edward Egan, by Imam Pasha from the Harlem Mosque of the Nation of Islam, and by Rabbi Alvin Kass from the New York Police Department. Another rabbi blew the shofar, the ritual ram's horn traditionally sounded at the end of the Day of Atonement, an imam sang the call to prayer, and a Christian church bell rang.

These services of remembrance doubled as patriotic rallies, with crosses and stars of David sometimes crowded out by American flags. The Jewish holidays of Rosh Hashanah and Yom Kippur were celebrated in the weeks after September 11, often with patriotic regalia on display in crowded synagogues. One rabbi told an interviewer that his Yom Kippur sermon would be "a public declaration of support and solidarity" for the nation and that he would break with tradition by singing "God Bless America" and other patriotic songs at the service.[14] Knoxville Christians likewise sang "God Bless America" after an interdenominational prayer service a week after the tragedy.

Sermons and conversations in church helped citizens decide how America should respond to the attacks. Some were belligerent. The National Conference of Catholic Bishops, the United Methodist Church, and the Evangelical

Lutheran Church all expressed support for a war against terrorism, even if it meant pursuing the adversary halfway around the world. A Southern Baptist leader added: "If you want to get rid of the malaria of international terrorism, you can't just swat mosquitoes; you have to drain the swamp." Bishop T. D. Jakes, pastor of the Potter's House, a Dallas megachurch, preached holy war:

> God has brought this country to its knees. But . . . do not think that to be on our knees is a posture of defeat. I dare say to you, my brothers and sisters, that to be on our knees is a posture of warfare. It is the best position that this country can ever take. And let Osama bin Laden and whosoever shall rise against this nation understand that we have not dropped to our knees because we are defeated, but we have dropped to our knees because we are armed and dangerous and ready to fight the good fight of faith. Glory to God.[15]

Many others agreed that a war against the perpetrators would be a just war, but they reminded themselves not to give way to feelings of hatred or thirst for revenge. "What we must fear most is not evil, it is becoming evil ourselves," said Rabbi Barry Starr at an interfaith service three days after the attack.[16] A Christian minister, Charles Kullman, echoed the theme: "God's love and our hatred cannot coexist in our hearts. . . . Jesus came to save all sinners, even terrorists."[17] How to react was particularly difficult for members of the historic peace churches; many Quakers admitted that in this situation they found it difficult to hold to their time-honored belief that war is always wrong. One Westchester, New York, Quaker told a reporter: "I think it's hard to oppose the military response here. And I'm kind of shocked to find myself feeling this way. But I feel personally threatened. I'm at a loss as to what a nonviolent response would be."[18]

The historic peace churches' leadership, along with such peace groups as Pax Christi (Catholic) and the Fellowship of Reconciliation (Protestant), however, emphasized in early statements that even an attack of this magnitude against innocent people did not change their belief that war was always wrong. "We know our message is not what a lot of people want to hear today," a Pax Christi representative admitted. Most Quakers agreed that September 11 must not change their historic peace witness, one noting that at a crowded meeting just after September 11 no one who had spoken had advocated war. "There was great fear that we would be adding to the number of innocent victims."[19] Another said that when she doubted the rightness of her Quaker tradition in this instance, "I think about bombs raining down on Afghanistan and I ask, 'Is this God's will?' Well, no. This is the clarifying question for me."[20]

The national mood as America prepared for war against Al Qaeda in Afghanistan frightened American Muslims. Some were attacked and beaten by enraged citizens who did not stop to reflect on distinctions within Islam or to inquire about their victims' beliefs. Three immigrants were murdered in the week after September 11, two of whom were wrongly identified as Muslims (the three were an Egyptian Christian in California, an Indian Sikh in Arizona, and a Pakistani Muslim in Dallas). Mosques in Atlanta, Washington, and Toronto were desecrated, the windows of a Texas mosque were shot out, and hundreds of Muslims reported threatening phone calls, E-mails, and letters. Attacks on turban-wearing Sikhs became so common (because at first glance they looked a little like press pictures of Al Qaeda leader Osama bin Laden) that some decided to break a religious rule by cutting their hair and going without the turban until the national mood was calmer. Others posted American flags in their taxis and shops, or signs that read: "God bless America" and "Sikh Americans Share the Pain and Grief."[21]

The majority of American Muslims had reacted to the attacks with the same sense of horror as everyone else, condemned them, and made statements emphasizing their solidarity with all other Americans. At the Yankee Stadium memorial service on September 23, the imam declared: "We stand today as Muslims, Americans with a heavy weight on our shoulders that those who would dare do such dastardly acts dare claim our faith. They are no believers in God at all, nor do they believe in his messenger Muhammed. We condemn them."[22] At the Islamic Academy of New England in Sharon, Connecticut, students began raising funds for the Red Cross and making posters to commiserate with the bereaved. Teachers emphasized to students that "Islam is a religion of peace and a religion of hope."[23] To help prevent hate crimes, President George W. Bush visited the Islamic Center of Washington, D.C., on September 17 and made a speech from the lectern, declaring that "the face of terror is not the true face of Islam" and that "Islam is peace."[24] Congress followed his example by passing a resolution for the protection of Arab Americans' civil rights. Government leaders were careful to avoid using the words "Islam" and "Muslim" in describing the enemy they faced.

Not everyone showed the same restraint as the nation's leaders. Some Christians jumped in where the president feared to tread, denouncing Islam and blaming it for the whole tragedy. Robert Morey, author of *The Islamic Invasion*, was one, and after September 11 he invited Christians to sign a pledge for a "spiritual crusade against Islam."[25] Rev. Albert Mohler, president of the Southern Baptist Theological Seminary in Louisville, Kentucky, declared that "the biggest problem with Islamic theology is that it kills the soul." He went on to argue that Islam "lies about God . . . and presents a false gospel."[26] Charles Colson agreed: "Islam's worldview sees God as remote, utterly transcendant. Christians worship a God who became flesh and intimately knowable and personal through the incarnation." Colson, like Mohler, hastened to add that he did not wish to "disparage moderate Muslims." At the same time, "like it or not, ancient worldviews are again struggling for domination; we do not all worship the same God."[27]

Ground Zero, meanwhile, became a religious place in its own right. Rescue workers spoke of it as "hallowed ground" (an echo of Lincoln's Gettysburg Address), and visitors from other parts of America and from around the world flocked in to see the disaster scene. By December 2001 it was a new kind of pilgrimage site, a modern counterpart to medieval Canterbury or nineteenth-century Lourdes. The City of New York built observation platforms overlooking the site so that visitors—many of whom were willing to wait for hours—could take turns gazing upon it. Fire stations around the city, many of which had lost firefighters in the disaster, became shrines too, with pictures of lost men posted beside flowers, memorabilia, and letters from families and friends.

Perhaps the most common way of coming to terms with the catastrophe was through the language of America as a chosen people. A powerful theme throughout the nation's history, it had figured largely in the language of early Puritan settlers, who thought of themselves as the new embodiment of God's Children of Israel. It had contributed to the justification of the Revolutionary generation of the 1770s and 1780s, and it had fired religious imaginations during the Civil War. Abraham Lincoln's rhetoric was full of references to God's will and to the idea that the war was the playing out of a divine plan for America. At Gettysburg he declared that the men who died there had "hallowed" and "consecrated" the ground more than he could hope to do. When New York mayor Rudi Giuliani gave his final mayoral speech three months after the attack on the World Trade Center, he chose to deliver it at the "miraculous" St. Paul's Chapel near Ground Zero, which had so strikingly escaped destruction. His rhetoric on the occasion was full of references to illustrious predecessors and to the nation's divine mission:

> The reason I chose this chapel is because this chapel is thrice-hallowed ground. . . . It is hallowed by the fact that it was consecrated as a house of God in 1766. . . . And in April of 1789 George Washington came here after he was inaugurated as the first president and he prayed right here in this church, which makes it a very sacred ground to people who feel what America is all about. But then it was consecrated one more time, in 2001, on September 11. . . . When the twin towers were viciously attacked and came crashing to the ground . . . this chapel remained not only not destroyed, not a single window was broken, not a single thing hurt. And I think there's some very, very special significance in that. The place where George Washington prayed when he first became President of the United States stood strong, powerful, undaunted by the attacks of these people who hate what we stand for. Because what we stand for is so much stronger than they are.

This speech, said a British journalist, Clifford Longley, "is manifestly a claim that faith in America is exactly like faith in a religion (or indeed *is* faith in a religion), and that America stands under God's special protection."[28]

Conclusion

Giuliani's remarks followed a time-honored formula, yet came straight from the heart. Americans' idea of their nation as one deserving of, and blessed by, God's special favor had persisted throughout American history and had not dimmed in the era since World War II. Other characteristics of American religion had persisted too. Americans remained far more involved in religious activities and groups than their counterparts in the rest of the industrialized world (indeed, American tourists were the salvation of such ancient centers of religious life as Canterbury Cathedral in England and Notre Dame in Paris, whose indigenous congregations were dwindling to nothing). At the start of the new millennium new immigrant groups—Hispanic Catholics, Muslims, Hindus, Buddhists, and others—were adapting their religions to American circumstances just as older generations of immigrants had done, changing and reshaping them to fit new circumstances even when the intention was to preserve them unchanged. Like their predecessors, they found religious organizations useful in bridging the gulf between their countries of origin and their new home, doubling as centers of religious observance and ethnic continuity.

In other respects, however, the situation was transformed between 1945 and 2001. The religious landscape that we surveyed in chapter 1 had changed. The mainline Protestant churches—Presbyterian, Methodist, Congregational, Unitarian, and Episcopalian—grew steadily weaker as cultural authorities through the second half of the twentieth century, while their membership aged and shrank. At the same time, the evangelical churches—especially the Southern Baptists and Assemblies of God—along with the Mormons and Pentecostalists, gained confidence, numbers, and cultural influence. Religious sociologists concluded that the more a church demanded of its members, the more likely it was to keep them. Those that structured an entire way of life, taught an exacting code of moral conduct, required an uncompromising adherence to the Bible, and demanded that members tithe were able to keep hold of existing congregations and to attract new recruits. Those, on the other hand, that emphasized moral permissiveness, counseled adaptation to new circumstances, and made few demands on their members were correspondingly likely to lose them.

Even among the thriving evangelicals, however, denominational loyalty was growing weaker, partly because Americans liked to experiment, shop around, and try different churches at different times in their lives and partly because they were attracted to charismatic leaders. The rise of evangelical superstars, on television and in the megachurches, accelerated the process. Outstanding figures like Billy Graham, Jerry Falwell, and Oral Roberts gathered massive followings, sometimes in parallel with but sometimes at the expense of local churches. The Bakker-Swaggart televangelist scandals of the late 1980s, meanwhile, reminded fundamentalists that even their leaders had feet of clay and that the age-old temptations of sex and money were as powerful as ever.

The Catholic Church no less than its Protestant rivals went through a series of unsettling changes between the Second World War and the new century. Immensely powerful internally in the 1940s and 1950s, centralized, unified, and self-confident, it was still marginal to American national life. The election of John F. Kennedy to the presidency in 1960 gave it greater political authority in America than ever before, even though Kennedy was careful to keep his religion and politics separate. The Second Vatican Council (1962–1965) transformed Catholicism internally, making it less "triumphal," more hospitable to ecumenism, and (in the decision to switch to vernacular languages) more easily understood by parishioners.

These changes, and a greater openness to Protestants and Jews (now reconceptualized as the "separated brethren"), contributed to a reduction in anti-Catholicism, which had been one of the last socially respectable prejudices among the American middle classes. Catholics born after 1945 were more outspoken than their parents on matters of national policy, moving in some cases from staunch anti-Communism in the 1950s to challenging America's Vietnam policy in the 1960s, to denouncing nuclear deterrence policy in the 1980s. They were also more outspoken than their parents on Church matters. Some criticized the Church for not ordaining women; others investigated child-abuse scandals. Nearly all criticized *Humanae Vitae*, the 1968 papal encyclical banning contraceptives. Earlier generations of Catholics had usually been less well educated than their priests. The fully assimilated new generations were often as well or better educated than their priests and correspondingly reluctant to give docile obedience to policies they disliked.

Vatican II's unintended side effects were probably even greater than its intended outcome. Thousands of priests and nuns, encouraged to test their vocations against new standards, decided to leave their orders, and many of them married. A steady decline in the overall number of priests and nuns, a sharp decline in new recruits, and a gradual aging of the entire population in holy orders was the result, which by 2001 had reached crisis proportions. The crisis was aggravated by pedophilia scandals, which just kept getting worse as the new millennium dawned, intensifying pressure on the Church to admit married priests or to permit the ordination of women. American Catholic leaders, beholden to the pope, were unable to institute either reform (though some would probably have liked to), but the aging Pope John Paul II was determined to permit neither.

To add to Catholic woes, divorce and contraception continued to be, officially, forbidden. In reality, Catholics practiced contraception with the same frequency as all other Americans, while the process of annulment ("Catholic divorce"), which had once been immensely slow and complex, became increasingly quick and pro forma—so much so that it encouraged skepticism about the purposes of the ban in the first place. To complete this litany of sex-related problems, Catholics maintained a steady condemnation of homosexuality in the face of widespread gay identification among parishioners and (covertly) among priests.

American Jews, like Protestants and Catholics, endured profound changes between 1945 and 2001. Suburban synagogues enjoyed a steady growth in membership after World War II as part of the postwar religious revival, with the Conservative branch profiting most in larger memberships. Interest in the developing state of Israel, a nation that had to fight for its life against hostile neighbors from day one, and a growing awareness of the Holocaust as a central tragic event in Jewish history, enabled many American Jews to emphasize the cultural and historical aspect, rather than the strictly religious side, of their identity. Religious and secular Jews alike worried about growing rates of inter-marriage (it had reached 50 percent by 1980), and the possibility that Jews as a distinctive population would ultimately disappear, not in reaction to persecution, as they had long feared, but in consequence of unequaled opportunities in pluralistic America. Whether intermarriage brought more converts in from the outside or alienated more Jews to the outside was a hotly contested question over several decades. Apparently conclusive arguments on both sides were offered. Fear of dilution or disappearance contributed to a revival of Jewish Orthodoxy after about 1970 and its intensification in New York and other metropolitan areas. By 2001, American Jewry consisted of a religiously observant minority and a majority for whom Judaism was a source of pride, tradition, and selective cultural identification.

As the three major groupings experienced these shifts, they were joined by adherents of many other religions: Hindus, Muslims, Buddhists, Sikhs, and Confucians, mainly from abroad, and Goddess worshipers, New Age-ers, and UFO sectarians, mainly native born. The aftermath of the September 11 attacks shows that by 2001 Islam had been accepted as one of the American national faiths, at least by civic and national groups, which included imams in their memorial services and avoided identifying the nation's enemy as Islamic. The indiscriminate attacks on Muslims (and misidentified non-Muslims), by contrast, show that popular support for this fourth group in the national pantheon was not yet assured at the grassroots level.

Throughout the period from 1945 to 2001, religion and American politics interacted in complex ways. Religious groups rarely created the issues, but their involvement led the participants to understand them as matters of transcendent significance. Throughout the Cold War, for example, the intensity of American anti-Communism came from many religious citizens' belief that their adversary was not just a rival great power, the Soviet Union, but an aggressive secular ideology, "Godless Communism." It was, they believed, a threat to the spiritual values on which Western civilization itself (now reconceptualized as the "Judeo-Christian tradition") had been built.

Likewise, the passions aroused by the civil rights movement cannot be understood by considering it solely as a secular movement. Its activist phase, from the Montgomery bus boycott to the sit-ins and freedom rides, was led by ministers almost from the outset—Martin Luther King Jr., Ralph Abernathy, Fred Shuttlesworth, Jesse Jackson, and Andrew Young. The boycott occasioned King's most profound religious experience, bringing him the faith and will to continue in the face of threats to his and his family's lives. He and the other clergy maintained morale among activists with regular prayer, preaching, and gospel music services. The movement's greatest statements (King's "Letter from Birmingham Jail" and his "I Have a Dream" speech) were as much sermons as political declarations. The tactics of nonviolence used to such brilliant effect between 1955 and 1964 owed far more to participants' understanding of Jesus' message of peace and love than to their understanding of Gandhi, of whom most knew little. When "black power" advocates challenged nonviolence, many of them did it in the name of another religious philosophy, that of the Black Muslims.

Just as the civil rights movement pursued its objectives by mobilizing a large religious constituency, so did movements that argued for and against American participation in the Vietnam War. An idealistic young Catholic doctor, Tom Dooley, did as much as anyone to persuade a generation of American Christians that fighting Communism in Vietnam was a noble and righteous cause. New York's Cardinal Spellman amplified the claim and did all he could to boost troops' morale. Conversely, by 1965 it was the Catholic Worker Movement, the Fellowship of Reconciliation, and Quaker groups that led agitation against the draft and against America's steadily growing involvement in southeast Asia. By the late 1960s the opposition of respectable middle-class church groups as well as the opposition of angry radical students had persuaded politicians on both sides of the political divide that the nation had to disengage. Subsequent controversies over American policy in Latin America during the 1980s, over the nation's dependence on nuclear weapons, and over its Hispanic refugee policy, were debated in religiously supercharged rhetoric as well as the language of realpolitik.

Involvement and motivation were one thing; resolution of these issues was another. Neither in the Cold War, nor in Vietnam, nor in the civil rights movement, was religion ultimately decisive. The history of each has usually been told from a purely secular standpoint, with historians focusing on legislative maneuvers, court cases, and presidential decisions. The nature of American church-state separation—especially after the school prayer and Bible reading cases of 1962 and 1963—required any movement that was motivated by religious convictions to *translate* its convictions into the secular language of the national good. Indeed, advocates had to be careful to *exclude* from their political arguments the religious ideas that had motivated them in the first place. Otherwise they would be vulnerable to opponents' charges that they were seeking to establish their particular religion, in violation of the First Amendment's Establishment Clause. Accordingly, civil rights legislation said nothing about the Bible but invoked the venerable American principle of equality. Antinuclear campaigners could tell one another that nuclear weapons violated God's law, but they had to content themselves with telling their congressional representatives that they violated sound principles of strategic planning and the American tradition of sparing noncombatants in war.

This paradox of arguing for reforms on the basis of intense religious beliefs without being allowed to voice them in the public forum was most vividly illustrated in the 1980s on the issues of creationism and abortion. Christian lobbyists who wanted public school children to learn creation science along with (or instead of) evolution had to make the case for it on scientific grounds alone. Motivated by religious belief, they had to act in the legislature and the courtroom as though guided solely by scientific criteria. They were never able to convince the relevant judges that they were acting in good faith. Anti-abortion activists, likewise, mostly Catholics and fundamentalists, shared a religiously based belief that an embryo is a human being and that abortion should be forbidden because it is a form of homicide. They had stronger scientific support for this view than the creationists had for their claims, but their pro-choice opponents did everything they could to discredit them as First Amendment transgressors. The 1980s bore witness to the relentless frustration of Moral Majority, while the 1990s were scarcely better for its successor, the Christian Coalition. In each case the organization's membership and motivation marked it out from the start as a religious lobby, enabling adversaries to discredit it for crossing church-state boundaries.

In the 1970s and 1980s a long succession of social and foreign policy issues involved religious Americans, but along new lines of alliance. Conservative Protestants and conservative Catholics repeatedly found themselves on the same side of these issues (notably those relating to education, the family, foreign policy, and sexuality), just as liberal Catholics and liberal Protestants made common cause on the opposite side, with each group finding Jewish allies from a third, sharply divided constituency. By then anti-Catholicism and anti-Semitism, still appreciable forces in public life in 1945, had all but disappeared, and controversy within Protestantism and within Catholicism was fiercer than conflict between them.

Religion and politics mixed in countless ways, as most of the episodes examined here illustrate, and drew in tens of thousands of Americans. Religion as an intellectual preoccupation was, by contrast, the preserve of a tiny minority. Theology followed a paradoxical path. Probably more theological writing was published in America during the fifty-six years after World War II than in any other comparable period, but its cultural influence had never been slighter. Most theologians by then were academic specialists and were hermetically sealed off from the wider religious population. Their intended audience was other theologians, and they, like professors in the secular disciplines, were publishing largely to assure promotion and tenure rather than to nurture congregations and save souls. A few theological writers, notably Francis Schaeffer, achieved a wider audience, but the majority, especially those writing theology for particular identity groups—the black, feminist, womanist, liberationist, and queer theologians, for example—had negligible influence outside the universities and divinity schools. There was still a massive audience for books on religion and spirituality, but these were books written in a different idiom, often with a strong self-help message. Norman Vincent Peale's *Power of Positive Thinking* (1952), Marabel Morgan's *The Total Woman* (1973), and Rabbi Harold Kushner's *When Bad Things Happen to Good People* (1980) were all religious best-sellers but were scarcely recognizable as theology in the traditional sense. Ministers and rabbis in most churches and synagogues found counseling and therapeutic work more important than doctrinal rigor, and the right emotions more important to their members than dogmatic exactitude.

Between Hiroshima and Ground Zero, in other words, America's religious situation had changed to one of greater diversity and greater politicization, even though the separation between church and state was stronger than ever. Certain tensions were built into the religious situation. Evangelicals, for example, were able simultaneously to condemn the godless modern world, to anticipate imminent crisis, and yet to operate prosperously and successfully in a high-tech environment with a large following. Liberal Christians were able simultaneously to dread what seemed to them like the threat of intolerant fundamentalism seizing the nation yet send their children to schools in which no prayer was uttered and no mention made of Christmas, Rosh Hashanah, or Ramadan. Agnostics and atheists could live daily lives from which even the mention of religion was almost totally excluded. As the sociologist Peter Berger remarked, one element of late-twentieth-century America's diversity was its ability to shelter many groups whose members had completely different ideas of what the world was like; what he called competing "plausibility structures." The heat of religious-political disputes usually came from individuals speaking out of different plausibility structures and finding it difficult to believe that their adversaries—whose assumptions about reality were so different—were speaking and acting in good faith.

Luckily, the American taste for verbal combat continued to be tempered by a strong American faith in civility. Most religious Americans agreed to differ and accepted a situation in which they could pursue their religious lives, or their unreligious lives, without threat of external interference and far from the public spotlight. The supporters and defenders of particular religious groups, and of religion in general, could easily point to the educational, charitable, and spiritual benefits of America's religiosity. Detractors, equally, could point to religion as a force for obfuscation and intolerance. As a historian I am less concerned with assigning praise and blame than with describing what happened and explaining why, so that readers, whatever their own views, can understand this element of the American past a little better.

Notes

1. Anxious Victory: 1945–1952

1. Oppenheimer, quoted in Robert Jungk, *Brighter Than a Thousand Suns* (New York: Penguin, 1958), 183.

2. George B. Tindall and David E. Shi, *America: A Narrative History*, 4th ed. (New York: Norton, 1996), 2:1369.

3. "Bomb" editorial, *Christian Herald* 68 (October 1945): 9.

4. Twenty-two theologians, cited in Richard Fox, *Reinhold Niebuhr: A Biography* (San Francisco: Harper and Row, 1987), 224.

5. "The Atom Bomb," editorial, *Catholic World* 161 (September 1945): 449.

6. Harry Murray, "The Only Solution Is Love," Catholic Worker Web site www.catholicworker.org/roundtable/essaytext.cfm?Number=178.

7. Christopher Cross and William Arnold, *Soldiers of God: True Story of the U.S. Army Chaplains* (New York: Dutton, 1945), 75.

8. Ibid., 105–6.

9. Cross and Arnold, *Soldiers of God*, 114.

10. Joel Carpenter, *Revive Us Again: The Reawakening of American Fundamentalism* (New York: Oxford University Press, 1997), 138.

11. Billy Graham, *Just As I Am: The Autobiography of Billy Graham* (San Francisco: HarperCollins/Zondervan, 1997), 139.

12. Carpenter, *Revive Us Again*, 229.

13. Joshua Loth Liebman, *Peace of Mind* (New York: Simon and Schuster, 1946), 15.

14. Norman Vincent Peale, *A Guide to Confident Living* (New York: Prentice Hall, 1948), 6.

15. Fulton Sheen, *Peace of Soul* (New York: McGraw Hill, 1949), 3.

16. Thomas Merton, *The Seven Storey Mountain* (New York: Harcourt, Brace, 1948), 387.

17. Mark Massa, *Catholics and American Culture* (New York: Crossroad, 1999), 56.

18. Merton, quoted in Monica Furlong, *Merton: A Biography* (San Francisco: Harper and Row, 1980), 147.

2. Religion and Materialism: 1950–1970

1. Dorothy Day, speech in Memphis (1954), cited on Spartacus Schoolnet Web site www.spartacus.schoolnet.co.uk/Jday.htm.

2. Chambers, quoted in Sam Tanenhaus, *Whittaker Chambers* (New York: Random House, 1997), 468.

3. Quoted in Patrick Allitt, *Catholic Intellectuals and Conservative Politics in America, 1950–1985* (Ithaca, N.Y.: Cornell University Press, 1993), 25.

4. Ibid., 69.

5. Charles Morris, *American Catholic: The Saints and Sinners Who Built America's Most Powerful Church* (New York: Random House/Times Books, 1997), 229–30.

6. John Courtney Murray, *We Hold These Truths: Catholic Reflections on the American Proposition* (New York: Sheed and Ward, 1960), 245.

7. Fred Schwarz, *Beating the Unbeatable Foe: One Man's Victory Over Communism, Leviathan, and the Last Enemy* (Washington, D.C.: Regnery, 1996), 22.

8. "No Methodist Pink Fringe," *The Lutheran* 32 (May 3, 1950): 7–8.

9. Reinhold Niebuhr, *The Irony of American History* (New York: Scribner's, 1952), 7.

10. Paul Tillich, "Beyond the Usual Alternatives," *Christian Century* 75 (May 7, 1958): 555.

11. Paul Tillich, *The Courage to Be* (New Haven, Conn.: Yale University Press, 1952), 107–8.

12. Jacques Maritain, *Reflections on America* (New York: Scribner's, 1958), 83.

13. Herberg, quoted in John P. Diggins, *Up from Communism: Conservative Odysseys in American Intellectual History* (New York: Harper and Row, 1975), 270–71.

14. Will Herberg, *Protestant, Catholic, Jew: An Essay in American Religious Sociology* (1955; reprint, New York: Anchor Doubleday, 1960), 3.

15. Eisenhower, quoted in Mark Silk, *Spiritual Politics: Religion and America Since World War II* (New York: Simon and Schuster, 1988), 40.

16. Miller, quoted in Paul Carter, *Another Part of the Fifties* (New York: Columbia University Press, 1983), 124.

17. Dooley, quoted in James T. Fisher, *Dr. America: The Lives of Thomas A. Dooley, 1927–1961* (Amherst: University of Massachusetts Press, 1997), 78.

18. J. F. White, "Recent Trends in American Church Building," *Studia Liturgica* 4 (Spring 1965): 112–13.

19. Philip Gardner, "New Directions in Church Design," *Christian Century* 81 (April 1, 1964): 424.

20. William W. Watkin, *Planning and Building the Modern Church* (New York: Dodge, 1951), 57.

21. Martin Anderson, *Planning and Financing the New Church*, 2nd rev. ed. (Minneapolis: Augsburg, 1949), 39.

22. Watkin, *Planning and Building the Modern Church*, 5.

23. Mies van der Rohe, quoted in Roger G. Kennedy, *American Churches* (New York: Crossroad, 1982), 56.

24. Belluschi, quoted in Gardner, "New Directions in Church Design," 425.

25. Belluschi, quoted in Meredith L. Clausen, *Pietro Belluschi: Modern American Architect* (Cambridge, Mass.: MIT Press, 1994), 154.

26. John LaFarge, S.J., "The Church as Instrument and Expression," in *Architectural Record* 1953 (Building Types Study #205), 123.

27. Maurice Eisendrath, "An American Synagogue for Today and Tomorrow," in *Architectural Record* 1953 (Building Types Study #205), 119.

28. Reinhold Niebuhr, "Tradition and Today's Ethos," in *Architectural Record* 1953 (Building Types Study #205), 118.

29. Paul Tillich, "Contemporary Protestant Architecture," in Albert Christ-Janer and Mary Mix Foley, eds., *Modern Church Architecture* (New York: McGraw-Hill, 1962), 123.

30. Tillich, quoted in Clausen, *Pietro Belluschi*, 161.

31. Michael Novak, "The Nonbeliever and the New Liturgical Movement," reprinted in Novak, *A Time to Build* (New York: Macmillan, 1967), 74–75.

32. James P. Gaffey, "The Anatomy of Transition: Cathedral Building and Social Justice in San Francisco, 1962–1971," *Catholic Historical Review* 70 (January 1984): 71.

3. Religion, Respect, and Social Change: 1955–1968

1. Ralph Abernathy, *And the Walls Came Tumbling Down* (New York: Harper and Row, 1989), 94.

2. E. Franklin Frazier, *The Negro Church in America*, and C. Eric Lincoln, *The Black Church Since Frazier* (1963; reprint, New York: Schocken, 1974), 50, 51.

3. Albert Raboteau, *A Fire in the Bones: Reflections on African-American Religious History* (Boston: Beacon, 1995), 143–44.

4. Maya Angelou, *I Know Why the Caged Bird Sings* (1970; reprint, New York: Bantam, 1979), 32.

5. James Baldwin, *The Fire Next Time* (1963; reprint, New York: Laurel, 1979), 44–47.

6. Abernathy, *And the Walls Came Tumbling Down*, 118.

7. Mahalia Jackson with Evan McLeod Wylie, *Movin' on Up* (New York: Hawthorne, 1966), 63.

8. Leroy Davis, interview by Patrick Allitt, February 18, 2000, Emory University, Atlanta.

9. Abernathy, *And the Walls Came Tumbling Down*, 106.

10. Marshall Frady, *Jesse: The Life and Pilgrimage of Jesse Jackson* (New York: Random House, 1996), 103.

11. Jo-Ann Gibson Robinson, *The Montgomery Bus Boycott and the Women Who Started It* (Knoxville: University of Tennessee Press, 1987), 53–54.

12. King, quoted in David Garrow, *Bearing the Cross: Martin Luther King, Jr., and the Southern Christian Leadership Conference* (1986; reprint, New York: Vintage, 1988), 24.

13. Virginia Durr, *Outside the Magic Circle: The Autobiography of Virginia Foster Durr* (New York: Simon and Schuster/Touchstone, 1985), 280.

14. Martin Luther King, Jr., "Pilgrimage to Nonviolence," in *Strength to Love* (1963; reprint, Philadelphia: Fortress, 1981), 148.

15. King, quoted in David Garrow, "Martin Luther King, Jr., and the Spirit of Leadership," *Journal of American History* 74 (September 1987): 442.

16. King, quoted in George B. Tindall and David E. Shi, *America: A Narrative History*, 4th ed. (New York: Norton, 1996), 2:1380.

17. Abernathy, *And the Walls Came Tumbling Down*, 149.

18. Frazier, *The Negro Church in America*, 79.

19. SCLC, quoted in C. Eric Lincoln, *The Black Church Since Frazier*, in ibid., 117.

20. Abernathy, *And the Walls Came Tumbling Down*, 257.

21. Ibid., 114.

22. Louis Twomey, "Autobiographical Notes on the Race Problem," *Social Order* 13 (January 1963): 1–4.

23. R. Frederick West, *Preaching on Race* (St. Louis, Mo.: Bethany Press, 1962), 17.

24. Humphrey K. Ezell, *The Christian Problem of Racial Segregation* (New York: Greenwich Books, 1959), 23.

25. Lawrence W. Neff, *Jesus: Master Segregationist* (Atlanta: Banner, 1964), 13.

26. H. C. McGowan, *God's Garden of Segregation* (New York: Vintage, 1961), 90.

27. Martin Luther King, Jr., "Letter from Birmingham Jail," reprinted in Milton C. Sernett, ed., *Afro-American Religious History: A Documentary Witness* (Durham, N.C.: Duke University Press, 1985), 431.

28. Ibid., 441–42.

29. Mahalia Jackson, "Singing of Good Tidings and Freedom," in Sernett, *Afro-American Religious History*, 455.

30. King, quoted in Garrow, *Bearing the Cross*, 283–84.

31. Leonard Dinnerstein, *Antisemitism in America* (New York: Oxford University Press, 1994), 192.

32. Anne Moody, *Coming of Age in Mississippi* (1968; reprint, New York: Dell, 1976), 307.

33. Alex Haley, *Autobiography of Malcolm X* (1964; reprint, New York: Ballantine, 1978), 165–66.

34. Baldwin, *The Fire Next Time*, 87–88.

35. Haley, *Autobiography of Malcolm X*, 195.

36. Archie Epps, ed., *The Speeches of Malcolm X at Harvard* (New York: William Morrow, 1968), 116 (from a 1961 speech at Harvard Law School Forum).

37. George Breitman, ed., *Malcolm X Speaks: Selected Speeches and Statements* (1965; reprint, New York: Pathfinder, 1989), 13.

38. Tindall and Shi, *America*, 1534.

39. Frazier, *The Negro Church in America*, 76.

40. R. Laurence Moore, *Religious Outsiders and the Making of Americans* (New York: Oxford University Press, 1986), 45–46.

41. Richard N. Ostling and Joan K. Ostling, *Mormon America: The Power and the Promise* (San Francisco: HarperSanFrancisco, 1999), 97.

4. New Frontiers and Old Boundaries: 1960–1969

1. Robert S. Alley, *The Supreme Court on Church and State* (New York: Oxford University Press, 1988), 186.

2. Ibid., 195.

3. Ibid., 213.

4. Ibid., 207.

5. Madalyn Murray, quoted in Lawrence Wright, *Saints and Sinners* (New York: Knopf, 1993), 102.

6. Joseph Martin Hopkins, "The Separation of God and State," *Christian Herald* 86 (July 1963): 16.

7. Frances Fitzgerald, *Fire in the Lake* (1972; reprint, New York: Vintage, 1973), 180.

8. Daniel Berrigan, *To Dwell in Peace* (San Francisco: Harper and Row, 1987), 180.

9. Dietrich Bonhoeffer, *Letters and Papers from Prison*, ed. Eberhard Bethge, enlarged ed. (New York: Macmillan, 1971), 327 (from a letter dated June 6, 1944).

10. Gabriel Vahanian, *The Death of God: The Culture of Our Post-Christian Era* (New York: George Brazillier, 1961), xxxii.

11. Paul Van Buren, *The Secular Meaning of the Gospel* (New York: Macmillan, 1963), 198.

12. William Hamilton, "From Prufrock to Ringo," in Thomas Altizer and William Hamilton, *Radical Theology and the Death of God* (Indianapolis: Bobbs-Merrill, 1966), 160.

13. Robert Ellwood, *The Sixties Spiritual Awakening* (New Brunswick, N.J.: Rutgers University Press, 1994), 133.

14. John Cogley, "God Is Dead Debate Widens," *New York Times*, January 9, 1966.

15. James H. Johnson of AAAA, San Diego, letter to the editor, *Time*, April 22, 1966, 9.

16. Emil Criscitiello, letter to the editor, *Time*, April 15, 1966, 13.

17. Ellsworth, Colonel R., (Ret.) U.S. Army, letter to the editor, *Time*, April 29, 1966, 19.

18. Walter Rugaber, " 'God Is Dead' View Arouses College," *New York Times*, November 5, 1964, 34.

19. Billy Graham, quoted in "Toward a Hidden God," *Time*, April 8, 1966.

20. Peter Berger, *A Rumor of Angels: Modern Society and the Rediscovery of the Supernatural* (1969; reprint, New York: Anchor Doubleday, 1990), 78–79.

21. Anthony Towne, *Excerpts from the Diaries of the Late God* (New York: Harper and Row, 1968), 93, 19, 55.

22. Garry Wills, *Bare Ruined Choirs: Doubt, Prophecy, and Radical Religion* (Garden City, N.Y.: Doubleday, 1972), 15–16.

23. Richard Roesel, interview by Patrick Allitt, January 12, 2000, Covington, Georgia.

24. Ibid.

25. Robert Stone, "The Way the World Is," in Peter Occhiogrosso, ed., *Once a Catholic: Prominent Catholics and Ex-Catholics Discuss the Influence of the Church on Their Lives and Work* (Boston: Houghton Mifflin, 1987), 46.

26. Enrique Fernandez, "Metaphysical Rushes," in Occhiogrosso, *Once a Catholic*, 185.

27. Mary Gordon, "The Irish Catholic Church," in Occhiogrosso, *Once a Catholic*, 68.

28. Margaret Steinfels, interview by Patrick Allitt, March 11, 2000, Notre Dame.

29. Karen Stolley, interview by Patrick Allitt, January 19, 2000, Emory University, Atlanta.

30. Thomas Lanigan Schmidt, "Incarnation and Art," in Occhiogrosso, *Once a Catholic*, 236.

31. Christopher Buckley, "God and Man at the Yale Club," in Occhiogrosso, *Once a Catholic*, 236.

32. Eve Davis, interview by Patrick Allitt, January 17, 2000, Emory University, Atlanta.

33. Stephen Dubner, *Turbulent Souls* (New York: Bard Books, 1999), 121.

5. Shaking the Foundations: 1963–1970

1. Susman, Goldberg, and Greenberg, quoted in Myrna Katz Frommer and Harvey Frommer, eds., *Growing Up Jewish in America* (New York: Harcourt Brace, 1995), 122–23.

2. Nathan Glazer, *American Judaism*, 2nd ed., rev. (Chicago: University of Chicago Press, 1972), 172–73.

3. Philip Roth, "The Facts: A Novelist's Autobiography," in Jay David, ed., *Growing Up Jewish* (New York: William Morrow, 1996), 102.

4. Frommer and Frommer, *Growing Up Jewish in America*, 86–87.

5. Rachel Shilsky, quoted in James McBride, *The Color of Water* (New York: Riverhead, 1996), 81.

6. Leonard Dinnerstein, *Antisemitism in America* (New York: Oxford University Press, 1994), 194.

7. Goldman, quoted in Frommer and Frommer, *Growing Up Jewish in America*, 87.

8. Ibid., 73.

9. Quoted in Abraham J. Karp, *Jewish Continuity in America: Creative Survival in a Free Society* (Tuscaloosa: University of Alabama Press, 1998), 244.

10. Elizabeth Ehrlich, *Miriam's Kitchen* (1997; reprint, New York: Penguin, 1998), 178–79.

11. Glazer, *American Judaism*, 134.

12. Dinnerstein, *Antisemitism in America*, 166–67.

13. Frommer and Frommer, *Growing Up Jewish in America*, 106.

14. Dinnerstein, *Antisemitism in America*, 211.

15. Chaim Potok, *The Chosen* (New York: Fawcett, Crest, 1967), 187.

16. Quoted in Robert Ellwood, *The Sixties Spiritual Awakening* (New Brunswick, N.J.: Rutgers University Press, 1994), 244.

17. Samuel Heilman, *Portrait of American Jews* (Seattle: University of Washington Press, 1995), 62.

18. Michael Berger, interview by Patrick Allitt, March 15, 2000, Emory University, Atlanta.

19. Heilman, *Portrait of American Jews*, 72.

20. Chaim Potok, *My Name Is Asher Lev* (New York: Fawcett Columbine, 1972), 172.

21. Andrew Leroy Pratt, "Religious Faith and Civil Religion: Evangelical Responses to the Vietnam War, 1964–1973" (Ph.D. diss., Southern Baptist Theological Seminary, 1988), 167n.

22. Cdr. Herbert L. Bergsma, *Chaplains with Marines in Vietnam, 1962–1971* (Washington, D.C.: History and Museums Division, U.S. Marine Corps, 1985), 47.

23. William Sloane Coffin, *Once to Every Man: A Memoir* (New York: Atheneum, 1977), 224.

24. Berrigan, quoted in John Cooney, *The American Pope: The Life and Times of Francis Cardinal Spellman* (New York: Times Books, 1984), 287.

25. David Garrow, *Bearing the Cross: Martin Luther King, Jr. and the Southern Christian Leadership Conference* (1986; reprint, New York: Vintage, 1988), 552–53.

26. Bevel, quoted in Ellwood, *The Sixties Spiritual Awakening*, 205.

27. Daniel Berrigan, *To Dwell in Peace* (San Francisco: Harper and Row, 1987), 221.

28. Rice, quoted in Pratt, "Religious Faith and Civil Religion," 169n.

29. Bergsma, *Chaplains with Marines in Vietnam*, 162.

30. "A Symbolic Sanctuary," in Donald R. Cutler, ed., *The Religious Situation, 1969* (Boston: Beacon, 1969), 518.

31. Ray Abrams, *Preachers Present Arms* (Scottdale, Pa.: Herald, 1969), 287.

32. Zoller, quoted in Bergsma, *Chaplains with Marines in Vietnam*, 193.

33. Kathleen Joyce, interview by Patrick Allitt, January 5, 2000, Chicago.

34. Charles Curran, quoted in Patrick Allitt, *Catholic Intellectuals and Conservative Politics in America, 1950–1985* (Ithaca, N.Y.: Cornell University Press, 1993), 174–75.

35. National Conference of Black Churchmen, "Black Power Statement," July 31, 1966, in Gayraud Wilmore and James H. Cone, eds., *Black Theology: A Documentary History, 1966–1979* (Maryknoll, N.Y.: Orbis, 1979), 24.

36. Vincent Harding, "Black Power and the American Christ," in Wilmore and Cone, *Black Theology*, 41.

37. Albert Cleage, *The Black Messiah* (New York: Sheed and Ward, 1968), 3.

38. James Forman, "The Black Manifesto," in Wilmore and Cone, *Black Theology*, 84.

39. "Will the Black Manifesto Help Blacks?" editorial, *Christian Century* 86 (May 21, 1969): 701.

40. "James Forman's Black Manifesto," editorial, *America* 120 (May 24, 1969): 605.

41. James Cone, "The White Church and Black Power," from his *Black Theology and Black Power* (1969), reprinted in Wilmore and Cone, *Black Theology*, 117.

42. Gayraud Wilmore, "Introduction to Part II," in Wilmore and Cone, *Black Theology*, 78.

43. James Cone, quoted in Garry Dorrien, *Soul in Society: The Making and Renewal of Social Christianity* (Minneapolis: Fortress, 1995), 240.

44. James Cone, A *Black Theology of Liberation* (Philadelphia: Lippincott, 1970), 59–60.

6. Alternative Religious Worlds: 1967–1982

1. J. Gordon Melton, Jerome Clark, and Aidan A. Kelly, *New Age Almanac* (New York: Visible Ink, 1991), 136.

2. Leon Festinger, Henry W. Riecken, and Stanley Schachler, *When Prophecy Fails: A Social and Psychological Study of a Modern Group That Predicted the Destruction of the World* (1956; reprint, New York: Harper, 1964), 168.

3. Alison Lurie, *Imaginary Friends* (1967; reprint, New York: Avon, 1968), 18.

4. Norman Mailer, *Of a Fire on the Moon* (New York: Little Brown/Plume, 1970), 316.

5. Borman, quoted in Phil Long and Martin Merzer, "Moon Cast a Spell on Astronauts," *Bergen (N.J.) Record,* July 21, 1994, A24.

6. Ibid.

7. Roger Shinn, "Apollo as Ritual," *Christianity and Crisis* 29 (August 4, 1969): 223.

8. David Kucharsky, "The Lunar Landing," *Christianity Today* 13 (August 1, 1969): 996.

9. "Our Foothold in the Heavens," editorial, *Christianity Today* 13 (August 22, 1969): 1030–31.

10. Zeynep Almedar, "Going to the Mountain," *Washington Post,* August 13, 1986, C3.

11. Edgar Mitchell and Dwight Williams, *The Way of the Explorer: An Apollo Astronaut's Journey Through the Material and Mystical Worlds* (New York: Putnam, 1996), 3–4.

12. Carl J. Schneider and Dorothy Schneider, *In Their Own Right: The History of American Clergywomen* (New York: Crossroad, 1997), 190.

13. Allin, quoted in Norene Carter, "The Episcopalian Story," in Rosemary Ruether and Eleanor McLaughlin, eds., *Women of Spirit: Female Leadership in the Jewish and Christian Traditions,* 365 (New York: Simon and Schuster/Touchstone, 1979).

14. Ellen Umansky, "Women in Judaism: From the Reform Movement to Contemporary Jewish Religious Feminism," in Ruether and McLaughlin, *Women of Spirit,* 335.

15. Kelley Raab, *When Women Become Priests: The Catholic Women's Ordination Debate* (New York: Columbia University Press, 2000), 2.

16. Joy Charlton, quoted in Jackson Carroll, Barbara Hargrove, and Adair Lummis, *Women of the Cloth: A New Opportunity for the Church* (San Francisco: Harper and Row, 1983), 12.

17. Quoted in Susan Hill Lindley, *You Have Stept Out of Your Place: A History of Women and Religion in America* (Louisville: Westminster/John Knox, 1996), 362.

18. Quoted in Rosemary Ruether, "Entering the Sanctuary: The Roman Catholic Story," in Ruether and McLaughlin, *Women of Spirit,* 375.

19. Rosemary Ruether, "Christian Feminist Theology," in Yvonne Y. Haddad and John L. Esposito, eds., *Daughters of Abraham: Feminist Thought in Judaism, Christianity, and Islam,* 66–67 (Gainesville: University of Florida Press, 2001).

20. Rosemary Ruether, *Sexism and God Talk* (Boston: Beacon, 1983), 136.

21. Phyllis Trible, *God and the Rhetoric of Sexuality* (Philadelphia: Fortress, 1978), 98–99.

22. Phyllis Trible, "Feminist Hermeneutics and Biblical Studies," in Ann Loades, ed., *Feminist Theology: A Reader*, 25 (Louisville: Westminster/John Knox, 1990).

23. Carol P. Christ and Judith Plaskow, eds., *Weaving the Visions: New Patterns in Feminist Spirituality* (San Francisco: Harper and Row, 1989), 2.

24. Alice Walker, "God Is Inside You and Inside Everybody Else," in ibid., 102–3.

25. Mary Daly, *Beyond God the Father: Toward a Philosophy of Women's Liberation* (1973; reprint, Boston: Beacon, 1985), 195.

26. Mary Daly, *Gyn-Ecology* (Boston: Beacon, 1978), 7.

27. Charlene Spretnak, quoted in Anne M. Clifford, *Introducing Feminist Theology* (Maryknoll, N.Y.: Orbis, 2001), 235.

28. Starhawk, *The Spiral Dance: A Rebirth of the Ancient Religion of the Great Goddess* (San Francisco: Harper and Row, 1979), 4–5.

29. Carol Christ, "Rethinking Theology and Nature," in Christ and Plaskow, *Weaving the Visions*, 322–23.

30. Carol Christ, *The Laughter of Aphrodite: Reflections on a Journey to the Goddess* (San Francisco: Harper and Row, 1987), 188.

31. Aldous Huxley, quoted in Monica Furlong, *Zen Effects: The Life of Alan Watts* (Boston: Houghton Mifflin, 1986), 163.

32. Michael Novak, "The New Relativism in American Theology," in Donald Cutler, ed., *The Religious Situation, 1968*, 205–6 (Boston: Beacon, 1968). See also, in the same volume, Huston Smith's "Secularization and the Sacred: The Contemporary Scene," 583–600, which includes a survey of the resacralization of a secular world by the hippies.

33. Hinckle, quoted in Robert Ellwood, *The Sixties Spiritual Awakening* (New Brunswick, N.J.: Rutgers University Press, 1994), 193.

34. Arthur Blessitt, *Life's Greatest Trip* (Waco, Tex.: Word Books, 1970), 21–22.

35. Arthur Blessitt, *Turned On to Jesus* (New York: Hawthorn, 1971), 17.

36. Quoted in Roger C. Palms, *The Jesus Kids* (Valley Forge, Pa.: Judson, 1971), 31.

37. Sparks, quoted in Ronald M. Enroth, Edward E. Erickson Jr., and C. Breckinridge Peters, *The Jesus People: Old-Time Religion in the Age of Aquarius* (Grand Rapids, Mich.: Eerdman's, 1972), 110. On the work and life of the WCLF, see also Jack Sparks, *God's Forever Family* (Grand Rapids, Mich.: Zondervan, 1974).

38. John R. Hall, *Gone from the Promised Land: Jonestown in American Cultural History* (New Brunswick, N.J.: Transaction, 1987), 299.

39. Jacob Needleman, *The New Religions: The Teachings of the East* (1970; reprint, New York: Pocket Books, 1972), 133.

40. Harvey Cox, *Turning East: The Promise and the Peril of the New Orientalism* (New York: Simon and Schuster, 1977), 11.

41. Jack Kerouac, *The Dharma Bums* (1958; reprint, New York: Penguin, 1976), 97–98.

42. Saul Levine, "Life in the Cults," in Marc Galanter, ed., *Cults and New Religious Movements*, 102 (Washington D.C.: American Psychiatric Association, 1989).

43. Cox, *Turning East*, 141.

7. Evangelicals and Politics: 1976–1990

1. Jimmy Carter, *Keeping Faith: Memoirs of a President* (New York: Bantam, 1982), 20.

2. Peter G. Bourne, *Jimmy Carter: A Comprehensive Biography from Plains to Post-Presidency* (New York: Lisa Drew/Scribner, 1997), 178.

3. Ibid., 347.

4. Carter, *Keeping Faith*, 274.

5. Frances Fitzgerald, *Cities on a Hill: A Journey Through Contemporary American Cultures* (New York: Simon and Schuster, 1986), 129.

6. Walter Capps, *The New Religious Right: Piety, Patriotism, and Politics* (Columbia: University of South Carolina Press, 1990), 31.

7. Ibid., 29.

8. Weyrich, quoted in James Moffett, *Storm in the Mountains: A Case Study of Censorship, Conflict, and Consciousness* (Carbondale: Southern Illinois University Press, 1988), 191.

9. Bailey Smith, quoted in Mark Silk, *Spiritual Politics: Religion and America Since World War II* (New York: Simon and Schuster, 1988), 160.

10. Bob Jones, quoted in Capps, *The New Religious Right*, 99.

11. Ezra Graley, quoted in Moffett, *Storm in the Mountains*, 65.

12. President Reagan, quoted in Paul Boyer, *When Time Shall Be No More: Prophecy Belief in Modern American Culture* (Cambridge, Mass.: Belknap Press/Harvard University Press, 1992), 142.

13. Randall Balmer, *Mine Eyes Have Seen the Glory: A Journey Into the Evangelical Subculture in America* (New York: Oxford University Press, 1989), 58.

14. Francis Schaeffer, *The Great Evangelical Disaster* (Westchester, Ill.: Crossway, 1984), 23.

15. Francis Schaeffer, A Christian Manifesto (Westchester, Ill.: Crossway, 1981), 61–62.

16. Quoted in Daniel C. Maguire, *Sacred Choices: The Right to Contraception and Abortion in Ten World Religions* (Minneapolis: Fortress, 2001), 128.

17. J. Gordon Melton, ed., *The Churches Speak on Abortion* (Detroit: Gale, 1989), 168.

18. Kristin Luker, *Abortion and the Politics of Motherhood* (Berkeley: University of California Press, 1984), 196–97.

19. Joan Andrews, quoted in Mary Meehan, "Joan Andrews and Friends," *Human Life Review* 14 (Spring 1988): 9.

20. Beverly LaHaye, quoted in Susan Faludi, *Backlash: The Undeclared War Against American Women* (New York: Crown, 1991), 251.

21. Balmer, *Mine Eyes Have Seen the Glory*, 120.

22. Stephen Clark, *Man and Woman in Christ* (Ann Arbor, Mich.: Servant Press, 1980), 604.

23. Hindson, quoted in Fitzgerald, *Cities on a Hill*, 140.

24. Blu Greenberg, *On Women and Judaism: A View from Tradition* (Philadelphia: Publication Society of America, 1981), 6.

25. Lis Harris, *Holy Days: The World of a Hasidic Family* (New York: Summit, 1985), 132.

8. The Christian Quest for Justice and Wisdom: 1980–1995

1. Bishop John Warren, quoted in Donald L. Davidson, *Nuclear Weapons and the American Churches: Ethical Positions on Modern Warfare* (Boulder, Col.: Westview, 1983), 124.

2. Ann Crittenden, *Sanctuary: A Story of American Conscience and the Law in Collision* (New York: Weidenfeld and Nicolson, 1988), 15.

3. Robert Tomsho, *The American Sanctuary Movement* (Austin: Texas Monthly Press, 1987), 31.

4. Fife, quoted in Hilary Cunningham, *God and Caesar at the Rio Grande: Sanctuary and the Politics of Religion* (Minneapolis: University of Minnesota Press, 1995), 112.

5. Elliott Abrams, "Contending Views of the Future of Central America," in Maria H. Thomas, ed., *Sanctuary: Challenge to the Churches*, 51 (Washington, D.C.: Institute on Religion and Democracy, 1986).

6. Chicago Religious Task Force, quoted in Kerry Ptacek, "The Theological and Political Aspects of Sanctuary," in Thomas, *Sanctuary*, 75.

7. Sister Julie Sheatzley, C.S.J., quoted in Renny Golden, "Sanctuary and Women," *Journal of Feminist Studies in Religion* 2 (Spring 1986): 144.

8. Cunningham, *God and Caesar at the Rio Grande*, 52–53.

9. Crittenden, *Sanctuary*, 286.

10. Gish, quoted in Raymond Eve and Francis B. Harrold, *The Creationist Movement in Modern America* (Boston: Twayne, 1991), 1.

11. Frances Fitzgerald, *Cities on a Hill: A Journey Through Contemporary American Cultures* (New York: Simon and Schuster, 1986), 198.

12. James Moffett, *Storm in the Mountains: A Case Study of Censorship, Conflict, and Consciousness* (Carbondale: Southern Illinois University Press, 1988), 16.

13. Christine Stolba to Patrick Allitt, January 18, 2000.

14. Ibid.

15. Ibid.

16. Catherine Remick to Patrick Allitt, January 18, 2000.

17. Susan D. Rose, *Keeping Them Out of the Hands of Satan: Evangelical Schooling in America* (New York: Routledge, 1988), 42.

18. Quoted in Warren A. Nord, *Religion and American Education: Rethinking a National Dilemma* (Chapel Hill: University of North Carolina Press, 1995), 363.

19. Dean Merrill, "Schooling at Mother's Knee: Can It Compete?" *Christianity Today* 27 (September 2, 1983): 17.

20. Ibid., 19.

21. Mitchell Stevens, *Kingdom of Children: Culture and Controversy in the Homeschooling Movement* (Princeton, N.J.: Princeton University Press, 2001), 12.

9. Profits, Profligates, and Prophets: 1987–1995

1. Jim Bakker, quoted in Gary Tidwell, *Anatomy of a Fraud: Inside the Finances of the PTL Ministries* (New York: Wiley, 1993), 18.

2. Quentin Schultze, *Televangelism and American Culture: The Business of Popular Religion* (Grand Rapids, Mich.: Baker Book House, 1991), 114.

3. Falwell, quoted in Walter Capps, *The New Religious Right: Piety, Patriotism, and Politics* (Columbia: University of South Carolina Press, 1994), 137.

4. Ibid., 153–54.

5. Lawrence Wright, *Saints and Sinners* (New York: Knopf, 1993), 52.

6. "Roberts Drops Dying Fund Pitch," *Bergen (N.J.) Record*, January 16, 1987, A5.

7. Victoria Sackett, "Oral Roberts Bucks Eternity," *New York Times*, March 30, 1987, A19.

8. Jerry Horner, quoted in Capps, *The New Religious Right*, 165.

9. Randall Balmer, *Mine Eyes Have Seen the Glory: A Journey Into the Evangelical Subculture in America* (New York: Oxford University Press, 1989), 135.

10. Capps, *The New Religious Right*, 176.

11. George Bush Sr., quoted in Garry Wills, *Under God: Religion and American Politics* (New York: Simon and Schuster, 1990), 80.

12. Michael McTighe, "Jesse Jackson and the Dilemmas of a Prophet in Politics," *Journal of Church and State* 32 (Summer 1990): 594.

13. Ibid., 585.

14. Jackson, quoted in Wills, *Under God*, 242–43.

15. Ellen Goodman, "Goodbye, Moral Majority," *Bergen (N.J.) Record*, June 18, 1989, 2.

16. Warith Deen Muhammad, quoted in Mattias Gardell, "The Sun of Islam Will Rise in the West," in Y. Y. Haddad and Jane I. Smith, eds., *Muslim Communities in North America*, 23 (Albany, N.Y.: SUNY Press, 1994).

17. Michael Kotzin, "Louis Farrakhan's Anti-Semitism: A Look at the Record," *Christian Century* 111 (March 2, 1994): 224–26.

18. Gardell, "The Sun of Islam Will Rise in the West," 28.

19. Ali S. Asani, "Allah at Harvard," in Steven Barboza, ed., *American Jihad: Islam After Malcolm X*, 41 (New York: Doubleday, 1994).

20. Ron Kelley, "Muslims in Los Angeles," in Haddad and Smith, *Muslim Communities in North America*, 137.

21. Quoted in Asma Gull Hasan, *American Muslims: The New Generation* (New York: Continuum, 2000), 44.

22. Ibid., 169.

23. Kambiz GhaneaBassiri, *Competing Visions of Islam in the United States* (Westport, Conn.: Greenwood, 1988), 44.

24. Hasan, *American Muslims*, 46–47.

25. Richard Wormser, *American Islam: Growing Up Muslim in America* (New York: Walker, 1994), 49.

26. Sohail Humayun Hashmi, "Accidental Muslim," in Barboza, *American Jihad*, 54.

27. Wormser, *American Islam*, 52–53.

28. Schwarzkopf, quoted in Hasan, *American Muslims*, 84.

29. Steven Barboza, "Facing Mecca," *Essence* 26 (November 1995): 106.

30. Wormser, *American Islam*, 55.

31. Hashmi, "Accidental Muslim," 59.

10. The New World Order: 1989–1999

1. Billy Graham, *Just As I Am: The Autobiography of Billy Graham* (San Francisco: HarperCollins/Zondervan, 1997), 555.

2. Kathleen McClain, "Praising the Lord at the Berlin Wall," *Bergen (N.J.) Record*, March 9, 1990, B4.

3. McInerny, quoted in Patrick Allitt, "The Bitter Victory: Catholic Conservative Intellectuals in America, 1989–1993," in Thomas Ferraro, ed., *Catholic Lives, Contemporary America*, 141 (Durham, N.C.: Duke University Press, 1997).

4. Bush, quoted in Peter Steinfels, "Beliefs," *New York Times*, February 1, 1992, A10.

5. Law, quoted in Peter Steinfels, "Cardinal Says Iraquis' Acts Prove Bush Right," *New York Times*, January 26, 1991, A9.

6. Coffin, quoted in M. P. McQueen, "Old War Foes, New Forums," *Newsday*, January 7, 1991, 7.

7. Jesse Jackson, "War Must Not Deter Search for Peace," *Newsday*, January 21, 1991, 76.

8. Richard Higgins, "Muslims Fear a Tarnish on Their Faith," *Boston Globe*, January 19, 1991, 10.

9. Scott, quoted in Associated Press, "Confrontation in the Gulf," *New York Times*, December 28, 1990, A7.

10. Ari Goldman, Religion Notes, *New York Times*, December 5, 1992, A26.

11. Michael Barkun, "Reflections After Waco: Millennialists and the State," *Christian Century* 110 (June 2–9, 1993): 597.

12. James Risen and Judy L. Thomas, *Wrath of Angels: The American Abortion War* (New York: Basic, 1998), 344.

13. Barry Bearak, "Eyes on Glory: Pied Pipers of Heaven's Gate," *New York Times*, April 28, 1997, A1, B8–B10.

14. Heaven's Gate Web site, excerpted at www.vcu.edu/hasweb/psy/psy633/heaven2.htm.

15. Ibid.

16. Gary Snyder, quoted in Roderick Nash, *The Rights of Nature* (Madison: University of Wisconsin Press, 1989), 115.

17. David Ortman, quoted in Susan Gilmore, "A Spiritual Look at Ecology," *Seattle Times*, October 20, 1990, C9.

18. Russell Chandler, "Religions Join the Crusade to Save Earth from Pollution," *Los Angeles Times*, April 19, 1990, A3.

19. Patrick Allitt, "American Catholics and the Environment," *Catholic Historical Review* 84 (April 1998): 277.

20. Gorman, quoted in Jill Senschul, "Blessing Creatures Great and Small," *Bergen (N.J.) Record*, September 24, 1989, T1.

21. Richard C. Austin, "Preaching to Environmental Crisis," *Journal for Preachers* 15 (Decatur, Ga.: Pentecost, 1992), Web.

22. Harry Kissileff, "Finding God Through the Wonders of Nature," *Bergen (N.J.) Record*, June 12, 1997, H9.

23. Smart, quoted in Heather Dewar, "Putting Faith in the Environmental Fight," *Albany (N.Y.) Times Union*, April 14, 1996, G7.

24. Gorman, quoted in Mariko Thompson, "Interfaith Movement Aims to Protect God's Creation," *Quincy (Mass.) Patriot Ledger*, April 26, 1997, 28.

25. David Toolan, *At Home in the Cosmos* (Maryknoll, N.Y.: Orbis, 2001), 210.

26. Audrey Shenandoah, quoted in Ari Goldman, "Religions and Environment, Focus on a Worldly Concern," *New York Times*, September 17, 1990, A16.

27. George Cornell, "Blight Knows No Border, Clan Leader Says," *Los Angeles Times*, January 13, 1990, F20.

28. Sallie McFague, *The Body of God: An Ecological Theology* (Minneapolis: Fortress, 1993), vii.

29. Thomas Berry, The Dream of the Earth (San Francisco: Sierra Club Books, 1988), x, 215.

30. Berry, quoted in Toolan, *At Home in the Cosmos*, 37–38.

31. Kevin Delaney, "Saving Earth's Soul," *Seattle Post-Intelligencer*, April 21, 1991, D3.

32. Lawrence Wright, "Matthew Fox Rolls Away the Stone," in his *Saints and Sinners*, 209 (New York: Knopf, 1993).

33. Tim Carman, "Dance Fervor," *Houston Press*, December 23, 1999.

34. LeBlanc, quoted in ibid.

35. Robert B. Fowler, *The Greening of Protestant Thought* (Chapel Hill: University of North Carolina Press, 1995), 43.

36. Heather Dewar, "Putting Faith in the Environmental Fight," *Albany (N.Y.) Times Union*, April 14, 1996, G7.

37. Le Quire, quoted in Steve Kloehn, "Evangelicals Embracing the Environment," *Bergen (N.J.) Record*, March 27, 1997, H1.

38. Michael Barkey, ed., *Environmental Stewardship in the Judeo-Christian Tradition: Jewish, Catholic, and Protestant Wisdom on the Environment* (Grand Rapids, Mich.: Acton Institute, 2000), xiv.

39. George Cornell, "Today's Megachurches Able to Offer Younger Christians More Programs," *Memphis Commercial Appeal*, January 5, 1991, A10.

40. Angela Winter, "Young Adults Make Leap of Faith to Nondenominational Megachurches," *Baltimore Sun*, March 27, 1994, 1K.

41. Gustav Niebuhr, "Large Suburban Sanctuaries Are Using Country Music, Videos, and Whatever Else It Takes to Reach the Unchurched Masses," *Lakeland (Fla.) Ledger*, April 22, 1995, 1C.

42. Winter, "Young Adults Make Leap of Faith."

43. Dolly Patterson, "Churches and the Essential Few," *St. Petersburg Times*, August 31, 1991, 2E.

44. Hybels, quoted in Teresa Mask, "25 Years and Growing, Willow Creek," *Chicago Daily Herald*, October 1, 2000, 1.

45. New York Times News Service, "What Is Our Business?" *Wilmington Star-News*, April 18, 1995, 1A.

46. John Wilson, "Not Just Another Megachurch," *Christianity Today*, December 4, 2000 (Web).

47. Robert Kerr, "Rev. Rogers Rolls On," *Memphis Commercial Appeal*, September 29, 1991, E1.

11. Fears, Threats, and Promises: 1990–2000

1. Sobran, quoted in Patrick Allitt, *Catholic Intellectuals and Conservative Politics in America: 1950–1985* (Ithaca, N.Y.: Cornell University Press, 1993), 195.

2. David Shallenberger, *Reclaiming the Spirit: Gay Men and Lesbians Come to Terms with Religion* (New Brunswick, N.J.: Rutgers University Press, 1998), 11.

3. Michael Warner, "Tongues Untied: Memoirs of a Pentecostal Boyhood," in Gary D. Comstock and Susan E. Henking, eds., *Que(e)rying Religion: A Critical Anthology*, 228 (New York: Continuum, 1997).

4. Andrew Sullivan, "Virtually Normal," in Thomas J. Ferraro, ed., *Catholic Lives, Contemporary America*, 173–74 (Durham, N.C.: Duke University Press, 1997).

5. Quoted in Gary D. Comstock, *Unrepentant, Self-Affirming, Practicing: Lesbian/Bisexual/Gay People Within Organized Religion* (New York: Continuum, 1996), 53.

6. Toby Johnson, *Gay Spirituality: The Role of Gay Identity in the Transformation of Human Consciousness* (New York: Alyson Books, 2000), 50–51.

7. Saul M. Olyan, "And with a Male You Shall Not Lie the Lying Down of a Woman," in Comstock and Henking, *Que(e)rying Religion*, 414.

8. L. William Countryman, quoted in L. R. Holben, *What Christians Think About Homosexuality: Six Representative Viewpoints* (North Richland Hills, Tex.: Bibal Press, 1999), 235.

9. Robert Goss, *Jesus Acted Up: A Gay and Lesbian Manifesto* (San Francisco: HarperSanFrancisco, 1993), 85.

10. Quoted in Shawn Zeller, "Finding Their Religion," *National Journal* 32 (January 1, 2000), 52.

11. Harold Lindsell, quoted in Holben, *What Christians Think About Homosexuality*, 42.

12. "Walking in Truth," editorial, *Christianity Today* 44 (September 4, 2000): 46–47.

13. Harry Koslovsky, quoted in "Survey: Would You Feel Comfortable as a Congregant in the Synagogue of a Gay Rabbi?" *Moment* 24 (October 1999): 33.

14. Falwell, quoted in Mark Kowalewski, "Religious Constructions of the AIDS Crisis," in Comstock and Henking, *Que(e)rying Religion*, 367.

15. Kim Lawton, "Clinton Signs Law Backing Heterosexual Marriage," *Christianity Today* 40 (October 28, 1996): 80.

16. Spong, quoted in Ari Goldman, "Was St. Paul Gay? Claim Stirs Fury," *New York Times*, February 2, 1991, A27.

17. Righter, quoted in David Wilkison, "Congregation Savors End of Heresy Case," *Bergen (N.J.) Record*, May 20, 1996, A3.

18. Comstock, *Unrepentant, Self-Affirming, Practicing*, 14.

19. Rod Dreher, "The Gay Question," *National Review* 54 (April 22, 2002): 35.

20. Charles Morris, *American Catholic* (New York: Random House/Times Books, 1997), 379.

21. Pat Long, "Pullen Memorial Baptist Church: An Inside Look at a Journey of Affirmation," in Comstock and Henking, *Que(e)rying Religion*, 219.

22. Laura Olson and Wendy Cadge, "Talking About Homosexuality: The Views of Mainline Protestant Clergy," *Journal for the Scientific Study of Religion* 41 (Winter 2002), 154.

23. Holben, *What Christians Think*, 226–27.

24. Quoted in Comstock, *Unrepentant, Self-Affirming, Practicing*, 51.

25. Katherine Rosman, "Mormon Family Values," *The Nation* 274 (February 25, 2002): 18–21.

26. Shawn Zeller, "Gay Group Seeks Denied Rights," *National Journal* 32 (December 2, 2000): 3754–55.

27. Shallenberger, *Reclaiming the Spirit*, 12.

28. Richard Goldstein, "Fight Club," *Village Voice*, May 2, 2000, 47.

29. Ann Scales, "Weekend Gay Rights March Doesn't Sit Well with Some Grass Roots Activists," *Boston Globe*, April 29, 2000, A3.

30. Gustav Niebuhr, "Men Crowd Stadiums to Fulfill Their Souls," *New York Times*, August 6, 1995, A1.

31. Bruce Weber, "Football: Pep Talks with a Higher Purpose," *New York Times*, June 20, 1997, B9.

32. Gustav Niebuhr, "Religious Rally in Capital Is Test of Faith," *New York Times*, October 3, 1997, A1.

33. Laurie Goodstein, "For Christian Men's Group, Racial Harmony Starts at the Local Level," *New York Times*, September 29, 1997, A12.

34. Patricia Ireland, "A Look at Promise Keepers," *Washington Post*, September 7, 1997, C3.

35. Maureen Dowd, "Promises, Promises, Promises," *New York Times*, October 4, 1997, A15.

36. Douglas DeCelle, "Among the Promise Keepers: A Pastor's Reflections," *Christian Century* 113 (July 3–10, 1996): 695–96.

37. McCartney, quoted in "Standing in the Mall," *Christian Century* 114 (October 22, 1997): 934.

38. Mary Stewart Van Leeuwen, "Mixed Messages on the Mall," *Christian Century* 114 (October 22, 1997): 932–34.

39. "Standing in the Mall," 935.

40. Michael Janofsky, "Women, on the Rally's Edge, Mirror Divided View of Group," *New York Times*, October 5, 1997, A24.

41. Bruce Weber, "Pep Talks with a Higher Purpose."

42. Ross, quoted in Frank Rich, "Thank God I'm a Man," *New York Times*, September 25, 1996, A21.

43. Gustav Niebuhr, "Enthusiasts and Critics for Evangelical Men's Group," *New York Times*, August 2, 1997, A25.

44. Gustav Niebuhr, "Promise Keepers Still Draws Crowds," *New York Times*, May 21, 2001, A12.

45. Adam Pertman, "Time Has Come for Millennium Center," *Boston Globe*, January 2, 1999, A1.

46. Alex Heard and Peter Klebnikov, "Apocalypse Now. No, Really. Now!" *New York Times*, December 27, 1998, 6:41.

47. Gustav Niebuhr, "Church Seeks to Allay Fears of New Millennium," *New York Times*, November 7, 1998, A12.

48. Knight-Tribune News Service, "Some Cuban Exiles See Boy in Savior Role," *Jacksonville Florida Times-Union*, January 17, 2000, A3.

49. Madeline Baro Diaz, "Messenger of God?" Associated Press State and Local Wire, January 28, 2000.

50. Twila Decker, "The Miracle Child," *St. Petersburg Times*, June 14, 2000, 1D.

12. The New Millennium: 2001

1. Mae M. Cheng, "Where Faith Is Needed," *Newsday*, September 29, 2001, A2.

2. Gayle White, "Drawing on Faith," *Atlanta Journal-Constitution*, September 12, 2001, C1.

3. Associated Press, "Religion Sees Revival After Terrorist Attacks," September 23, 2001.

4. Julia Malone, "Need for Spiritual Care Won't End Soon," *Atlanta Journal-Constitution*, November 28, 2001, A8.

5. Richard Dujardin, "Where Was God When the Towers Came Down?" *Providence Journal-Bulletin*, November 3, 2001, D1.

6. John F. Harris, "God Gave U.S. What We Deserve, Falwell Says," *Washington Post*, September 14, 2001, C3.

7. Bruce Nolan, "America Blessed? Or Paradise Lost?" *New Orleans Times Picayune*, September 22, 2001, 4.

8. Sharon Tubbs, "Apocalypse Seen in Recent Events," *St. Petersburg Times*, September 14, 2001, A22.

9. Mae M. Cheng, "America's Ordeal: Cross Brings Spiritual Lift to Workers," *Newsday*, October 5 2001, A46.

10. Mike Kelly, "Hundreds Toil at Task Both Sacred and Hellish," *Bergen (N.J.) Record*, October 14, 2001, 1.

11. David Abel, "A Chapel Spared Stirs Talk of Miracle," *Boston Globe*, September 26, 2001, A12.

12. Wolf, quoted in Richard Dujardin, "Visit to Ground Zero Moves, Inspires Bishop," *Providence Journal-Bulletin*, October 13, 2001, A7.

13. Billy Graham, "The Mystery of Evil," in Editors of Beliefnet, eds., *From the Ashes: A Spiritual Response to the Attack on America*, 109 (New York: Rodale, 2001).

14. Nedra Rhone, "Somber Beginning to Jewish New Year," *Newsday*, September 16, 2001, W19.

15. Bishop T. D. Jakes, "Awake from Your Slumber" in Editors of Beliefnet, *From the Ashes*, 3–4.

16. Associated Press, "After the Attacks," *New York Times*, September 14, 2001, A15.

17. Jay Maeder, "All Over the City, Healing Sought Through Prayer," *New York Daily News*, September 17, 2001, 40.

18. Merri Rosenberg, "Private Crises of Conscience," *New York Times*, December 30, 2001, 14:5.

19. Charles Austin, "Pacifists Know They Go Against the Grain," *Bergen (N.J.) Record*, September 23, 2001, A16.

20. Rosenberg, "Private Crises of Conscience."

21. Halimah Abdullah, "Sikhs Face Attacks, Discrimination," *Newsday*, September 24, 2001, A31.

22. Bob Heisler, "Memorial at Stadium Joins All Faiths," *New York Daily News*, September 24, 2001, 8.

23. Marie Franklin, "Classrooms Cope with Terror's Toll," *Boston Globe*, September 23, 2001, B13.

24. Dana Milbank and Emily Wax, "Bush Visits Mosque," *Washington Post*, September 18, 2001, A1.

25. James Beverley, "Is Islam a Religion of Peace?" *Christianity Today* 46 (January 7, 2002): 32–40.

26. "Baptist Group Shuns Call for Shared Worship," *Charleston (W. Va.) Gazette*, November 18, 2001, P4.

27. Charles Colson, "Drawing the Battle Lines," *Christianity Today* 46 (January 7, 2002), 80.

28. Clifford Longley, *Chosen People* (London: Hodder and Stoughton, 2002), 20–21.

Bibliography

Only direct quotations have been end-noted in the text. On many of the issues discussed there is, however, a vast literature by historians, sociologists, anthropologists, theologians, scholars of religion, and journalists. The following bibliography is meant to be selective rather than exhaustive, usually providing a few suggestions (the most readable and accessible) on each theme. For the post-1980 chapters, especially in creating a narrative, I was increasingly dependent on periodical literature and newspaper accounts.

General

There are, so far as I know, no other books on American religious history for the years 1945–2001, though there are many devoted to American religious history as a whole. Sydney Ahlstrom's big classic, *A Religious History of the American People* (New Haven, Conn.: Yale University Press, 1972), is probably still the most comprehensive. Mark Noll's *A History of Christianity in the United States and Canada* (Grand Rapids, Mich.: Eerdman's, 1992) is shorter and more readable but does not cover the proliferation of non-Christian religions. Martin Marty's *Pilgrims in Their Own Land: 500 Years of Religion in America* (Boston: Little, Brown, 1984) is good and takes in more groups, as does J. Gordon Melton's *American Religions: An Illustrated History* (Santa Barbara, Calif.: ABC-CLIO, 2000). Catherine Albanese, approaching the subject as a student of religion rather than as a historian, offers a different and very useful vantage point in *America: Religion and Religions*, 2nd ed. (Belmont, Calif.: Wadsworth, 1992). Roger Finke and

Rodney Starke's *The Churching of America, 1776–1990: Winners and Losers in Our Religious Economy* (New Brunswick, N.J.: Rutgers University Press, 1992) traces long-term rises and declines in church membership and theorizes about the factors that enabled certain groups to gain power, influence, and membership. For statistics on membership and attitudes to religion, see George Gallup Jr. and Jim Castelli, *The People's Religion: American Faith in the 1990s* (New York: Macmillan, 1989). William M. Newman and Peter L. Halvorson's *Atlas of American Religion: The Denominational Era, 1776–1990* (Walnut Creek, Calif.: Altamira, 2000) maps the distribution of religious groups across the United States and shows how population concentrations have changed through the last two centuries.

Charles Lippy's *Being Religious: American Style* (Westport, Conn.: Praeger, 1994) and Bruce David Forbes and Jeffrey H. Mahan's edited volume, *Religion and Popular Culture in America* (Berkeley: University of California Press, 2000), survey the history of popular religiosity. Daniel Sack's *Whitebread Protestantism: Food and Religion in American Culture* (New York: St. Martin's, 2000) examines the relationship of food to faith, while Colleen McDannell's *Material Christianity: Religion and Popular Culture in America* (New Haven, Conn.: Yale University Press, 1995) considers the history of religious clothes and objects. A compact and user-friendly two-volume reference work is Edward Queen II, Stephen Prothero, and Gardiner Shattuck Jr., eds., *The Encyclopedia of American Religious History* (New York: Columbia University Press, 1996).

Many good religious histories cover parts of this era. See, for example, Martin Marty's *Under God, Indivisible, 1941–1960*, volume 3 of *Modern American Religion* (Chicago: University of Chicago Press, 1996); Robert Ellwood's *The Sixties Spiritual Awakening* (New Brunswick, N.J.: Rutgers University Press, 1994); Mark Silk, *Spiritual Politics: Religion and America Since World War II* (New York: Simon and Schuster, 1988); and Ferenc Szasz's *Religion in the Modern American West* (Tucson: University of Arizona Press, 2000).

I mention in the introduction a few works that influenced my ideas about the whole period. They are Robert Wuthnow, *The Restructuring of American Religion: Society and Faith Since World War II* (Princeton, N.J.: Princeton University Press, 1988); Peter Berger, *A Rumor of Angels: Modern Society and the Rediscovery of the Supernatural* (1969; reprint, New York: Anchor Doubleday, 1990); Peter Berger, *The Heretical Imperative* (Garden City, N.Y.: Anchor/Doubleday, 1979); and R. Laurence Moore, *Selling God: American Religion in the Marketplace of Culture* (New York: Oxford University Press, 1994). Moore's *Religious Outsiders and the Making of Americans* (New York: Oxford University Press, 1986) is also conceptually valuable in pointing out that being perceived as "outsiders" has always had benefits as well as drawbacks for such American religious groups as the Catholics and the Mormons.

1. Anxious Victory: 1945–1952

On World War II and religious groups, see Christopher Cross and William Arnold, *Soldiers of God: True Story of the U.S. Army Chaplains* (New York: Dutton, 1945). For early Christian reactions to Hiroshima, Nagasaki, and the Cold War nuclear standoff, see Edward L. Long, *The Christian Response to the Atomic Crisis* (Philadelphia: Westminster, 1950). On the pacifist churches, see R. L. Moellering, *Modern War and the American Churches* (New York: American Press, 1956), and Perry Bush, *Two Kingdoms, Two Loyalties: Mennonite Pacifism in Modern America* (Baltimore: Johns Hopkins University Press, 1998). Among studies of the pacifist Dorothy Day, the most insightful works are William Miller, *Dorothy Day: A Biography* (San Francisco: Harper and Row, 1982), and James Fisher, *The Catholic Counterculture in America: 1933–1962* (Chapel Hill: University of North Carolina Press, 1990).

The survey of American religious history prior to 1945 is based mainly on the general works mentioned above. On the development of fundamentalism, see in particular George Marsden, *Fundamentalism and American Culture* (New York: Oxford University Press, 1980) and his *Understanding Fundamentalism and Evangelicalism* (Grand Rapids, Mich.: Eerdman's, 1991). Good general introductions to American Catholicism are Charles Morris, *American Catholic: The Saints and Sinners Who Built America's Most Powerful Church* (New York: Random House/Times Books, 1997), and Jay P. Dolan, *The American Catholic Experience* (Garden City, N.Y.: Doubleday, 1985). Good general introductions to American Judaism can be found in Nathan Glazer, *American Judaism*, 2nd ed., rev. (Chicago: University of Chicago Press, 1972); Marc Lee Raphael, *Profiles in American Judaism: The Reform, Conservative, Orthodox, and Reconstructionist Traditions in Historical Perspective* (San Francisco: Harper and Row, 1985); and Jack Wertheimer, *A People Divided: Judaism in Contemporary America* (New York: Basic, 1993). On the idea of America as God's chosen nation, see Clifford Longley, *Chosen People* (London: Hodder and Stoughton, 2002).

On the evangelical revival of the immediate postwar years, and the emergence of Billy Graham, see Joel Carpenter, *Revive Us Again: The Reawakening of American Fundamentalism* (New York: Oxford University Press, 1997), and Billy Graham's sometimes naive but sometimes revealing autobiography, *Just As I Am* (San Francisco: HarperSanFrancisco/Zondervan, 1997). On the spiritual peace writers, see Donald Meyer, *The Positive Thinkers: Religion as Pop Psychology from Mary Baker Eddy to Oral Roberts*, rev. ed. (New York: Pantheon, 1980); Carol V. George, *God's Salesman: Norman Vincent Peale and the Power of Positive Thinking* (New York: Oxford University Press, 1993); Mark Silk, *Spiritual Politics* (on Liebman), and Mark Massa, *Catholics and American Culture* (New York: Crossroad, 1999), on Sheen. There is no substitute for reading Thomas Merton's *Seven Storey Mountain* (New York: Harcourt Brace, 1948), but numerous biographies of the famous monk are available. The most thorough is Stephen Mott, *The Seven Mountains of Thomas Merton* (Boston: Houghton Mifflin, 1984), and the most manageable is Monica Furlong, *Merton: A Biography* (San Francisco: Harper and Row, 1980).

2. Religion and Materialism: 1950–1970

On Communism and fear of Communism, see Richard M. Freid, *Nightmare in Red: The McCarthy Era in Perspective* (New York: Oxford University Press, 1990). For its effects on religious groups, especially Catholics, see Donald Crosby, *God, Church, and Flag: Senator Joseph McCarthy and the Catholic Church* (Chapel Hill: University of North Carolina Press, 1978); Thomas Kselman and Steven Avella, "Marian Piety and the Cold War in the United States," *Catholic Historical Review* 72 (1986): 403–24; and Patrick Allitt,

Catholic Intellectuals and Conservative Politics, 1950–1985 (Ithaca, N.Y.: Cornell University Press, 1993). Paul Blanshard's *Communism, Democracy, and Catholic Power* (Boston: Beacon, 1951) argues the essential similarity between Soviet and Vatican power, and was perhaps the last highbrow anti-Catholic tract in American history. Whittaker Chambers's autobiography, *Witness* (New York: Random House, 1952), brilliantly re-creates the feverish mood of the midcentury conflict over Communism and its religious overtones. On Tom Dooley, see James T. Fisher, *Dr. America: The Lives of Thomas A. Dooley, 1927–1961* (Amherst: University of Massachusetts Press, 1997).

For critical contemporaneous evaluations of the 1950s religious revival, see Peter Berger, *The Noise of Solemn Assemblies* (Garden City, N.Y.: Doubleday, 1961); Gibson Winter, *The Suburban Captivity of the Churches* (Garden City, N.Y.: Doubleday, 1961); and Albert I. Gordon, *Jews in Suburbia* (Boston: Beacon, 1959). Paul Carter provides a retrospective in *Another Part of the Fifties* (New York: Columbia University Press, 1983), as does Robert Ellwood in *1950: Crossroads of American Religious Life* (Louisville: Westminster/John Knox, 2000).

On the religious intellectuals Niebuhr, Tillich, Maritain, and Herberg, see their own extensive works, particularly Niebuhr's *Moral Man and Immoral Society* (New York: Scribner's, 1932) and *The Irony of American History* (New York: Scribner's, 1952); Tillich's *The Courage to Be* (New Haven, Conn.: Yale University Press, 1952) and *On the Boundary: An Autobiographical Sketch* (London: Collins, 1967); Maritain's *Reflections on America* (New York: Scribner's, 1958) and his *Integral Humanism: Temporal and Spiritual Problems of a New Christendom*, translated by Joseph W. Evans (1936; reprint, New York: Scribner, 1968); and Herberg's *Protestant, Catholic, Jew: An Essay in American Religious Sociology* (Garden City, N.Y.: Doubleday, 1955) and *Four Existentialist Theologians* (Garden City, N.Y.: Doubleday, 1958). On their lives, see Richard W. Fox, *Reinhold Niebuhr: A Biography* (San Franciso: Harper and Row, 1987); John H. Thomas, *Tillich* (New York: Continuum, 2000); John M. Dunaway, *Jacques Maritain* (Boston: Twayne, 1978); Deal Hudson and Matthew J. Mancini, eds., *Understanding Maritain* (Macon, Ga.: Mercer University Press, 1987); Harry Ausmus, *Will Herberg: From Right to Right* (Chapel Hill: University of North Carolina Press, 1987); John P. Diggins, *Up From Communism: Conservative Odysseys in American Intellectual History* (New York: Harper and Row, 1975); and John Murray Cuddihy, *No Offense: Civil Religion and Protestant Taste* (New York: Seabury, 1978).

On church buildings, there is not much historical (as opposed to narrowly architectural) literature. See, however, Peter Williams, *Houses of God: Region, Religion, and Architecture in the United States* (Urbana: University of Illinois Press, 1997); Albert Christ-Janer and Mary Mix Foley, eds., *Modern Church Architecture* (New York: McGraw-Hill, 1962); and George A. Lane, *Chicago Churches and Synagogues* (Chicago: Loyola University Press, 1981). For superb photographs of the most innovative church designs, see Roger G. Kennedy, *American Churches* (New York: Stewart, Tabori and Chang, 1982). Books written in the 1940s and 1950s about problems related to planning and building churches explain the obstacles a congregation needed to overcome; they include William Harrell, *Planning Better Church Buildings* (Nashville: Broadman, 1947); Martin Anderson, *Planning and Financing the New Church*, 2nd ed., rev. (Minneapolis: Augsburg, 1949); William Watkin, *Planning and Building the Mod-*

ern Church (New York: Dodge, 1951); and Katharine Morrison McClinton, *The Changing Church: Its Architecture, Art, and Decoration* (New York: Morehouse-Gorham,
1957). Architecture journals such as *Architectural Record* also followed developments in
church design and construction.

3. Religion, Respect, and Social Change: 1955–1968

Books on African American Christianity and its relationship to the civil rights movement
abound. David Garrow's *Bearing the Cross: Martin Luther King, Jr., and the Southern
Christian Leadership Conference* (1986; reprint, New York: Vintage, 1988) is still
unbeatable as a history of King's own role in the movement. Of King's own books, *Stride
Toward Freedom: The Montgomery Story* (New York: Harper, 1958) was partially ghost-
written. Collections of his speeches, articles, and sermons—*Strength to Love* (New York:
Harper and Row, 1963) and *Why We Can't Wait* (New York: Signet, 1964)—give a representative sample of his outlook and rhetorical style. On his plagiarism, see David Garrow, "King's Plagiarism: Imitation, Insecurity, and Transformation," *Journal of American
History* 78 (1991): 86–92. Ralph Abernathy's memoir, *And the Walls Came Tumbling
Down* (New York: Harper and Row, 1989) and Marshall Frady's *Jesse: The Life and Pil-
grimage of Jesse Jackson* (New York: Random House, 1996) describe events in the civil
rights movement from the point of view of King's closest collaborators. On the context
of the movement as it appeared at the time, see also E. Franklin Frazier, *The Negro
Church in America* (New York: Schocken, 1963). For later interpretations, see Charles
Hamilton, *The Black Preacher in America* (New York: William Morrow, 1972); C. Eric
Lincoln and Lawrence H. Mamiya, *The Black Church in the African American Experi-
ence* (Durham, N.C.: Duke University Press, 1990); Paul E. Johnson, *African American
Christianity: Essays in History* (Berkeley: University of California Press, 1994); and
Albert Raboteau, *A Fire in the Bones: Reflections on African-American Religious History*
(Boston: Beacon, 1995).

On the white clergy reaction to the civil rights movement, see S. Jonathan Bass,
*Blessed Are the Peacemakers: Eight White Religious Leaders and the "Letter from Birm-
ingham Jail"* (Baton Rouge: Louisiana State University Press, 2001). For works on the
Nation of Islam, see bibliography for chapter 9 below. Alex Haley's *The Autobiography
of Malcolm X* (New York: Random House, 1964) is a riveting, and still unequaled,
account of the Black Muslim leader's life. James Baldwin's *The Fire Next Time* (New
York: Dial Press, 1963) includes a vivid portrait of his storefront-church upbringing and
of Nation of Islam leader Elijah Muhammad in the early 1960s.

On Mormon history, a good general introduction is Richard N. Ostling and Joan K.
Ostling, *Mormon America: The Power and the Promise* (San Francisco: HarperSanFran-
cisco, 1999). The best insider's account comes from Leonard J. Arrington, *The Mormon
Experience: A History of the Latter-Day Saints* (New York: Knopf, 1979), while a shrewd
outsider's view is Jan Shipps, *Mormonism: The Story of a New Religious Tradition*
(Urbana: University of Illinois Press, 1985). On recent issues in Mormon history, see also
Armand L. Mauss, *The Angel and the Beehive: The Mormon Struggle with Assimilation*
(Urbana: University of Illinois Press, 1994), and Bryan Waterman and Brian Kagel, *The
Lord's University: Freedom and Authority at BYU* (Salt Lake City: Signature Books,
1998).

4. New Frontiers and Old Boundaries: 1960–1969

On the Kennedy presidency and the religion issue, see Lawrence Fuchs, *John F. Kennedy and American Catholicism* (New York: Meredith, 1967). A representative anti-Kennedy argument, written before the election by an ex-Catholic who had become an Episcopalian bishop, was James Pike's *A Catholic in the White House* (Garden City, N.Y.: Doubleday, 1960).

On church-state relations and the Supreme Court cases, see John T. Noonan, ed., *The Believer and the Powers That Are* (New York: Macmillan, 1987); Terry Eastland, ed., *Religious Liberty in the Supreme Court: The Cases that Define the Debate Over Church and State* (Grand Rapids, Mich.: Eerdman's, 1993); Robert Alley, ed., *The Supreme Court on Church and State* (New York: Oxford University Press, 1988); Marvin Frankel, *Faith and Freedom: Religious Liberty in America* (New York: Hill and Wang, 1994); George Goldberg, *Reconsecrating America* (Grand Rapids, Mich.: Eerdman's 1984); Albert Menendez, *The December Wars: Religious Symbols and Ceremonies in the Public Square* (Buffalo, N.Y.: Prometheus, 1993), and many others.

Ved Mehta's articles on theology in the *New Yorker*, published as *The New Theologian* (New York: Harper and Row, 1965), gave an accurate and readable portrait of the Protestant theological landscape in the early 1960s. The great texts of the "God is dead" movement were Gabriel Vahanian, *The Death of God: The Culture of Our Post-Christian Era* (New York: George Brazillier, 1961); Paul Van Buren, *The Secular Meaning of the Gospel* (New York: Macmillan, 1963); Thomas Altizer and William Hamilton, *Radical Theology and the Death of God* (Indianapolis: Bobbs-Merrill, 1966); and Harvey Cox, *The Secular City: Secularization and Urbanization in Theological Perspective* (New York: Macmillan, 1965). Main lines of response to, and criticism of, the radical theologians' work can be found in Jackson Lee Ice and John J. Carey, eds., *The Death of God Debate* (Philadelphia: Westminster, 1967); and James F. Childress and David B. Harned, eds., *Secularization and the Protestant Prospect* (Philadelphia: Westminster, 1970). The most profound response to the affair came many years later in Michael Harrington's *The Politics at God's Funeral: The Spiritual Crisis of Western Civilization* (New York: Holt, Reinhart, and Winston, 1983).

For literature on religion and the Vietnam War, see discussion at chapter 5, below.

On the transformation of American Catholicism in the 1960s, and the impact of Vatican II, see John McGreevy, *Parish Boundaries: The Catholic Encounter with Race in the Twentieth-Century Urban North* (Chicago: University of Chicago Press, 1996), and his *Catholicism and American Freedom* (New York: Norton, 2003); Allitt, *Catholic Intellectuals and Conservative Politics, 1950–1985* (Ithaca, N.Y.: Cornell University Press, 1993); Garry Wills, *Bare Ruined Choirs: Doubt, Prophecy, and Radical Religion* (Garden City, N.Y.: Doubleday, 1972); Peter Occhiogrosso, ed., *Once a Catholic: Prominent Catholics and Ex-Catholics Discuss the Influence of the Church on Their Lives and Work* (Boston: Houghton Mifflin, 1987); Robert Orsi, "Mildred, Is It Fun to Be a Cripple?" in *Catholic Lives, Contemporary America*, Thomas J. Ferraro, ed. (Durham, N.C.: Duke University Press, 1977), 19–64; and Philip Gleason, *Contending with Modernity: Catholic Higher Education in the Twentieth Century* (New York: Oxford University Press, 1995).

5. Shaking the Foundations: 1963–1972

General studies of recent Jewish history include Samuel Heilman, *Portrait of American Jews* (Seattle: University of Washington Press, 1995); Jack Wertheimer, *A People Divided: Judaism in Contemporary America* (New York: Basic, 1993); Naomi Cohen, *Jews in Christian America* (New York: Oxford University Press, 1992); Abraham Karp, *Jewish Continuity in America: Creative Survival in a Free Society* (Tuscaloosa: University of Alabama Press, 1998); and Leonard Dinnerstein, *Antisemitism in America* (New York: Oxford University Press, 1994). Oral history anthologies about Jewish childhood include Jay David, ed., *Growing Up Jewish* (New York: William Morrow, 1996) and Myrna Katz Frommer and Harvey Frommer, eds., *Growing Up Jewish in America* (New York: Harcourt Brace, 1995). Harvey Cox's *Common Prayers: Faith, Family, and a Christian's Journey Through the Jewish Year* (Boston: Houghton Mifflin, 2001) is a sympathetic outsider's guide through, and explanation of, the rituals that mark the Jewish calendar. Lis Harris, *Holy Days: The World of a Hasidic Family* (New York: Summit, 1985), and Elizabeth Ehrlich's *Miriam's Kitchen* (New York: Viking, 1997) explain the increasing allure of Orthodox Judaism to secularized American Jews in the later decades of the twentieth century. Current dilemmas and possible future directions for Judaism are explored in Steven M. Cohen and Arnold M. Eisen, *The Jew Within: Self, Family, and Community in America* (Bloomington: University of Indiana Press, 2001).

The religious dimensions of the Vietnam War are explained by Mitchell K. Hall, *Because of Their Faith: CALCAV and Religious Opposition to the Vietnam War* (New York: Columbia University Press, 1990). Daniel Berrigan's autobiography, *To Dwell in Peace* (San Francisco: Harper and Row, 1987); William Sloane Coffin, *Once to Every Man: A Memoir* (New York: Atheneum, 1977); and Francine DuPlessix Gray, *Divine Disobedience: Profiles in Catholic Radicalism* (New York: Knopf, 1970), give vivid accounts of the antiwar clergy's "actions." Andrew Leroy Pratt, "Religious Faith and Civil Religion: Evangelical Responses to the Vietnam War, 1964–1973" (Ph.D. diss., Southern Baptist Theological Seminary, 1988), explains the generally pro-Vietnam views of evangelicals in the same era.

Post–Vatican II Catholic controversies produced numerous historical polemics, which, if read with a measure of skepticism and detachment, can be highly informative. See, for example, Monsignor George Kelly, *The Battle for the American Church* (Garden City, N.Y.: Doubleday, 1979), and E. Michael Jones, *John Cardinal Krol and the Cultural Revolution* (South Bend, Ind.: Fidelity Press, 1995).

For African American religion in the late 1960s and after, see James Cone, *Black Theology and Black Power* (New York: Seabury, 1969); Cone, *Speaking the Truth: Ecumenism, Liberation, and Black Theology* (Grand Rapids, Mich.: Eerdman's, 1986); and Gayraud Wilmore and James H. Cone, eds., *Black Theology: A Docmentary History, 1966–1979* (Maryknoll, N.Y.: Orbis, 1979).

6. Alternative Religious Worlds: 1967–1982

For the religious UFO scene in the 1950s, start with Leon Festinger, Henry W. Riecken, and Stanley Schachter, *When Prophecy Fails: A Social and Psychological Study of a Modern Group That Predicted the Destruction of the World* (New York: Harper, 1956), then go to Alison Lurie, *Invisible Friends* (1967; reprint, New York: Avon, 1968). For ex–Moon walkers' spiritual journeys, see Edgar Mitchell and Dwight Williams, *The Way of the Explorer: An Apollo Astronaut's Journey Through the Material and Mystical Worlds* (New York: Putnam, 1996).

Learn about women and ministry from Carl J. Schneider and Dorothy Schneider, *In Their Own Right: The History of American Clergywomen* (New York: Crossroad, 1997); Susan Hill Lindley, *You Have Stept Out of Your Place: A History of Women and Religion in America* (Louisville: Westminster/John Knox, 1996); Jackson Carroll, Barbara Hargrove, and Adair Lummis, eds., *Women of the Cloth: A New Opportunity for the Church* (San Francisco: Harper and Row, 1983); and Rosemary Ruether and Eleanor McLaughlin, eds., *Women of Spirit: Female Leadership in the Jewish and Christian Traditions* (New York: Simon and Schuster/Touchstone, 1979). For a Catholic view in favor of women's ordination, see Mary Jo Weaver, *New Catholic Women: A Contemporary Challenge to Traditional Religious Authority* (New York: Harper and Row, 1986). For the traditionalist rebuttal, see Donna Steichen, *Ungodly Rage: The Hidden Face of Catholic Feminism* (San Francisco: Ignatius, 1991). The first female Reform rabbi wrote her own story: Sally Priesand, *Judaism and the New Woman* (New York: Behrman House, 1975). The larger story of which she was an element is told in Pamela S. Nadell, *Women Who Would Be Rabbis: A History of Women's Ordination, 1889–1985* (Boston: Beacon, 1998).

The nature and history of feminist theology are ably explained in Anne M. Clifford, *Introducing Feminist Theology* (Maryknoll, N.Y.: Orbis, 2001). Mary Daly's *The Church and the Second Sex* (Boston: Beacon, 1968) lit the fuse of feminist theology. Her own subsequent works, *Beyond God the Father* (Boston: Beacon, 1973); *Gyn-Ecology: The Metaethics of Radical Feminism* (Boston: Beacon, 1978); and *Pure Lust: Elemental Feminist Philosophy* (Boston: Beacon, 1984), became some of its central texts. Get a sense of the rich variety of feminist approaches to spirituality from Carol P. Christ and Judith Plaskow, eds., *Weaving the Visions: New Patterns of Feminist Spirituality* (San Francisco: Harper and Row, 1989); Ellen Umansky and Dianne Ashton, eds., *Four Centuries of Jewish Women's Spirituality: A Sourcebook* (Boston: Beacon, 1992); Rosemary R. Ruether, *Woman-Church: Theology and Practice of Feminist Liturgical Communities* (San Francisco: Harper and Row, 1988); Naomi Goldenberg, *The Changing of the Gods: Feminism and the End of Traditional Religion* (Boston: Beacon, 1979); Starhawk (née Miriam Simos), *The Spiral Dance: A Rebirth of the Ancient Religion of the Great Goddess* (San Francisco: Harper and Row, 1979); and Carol Christ, *The Laughter of Aphrodite: Reflections on a Journey to the Goddess* (San Francisco: Harper and Row, 1987). On reinterpreting familiar biblical stories in light of feminist insights, see Leonard Swidler, *Biblical Affirmations of Woman* (Philadelphia: Westminster, 1979). The essays in Yvonne Y. Haddad and John L. Esposito, eds., *Daughters of Abraham: Feminist Thought in Judaism, Christianity, and Islam* (Gainesville: University of Florida Press, 2001), indicate the potential relevance of feminist ideas to other parts of the religious spectrum.

Religion, the counterculture, and the hippie movement were explored by numerous sociologists and anthropologists, though there has not been much historical study in this area since the early 1980s. See, for example, Roger C. Palms, *The Jesus Kids* (Valley Forge, Pa.: Judson, 1971); Ronald Enroth, Edward E. Ericson Jr., and C. Breckinridge

Peters, *The Jesus People: Old-Time Religion in the Age of Aquarius* (Grand Rapids, Mich.: Eerdman's, 1972); Hiley Ward, *The Far-Out Saints of the Jesus Communes* (New York: Association Press, 1972); and Erling Jorstad, *That New-Time Religion: The Jesus Revival in America* (Minneapolis: Augsburg, 1972). Representative of the era's mood and rhetoric are Arthur Blessitt with Walter Wagner, *Turned On to Jesus* (New York: Hawthorne, 1971) and Jack Sparks, *God's Forever Family* (Grand Rapids, Mich.: Zondervan, 1974). The best work setting them in a larger context is Ronald B. Flowers, *Religion in Strange Times: The 1960s and 1970s* (Macon, Ga.: Mercer University Press, 1984).

On Jim Jones and Jonestown, see John R. Hall, *Gone from the Promised Land: Jonestown in American Cultural History* (New Brunswick, N.J.: Transaction, 1987); David Chidester, *Salvation and Suicide* (Bloomington: University of Indiana Press, 1988); Marshall Kilduff and Ron Javers, *The Suicide Cult* (New York: Bantam, 1978); and James Reston Jr., *Our Father Who Art in Hell* (New York: Times Books, 1981).

On new religious movements and "cults," begin with Philip Jenkins, *Mystics and Messiahs: Cults and New Religious Movements in American History* (New York: Oxford University Press, 2000), then go on to I. I. Zaretsky and M. P. Leone, eds., *Religious Movements in Contemporary America* (Princeton, N.J.: Princeton University Press, 1974), and Marc Galanter, ed., *Cults and New Religious Movements* (Washington, D.C.: American Psychiatric Association, 1989). For cult deprogramming, see Ted Patrick and Tom Dulack, *Let Our Children Go* (New York: Dutton, 1976); F. Conway and J. Siegelman, *Snapping: America's Epidemic of Sudden Personality Change* (New York: Dell, 1978); and Michael Langone, *Recovery from Cults: Help for Victims of Psychological and Spiritual Abuse* (New York: Norton, 1993). On exaggerated fears of the new religions, see Larry Shin, *The Dark Lord: Cult Images and the Hare Krishnas in America* (Philadelphia: Westminster, 1987); D. G. Bromley and A. D. Shupe Jr., *Strange Gods: The Great American Cult Scare* (1982); and the same two authors' book *The Moonies in America: Cult, Church, and Crusade* (Beverly Hills, Calif.: Sage, 1979). On the Rajneeshis, see James S. Gordon, *The Golden Guru* (Lexington, Mass.: S. Greene Press, 1988), and Hugh Milne, *Bhagwan: The God That Failed* (New York: St. Martin's, 1986).

Jacob Needleman's *The New Religions: The Teachings of the East* (Garden City, N.Y.: Doubleday, 1970) is an accessible introduction to Asian spirituality in America and a thoughtful analysis of why Americans had become so susceptible to its appeal. Monica Furlong's *Zen Effects: The Life of Alan Watts* (Boston: Houghton Mifflin, 1986) introduces one of the early leaders. Harvey Cox's *Turning East: The Promise and Peril of the New Orientalism* (New York: Simon and Schuster, 1977) is a liberal Protestant participant observer's account of its strengths and weaknesses. Robert Ellwood's *Alternative Altars: Unconventional and Eastern Spirituality in America* (Chicago: University of Chicago Press, 1979) adds a historical dimension, while Michael Downing's *Shoes Outside the Door: Desire, Devotion, and Excess at San Francisco Zen Center* (Washington, D.C.: Counterpoint, 2001) shows that even Buddhists can have feet of clay.

7. Evangelicals and Politics: 1976–1990

President Carter describes his own religious outlook in *Keeping Faith: Memoirs of a President* (New York: Bantam, 1982), while Peter G. Bourne's *Jimmy Carter: A Comprehen-*

sive Biography from Plains to Post-Presidency (New York: Lisa Drew/Scribner, 1997) explains how it affected his approach to politics.

On the early history of religious television, see Christopher O. Lynch, *Selling Catholicism; Bishop Sheen and the Power of Television* (Lexington: University of Kentucky Press, 1998). Jeffrey Hadden and Charles E. Swann, *Prime Time Preachers* (Reading, Mass.: Addison-Wesley, 1981), and Quentin Schultze, *Televangelism and American Culture: The Business of Popular Religion* (Grand Rapids, Mich.: Baker Book House, 1991), pick up the story in its evangelical phase.

On Falwell, the New Religious Right, and the evangelical resurgence, see Mark Noll, *American Evangelical Christianity: An Introduction* (Malden, Mass.: Blackwell, 2001); Walter Capps, *The New Religious Right: Piety, Patriotism, and Politics* (Columbia: University of South Carolina Press, 1990); Dinesh D'Souza, *Falwell Before the Millennium: A Critical Biography* (Chicago: Regnery, 1984); Randall Balmer, *Mine Eyes Have Seen the Glory: A Journey Into the Evangelical Subculture in America* (New York: Oxford University Press, 1989); Michael Lienesch, *Redeeming America: Piety and Politics in the New Christian Right* (Chapel Hill: University of North Carolina Press, 1993); and Harvey Cox, *Religion in the Secular City: Toward a Postmodern Theology* (New York: Simon and Schuster, 1984). On visions of the Apocalypse and the Rapture, see Paul Boyer, *When Time Shall Be No More: Prophecy Belief in Modern American Culture* (Cambridge, Mass.: Belknap Press/Harvard University Press, 1992). For evangelical theological developments, try Francis Schaeffer, *A Christian Manifesto* (Westchester, Ill.: Crossway, 1981), and Lane T. Dennis, ed., *Francis A. Schaeffer: Portraits of the Man and His Work* (Westchester, Ill.: Crossway, 1986).

The literature on the abortion controversy is immense. Good introductions to the issue and its religious aspects include Kristin Luker, *Abortion and the Politics of Motherhood* (Berkeley: University of California Press, 1984); J. Gordon Melton, ed., *The Churches Speak on Abortion* (Detroit: Gale, 1989); John T. Noonan, *A Private Choice: Abortion in America in the Seventies* (New York: Free Press, 1979); Peter S. Wenz, *Abortion Rights as Religious Freedom* (Philadelphia: Temple University Press, 1992); James Risen and Judy L. Thomas, *Wrath of Angels: The American Abortion War* (New York: Basic, 1998); Daniel C. Maguire, *Sacred Choices: The Right to Contraception and Abortion in Ten World Religions* (Minneapolis: Fortress, 2001).

On evangelical ideas about gender, see Tim and Beverly LaHaye, *The Act of Marriage: The Beauty of Sexual Love* (Grand Rapids, Mich.: Zondervan, 1976); Ruth Murray Brown, *For a Christian America: A History of the Religious Right* (Amherst, N.Y.: Prometheus, 2002); Christel Manning, *God Gave Us the Right: Conservative Catholic, Evangelical Protestant, and Orthodox Jewish Women Grapple with Feminism* (New Brunswick, N.J.: Rutgers University Press, 1999). On Phyllis Schlafly and Stop ERA, see Carol Felsenthal, *Phyllis Schlafly: The Sweetheart of the Silent Majority* (Garden City, N.Y.: Doubleday, 1981). For a critical assessment, see Susan Faludi, *Backlash: The Undeclared War Against American Women* (New York: Crown, 1991).

8. The Christian Quest for Justice and Wisdom: 1980–1995

The Catholic bishops' pastoral letter, *The Challenge of Peace: God's Promise and Our Response* (Washington, D.C.: National Conference of Catholic Bishops, 1983), was the central document of the religious antinuclear protest. Michael Novak's *Moral Clarity in the Nuclear Age* (Nashville: Thomas Nelson, 1983) is a Catholic neoconservative's rebuttal. Other accessible works on the controversy include Donald L. Davidson, *Nuclear Weapons and the American Churches: Ethical Positions on Modern Warfare* (Boulder, Col.: Westview, 1983); Robert Spaeth, *No Easy Answers: Christians Debate Nuclear Arms* (Minneapolis: Winston, 1983); and George Weigel's magisterial *Tranquillitas Ordinis: The Present Failure and Future Promise of American Catholic Thought on War and Peace* (New York: Oxford University Press, 1987).

Learn the principal themes of liberation theology from Arthur F. McGovern, *Liberation Theology and Its Critics: Toward an Assessment* (Maryknoll, N.Y.: Orbis, 1990), and Paul Sigmund, *Liberation Theology at the Crossroads: Democracy or Revolution?* (New York: Oxford University Press, 1990). On the Sanctuary movement, the most useful works are Robert Tomsho, *The American Sanctuary Movement* (Austin: Texas Monthly Press, 1987); Hilary Cunningham, *God and Caesar at the Rio Grande: Sanctuary and the Politics of Religion* (Minneapolis: University of Minnesota Press, 1995); Maria H. Thomas, ed., *Sanctuary: Challenge to the Churches* (Washington, D.C.: Institute on Religion and Democracy, 1986); and Penny Lernoux, *People of God: The Struggle for World Catholicism* (New York: Viking, 1989).

On creationism, begin with Raymond Eve and Francis B. Harrold, *The Creationist Movement in Modern America* (Boston: Twayne, 1991), then move on to Roland M. Frye, *Is God a Creationist? The Religious Case Against Creation Science* (New York: Scribner's, 1983), and Langdon Gilkey, *Creationism on Trial: Evolution and God at Little Rock* (Minneapolis: Winston, 1985). On textbook controversies, see James Moffett, *Storm in the Mountains: A Case Study of Censorship, Conflict, and Consciousness* (Carbondale: Southern Illinois University Press, 1988).

There is plenty of promotional literature on Christian academies and home schooling but not much that is analytical. See, however, Susan D. Rose, *Keeping Them Out of the Hands of Satan: Evangelical Schooling in America* (New York: Routledge, 1988); Mitchell Stevens, *Kingdom of Children: Culture and Controversy in the Homeschooling Movement* (Princeton, N.J.: Princeton University Press, 2001); David Guterson, *Family Matters: Why Homeschooling Makes Sense* (New York: Harcourt Brace Jovanovich, 1992); and Warren A. Nord, *Religion and American Education: Rethinking a National Dilemma* (Chapel Hill: University of North Carolina Press, 1995).

9. Profits, Profligates, and Prophets: 1987–1995

For an entertaining journalistic account of the unraveling of Jim and Tammy Bakker's evangelical empire, see Charles Shepard, *Forgiven: The Rise and Fall of Jim Bakker and the PTL Ministry* (New York: Atlantic Monthly Press, 1989), or Hunter James, *Smile Pretty and Say Jesus: The Last Great Days of PTL* (Athens: University of Georgia Press, 1993). For a more sober telling of the story, see Gary Tidwell, *Anatomy of a Fraud: Inside the Finances of the PTL Ministry* (New York: Wiley, 1993). For a lament over the internal deterioration of evangelicals' intellectual standards, see David F. Wells, *No Place for Truth: Or, Whatever Happened to Evangelical Theology?* (Grand Rapids, Mich.: Eerdman's, 1993). For a vivid sketch of Jimmy Swaggart, see Lawrence Wright, *Saints and Sinners* (New York: Knopf, 1993). On the growing importance of pentecostalism, see

Harvey Cox, *Fire from Heaven: The Rise of Pentecostal Spirituality and the Reshaping of Religion in the Twenty-first Century* (Cambridge, Mass.: Da Capo, 2001).

Neoconservative authors were skeptical about the idea of a "secular humanist" conspiracy, but several of them argued in the 1980s and 1990s that the separation between religion and politics had indeed gone too far. See, in particular, Richard John Neuhaus, *The Naked Public Square* (Grand Rapids, Mich.: Eerdman's, 1984), and Stephen Carter, *The Culture of Disbelief: How American Law and Politics Trivialize Religious Devotion* (New York: Anchor Doubleday, 1993). Garry Wills's *Under God: Religion and American Politics* (New York: Simon and Schuster, 1990) explains the religious issues at stake in the presidential election campaign of 1988.

There is not yet much historical literature on American Islam, so I was dependent mainly on sociological studies, memoirs, and journalism. The best starting point is Jane Smith, *Islam in America* (New York: Columbia University Press, 1999). Ms. Smith is also coeditor, with Yvonne Yazbeck Haddad, of *Muslim Communities in North America* (Albany, N.Y.: SUNY Press, 1994), which contains more than twenty useful essays on aspects of American Islam. Other informative studies include Yvonne Y. Haddad and Adair Lummis, *Islamic Values in the United States: A Comparative Study* (New York: Oxford University Press, 1987); Kambiz GhaneaBassiri, *Competing Visions of Islam in the United States* (Westport, Conn.: Greenwood, 1988); Steven Barboza, *American Jihad: Islam After Malcolm X* (New York: Doubleday, 1994); and Richard Wormser, *American Islam: Growing Up Muslim in America* (New York: Walker, 1994); Robert Singh, *The Farrakhan Phenomenon* (Washington, D.C.: Georgetown University Press, 1997); Asma Gull Hasan, *American Muslims: The New Generation* (New York: Continuum, 2000); and Vibert White Jr., *Inside the Nation of Islam: A Historical and Personal Testimony by a Black Muslim* (Gainesville: University of Florida Press, 2001).

10. The New World Order: 1989–1999

George Weigel's *The Final Revolution* (New York: Oxford University Press, 1992) explains the end of the Cold War in religious terms. On the development of evangelicalism in post–Cold War Russia, see Sharon Linzey and Ken Kaisch, *God in Russia: The Challenge of Freedom* (Lanham, Md.: University Press of America, 1999).

Michael Barkun, *Religion and the Racist Right: The Origins of the Christian Identity Movement* (Chapel Hill: University of North Carolina Press, 1994), explains the outlook of Randy Weaver and other Christian survivalists. For the Branch Davidians and the Waco catastrophe, see Stuart Wright, ed., *Armageddon in Waco: Critical Perspectives on the Branch Davidian Conflict* (Chicago: University of Chicago Press, 1995); James D. Tabor, *Why Waco? Cults and the Battle for Religious Freedom in America* (Berkeley: University of California Press, 1995); and James D. Faubion, *The Shadows and Lights of Waco: Millennialism Today* (Princeton, N.J.: Princeton University Press, 2001).

On the environment, begin with Robert Booth Fowler, *The Greening of Protestant Thought* (Chapel Hill: University of North Carolina Press, 1995). Advocacy sources include Francis Schaeffer, *Pollution and the Death of Man: The Christian View of Ecology* (Wheaton, Ill.: Tyndale House, 1970); Thomas Berry, *The Dream of the Earth* (San

Francisco: Sierra Club Books, 1988); Rosemary R. Ruether, *Gaia and God: An Ecofeminist Theology of Earth Healing* (San Francisco: HarperSanFrancisco, 1992); Sallie McFague, *The Body of God: An Ecological Theology* (Minneapolis: Fortress, 1993); Gary Cochran, *Shaping Our Environmental Conscience: The Caring Christian's Environmental Guide* (Alpharetta, Ga.: Old Rugged Cross Press, 1995); Matthew Fox, *Confessions: The Making of a Postdenominational Priest* (San Francisco: HarperSanFrancisco, 1996); and the much more skeptical Michael Barkey, ed., *Environmental Stewardship in the Judeo-Christian Tradition: Jewish, Catholic, and Protestant Wisdom on the Environment* (Grand Rapids, Mich.: Acton Institute, 2000).

The megachurch phenomenon has attracted more attackers than defenders, at least among writers. See, for example, Joel Gregory, *Too Great a Temptation: The Seductive Power of America's Super Church* (Fort Worth, Tex.: Summit Group, 1994), and a large periodical literature. More analytical are Scott Thumma, "The Kingdom, the Power, and the Glory: The Megachurch in Modern American Society" (Ph.D. diss., Emory University, 1996); and Stewart M. Hoover, "The Cross at Willow Creek: Seeker Religion and the Contemporary Marketplace," in Bruce David Forbes and Jeffrey H. Mahan, eds., *Religion and Popular Culture in America*, 145–59 (Berkeley: University of California Press, 2000).

11. Fears, Threats, and Promises: 1990–2000

The best introductory history to the American gay liberation movement is John D'Emilio, *Sexual Politics, Sexual Communities: The Making of a Homosexual Minority in the United States, 1940–1970* (Chicago: University of Chicago Press, 1983). John Boswell's *Christianity, Social Tolerance, and Homosexuality* (Chicago: University of Chicago Press, 1980) put the study of homosexuality and religion squarely on the map as a scholarly issue. Despite acute controversy, it has become a classic on the long relationship between the Judeo-Christian religions and homosexuality. There is as yet little historical literature on the subject of religion and homosexuality in recent America. The way to begin a study of the issue, I think, is to browse the articles in Gary D. Comstock and Susan E. Henking, eds., *Que(e)rying Religion: A Critical Anthology* (New York: Continuum, 1997). Other useful titles on homosexuality and religion include Robert Goss, *Jesus Acted Up: A Gay and Lesbian Manifesto* (San Francisco: Harper SanFrancisco, 1993); Gary David Comstock, *Unrepentant, Self-Affirming, Practicing: Lesbian/Bisexual/Gay People Within Organized Religion* (New York: Continuum, 1996); Peter Sweasy, *From Queer to Eternity: Spirituality in the Lives of Lesbian, Gay, and Bisexual People* (Herndon, Va.: Cassell, 1997); Kathy Rudy, *Sex and the Church: Gender, Homosexuality, and the Transformation of Christian Ethics* (Boston: Beacon, 1997); David Shallenberger, *Reclaiming the Spirit: Gay Men and Lesbians Come to Terms with Religion* (New Brunswick, N.J.: Rutgers University Press, 1998); L. R. Holben, *What Christians Think About Homosexuality: Six Representative Viewpoints* (North Richland Hills, Tex.: Bibal Press, 2000); and Toby Johnson, *Gay Spirituality: The Role of Gay Identity in the Transformation of Human Consciousness* (Los Angeles: Alyson Books, 2000).

On Promise Keepers, see Ken Abraham, *Who Are the Promise Keepers? Understanding the Christian Men's Movement* (New York: Doubleday, 1997); Dane S. Clausen, ed., *Standing on the Promises: The Promise Keepers and the Revival of Manhood* (Cleveland:

Pilgrim, 1999); George N. Lundskow, *Awakening to an Uncertain Future: A Case Study of the Promise Keepers* (New York: Peter Lang, 2001); and the founder's own book, Bill McCartney, *Sold Out: Becoming Man Enough to Make a Difference* (Dallas: Word, 1997).

On the approach of the millennium, there is little permanent literature. The sense of momentous events unfolding contributed to the astonishing popularity of Tim LaHaye and Jerry Jenkins's series of apocalyptic novels, beginning with *Left Behind* (Wheaton, Ill.: Tyndale House, 1995). There are, unfortunately, no good books on the Elian Gonzalez affair.

12. The New Millennium: 2001

The first generation of studies relating to the attacks on the World Trade Center is just now being published as this book goes to press. See, on religious aspects of the tragedy, Editors of Beliefnet, eds., *From the Ashes: A Spiritual Response to the Attack on America* (New York: Rodale, 2001); Jon L. Berquist, *Strike Terror No More: Theology, Ethics, and the New War* (St. Louis: Chalice Press, 2002); Anonymous, *Through Our Enemies' Eyes: Osama Bin Laden, Radical Islam, and the Future of America* (Washington, D.C.: Brassey's, 2002); and the film *Ground Zero Spirituality at Trinity Church, Wall Street*, by Paul Brubaker (New York: Trinity Television, 2002).

Interviews and Correspondence

I interviewed and corresponded with many individuals about their religious experiences as children. Those cited here are Michael Berger, Pete Daniel, Eve Davis, Leroy Davis, Kathleen Joyce, Catherine Remick, Richard Roesel, Margaret Steinfels, Christine Stolba, and Karen Stolley.

Periodicals

For research on liberal Protestant topics, the most useful journals are *Christian Century* and *Christianity and Crisis*. On evangelical topics, turn to *Christianity Today* and *Sojourners*. Most of the denominations have, or had, national and regional periodicals of their own. Catholic journals running throughout the decades covered in this book include *Commonweal* (moderately liberal), *America* (liberal, but with a Jesuit slant), *National Catholic Reporter* (from 1964, distinctly to the left of the first two), and the *National Catholic Register* (distinctly to the right). The best Jewish journal, which also covered affairs of national significance, was *Commentary*. On ecumenical (interreligious) issues, especially relating to politics, *First Things* (founded in 1990) is also very good. When religious stories became nationally significant, they were usually covered in *Time, Newsweek*, the *New York Times*, and the *Washington Post*.

The Lexis-Nexis Web site has enabled historians in the last decade to gain easy access to all newspaper articles published since the early 1980s. I found it indispensable, especially for post-1990 research.

Other periodicals consulted included:
Albany (N.Y.) Times Union
Architectural Record
Atlanta Journal-Constitution

Baltimore Sun
Bergen (N.J.) Record
Books and Culture
Boston Globe
Catholic Historical Review
Catholic World
Chattanooga Times
Chicago Daily Herald
Christian Herald
Denver Post
Essence
Hartford Courant
Houston Press
Insight
Jacksonville Florida Times-Union
Journal of American History
Journal of Church and State
Journal of Feminist Studies in Religion
Journal for Preachers
Journal for the Scientific Study of Religion
Journalism Quarterly
Knoxville News-Sentinel
Lakeland (Fla.) Ledger
Los Angeles Times
The Lutheran
Memphis Commercial Appeal
Moment
The Nation
National Journal
National Review
New Orleans Times Picayune
New York Daily News
Newsday
Pittsburgh Post-Gazette
Providence Journal-Bulletin
Quincy (Mass.) Patriot Ledger
San Francisco Chronicle
Seattle Post-Intelligencer
Seattle Times
Social Order
South Atlantic Quarterly
St. Petersburg Times
Studia Liturgica
U.S. News and World Report
Wilmington Star-News

Index